Govind Narayan's Mumbai

Anthem South Asian Studies

Banerjee-Dube, Ishita *Religion, Law and Power* (2007)
Fraser, Bashabi (ed.) *Bengal Partition Stories* (2007)
Osella, Filippo and Caroline *Men and Masculinities in India* (2006)
Chattopadhyaya, Brajadulal *Studying Early India* (2006)
Brosius, Christiane *Empowering Visions* (2005)
Mills, James (ed.) *Subaltern Sports: Politics and Sport in South Asia* (2005)
Joshi, Chitra *Lost Worlds: Indian Labour and its Forgotten Histories* (2005)
Dasgupta, Biplab *European Trade and Colonial Conquest* (2005)
Kaur, Raminder *Performative Politics and the Cultures of Hinduism* (2005)
Rosenstein, Lucy *New Poetry in Hindi* (2004)
Shah, Ghanshyam *Caste and Democratic Politics in India* (2004)
Van Schendel, Willem *The Bengal Borderland* (2004)

Govind Narayan's Mumbai

An Urban Biography from 1863

Edited and Translated by
Murali Ranganathan

With a Foreword by Gyan Prakash

ANTHEM PRESS
LONDON · NEW YORK · DELHI

Anthem Press
An imprint of Wimbledon Publishing Company
www.anthempress.com

This edition first published in UK and USA 2008
by ANTHEM PRESS

75-76 Blackfriars Road, London SE1 8HA, UK
or PO Box 9779, London SW19 7ZG, UK and
244 Madison Ave. #116, New York, NY 10016, USA

British Library Cataloguing in Publication Data
A catalogue record for this book is available from the British Library.

Library of Congress Cataloguing in Publication Data

Madagāvakara, Govinda Narayana, 1815–1865.
[Mumbaice varnana. English]
Govind Narayan's Mumbai : an urban biography from 1863 /
edited and translated by Murali Ranganathan with a foreword by Gyan Prakash.
p. cm.—(Anthem South Asian studies)
Includes bibliographical references and index.
ISBN 978-1-84331-277-2 (hardback)
1. Bombay (India)—History. I. Ranganathan, Murali. II. Title.

DS486.B7M2213 2008
954'.79203510922--dc22
2007042078

With thanks to the DeGoyler Library at Southern Methodist
University for the use of the images in this volume.

Map courtesy of the Royal Geographical Society.

ISBN-10: 1 84331 277 8 (Hbk)
ISBN-13: 978 1 84331 277 2 (Hbk)

1 3 5 7 9 10 8 6 4 2

Printed in India

To my parents

CONTENTS

LIST OF ILLUSTRATIONS

List of Illustrations

The illustrations used in this book have been selected from a three-volume photographically-illustrated book with original tipped-in albumen photographs titled Photographs of Western India *with the volumes bearing the titles, vol I., 'Costumes and Characters', vol. II., 'Scenery, Public Buildings', and vol. III., 'Scenery, Public Buildings'. It contains nearly 200 photographs, mainly of Mumbai and the surrounding region and its inhabitants. The volumes bear the book-plate of Sir H. B. E. Frere, Governor of Bombay from 1862–67. They were recently discovered at the DeGolyer Library of the Southern Methodist University, Texas and had been purchased many decades ago by Everett L. DeGolyer, Jr.*

The sixteen illustrations capture Mumbai during the period 1855–61, prior to the demolition of the Fort and the rebuilding of large parts of Mumbai. This closely corresponds with the period in which Mumbaiche Varnan *was conceptualized and written. Many of the photographs selected seem to have been earlier published in the* Indian Amateur's Photographic Album *by William Johnson (see biographical note for more details) and William Henderson. The Album appeared monthly for three years from November 1856 to October 1859, each issue containing three photographs and a page of letterpress describing them. Some, but not all of the photographers have been identified in the* Album.

1. Temples at Walkeshwar with the Banganga Tank in the foreground; the temple of Rameshwar Shiva (left) and Ganesh (right) with a devotee standing on the bathing ghats (see page 79).

2. A view of the beach at Chowpatty with timber stacked in the foreground. It was beginning to be 'populated with beautiful houses and gardens' visible in the background (see page 82).

3. The temple at Mahalaxmi (see page 83).

4. The Mankeshwar Temple built by Ranmull Lakha near the Byculla station (see page 90).

ACKNOWLEDGEMENTS

This book has essentially been a solitary effort and all its many shortcomings are my responsibility. However I would like to acknowledge all those who helped me in the process of writing this book.

Firstly, I would like to thank my sister, Meera Ranganathan, for reading and commenting on the various drafts of this book. Her help and support during this period has been unstinting and more valued because it had to traverse inter-continental distances.

The Asiatic Society of Mumbai awarded the Gulestan Billimoria Fellowship, conferred annually on research undertaken on Mumbai and the surrounding region, for research related to this book. Their recognition of this effort is highly appreciated.

Help received at the libraries of the following institutions in Mumbai is gratefully acknowledged – *Asiatic Society of Mumbai*; *Department of Archives, Government of Maharashtra*; *K. R. Cama Oriental Institute*; *University of Mumbai*; *Mumbai Marathi Granth Sangrahalaya*; *Wilson College*; *Forbes Gujarati Sabha*; *Heras Institute of Indian History and Culture, St. Xavier's College*; *Mumbai Marathi Sahitya Sangh*; and the *Chhatrapati Shivaji Maharaj Vastu Sangrahalaya* (formerly the *Prince of Wales Museum*). Libraries outside Mumbai include the *Marathi Granth Sangrahalaya*, Thane and the *National Library*, Calcutta.

The *DeGolyer Library* at *Southern Methodist University*, Texas provided the photographs of pre-1860 Mumbai; their cooperation, especially that of Anne Peterson, Curator of photographs is much appreciated. The staff at Anthem Press provided me with useful help in producing this book. And lastly, thanks to numerous friends and acquaintances who, knowingly or unknowingly, helped me when this book was being written.

Foreword

Gyan Prakash
Dayton-Stockton Professor of History
Princeton University

The city is dead. Urban theorists tell us that the city no longer exists as a distinct, bounded entity. Urban sprawl and globalization have turned cities into barely legible nodes in vast urbanized systems of communication, transnational flows of people, capital, commodities, images, and ideas. The world is now comprised of megacities with ever-extending reach and rapidly diminishing inner unity. Increasingly obsolete is the idea of the bounded city, defined by an internally coherent civic life, organized as a public space inhabited by rational citizens, and structured by clear relationships to the region, nation, and the wider world.

Mumbai is often described in similar terms. Newspaper and magazine commentaries, and literary and academic writings frequently portray the great city in ruins. Where once textile mills and docks had hummed to an industrial rhythm, there is now the cacophony of the post-industrial megalopolis. In place of the clearly defined city of mills, dockworkers, employees, and trade unions, there is now the socially amorphous world of the megacity strung out tight between its rich and poor ends. Civic services are bursting at the seams under the pressure exerted by explosive and unplanned growth. Nativist passions, communal riots, the nexus between corrupt politicians and greedy businessmen, have destroyed civic consciousness and wrecked the city as a coherent and cosmopolitan space. So when the Shiv Sena officially renamed Bombay as Mumbai in 1996, to many the re-christening seemed to formalize the transformation that had already occurred. The flood in 2005, when large parts of the city went under water, only darkened the sense of doom. The human bodies, animal carcasses, and garbage floating in the water appeared to expose the malaise set deep in the city's body.

Etched in this portrait of death and ruin are the outlines of a remembered city. Its shape peers through the images of the creaking infrastructure, eroded institutions, and ethnic eruptions on the city's cosmopolitan skin. Yes, the city has changed, but also identifiable in accounts of transformations wrought by post-industrial growth and globalization is the idea of Mumbai as a specific place. The city's residents experience their globally situated and connected environments as decidedly local lifeworlds, thick with particular experiences, practices, imaginations, and memories. In fact, the awareness of change has only sharpened Mumbai's urban consciousness and produced a surfeit of interest in the city. Consider the recent proliferation in the number of novels, nonfiction works, and films about Mumbai. Architectural historians have retrieved records and photographs to produce portraits of the history of the Island City's built environment. A renaissance of scholarly interest in Mumbai is clearly evident in the spurt of studies by historians, anthropologists, and urban researchers. The enhanced focus on Mumbai not only reflects the growing importance of urbanization, but also draws attention to the question of the modern city as society.

The English translation and publication of Govind Narayan's *Mumbaiche Varnan* as *Govind Narayan's Mumbai: An Urban Biography from 1863* should be seen in the light of this growing interest in the city. The first full account of Mumbai written in any language, Govind Narayan's text is well known among students of the city's history. It was composed before the ramparts of the Fort were torn down to accommodate the city's growth. Yet, even at this early date, the text registers an urban consciousness. It describes Mumbai as an urban society, not as a subset of the nation or region. The Island City appears as a spectacle, a visual object to behold and appreciate. As Govind Narayan describes Mumbai's sights and sounds, he suggests that we are witnessing the emergence of something new. He presents himself as an observer of this emergent reality, taking us on a guided tour of its wondrous social and cultural landscape.

Combining observations of daily life with accounts of the city's built environment, institutions, and people, and interspersing historical details with legends and myths, Govind Narayan writes excitedly of Mumbai as a dynamic city, as a marvellous metropolis of cultural and linguistic diversity. He depicts the cotton trade and cotton mills, describes the city's religious patterns and festivals, provides a view of its drinking and gambling dens and criminal life, and paints pictures of its street life. These descriptions anticipate the representations that we now associate with Mumbai. Thus, he writes of the presence of a cosmopolitan array of religions, ethnicities, languages, classes, castes, and communities in the city. The Hindus, he says, consist of over a hundred castes, 'with no end of differences and variations within these castes.' Then, there are 'other castes – the Parsi, Mussalman, Moghul, Yahudi, Israeli, Bohra, Khoja, Memon, Arab, Kandhari'. Also listed are the 'hatted races', – the English, Portuguese, French, Greek, Dutch, Turkish, German, Armenian, and Chinese (p. 50). Diverse and complex, Mumbai is also presented as a dynamic city of opportunities, a place that attracts people from all over in search of work and fortunes. Accounts of its famous Parsi merchants and traders serve as evidence of the chance for advancement and wealth that the city offers. So great are these opportunities that no one need go hungry. 'In this City of Mumbai, the poor and the maimed, the lame and the crippled, the deaf and the dumb, the blind and the maimed, the good and the bad, the thief and the scavenger, the fool and the fraud, whoever one may be, is deprived neither of food nor clothing' (p. 58). Obviously, this is not meant to describe an actual situation but to convey his image of the possibilities that Mumbai offered.

In fact, a striking feature of Govind Narayan's text is its unalloyed enthusiasm for the city. As he moves from topic to topic, now describing its urban form and then sketching its social architecture, a strong undercurrent of admiration for the city runs through the text. He strongly appreciates the environment of the modern city that he identifies in the mint, the telegraphs, metalled roads, railways, docks, cotton mills, Town Hall, the courts and the police, and street life. Recognizing the formation of a new society in these spatial forms, he registers the development as a doubly colonial project. Thus, while expressing support for British efforts to develop and manage Mumbai, he also records its history as a colonial project, i.e., as an attempt to establish mastery over nature. He writes about the filling of breaches and the cutting down of trees as part of the city's growth. We learn about the construction of docks and piers, and roadways and embankments as acts of human artifice to bend nature to culture. But these acts of progress were also acts of destruction. They involved, for example, the imposition of an abstract geographical grid over lands infused with religious and customary meanings. Govind Narayan's meticulous recording of this process, however, also reveals that these acts of erasure were not complete. Consider, for example, his account of the construction of the Worli embankment. In describing the embankment's erection, he recounts a legend according to which the project did not succeed until the engineer followed goddess

Mahalaxmi's instructions that he received in a dream. She told him to retrieve her idol buried in the seabed and install it in a temple. Once this was done, the embankment project was successful (pp. 74–75). Whether or not historically accurate, the legend undercuts the story of a relentless march to progress. Gods and goddesses do not go away but return to haunt the site of their expulsion.

As a record of Mumbai's nineteenth century history, as a text of urban consciousness, *Mumbaiche Varnan* is superb. Its unavailability in English so far has meant that this fascinating indigenous account of Mumbai has remained inaccessible to readers without the knowledge of Marathi. We owe a debt of gratitude to Murali Ranganathan for translating this text and making it available to the wider readership that it so richly deserves.

INTRODUCTION

The growth and history of Mumbai over the last four centuries has been documented in copious detail, by both contemporary writers and historians. The change of name from Bombay to Mumbai on the eve of the twenty-first century has produced a slew of books – in a variety of shapes and sizes and focussing on Mumbai from various angles. Straightforward urban biographies compete for attention with racy novels set in Mumbai's legendary underworld. Essayists debate the future of the city in numerous volumes while photographers try to capture every mood of the city. This mirrors the attention which Mumbai has received in the previous centuries from residents and visitors alike.

When the English first acquired Mumbai in the mid-seventeenth century from the Portuguese, the employees of the East India Company were the first to write about the strange world which they encountered in a small island off the mainland of India. The likes of Fryer and Ovington, a doctor and a chaplain respectively, recount their experiences in Mumbai, providing an account of the fledgling town. As the initial enthusiasm for the new settlement waned, the harsh ground realities of staying in Mumbai in the early eighteenth century did not allow for enthusiastic documentation. Outsiders (that is, those not linked with the East India Company) like Alexander Hamilton and a few foreign visitors like John Grose however kept track of the city's fortunes.

By the end of the eighteenth century, life in Mumbai was more settled as the English consolidated their command over India. The advent of the printing press in Mumbai by the 1780s allowed the contemporary documentation of the city in the forms of calendars and almanacs. Histories of the East India Company's acquisition of India began to be written by annalists like Bruce while gazetteers were compiled by the likes of Walter Hamilton; these typically included detailed accounts of settlement of Mumbai. More than the gentlemen, the ladies – Maria Graham, Mrs. Elwood, Mrs. Postans and Lady Falkland – began to document both the journey to Mumbai and the destination itself. Old India hands like James Forbes and T. Erskine Perry also shared their reminiscences.

By the 1850s, there was practically a deluge of books related to India, and especially to Mumbai. The traffic to Mumbai had increased and there were numerous strangers who needed handbooks to successfully negotiate their visits to India. The first in a long series of John Murray handbooks on India – written by Edward Eastwick in 1859 – provides a detailed account of the city of Mumbai. Critical accounts of English rule in India were finally being written by both residents like Philip Anderson and professional historians like Kaye and Mill. Scholarly societies, both in Mumbai and elsewhere, were also publishing the latest research on the city. Daily events were being documented by a multitude of newspapers, not just in English, but also in local languages such as Marathi and Gujarati. The closest attempt to write a biography of Mumbai was made in 1855 by George Buist, a newspaperman, who however had to present it as a 'Guide to Bombay', embedded in the *Bombay Calendar and Almanac* for that year.

This was the long build-up leading to the first urban biography of Mumbai, *Mumbaiche Varnan*, written by Govind Narayan in Marathi, and published in 1863. In many ways, 1863 was a turning point for Mumbai. The old city, which Govind Narayan describes, was gradually pulled down and enlarged and rebuilt. The old Fort, the most dominant structure in Mumbai, was demolished; architectural edifices which identify present-day Mumbai gradually took form; the familiar outline of Mumbai came to be redefined through numerous reclamations; new industries were mushrooming at a rapid rate. The city had already begin to change and acquire the trappings of a modern metropolis – railways, piped water, covered sewers, and increasingly distant suburbs – but the boom of the early 1860s enabled a complete makeover. In a sense, Govind Narayan is describing the pre-industrial city as it prepares to usher in the next age. However, in some ways, more inscrutable and less capable of being described, the city remains the same. Its uncomplaining acceptance of new arrivals, its ability to provide means of livelihood to everybody who wants it, its superficial mayhem and unceasing activity – all these have survived into the twenty-first century.

It is indeed surprising, for many reasons, that the the first urban biography of Mumbai, in the modern sense of the word, came to be written in Marathi. It combines written history, oral accounts, contemporary narratives, and elements of the guidebook in a manner that had never been done before. When this book first appeared in 1863, it was a landmark in many ways – both in its breadth of scope and depth of knowledge and the language in which it was written.

Though an ancient language, Marathi had to be reinvented in the nineteenth century to fit the requirements of writing prose in a new era dominated by Western thought and education. This began to happen from the 1830s through a series of translations into Marathi from English and Sanskrit, followed by a multitude of text-books in a variety of subjects and Christian missionary literature. By the 1860s, the language had achieved a certain level of standardization and an evolving sense of style. There were, however hardly any books, that could match *Mumbaiche Varnan* either in terms of originality or compare with it in terms of size and scope. The 'simple and straightforward style' in which he seeks to write is still very easy to read even though a century and a half have elapsed since the book was written.

However, more important than either the language and the scope of the biography is Govind Narayan's personal imprint on the narrative. The vivid descriptions of places and people, the keen eye for detail, the constant emphasis on social reform, the occasional anecdote – all these have ensured that the book has not dated. Its not as much a record of the past as a recreation of the city. This truly makes the book, *Govind Narayan's Mumbai*.

Only an author confident about both his writing skills and his knowledge of the subject could have attempted to undertake such an onerous task. He takes on the responsibility with patriotic fervour 'to benefit the nation' and because 'the history of a country ... is best written by its offspring.' While he explicitly states the reason for writing the book, he does not define his audience. The 'our people' to whom the book addresses itself frequently are the 'Dakshini Hindus', Hindus from the South, that is from the Maratha country south of Mumbai, from where Govind Narayan migrated to Mumbai in the 1820s and whose interest was the closest to his heart. Govind Narayan had written and published 14 books and managed the publication of two magazines for many years before he undertook to write *Mumbaiche Varnan,* unarguably his *magnum opus.* As an independent writer, he also had to publish most of his books himself and must have been fairly familiar with both the process and risks involved in producing this book.

Early drafts of the book must have been completed by the start of 1862, though he continued to add material through most of 1862, including details of events which happened in December 1862. He sent the manuscript to Mahadeo Govindshastri Kolhatkar, a high-ranking Indian in the employ of the Bombay Government, whose help he acknowledges in the preface. Kolhatkar wrote back on 18 March 1862 saying that he thought 'the work a very meritorious one and fittest to be both interesting and useful to the Natives. It is written in a plain and attractive manner and has some excellent and original features'. In the meanwhile, Govind Narayan had selected the *Induprakash Press* for printing the book and circulated a prospectus in both English and Marathi to enrol advance buyers for his book (extracted from Department of Archives, Government of Maharashtra, Mumbai: Dakshina Prize Committee, Poona. From Jan 1860 to Dec 1862. Inward Volume No. 6).

PROSPECTUS

The Island of Bombay in superficial extent is small, but it is so greatly distinguished by its rapid increase in population, wealth, commerce, literature, and all the useful arts, that every thing connected with its history and progress must be a subject of daily increasing interest. The author of this work, for which the patronage of the reading public is solicited, has, on not a few former occasions, had gratefully to acknowledge the favorable reception given to the humble efforts of his pen; and he is encouraged to hope that this will be as favorably received. It is a work in Marathi on 'Bombay Past and Present' and contains a topographical and historical account of Bombay. The book will consist of about 400 pages octavo and will be bound in an embossed cover with a map of the Island of Bombay as a frontispiece. The price to subscribers will be three rupees and non-subscribers three rupees and a half.

In laying this prospectus before the public, especially before the Marathi reading community, the author solicits their patronage to enable him to carry the work through the press.

GOVIND NA'RA'YAN

He also wrote to the Dakshina Prize Committee in May 1862 asking for financial patronage to finance the publication of the book. Perhaps because the Committee was itself being restructured during this period, Govind Narayan never heard from them until after the book was published; they then awarded him a prize of seventy-five rupees, a meagre sum considering the merits of the book and the value of prizes awarded to decidedly inferior efforts. The book does not seem to have been a commercial success either, perhaps only serving to emphasize the fact that the book was written ahead of its time.

Govind Narayan does not venture to make too many predictions about the future of Mumbai but even he would have been surprised by the accuracy of his assertion that 'when Sashtee (Salsette) and other villages are merged with Mumbai, it will never occur to anybody that Mumbai was an island once.' Similarly, his confidence that Marathi could develop as a literary language 'only when dictionaries of our language are compiled and thousands of books of both prose and poetry are composed and critically reviewed ...' was not misplaced.

Whenever the context presents itself and sometimes even when it is not called for, Govind Narayan is highly vocal about the need for social reform in Hindu society. He is openly critical of the caste system but he does not seem to have wholly abandoned them, as evidenced by his reactions to the radical Paramahansa Sabha. He is very critical about certain social practices of the Hindus – their ostentatious marriages, their obsession with rituals, their fascination for jewellery, and their lack of yearning for knowledge. Many of his views must have made him unpopular amongst many sections of Mumbai society.

His reaction to English rule is more positive though he condemns the Indian kings for having handed over their kingdoms to the English on a platter. He sees their rule as reformative and beneficial to the country, especially after the profligacy of the earlier incumbents. He admires their skill in business and their scholarship. In spite of all this, he ultimately concludes that unless representatives of the people have a say in government, the country will not prosper.

The publication of *Mumbaiche Varnan* spawned many books on Mumbai. The first Gujarati book on Mumbai was published soon after in 1867 and titled *Mumbaino bhomiyo* or literally a guide to Mumbai. It was 'designed as a *Guide* to persons who continually pour into Bombay from Gujarat and its adjacent provinces for commercial and other purposes.' This was followed in 1874 by *Mumbaino bahar,* another Gujarati book which was an account of the ancient leading families of Mumbai. The first independent guide to the city in English was Maclean's *A Guide to Bombay* which was published annually from 1875 to 1902. Another important book in Marathi which completes our brief review of books on Mumbai in the nineteenth century was *Mumbaicha vrittant,* literally an account of Mumbai which appeared in 1889.

The translation includes the entire text of the original book except for an extended section on prayers which were sung during 1857 during the 'Sepoy Mutiny'. A few Sanskrit couplets which have been sprinkled at various points in the text have also been excluded.

While writing the book, Govind Narayan has relied on 'either personal observation or ... books written about this famous city'. He tracks down obscure Marathi manuscripts in the possession of families resident in Mumbai for many years and includes extracts from both English and Marathi newspapers. He identifies some of his sources in a haphazard manner but leaves a large majority of them unmentioned. His principal source for the early history of the city seems to be Philip Anderson's *English in Western India*. He mentions other sources like Murphy on whose article in the *Transactions of the Bombay Geographical Society* he relies on for information on the pre-history of Mumbai. The 'Bibliography' contains a section on books published prior to 1863 which could have been used by Govind Narayan while writing this book.

The temptation to write a running commentary on the book and provide an update on the various aspects of Mumbai has been resisted. The notes, which have been bunched together at the end of the text, only touch on a few aspects which require further elucidation or where reference is provided to the original source of information. The book takes a virtual roll-call of eminent Mumbai citizens of the nineteenth century, many of whom have become completely obscure with the passage of time. The section 'Mumbai Men of the Nineteenth Century' provides short biographical notes on nearly 75 of the them – still leaving out a similar number on whom adequate information could not be collected. Similarly 'Mumbai Institutions of the Nineteenth Century' documents the main institutions in Mumbai during the same period.

The life and literary career of Govind Narayan have never been studied or written about in the English language. Short biographies have been published in Marathi at regular intervals since his death in 1865. A brief notice of his life is taken in 'Govind Narayan: A Preliminary Bio-bibliography' which could form the basis for a more detailed study of the man and his times.

Govind Narayan: A Preliminary Bio-Bibliography

Govind Narayan: A Preliminary
Bio-Bibliography

In 1824, Govind Narayan, as a young boy of nine, accompanied his family
on the one-way journey to Mumbai in search of education and economic
prosperity – like many generations before his and all succeeding generations
thereafter. The Mumbai of the 1820s was however hardly the city it had
transformed itself into by the 1860s when Govind Narayan finally gathered
together the observations and studies of a life-time in his book, *Mumbaiche
Varnan*. A long-time observer of India reminiscing in the 1870s about the
state of Mumbai half a century earlier provides an European perspective:
'To the present generation it would be difficult to convey an idea of the
aspect of Bombay in 1822. It can only be done by negatives. There was no
Town Hall; no educational establishment of any kind for the natives, no
boarding houses, no banks, one old hotel to which scarcely any one ever
resorted, no Mechanics' Institution, no Mint, no daily newspaper, no
communication with Colaba except at low water, no steam engines of any
kind, and of course no railroad. That only existed in the imagination of
George Stephenson, the first railroad in England had not been commenced.
Civilization, as we now understand, was positively stagnant. There was no
supreme court of judicature, and only one English and one Scottish church.'[1]

Though the English had acquired Mumbai (or Bombay as they called it)
from the Portuguese in 1661, their hold on the island during the seventeenth
and for a large part of the eighteenth century was, at best tenuous and their
security depended on the indulgence of the military powers on the
surrounding mainland, the Mughals and the Marathas. As their political
fortunes improved, they began consolidating their hold on the island and
developing it as the centre of commerce in the Eastern part of the world. By
the end of the eighteenth century, Mumbai had emerged as a relatively
peaceful haven from the continuous upheavals and military skirmishes
which ravaged most parts of the surrounding country and to which the
English contributed not a little. The English also actively encouraged the

settlement of the island of Mumbai by various inducements; this led to an influx of people into Mumbai from most of the surrounding countryside and especially the coastal areas of the Konkan by water, which was the easiest mode of travel into Mumbai in those days. The population of Mumbai had swelled to over 200,000 by the early 1800s from a paltry 16,000 as recorded by Fryer in the 1670s.

With the capitulation of the Maratha Peshwas, the last great Indian power, in 1818, the English became the undisputed overlords of the Indian sub-continent and Mumbai, the long-established seat of the English on the Western coast of India emerged as the *de facto* capital of Western India and the capital of the eponymous Presidency of Bombay. This position of leadership further enhanced the reputation of Mumbai as a place where fortunes could be made. Furthermore, with a basic knowledge of English, one could obtain employment with the English government, which ensured a regular income and, perhaps, a much-needed sense of power to the recently emasculated ruling classes.

Much of Govind Narayan's life can be inextricably linked with the development of a modern education system in Mumbai and the emergence of an intellectual class amongst the citizens of Mumbai. He describes both these advancements as he sees them happening in his book, *Mumbaiche Varnan,* in an episodic fashion, and in most cases, without passing judgement. These developments have been briefly reviewed below as they provided a necessary background to Govind Narayan's life. The development of modern Marathi literature is also intertwined with the new education system, which demanded a constant supply of new books in Marathi; the assimilation of these books as well as those in English contributed to the emergence of an intellectual class. An account of the early development of modern Marathi literature is beyond the scope of this paper.[2]

His life can be split into three distinct phases – the initial phase comprising of the formative years of education, a long literary foreground spent in teaching, and the final phase when he embarked on his literary career. This narrative is followed by a discussion of Govind Narayan's involvement with the intellectual scene in Mumbai, his relationships with many of Mumbai's elite, and his opinions on the important issues which loomed large in the socio-cultural life of Mumbai in the mid-nineteenth century, followed by a bibliography of his works.

Up until the establishment of the University at Mumbai in 1857, it was not the general practice among the Hindus to use a family name or caste denominator or a suffix denoting their place of origin in their appellations. The name only consisted of the person's given name and his father's name as in the case of Govind Narayan. However, with the increasing spread of Western-style education, the use of surnames in the application forms became, to a certain extent, mandatory and very quickly came into popular practice. Govind Narayan's family chose to use Madgaonkar as their surname denoting their origin from Madgaon in Goa. Govind Narayan himself used the surname Shenvi in the first two editions of his earliest book, *Suchirbhutpana*, published in 1849 and 1853 respectively. He was generally addressed as 'Govindji' by his colleagues as a mark of respect and this style is used in the book *Srushtitil Chamatkar* published in 1851. He is also variously styled 'Govindji Narayn', 'Govindjee Narrayan', and 'Govindji Narayan'. All his works published in the twentieth century carry the name of the author as Govind Narayan Madgaonkar. I have however generally referred to him by the appellation which he himself used – Govind Narayan.

Education in Mumbai: 1815–65

The new English regime inevitably changed the traditional way of life and many of the old institutions and practices of the Maratha regime were either immediately replaced or they slowly degraded due to neglect and economic pressures. One of the major institutions which crumbled because of government apathy were the old-style *pathshalas* of the Hindus and the *madrasas* of the Muslims. This was however accompanied by a development of schools modelled on the Western model teaching English and other modern sciences. The development of a modern education system in Mumbai was eventually followed by the creation of a new intellectual climate, further aided by the development of printing technology, the emergence of a local press, and the creation of a body of literature in the local languages of Marathi and Gujarati.

In 1815 itself, the *Society for Promoting the Education of the Poor within the Government of Bombay*, better known as the *Bombay Education Society*, was formed to manage a school for poor Anglo-Indian children, born of European soldiers and sailors and Indian mothers. By the early 1820s, there were quite a few schools in Bombay imparting education in Marathi, Gujarati and English. Besides, many rich men engaged private teachers to teach their children at home. However, there was neither a central body which oversaw the education process, nor was there any text-books or any other books for that matter. The printing press had arrived in Mumbai only at the fag end of the eighteenth century; however printing in Marathi and Gujarati was still at a very nascent stage and casting types was still being learnt in the 1820s.

When the Charter of the East India Company was renewed in 1813, it undertook to allocate a portion of its budget for 'the revival and improvement of literature and the encouragement of the learned natives of India and for the introduction and promotion of knowledge of the sciences among the inhabitants of the British territories in India.'[3] In the Western Presidency of Bombay, which was created after the annexation of the Peshwa territories, Governor Mountstuart Elphinstone provided the necessary impetus for streamlining the system of education to meet the evolving needs of the English government while also keeping in mind the need for reformation among the local communities.

After Elphinstone became the President of the *Bombay Education Society*, he broadened its activities by establishing the *Native School and School-Book Committee* to promote education amongst the Hindus, Muslims, and Parsis. With a view to provide a framework for the development of the new education system, the committee was reconstituted as the *Bombay Native School and School-Book Society* in 1822 with Mountstuart Elphinstone as the first President; a 'European Secretary' managed the activities while the 'Native Secretary' was to be the link between the Society and its intended audience, the Indian population in Mumbai and the prominent members of Mumbai, who funded its activities. Only after Captain George Jervis took over as the European Secretary did the Society begin to show results; he was ably assisted by Sadashiv Kashinath Chhatre. The Society believed that education must be imparted to the people in their native language and consequently its schools taught in English as well as the two principal languages of Mumbai – Marathi and Gujarati. While Jervis adapted from English text-books and produced a number of books in both these languages, Chhatre also wrote a number of Marathi books for use in schools, mainly translations from Sanskrit.

Chhatre was also instrumental in attracting to Mumbai, the brightest Indian students like Bal Gangadharshastri Jambhekar and Govind Vithal Kunte who went on to shape the intellectual climate of Mumbai in the next few decades. By 1826, the Society had published ten books in Marathi and manuscripts of a further twelve books were readied for publication. Most of the students in this school were from the upper castes or from the Prabhu community, traditionally clerks in government or private offices, to which Govind Narayan belonged.

This Society was renamed as the *Bombay Native Education Society* in 1827 and continued its activities as an independent organization with the establishment of the *Elphinstone Institution* to commemorate the departure to England of the Governor, Mountstuart Elphinstone. It was established with funds gathered from the prominent citizens of Mumbai to teach the English language and other branches of Western knowledge. In 1856, the *Elphinstone Institution* was bifurcated into the *Elphinstone High School* and the *Elphinstone College*, both of which continue to function under the same name today.

The *Bombay Native Education Society* continued the programme of publishing books in Marathi, both translations and original compositions, which could be used in schools across the Bombay Presidency.

Many books on Marathi Grammar were written (the most famous being the one by Dadoba Pandurang Tarkhadkar, an associate of Govind Narayan) and Marathi dictionaries were compiled (the most enduring being that of Molesworth, whom Govind Narayan quotes as an authority). Histories of the Maratha nation as well as that of England were prepared with a view to help students better understand their past as well as their current rulers.

Parallel to these quasi-governmental efforts, was the education movement started by Christian missionaries. The first missionaries to arrive in Mumbai in 1813 were American Protestants, who established the *American Marathi Mission*. They started the first Marathi school for girls soon after they reached Mumbai. As successive missions were established in Mumbai, many of them emulated the Americans by setting up schools, with the *General Assembly's Institution*, a school started by Dr. John Wilson, building a reputation of offering the best education that could be had in Mumbai. These schools emphasized the role of native languages rather than English in school education; independent text-books were also written by the missionaries for use in these schools.

Along with the establishment of schools for basic education, institutions for higher learning were also founded. An *Engineer's Institution* or *Ganeet Shilpa Vidyalaya* was established in 1825 and Captain Jervis produced numerous books on mathematics and science in Marathi and Gujarati for use in this institution. This institution was later moved to Pune and eventually became defunct in the 1850s. A *Native Medical School* was established in 1826 which was the forerunner to the *Grant Medical College*, founded in 1845 with the assistance of Sir Jamsetjee Jejeebhoy; the latter is still in existence. The same gentleman also provided funds for starting a *School of Art* in 1857 which is now known as the *J.J. School of Arts*.

In 1840, the *Bombay Native Education Society* was replaced by the *Board of Education* which was now a full-fledged government department. The Board soon realized that the development of the school curriculum and text-books had been necessarily haphazard in the past twenty years. They invited suggestions from a committee consisting of, among others, Professor Orlebar,

Professor Bell, Major Candy, and Bal Gangadharshastri Jambhekar. While this committee recommended a complete revision of the text-books, matters did not progress for the next four years until Jambhekar was entrusted with the responsibility of revising the text-books in 1845, but he died in the following year. Major Candy, already the Inspector of Marathi Schools in the Konkan and Principal of the *Poona Sanskrit College*, was therefore appointed as Marathi Translator and Referee in 1847, a position he held for the next three decades.

In the following years, he exercised tight control over 'Mahratta publications, with the view of removing everything that may be found objectionable, previous to passing new editions through the press, and of striking off the list any work which may be found to contain either false morality or false science.'[4] He had quite a few critics but the vast majority of Marathi scholars did not take issue with him either because of his perceived close proximity to the ruling authority or because they found his comments and suggestions truly useful in improving their writing in Marathi.

In 1855, a Director of Public Instruction was appointed to centrally control all aspects of education in the Bombay Presidency in the newly formed Department of Education. The Director, E. I. Howard, in one of his early reports sums up the thorny issue of European supervision over Marathi books very perspicaciously. 'As yet, it is apparently impossible to dispense with European superintendence in getting up vernacular treatises of general knowledge. There is no doubt the books are the worse in point of style from this circumstance. Natives complain that at the best they are stiff, and ungainly; and probably it must needs be so. A council of pundits may correct and retouch, but the original foreign air will never entirely disappear. And the very merits of the European scholar – his logical precision of thought, his taste for grammatical analysis, and love of symmetry – become defects in as much as they tend to sweep away the racy anomalies which grow up in the structure of every language, and to a native ear constitute some of its greatest attractions'.[5] He played the role of moderator in the ensuing conflicts between Major Candy and various Marathi scholars, and felt that a difference of opinion was an indication of the robust health of the language.

He appointed a *Graded Text-Book Committee* which consisted of eminent European and Indian members, including Govind Narayan, to evaluate Marathi text-books and prepare a series of graded text-books which could be used in Marathi schools. Though the committee was established, the bulk of the work was done by Candy who exercised direct control over the production of books; a series of six books were produced between 1857 and 1861. These text-books were again completely revised and enlarged in 1868.

An important event in the final years of the period under review was the establishment of the *University of Bombay* in 1857, with funds from numerous prominent citizens of Mumbai. It opened a new chapter in education in Mumbai and was mainly intended to impart education in English in the style of European universities and award degrees upon completion of education courses. Marathi, though initially taught in the university, was, by the late 1860s, discarded from the curriculum, much to the anguish and disgust of Marathi patriots, both Indian and English.

The intellectual climate of Mumbai

Much of the intellectual climate of Bombay in the nineteenth century was shaped by the activities of Europeans, though much of it was sponsored by rich Indian merchants.[6] The *Literary Society of Bombay*, formed in 1804 at the initiative of Sir James Mackintosh was the first organization where Europeans gathered to share information about various parts of India, which had recently come under English rule. This Society affiliated itself to the Royal Asiatic Society in 1829 and was renamed the *Bombay Branch of the Royal Asiactic Society* (BBRAS). Organizations like the *Bombay Geographical Society*, the *Medical and Physical Society of Bombay* also worked on similar lines. In the initial years, there were no Indian members, most probably because none could be found who had mastered the English language and was interested enough in the acquisition of knowledge in the Western style. The first Indian member, a Parsi named Maneckjee Cursetjee, joined the BBRAS in 1840; Indian membership continued to remain very minuscule for a long time (totalling less than 20 until the 1860s), perhaps because the annual fees of rupees fifty could be afforded only by the very rich. School-teachers like Govind Narayan, who may have wanted to become members to access the Society's rich collection of books not available elsewhere in Mumbai for a very long time, could not afford to do so. Dr. Bhau Daji Lad, a private student of Govind Narayan, and very active in all aspects of Mumbai life, became the first Indian Vice-President of the BBRAS in 1864.

Notwithstanding the lack of Indian membership in such organizations, there were many educated Mumbaikars who had read modern European texts, were inspired by the recent upheavals in France, Germany and Italy, absorbed concepts like liberty, equality, and fraternity and applied it to their own circumstances in Mumbai. Initiatives were also taken for the establishment of libraries in Mumbai where locals would have easier access to books, most notably the *Native General Library*, started in 1845 and *Juvenile Improvement Library*, established in 1852.

The formation of new opinion was aided by the development of printing technology in Mumbai. In the last decade of the eighteenth century, the art of printing was finally established in Mumbai and a few English newspapers, notably the *Bombay Gazette* and the *Bombay Courier,* had commenced publication. The *Courier Press* created types in Gujarati and started using them in 1797 for printing advertisements; similarly, Marathi types came into use in 1802. The first Gujarati press in Mumbai was started in 1812 by Fardunji Marzaban while the *American Marathi Mission* established the first exclusively Marathi press in 1816, mainly to print their religious tracts and text-books for use in their schools. The government also began to feel the need to establish a printing press, especially for the publication of Gujarati and Marathi books being produced by the *Bombay Native Education Society.* Both lithographic and typographic presses were in use and soon there was enough demand for this business to attract private enterprise. Constant improvements were made in the type used for printing in Marathi and Gujarati and the *Ganpat Krishnaji Press,* established in 1840 came to represent the acme of local printing.[7]

An immediate fall-out of the development of printing technology was the foundation of a local vernacular press. The *Bombay Samachar,* a business newspaper in Gujarati was the first entrant in 1822. In 1832, the Anglo-Marathi newspaper, *Bombay Durpun,* was started by Bal Gangadharshastri Jambhekar 'to open a field of inquiry for free public discussion on points connected with the prosperity of the country and happiness of its inhabitants'.[8] This spirit of inquiry, aided by other newspapers, soon encompassed every field of life, from stagnation in the Hindu religion to evaluation of British rule. While most of the educated men who participated in these debates were essentially conservative who advocated reform within the existing framework and accepted British rule as beneficial to India, there were others who began to move in an opposite direction. Bhau Mahajan started the *Prabhakar* in 1841 which soon emerged as the pre-eminent vernacular newspaper on account of its trenchant treatment of political and economic issues.

The English had been careful to censor the press from its very inception but that was mainly to control disgruntled elements amongst the Europeans. During a brief period starting in 1835 when the censor laws were relaxed, there were many voices in the English and Marathi press which vehemently criticized the English rule on various accounts, especially on grounds of discrimination against Indians and the impoverishment of India.[9]

In the social arena, fledgling movements to reform Hinduism were floated by the newly educated young men of Mumbai. The most famous one was the *Paramahansa Sabha,* a secret society inspired in 1847 by Dadoba Pandurang Tarkhadkar with a view to dismantling the caste system and other evils of Hindu society. This Sabha was short-lived mainly because of its secret nature and strong opposition from Hindu society. The *Marathi Dnyanaprasarak Sabha,* formed in 1848, under the auspices of the Students' Literary and Scientific Society, with Dadoba Pandurang Tarkhadkar as its first President, could well be construed as the public arm of the *Paramahansa Sabha,* and provided a very liberal environment, though it specifically eschewed religious and political issues. It contributed significantly to the development of the Marathi language as well as a corpus of knowledge in Marathi.

The *Bombay Association* was the first overtly political organization formed by eminent Indian citizens of Mumbai in 1852 to formally represent the views of Indians in the British Parliament. While it did not achieve anything substantial, it did manage to create a political forum in Mumbai and was the predecessor of all other organised political movements in Western India.

With the First Indian War of Independence or 'Sepoy Mutiny' of 1857 as it was then known, there were stricter clampdowns on the press and on freedom of opinion. This was accompanied by a marked chilling in the relationship between Indians and Europeans in general and an increase in the level of mistrust and polarity.

In the early 1860s, with Mumbai enjoying a boom because of unsustainably high prices for cotton (a fall-out of the American Civil War), plans for a complete redevelopment of Mumbai were being implemented; new monumental structures and public spaces were being designed; modern conveniences like public transport and water supply were finally becoming a reality; new companies were being floated for ambitious business ventures; and there was a sheen of prosperity on the entire city.

Getting an education: 1815–34

It was to such a Mumbai that Govind Narayan's family made the move from Madgaon in Goa. The Portuguese territory of Goa, from which Govind Narayan's family hailed, had witnessed a marked change in its fortunes. The Portuguese were no longer the world power they once were and the economic opportunities in Goa were increasingly limited. Govind's father, Narayan was an apothecary of sorts and dispensed various medicines. He also was a vendor of snuff, a derivative of tobacco – tobacco imported from Brazil, another Portuguese colony would be processed into snuff in Portugal before being exported to Goa. As a small-time trader, he may have well felt that he had better options in Mumbai, both for himself and for the education of his three sons. He set up a shop to conduct his business on Kalikadevi Road, a major thoroughfare in the 'Black Town'[10] of Mumbai. By all accounts, he successfully ran this business until his death in 1833. He was assisted in the shop by his eldest son, Vishnu, who does not seem to have obtained any formal education in Mumbai.

The other two sons, Gopinath and Govind, having started their formal education in Goa, continued it in Mumbai. They may well have joined the *Central Marathi School* which was located near the Esplanade and managed by the *Bombay Native School-Book and School Society*. A contemporary report says that 'The Central Marathi School possesses some boys, who fluently read and write the Language, both in the Balbodh and Moree character; and are prepared to commence the study of the grammatical structure of this language'.[11]

It is not clear for how long Govind Narayan continued in this school. It is likely that he studied there for three to four years before joining the *Central English School* stared by the *Bombay Native Education Society* in 1827. Govind Narayan, aged about thirteen, must have acquired a fair knowledge of the Marathi language and such other sciences, as were included in the curriculum and met the standards set for admission to the *Elphinstone Institution*. A later report gives guidelines for admissions: 'No boy can be now admitted into the English School who has not previously passed an examination as to his grammatical acquirements in his own language and his acquaintance with the rules of Arithmetic. Should his examination prove satisfactory, a written order for his admission is given.'[12]

Govind and his elder brother, Gopinath were both students of this Institution. Gopinath however soon left the School in 1828 and became an assistant teacher in Dr. Wilson's school (then called the *General Assembly's Institution*) which was founded in 1832. He went on to work in various departments of the government, finally retiring from the Military Department. Govind continued in the *Elphinstone Institution* until 1834.[13] He then left the Institution once he had completed the most senior of the seven classes conducted in the school because there were no facilities for advanced learning. Though, in 1827, it was proposed to institute professorships 'to be held by learned men from Great Britain, who could teach the English language, the arts and sciences, and literature of Europe, until the happy period arrived, when the Natives of this Country might be found perfectly competent to undertake this office',[14] no candidates seem to have offered themselves until 1835 when Arthur Orlebar and John Harkness arrived in Mumbai to take up the Elphinstone professorships in natural philosophy and general literature respectively.

Though Govind Narayan was already nineteen years old and could have obtained a well-paying government job with his knowledge of English, he might have felt that he needed to have a deeper education than that offered by the basic curriculum at the *Elphinstone Institution*. On the other hand, the *General Assembly's Institution* seemed to hold a lot of promise, especially as it was run by a learned scholar like Dr. Wilson. Additionally Govind's elder brother, Gopinath was a teacher in that school which may have allayed any apprehensions his family might have felt about him joining a Christian-run school. He thus followed in his brother's footsteps and joined Dr. Wilson's school, most likely as a student in the senior classes; he may also have assisted in teaching the lower classes as a 'monitor'.

The long foreground: 1834–48

When Govind Narayan joined the *General Assembly's Institution* in 1834, it had 50 students – 37 Hindus, 9 Parsis, and 4 Muslims, and functioned from a room in Dr. Wilson's house at Ambroli, a place in the Girgaon area of Mumbai. It made quick progress and by 1837, there were 216 boys in the 'School Division' and 14 in the 'Upper Division'[15] which was formed in 1836. In 1837, Govind Narayan was teacher for the Fifth Class in the School Division and taught subjects like reading, geography and religious knowledge. A report of the public examination for that year remarks that 'the boys of the fifth class were noticed as making rapid progress under a native teacher'.[16] Govind Narayan was also a student of the 'Upper Division' (soon called the 'College Division') where he won a prize in one subject – grammar and composition.

In 1838, Govind Narayan finished his education and graduated from the 'College Division' of the *General Assembly's Institution* at the age of twenty-four. He won prizes in the subjects of natural history, natural theology, and translations into Indian languages but did not get any prizes in the other three subjects – English classics, mathematics, and mental and moral philosophy.[17] By all accounts, this was a late age to finish one's education, but in the initial stages of both a new system of education and a new body of literature in Marathi, this could perhaps not be helped and was fairly common-place. For example, Dr. Bhau Daji Lad after having finished his studies at the *Elphinstone Institution* in 1841, joined the newly opened *Grant Medical College* in 1845 and graduated in 1851, when he was twenty-seven.

In all probability, while he continued his education in the 'College Division', Govind Narayan had started teaching at the primary and secondary levels of the 'School Division'. For instance, he is listed as taught

'Idiomatical Exercises in English and Marathi' to the Third Class of the School Division in 1853.[18] By 1839, he was already the book agent for the *General Assembly's Institution* and his name appeared on the cover of books written by Dr. Wilson and others and published by this organization.[19]

In the initial years, Dr. Wilson personally taught most of the subjects, framed the syllabus of instruction and also wrote a few of the text-books. A Hindu, most probably Gopinath Narayan and an Anglo-Indian made up the teaching staff. In the late 1830s, Dr. Wilson was joined by two other Scottish missionaries, Rev. J. Murray Mitchell and Rev. Robert Nesbit who taught with much dedication. The reputation of the school continued to grow by leaps and bounds over the years, and even *Prabhakar,* one of the leading Marathi newspapers which viewed all activities of the missionaries with intense suspicion, had to acknowledge the fact that the teaching in the missionary institution (which was now called the Free *General Assembly's Institution* after the Disruption of the Church of Scotland in 1843) was better than the government schools.[20] It can be surmised that Govind Narayan must have contributed in no small measure to the building of this reputation. For instance, as early as 1838, he is recorded as having collected rupees thirty-five for the Building Fund.[21]

The middle quarter of the nineteenth century was the years of formation of modern Marathi literature; it was also the scene for many controversies regarding the medium of instruction, the standardization of the language and other aspects of development of a nascent language. This period has been characterised as the 'Age of Translation' in Marathi literature,[22] with many works in English and Sanskrit being translated into English and many new words and a whole body of scientific literature being created in Marathi. Numerous dictionaries and grammars were compiled by various scholars and standardised text-books were being constantly introduced across schools in the Marathi-speaking territories of the Bombay Presidency.

This period can also be seen as a long foreground for Govind Narayan's later literary career. Unlike many of his other English-educated contemporaries who promptly took up the relatively lucrative government service once they finished their education, Govind Narayan seems to have been content to work in the same mission school until his retirement and supplement his necessarily meagre income with private tuitions. He emerged as a trusted associate of Dr. John Wilson, though his continued non-acceptance of Christianity must have chilled their relationship, as Wilson was an indefatigable missionary, ever intent on obtaining conscientious converts to the Christian religion.

Govind Narayan, having been mainly educated in English, became a strong believer in the supremacy of English over other Indian languages, especially Marathi, as a medium of instruction in India. This was accompanied by a strong level of disinterest in and a complete disdain for Marathi as a literary language. It required the inspiration and example of a few Englishmen for Govind Narayan to change his mind and begin to appreciate the potential of Marathi. He describes his conversion in a candid manner in the foreword of one his books, *Udbhiddajanyapadarth*, first published in 1856. 'After having started to learn English, I, like many others, developed a strong dislike for the language of Maharashtra. I felt disgusted to read a Marathi book or to even hold one in my hands. However, after I joined the Free Church School, I had to make some efforts to study Marathi because both Dr. Wilson and the late Reverend Robert Nesbit were very devoted to the language and strove very hard to ensure that the local children learnt the language in a proper manner. In 1847, another fortunate incident happened; Dr. Leith who used to visit the school occasionally believed that a strong understanding of one's native language enabled students to learn foreign languages easily, and generously announced a prize of hundred rupees for an essay competition in which participants had to write an impromptu essay on a given subject in the Maharashtra language without reference to any books. This praiseworthy deed automatically led many of the students and teachers to study their native tongue. I was also greatly inspired to learn Marathi and made a lot of efforts in that direction. This is how I developed an interest in the Marathi language, and I am grateful to these three gentlemen for whatever little knowledge I now have of the language.'[23] These episodes led to a kindling of interest in Govind Narayan and a subsequent liking for the Marathi language in which he went on to make a literary career.

A prodigious literary output: 1849–65

Reviewing the career of Govind Narayan, Dr. John Wilson comments 'on the success which, in the view of all readers of Marathi and Gujarati, he had obtained in the seventeen[24] popular original works, great and small, with which he had enriched the vernacular literature of the West of India'.[25] A large number of these works are small in scope; there are three or four which can be classified as major works. However all of them display a measure of original thought and a freshness of approach, both of which were singularly rare in Marathi books published in that era.

In the first phase of his literary career, Govind Narayan mainly wrote a number of essays which were prescriptive in their content and reformatory in nature. In the second phase, his focus shifted towards scientific subjects while in the third and final phase of his literary career, the subjects were more general in nature and culminated in *Mumbaiche Varnan*. During this period, he was also associated with two monthly periodicals. The first was the *Oriental Christian Spectator* which had been started in 1830 by Dr. Wilson, who edited it for most of the four decades of its existence. It was avowedly a missionary publication with the furtherance of Christianity as its main objective. Govind Narayan was the 'Agent' (or manager) and publisher of this monthly magazine from 1844 to 1861. He might well have written a few stray snippets in English for this magazine but they are not identifiable. Around 1856, he increased his involvement with the Marathi *Dnyanaprasarak Sabha* and its magazine, the *Marathi Dnyanaprasarak*. He was the moving spirit behind this publication until about a year before his death in 1865.

A survey of his literary output

Govind Narayan's literary development can be discerned over three phases, each reflective of the development in style and innovation in the author, and responsive to the demand for specific books in those periods. In the first phase, he mainly wrote essays which were calculated to shake Hindu society out of its lassitude and complacence.

The first few books which appeared between 1849 and 1855 were mainly exhortative essays which called upon his fellow countrymen to reform themselves whether it be in matters of personal hygiene and the handling of domestic issues, or warning them about the evils of drink and debt. They were written in what can be best described as the typical school-master style, but they were modern in their outlook and advocated a substantial change in the traditional practices of the Hindus. Govind Narayan could never resist giving words of advice to his readers and slips it in even in his later books about trees and Mumbai. His language is very serious in tone, with not a trace of humour, perhaps reflective of the man in the classroom.

The first book which was published in 1849, when he was 34 years old, was *Suchirbhutpana*, a 'Treatise on Cleanliness' which was most likely written in response to the call for Marathi essays issued by the aforementioned Dr. Leith. This book was published by the Board of Education at Mumbai and printed at the *American Mission Press*. A Gujarati translation was published in Ahmedabad soon after the Marathi edition. Two more Marathi editions of this book were published during his life-time.

This short essay was immediately followed in 1850 by *Rinn-Nishedhak Bodh* or the 'Evils of Debt'. He condemns the practice of spending beyond ones means and getting into a debt spiral which seems to have been very common amongst the citizens of Mumbai. The book's 'lively and happy style' particularly appealed the reviewer in the *Oriental Christian Spectator*.[26] He also discourses about the same topic in *Mumbaiche Varnan* when he describes the life-style of the Hindus.

Another essay in the same vein is *Hindu Lokanchya Reeti Sudharnyacha Bodh* or 'Domestic Reform among the Hindus' which appeared in 1851 in Mumbai. He comments on the traditional practices of the Hindus and exhorts them to change with the times. It is noticed as an 'excellent tract' in the *Oriental Christian Spectator*.[27]

Govind Narayan presented these three books to the *Bombay Branch of the Royal Asiatic Society* as is noted in the extracts from the Proceedings of the Society for the year 1850–51, though he was not a member of the Society.[28] These books are not forthcoming at the present time. He is referred to as 'Govindji Narayn' in the report.

He also published another small essay, *Nitisanvad*, a 'Discourse on Ethics' in 1850 which is dedicated to his student, Dr. Bhau Daji, who went on to become one of the leading citizens of Mumbai.

Satyanirupan, 'An Exposition of Truth' was published in 1852. This was written in response to a competition announced in October 1851 by John Willoughby, member of the Governor's Council in the Government of Bombay for essays in the Marathi or Gujarati languages on the 'Observance of Truth with special reference to the administration of justice and the advancement of the best interests of Society'[29]; prizes of rupees 150, rupees 60 and rupees 40 were announced. Govind Narayan's essay won one of these prizes. The book also contains a list of the advance subscribers to the book and includes all the leading citizens of Mumbai like the then Governor of Bombay, Lord Falkland, the Chief Justice Sir Erskine Perry, Major le Grand Jacob and Sir Jamsetjee Jejeebhoy. The *Dakshina Prize Committee* purchased 100 copies of this book.[30]

The last in the series of reformatory essays was *Darupasun Anarth* or 'The Evils of Drink' which was published in 1855. This was written in response to the growing spread of alcoholism amongst the younger generation under the rule of the English and may well have been written under the aegis of the *Bombay Temperance Union*. The essay was awarded a prize by the *American Marathi Mission*, who also published it.

In this first phase, he also published *Srushtitil Chamatkar*, a translation of the book, 'Natural Phenomena with Pictorial Illustrations'. This book was in response to a call given by the *Deccan Vernacular Translation Society* which was formed in 1849 with a view to publish books in the Marathi and Gujarati lanuages. In its first meeting, it was decided to publish translations of three books: 'Elphinstone's History of India', 'The Pictorial Museum of Animated Nature in 27 parts', and 'Natural Phenomena with Pictorial Illustrations'. However, at the end of one year it was realized that in spite of their being many Marathi-speaking individuals who were fluent in English, there had been no progress in these translations.[31] Govind Narayan must have taken up the translation of the last-mentioned book a short while thereafter and this book was published in 1851 by the *Deccan Vernacular Translation Society*. It was printed in the *Gunput Krishnaji Press* and bound with the original English version published by the *Society for Promoting Christian Knowledge*.

In the second phase of his literary career, he changed his focus to scientific subjects. There was a strong demand for Marathi books on various scientific subjects from the various organizations which were charged with the responsibility of producing books in Marathi and from the increasing number of educational institutions which were being established in Western India. Govind Narayan chose to focus on flora in both of his major works and this is clearly linked to a deep love for nature and many years of observation in the field. Characteristic to his style, he hardly ever lets escape his deep personal interest in plants and trees in any of his other works. However, an estimate of his fascination with trees may be made from a visit he refers to in his introduction to the book, *Udbhiddajanyapadarth*. He mentions a trip he especially made to Thane (about 30 kilometres from Mumbai) to visit and measure a fallen baobab (*Adansonia digitata)* tree which had stood in the vicinity of the old fort there, and count the number of rings in its trunk to estimate its age. Before the advent of the train, even this short journey would have involved considerable planning and hardship and could have been undertaken only by the most committed observer.

Both the books – *Udbhiddajanyapadarth* or 'Vegetable Substances' and *Vrikshavarnan* or 'Description of Trees' – were published in 1856 and 1857 respectively and were intended to be used as a text-books. However, both of them are too vast in their scope and detailed in their treatment to be termed as text-books and can well be termed as the first botanical reference books in Marathi. Though *Vrikshavarnan* was published later, it is referred to in the former book; this suggests that they were written in the same period and were designed to be companion volumes.

The first book, *Udbhiddajanyapadarth,* is an encyclopaedic reference manual on all agricultural plants grown in Western India with a small section providing an introduction to plants grown in other parts of the world. While he may have well have had access to books on agriculture in English, this is an original compilation of all edible substances of Western India. The work has twelve sections for various categories of vegetable substances – grains, cereals, tubers, vegetables from creepers, vegetables from plants, root vegetables, leafy vegetables, forest fruits, forest vegetables, vegetables grown in salt grounds, vegetables suitable for pickling, and foreign edible substance – and a final section where Govind Narayan expresses his views on agriculture. For each plant, he covers its nutritive aspects, the importance of the plant in the local diet and culture, the mode of cultivation and other anecdotal details. In the introductory chapter of this book, Govind Narayan provides detailed instructions on how to use the book as a teaching aid and provides a good description of his brand of pedagogy. This book figures in the list of books being used in schools for the years 1858–59.[32] It was dedicated to the then Governor of Bombay, Lord Elphinstone. He received a sum of rupees five hundred from the Bombay Government which purchased the rights to the book. The government also proposed to translate this book into Hindi but this plan was not perhaps acted upon.[33]

Vrikshavarnan is structured as a popular book on trees, both Indian and foreign, and is modelled on the lines of any modern book on trees but without any illustrations, which were dropped because its publishers, the *Dakshina Prize Committee* felt they were too expensive.[34] The *Dakshina Prize Committee* awarded a cash prize to Govind Narayan for this book. However, both these books now seem to be lost from the tradition of Marathi literature on natural history and there is clearly a need to rehabilitate them in recognition of their pioneering content.

The third book, which also may be termed scientific, reported on the coming of the railway – viewed as a miracle in India, as it was in other parts of the world. This small book, *Lokhandi Sadakache Chamatkar* (translated by Govind Narayan himself as the 'Wonders of the Railway') describes the planning, building and the grand opening of the railway in India with the completion of the first section between Mumbai and Thane. Though it is unlikely that Govind Narayan may have been one of the important personages who made the triumphant journey on 16 April 1853, he must have travelled by the railways soon after. The book is based on a lecture given by Govind Narayan at the *United Students' Association* on 15 March 1858 and is dedicated to Rev. Adam White, the convenor of this organization. The Bombay Government bought 100 copies of this book.[35]

During the same phase, he also wrote numerous articles in the *Marathi Dnyanaprasarak* on subjects related to nature in a manner reminiscent of Thoreau. His essays on bee-hives and nests of crows can well be compared with Thoreau's classic essay on wild apples. These continued to appear in the magazine until 1865.

The only book he published after 1860 was *Mumbaiche Varnan* which appeared in 1863, the product of many years of hard work of research and writing. It is quite clearly intended to be his *magnum opus*. Though it was awarded a prize of rupees seventy-five by the *Dakshina Prize Committee* in 1864, it does not seem to have been then recognised as a landmark in Marathi literature by contemporary critics. The book was dedicated to E. I. Howard, the then Director of Public Instruction.

Govind Narayan and the Marathi *Dnyanaprasarak Sabha*

Some of the past students of the *Elphinstone Institution* in which Govind Narayan had initially studied established the *Students' Literary and Scientific Society* in June 1848. The *Upayukt Dnyanaprasarak Sabha* was formed in September 1848 under the auspices of this organization to work towards the diffusion of useful knowledge (as its name denoted) amongst Marathi-speaking Hindus and was perhaps modeled on the *Society for Diffusion of Universal Knowledge*. Dadoba Pandurang Tarkhadkar, the eminent Marathi grammarian was its first President while its first Secretary was Mahadeo Govindshastri Kolhatkar, a close associate of Govind Narayan, whose contribution to the *Mumbaiche Varnan* is acknowledged in the preface. This Society, after being renamed as *Marathi Dnyanaprasarak Sabha*, met twice a month in the premises of *Elphinstone Institution* where members delivered lectures in Marathi. These were subsequently published in the *Marathi Dnyanaprasarak*, a monthly magazine which the Sabha started publishing in April 1850. A range of subjects – scientific, historical, geographical, and social – were covered in the magazine and occasionally stories and plays would be serialised. Overtly political subjects and religious themes were prohibited. The magazine ran uninterruptedly for seventeen years, a major achievement in those years when most publications were short-lived, not least because of the energy and efforts of the men behind the Sabha.

While it is not clear when Govind Narayan became a member of the *Marathi Dnyanaprasarak Sabha*, he could well have joined it at its inception. His active involvement with the Sabha can however be linked to the appearance of his articles in the magazine, *Marathi Dnyanaprasarak* from 1856. In 1857, he was the Vice-President of the Sabha and his services to the Society were highly appreciated in their annual report for that year.[36] From 1858 onwards, he was, by popular opinion, the obvious choice for the President of the *Marathi Dnyanaprasarak Sabha*[37] but was elected as President only in 1863–64.[38] By virtue of this position, he was also the Vice-President of the *Students' Literary and Scientific Society* under the presidency of Dr. Bhau Daji.

He delivered a number of lectures at the *Marathi Dnyanaprasarak Sabha*, a few of which were published in the society's magazine. Many of these lectures urged the members, who seem to have been apathetic to the affairs of the society, to participate whole-heartedly in the affairs of the Sabha, to devote themselves to its objectives, and ensure the development of the Marathi language. One of the projects he suggested before the Sabha was the compilation of a *Sarvasangrah* in Marathi which as its name suggested was to be encyclopaedic in nature. He was of the opinion that a language could be considered developed only if it had books like encyclopaedias in its literature. The Sabha, perhaps because of the lack of keen interest among its members, could not undertake such a gargantuan undertaking. The Marathi encyclopaedia had to wait for another seventy years before Dr. S.V. Ketkar completed his monumental 26-volume 'Marathi Encyclopaedia' in 1926.[39]

Soon after his death, the *Marathi Dnyanaprasarak* also folded up in 1867 after a long and seminal contribution to the cause of Marathi literature. The baton was picked up by *Vividhadnyanavistaar*, a Marathi monthly magazine founded by Ramachandra Bhikaji Gunjikar, and devoted to the expansion of knowledge in various areas, as its name suggested.[40]

The *Students' Literary and Scientific Society* also ran a Marathi primary school for girls. It may well be conjectured that Govind Narayan was also involved in this activity, given his natural proclivity for teaching and long years of experience in a school which had the highest reputation in Mumbai. The *Marathi Dnyanaprasarak Sabha* undertook to prepare a series of graded text-books for use in this school. In response to criticism of the first book, their response was as follows. 'The object of the little book is to supply for Indian schools a series of short and easy sentences, written not merely for the purpose of exercising the tongue in pronunciation and reading, but also with a view to convey to the mind such pleasing, instructive, and above all definite ideas, as the child may without efforts retain.'

The writer is most likely Govind Narayan as the language and sentiments expressed in this letter are so similar to those expressed by Govind Narayan in his comments on the first primer published by the government.

Govind Narayan and Major Thomas Candy

Major Thomas Candy, through his various official positions was, for over three decades from the 1840s, the final arbiter on all aspects of Marathi literature in which the Bombay Government had a role to play. This included most books related to education and used in government schools and books published by organizations funded by the government like the

Deccan Vernacular Translation Society and the *Dakshina Prize Committee*. While his dedication to the cause of Marathi literature was not questioned by even his most vehement detractors, the unbridled exercise of his absolute power did raise a lot of hackles, especially among those who patriotically felt that they did not have to learn their native language from a foreigner. He did make many important contributions to the standardization of the Marathi language and developed a rigorous procedure for examining new books. However, it was felt that any Marathi writer who persistently crossed swords with him was more than likely to find that his books remained unpublished.

This period completely overlapped with Govind Narayan's literary career and they perforce came into contact fairly regularly as members of various committees, and could well have been correspondents for a certain period. Like all books written for use in schools, Govind Narayan's *Udbhiddajanyapadarth* was sent to Major Candy for his evaluation and comments before it was printed. Major Candy says that 'With regard to the style of the work, it is pretty fluent and pleasing, but I have noticed a number of minor errors of grammar and composition, a few of which I will append as a specimen, that the author may correct them if he thinks fit'.[41]

He goes on to list a number of points ranging from the spelling of Sanskrit words and sentence constructions to grammatical errors and conjugations; Govind Narayan seems to have graciously accepted many of the suggestions and the published book reflects these corrections.

In 1856, both were nominated as members of the *Graded Text-Book Committee* formed by E.I. Howard, the Director of Public Instruction to bring order to the random collection of books which had been produced in the preceding three decades and were being used in schools. The European members of the Committee included Howard himself, Major Candy, Dr. Wilson, Rev. Glasgow, Rev. Murray Mitchell, Rev. Aitkin, John Harkness, and four others while the Indian members were Govind Narayan, Bhaskar Damodar Palande, Vinayak Vasudeo Kirtikar, Vishwanath Narayan Mandlik and Dadoba Pandurang Tarkhadkar. The large committee was obviously unwieldy and many of the members unsuited to the work on hand – Major Candy was expected to shoulder most of the responsibility but he proceeded on leave and returned towards the end of 1857. In the meanwhile the first book[42] was published under the initiative of Bhaskar Damodar Palande and sent to the members for their comments. In a letter dated 15 March 1858, Govind Narayan writes that 'I am sorry, however, that I cannot approve of the high Sanskrit and foreign words, which are introduced in the Primer. In my opinion, the First Reading Book for children should contain neither difficult Sanskrit words nor foreign idioms, but plain simple current words and idiomatic sentences that a child of three or four years may comprehend and repeat them without any mental effort'.[43]

When the second edition of this book was to be readied for the press, Major Candy was back in Bombay and had taken over the role of final arbiter and judge. His response to the suggestions received from Govind Narayan and other members of the committee can only be termed self-righteous.

'I do not suppose that it is your [Howard] wish that I should adopt the suggestions of any member of the Class-Book Committee except I see them to be correct. I am very desirous to consider every suggestion in a spirit of candour, but I must finally be guided by my own convictions.

'I have looked over the observations of Messrs. Govind Narayan and Dadoba Pandurang, and am prepared to adopt a few of these suggestions; but from most of them I am compelled to dissent ...

'I have thankfully adopted such of all alterations proposed by Messrs. Govind Narayan and Dadoba Pandurang as seemed to me to be improvements; and to show my readiness to meet the wishes of others, I have adopted a few more of their alterations though I consider the original phrases or clauses to be idiomatic and right. But the great majority of the alterations they propose I feel compelled to reject.'[44]

Govind Narayan was again a target of Major Candy's vitriolic comments, albeit indirectly, on account of his work as editor of the *Marathi Dnyanaprasarak*. As the government bought 124 copies of every issue of the magazine for distribution in schools, they asked Major Candy to examine the magazine. He severely criticized the July 1857 issue of the magazine, 'I feel it my duty to report that judging from the specimens before me, I consider ... *The Dnyan Prasarak* ... to lie open to objection on the ground of bad style, violations of grammar and idiom, and solecisms of various kinds ...'[45]

Not to take such a damning criticism lightly, the publishers of *Marathi Dnyanaprasarak* took issue with Major Candy on the various points raised by him related to correct usage in Marathi. This led to a protracted war of words between the *Marathi Dnyanaprasarak* and Major Candy on various questions related to Marathi grammar. Other notables including the Principal of *Poona Sanskrit College*, Krishnashastri Chiplunkar were called in to present their views. While no agreement was finally reached between the parties, Major Candy had the last word; the voluminous correspondence was gathered together and published in 1858 as a book titled 'Correspondence on the subject of the Dnyanprasarak' to present a complete picture to students of the Marathi language.[46]

Govind Narayan sums up his perspective by advising Major Candy to 'render service to the Committee and to vernacular literature by noticing these (faults) in a friendly and indulgent spirit, so as to encourage rather than suppress juvenile aspirations after literary distinction'.[47] These are exactly the same sentiments he expresses to any potential critics of his book, *Mumbaiche Varnan*, in the preface.

Controversies relating to Christian conversions

One of the major issues which simmered and sometimes exploded in the social life of those times, as it continues to do so even to this day, was the proselytising activities of the missionaries and conversions to Christianity. For a long while, the East India Company banned all forms of missionary activity in their Indian territories but the Charter Act of 1813 provided for the entry of missionaries and allowed them to introduce 'useful knowledge for religious and moral improvement' of India. The first missionaries to arrive in Mumbai where Americans and their early struggles are vividly described by Govind Narayan in his book, *Mumbaiche Varnan*, and he strongly commends their commitment to the improvement of Indian society. They where followed by representatives of a variety of missions from numerous denominations.

One of the foremost methods of reaching out to the local population was the setting up of schools; the American Mission was the first in this regard and most well-funded missions emulated them. Many of the leading citizens, be they Hindu, Muslim or Parsi, hesitated to send their children to these mission schools for the fear of the Christian religious education and the possible conversion of their children into Christianity.

While the conversion of the poor was condemned in general, the conversion of an educated person caused a great uproar. In May 1839, by which time Govind Narayan was already a teacher in the Free *General Assembly's Institution*, two of its Parsi students were converted to Christianity. This caused a great uproar among the Parsi community who withdrew their children in large numbers. An even greater turmoil resulted with the conversion of another student, a Hindu Brahmin, Narayan Sheshadri in 1843 followed by his brother soon after. Many Hindus, vocal in the nascent local press, strongly objected to these intellectual conversions and tried to win the new converts over, and vehemently criticized the proselytising work of the missionaries.

Through all these controversies, Govind Narayan continued to work closely with Dr. Wilson. In *Mumbaiche Varnan*, he describes the conversion of the two Parsis in a matter-of-fact manner, the associated controversy and implies that Dr. Wilson could emerge unscathed from the imbroglio because of his fame, reputation, and close connections with the government. Govind

Narayan, so very rooted to the soil and completely identifying himself with his Hinduism, may have never felt the need for conversion. He was so naturally religious-minded and pious that he seemed almost like a true Christian in the eyes of the missionaries, much like Mahatma Gandhi who was considered as the most Christian of men by his missionary friends. Baba Padmanji, another Hindu student who converted to Christianity in 1854 and a close associate and colleague of Govind Narayan, may not have been far off the mark, when he recalls in his autobiography[48] that he justified his decision to embrace Christianity to his father by stating that the only difference between him and Govind Narayan was that the latter was not baptised.

Govind Narayan and his family

Very little is known about the personal life of Govind Narayan. As already mentioned, he had two brothers, Vishnu and Gopinath. Neither his mother's name nor his wife's is recorded.

He had two sons, Jagannath and Narayan, the latter named after his grandfather, as per the practice generally followed among Hindus. His literary heirs were however his nephews, Ramchandra and Dinanath, sons of his eldest brother, Vishnu Narayan. Govind Narayan acted as their guardian and involved himself deeply in their education. Both of them completed their Bachelor of Arts degree from the *Elphinstone College*. In 1862, Ramachandra joined as a trader with a private English company, Graham & Co. He rose to a senior position with this company and was transferred to London in 1893 where he settled permanently after his retirement. He was deeply interested in the literature of the great saints of Maharashtra and very carefully edited and published their works, with the help of his brother, Dinanath. Their edited books include the works of the leading poet-saints of Maharashtra, Sant Dnyaneshwar, Sant Tukaram, and Sant Ramdas, accompanied by well-researched biographies. This work has been acknowledged as an important step in the study of the ancient literature of the Marathi language.

Sir Govind Dinanath Madgaonkar, a grand-nephew of Govind Narayan joined the Indian Civil Service and was knighted for his services to the British empire. The Madgaonkar family continued to interest itself in the development of Marathi literature. An endowment by Sir Govind to the *Mumbai Marathi Granth Sangrahalaya* enabled publication of Govind Narayan's collected works in the 1960s.

A farewell to Govind Narayan

Many of his biographers have surmised that Govind Narayan did not aggressively work towards a career in government or business because of his delicate constitution. Be that as it may, one of his early books could not be completely revised as he was very ill.[49] Towards the end of 1863, Govind Narayan retired from public life because of his indifferent health. He resigned his position as Head Master with the Free *General Assembly's Institution* and also as President of *Marathi Dnyanaprasarak Sabha*. His long-time associate and mentor, Dr. Wilson, proposed a public felicitation ceremony to honour Govind Narayan's long years of public service; self-effacing as he was, Govind Narayan asked him not to trouble himself in this regard. Notwithstanding his protests, the felicitation ceremony was held on 24 January 1864 with Dr. Wilson acting as Chairman. A contemporary report on the function is included in one of his early biographical sketches.

> Dr. Wilson mentioned that he had called the meeting on the requisition of a large number of friends of Mr. Govindji Narayan, anxious to present him with a testimonial, on the occasion of his withdrawing from active duty in the Free *General Assembly's Institution*, of which he was one of the earliest pupils, and a monitor and teacher for thirty years. He dwelt with such interest on his promise as a learner and his ability, fidelity, judiciousness, kindness, and perseverance as a teacher and Superintendent of some of the classes of the Institution; on his accuracy and order in keeping the lists and accounts which were under his care; on his constant endeavours, by essays and addresses, to promote the great cause of native reform and advancement; on the success which in the view of all readers of Marathi and Gujarati, he had obtained in the seventeen popular original works, great and small, with which he had enriched the vernacular literature of the West of India; and on the amiability and respectability of his character, observed and admired by all his friends and acquaintances.[50]

Govind Narayan was presented with a citation and a purse containing six[51] thousand rupees. The assembly also passed two resolutions; firstly, it commended Govind Narayan on his thirty years of uninterrupted service in education, his efforts for the development of society, and his literary works and conveyed its gratitude to him; secondly, it was agreed to institute a scholarship to perpetuate the memory of Govind Narayan and a committee was nominated. The members of the committee included Dr. Bhau Daji, Vishwanath Narayan Mandlik, Rao Bahadur Ramchandra Balkrishnaji,

Rao Bahadur Trimalrao Venkatesh Inamdar, Dadoba Pandurang, Rev. Narayan Sheshadri, Baba Padmanji, Vincent de Cruz, Joseph Ezekiel, John Crisp, Shapoorji Edulji, Dina Moroba, Goolam Mohiuddin Dehalvi, and Moroba Vinoba. They represented the cream of Bombay intelligensia, encompassing practically all the prominent communities and professions. Many of them had been his past students or colleagues in the various organizations he worked for. However, it seems that they could not collect sufficient funds to institute the scholarship as no records are forthcoming.

The literary heritage of Govind Narayan

By all accounts, Govind Narayan was considered a prominent man by the other notable citizens of Mumbai. His teaching career and literary activities provided many opportunities for building relationships with a range of influential people – senior government officers, prominent Indian citizens with whom he served on committees and other organizations, and missionaries with whom he was associated through his school – and he seems to have used them. However, he seems to have maintained a very low profile, with hardly any articles about him or reviews of his books having been published in the Marathi newspapers, let alone the English publications. His death, at the height of a prolific and path-breaking literary career, went almost unnoticed.

Govind Narayan is himself extremely reticent about his personal life in most of his writing. The entire text of *Mumbaiche Varnan* is written in a completely impersonal style and he never lets escape the fact that he is closely connected with many of the institutions and individuals he writes about in the book. He however seems to have carried on a long-standing correspondence with a variety of people as has been noticed by one of his early biographers who had access to this collection of letters; it has now been lost.

Govind Narayan wrote most of his books in direct response to a felt need in a particular subject; in that sense, he was a man of his times, and in the opinion of his earliest biographer, his works were already dated in 1918. On the contrary, the historical value of his works have, of course, only increased in the hundred years since, but one cannot help get the feeling, that many of his reformatory essays are still relevant to those sections of society which he addressed and they would do well to heed his advice.

Many of his works went through multiple editions during his lifetime, and at least four of his books were translated into Gujarati. It is not possible to determine the print-run of these editions, but it quite probable that they did not ever exceed a thousand. However, he was soon forgotten by the

Marathi-speaking society at large; as Marathi rapidly developed as a literary language in the years leading to the twentieth century, many more literary luminaries took centre-stage and Govind Narayan and others who provided the strong foundation for modern Marathi disappeared from the Marathi literary tradition. His son, Jagannath Govind Madgaonkar, republished one of his books in 1877. In the 1890s, another eight of his smaller books were republished, most probably at the initiative of another son, Narayan Govind Madgaonkar. The last of these books was published in 1895 and contained a small biographical sketch. This may well have been the brief article on Govind Narayan written by Vinayak Konddeo Oak which appeared in the November 1887 issue of the magazine, *Balabodh*. He went into literary oblivion thereafter for a long period until his death centenary in 1960s.

The only exception was a relatively detailed biography published by Balkrishna Narayan Deo in the literary magazine, *Vividhadynanavistaar* in September 1918 which was based on a study of the personal papers and letters of Govind Narayan as well as information provided by his son, Narayan Govind Madgaonkar, who died as late as 1924.[52] No well-researched biographical work is forthcoming for the next four decades. An article titled *Govind Narayan Shenoy Madgaonkar*[53] appeared in the Marathi magazine *Swayamsevak* by famous Konkani writer, 'Shenoy Goembab' Varde Valaulicar but the article has very little to do with Govind Narayan. The article which appeared in response to Deo's biography mainly contains arguments on the bitter debate (still ongoing) between Marathi and Konkani, and the contention of the latter's advocates that it is an independent language as opposed to being a dialect of Marathi. He also criticizes Govind Narayan, a native of Goa, for writing in Marathi rather than in Konkani.

By the middle of the twentieth century, the historical study of the growth of Marathi as a literary language received a strong impetus with the work of Professor Anant Kakba Priolkar at the *Marathi Samshodan Mandal* and other scholars. Lengthy biographies of many of the leaders of Marathi literature were being written and a historical and critical analysis of their work was being undertaken. Through these works, Govind Narayan began to be identified as one of the founding fathers of modern Marathi literature in the company of Sadashiv Kashinath Chhatre, Bal Gangadhar Shastri Jambhekar, and Bhau Mahajan.

C. G. Karve devotes a chapter to Govind Narayan in his book[54] on marginalised Marathi littérateurs but does not cover any new ground. In his monumental eight-volume directory of the makers of modern Marathi literature,[55] G. D. Khanolkar inserts a long and well-researched entry on Govind Narayan with a bibliography.

However, not until the lecture given by Professor A. K. Priolkar in 1965 to mark the centenary death anniversary of Govind Narayan, was any comprehensive biographical work on Govind Narayan forthcoming. This lecture was subsequently published as an independent book with a comprehensive bibliography.[56] Professor Priolkar, an indefatigable researcher of the Marathi language, through many decades of work at the *Marathi Samshodan Mandal* documented the development of modern Marathi literature in the nineteenth century. He accessed all possible primary sources of information and unearthed much new information which enable the reconstruction of Govind Narayan's life.

There was also a resurgence in the republication of his writing to coincide with his death centenary. In 1962, *Mumbaiche Varnan* was republished with an introductory essay by Dr. N. R. Phatak. In 1968, the first volume of the collected works of Govind Narayan was edited by Professor A. K. Priolkar and this was followed by two more volumes in the succeeding years. These three volumes bring together all the known works of Govind Narayan except for *Mumbaiche Varnan* which had been republished a few years before and *Srushtitil Chamatkar* which was to have been the fourth volume in the series, but was apparently never published. These volumes provide the Marathi scholar with easy access to his works but are not geared to reach the intended audience for his books, especially his books on botany.

In terms of critical studies of Madgaonkar's work, very little work has been done. There was hardly any tradition of critical reviews in Marathi literature until the establishment of the magazine *Vividhadnyanavistaar* in 1867. No contemporary reviews of his work are forthcoming except for a few notices.[57] In 1962, Gangadhar Gadgil published a long critical essay on *Mumbaiche Varnan* in the magazine, *Manohar Masik* in which he describes it as a unique and pioneering effort. Meera Kosambi, a Mumbai-based researcher in urban studies, draws upon Govind Narayan's *Mumbaiche Varnan* to support her various theses on Mumbai in the nineteenth century. She extensively quotes from the book (translating the sections herself) to illustrate Indian perceptions of Mumbai in the 1800s in her contribution to the book, *Bombay: Mosaic of Modern Culture*.[58]

A major credit for Govind Narayan's literary rehabilitation should go to Professor Priolkar and the Marathi Samshodhan Mandal. Further critical work by Marathi and Mumbai scholars is required if Govind Narayan is to be fully restored to the venerable position in Marathi literature that he fully deserves.

Bibliography

Govind Narayan's bibliography includes fifteen independent books published during his life-time and the three-volume collected edition of his works published to commemorate his death centenary. His articles, essays and speeches appeared only in the magazine *Marathi Dnyanaprasarak*. Any article in English which may have appeared in the *Oriental Christian Spectator* or other contemporary magazines have not been traced. Posthumous reprints of articles in other magazines have not been listed. The last section of the bibliography includes biographies and criticisms, all of them published only in Marathi.

Books

The books are listed chronologically from the date of their first publication. Further editions are also noted where information is available.

1. *Suchirbhutpana* [Treatise on Cleanliness], Board of Education, Mumbai, 1849, printed at the American Mission Press; Second edition, 1853; Third edition, 1856; Fourth edition, 1891, printed at the Tattvavivechak Chapkhana. Also translated into Gujarati and published in Ahmedabad.
2. *Rinn-Nishedhak Bodh* [Evils of Debt], Deccan Vernacular Translation Society, Mumbai, 1850. Also translated into Gujarati and published in Ahmedabad.
3. *Nitisanvad* [Discourse on Ethics], Mumbai, 1850, printed at the Thomas Graham Press; Second edition, 1868, printed at Gunput Krishnaji Press.
4. *Hindu Lokanchya Reeti Sudharnyacha Bodh* [Domestic Reform among the Hindus], Bombay Tract and Book Society, Mumbai, 1851; Second edition, 1891, published by the author's son Narayan Govind Madgaonkar as *Kutumbsudharana* [Family Welfare], printed at Tattvavivechak Chapkhana, Mumbai.
5. *Srushtitil Chamatkar* [Natural Phenomena], Deccan Vernacular Translation Society, Mumbai, 1851, printed at the Gunput Krishnaji Press; translation from the original English book (published by The Committee of General Literature and Education, appointed by the Society for Promoting Christian Knowledge) and bound with it. Also translated into Gujarati.
6. *Satyanirupan* [An Exposition of Truth], Mumbai 1852, printed at the *American Mission Press*; Second edition, 1856; Third edition, 1877, published by the author's son Jagannath Govind Madgaonkar, printed

at the *Nirnayasagar Chapkhana*, Mumbai. Also translated into Gujarati and two editions published.

7. *Darupasun Anarth* [The Evils of Drink], Mumbai, 1855, printed at the *American Mission Press*; Second edition, 1890.

8. *Udbhiddajanyapadarth* [Vegetable Substances], Mumbai, 1856, printed at the *Thomas Graham Press*; Gujarati translation published in 1859.

9. *Vrikshavarnan* [Description of Trees], Dakshina Prize Committee, Mumbai, 1857, printed at the Thomas Graham Press; Second edition, 1895, printed at Tattvavivechak Chapkhana, Mumbai.

10. *Lokhandi Sadakache Chamatkar* [Wonders of the Railway], Mumbai, 1858, printed at the Thomas Graham Press; lecture delivered at the United Students Association on 15 March 1858.

11. *Vyavaharupayogi Natak* [Drama on a Practical Subject], Mumbai, 1859; Third edition, 1864, printed at the Oriental Press, Mumbai; Fourth edition, 1890, printed at Nirnayasagar Chapkhana, Mumbai.

12. *Bhojanbandhu Pantambaku* [Aids to Digestion], Mumbai, 1860, printed at the Thomas Graham Press; Second edition, 1891, printed at Tattvavivechak Chapkhana, Mumbai.

13. *Sulekhanvidya* [The Art of Handwriting], Mumbai, 1860, printed at the Thomas Graham Press; Second edition, 1891, printed at Tattvavivechak Chapkhana, Mumbai.

14. *Patravali va Dron* [Plates and Cups made from Leaves], First edition not forthcoming; Second edition, 1891, printed at Tattvavivechak Chapkhana, Mumbai. *Patravali* first published in the magazine *Marathi Dnyanaprasarak*, Vol. 8, No. 2, (1857) and *Dron* first published in Vol. 12, No. 2 (1861).

15. *Mumbaiche Varnan* [Bombay Past and Present], Mumbai, 1863, printed at the Induprakash Chapkhana; Second edition, Itihaas Samshodhan Mandal, Mumbai Marathi Granth Sangrahalaya, Mumbai, 1963 (with an introduction by Dr. N. R. Pathak); Third edition, Varda Books, Pune, 1992 (Facsimile of Second edition without maps); Fourth edition, Varda Books, Pune, 2002 (Reprint of Third edition).

16. *Madgaonkaranche Sankalit Vangmaya: Khand Pahila* [The Collected Works of Madgaonkar: Volume 1], Editors: A. K. Priolkar and S. G. Malshe, Marathi Samshodhan Mandal, Mumbai Marathi Granth Sangrahalaya, Mumbai, 1968.

17. *Madgaonkaranche Sankalit Vangmaya: Khand Doosra* [The Collected Works of Madgaonkar: Volume 2], Editor: S. G. Malshe, Marathi Samshodhan Mandal, Mumbai Marathi Granth Sangrahalaya, Mumbai, 1969.

18. *Madgaonkaranche Sankalit Vangmaya: Khand Teesra* [The Collected Works of Madgaonkar: Volume 3], Editors: S. G. Malshe and S. R. Chunekar, Marathi Samshodhan Mandal, Mumbai Marathi Granth Sangrahalaya, Mumbai, 1970. Includes *Vrikshavarnan, Lokhandi Sadakache Chamatkar, and Udbhiddajanyapadarth.*

Essays, articles, and speeches

1. *'Marathi bhashet Sarvasangraha namak granth vhavha'* Marathi Dnyanaprasarak 7, Nos. 7–8.
2. *'Udbhijja vidya'* [Agricultural Science], *Marathi Dnyanaprasarak* 7, Nos. 1, 4, 6–8 and 10.
3. *'Dnyanaprasarak mandalichya varshik sabhet kelele bhashan (January 1857)'* Marathi Dnyanaprasarak 7, No. 11.
4. *'Patravali'* [Plates from Leaves], *Marathi Dnyanaprasarak* 8, No. 2.
5. *'Anna'* [Diet], *Marathi Dnyanaprasarak* 8, Nos. 5 and 8.
6. *'Manushyache Aachhadan'* [Human Hygiene], *Marathi Dnyanaprasarak* 8, No. 7.
7. *'Varshik sabhe pudhe bhashan (December 1857)'*, *Marathi Dnyanaprasarak* 8, No. 10.
8. *'Dnyanaprasarak sabhet kelele bhashan' (August 1859)*, Marathi Dnyanaprasarak 10, No. 6.
9. *'Reshmi Roomal'* [The Silk Kerchief], *Marathi Dnyanaprasarak* 10, No. 10.
10. *'Kavlyacha Gharta'* [The Crow's Nest], *Marathi Dnyanaprasarak* 12, No. 3.
11. *'Achaat Khaane Masnaat Jaane'* [Gluttony], *Marathi Dnyanaprasarak* 12, No. 9.
12. *'Madhmashache Pole'* [Bee-hives], *Marathi Dnyanaprasarak* 12, No. 10.
13. *'Bharatkhandatil Karigar'* [The Craftsmen of India], *Marathi Dnyanaprasarak* 13, Nos. 5–6.
14. *'Aatmashikshan'* [Self-instruction], *Marathi Dnyanaprasarak* 13, Nos. 8–9 and 14, No. 1.
15. *'Mahadeo Govind Shastri yanchya nitishastravaril vykhyanavar bhashan'*, *Marathi Dnyanaprasarak* 14, No. 4.
16. *'Kaapus'* [Cotton], *Marathi Dnyanaprasarak* 14, No. 6.
17. *'Yatnena ki durlabham'*, *Marathi Dnyanaprasarak* 14, No. 10.
18. *'Draveyna Sarve Vashah'*, *Marathi Dnyanaprasarak* 15, No. 4.
19. *'Ati sarvatra Varjyet'*, *Marathi Dnyanaprasarak* 15, No. 9.

Biographies, Criticism, etc.

Deo, B. N. *'Govind Narayan Madgaonkar.'* *Vividhdnyanavistaar* 49, No. 5, (September 1918): pp. 109–21.

Gadgil, Gangadhar. *'Govind Narayan Madgaonkar: Mumbaiche Varnan.'* in *Sahityache mandand*. Mumbai: Popular Prakashan, 1964.

'Govind Narayan Madgaonkar.' *Maharashtra Saraswat* 5 (2 April 1921): pp. 42–8.

'Junya Mandalichi Olakh – Govind Narayan Madgaonkar.' *Navayug* 2 (10 August 1964): p. 731.

Karve, C. G. *Marathi Sahityatil Upekshit Mankari*. Pune: Venus Prakashan, 1957. pp. 15–22.

Khanolkar, G. D. *Arvachin Marathi Vangmayasevak: Pancham Khand*, Pune: Venus Prakashan, 1962. pp. 122–35.

Oak, Vinayak Konddeo. *'Govind Narayan Madgaonkar.'* *Balabodh* (November 1887): pp. 169–73.

Priolkar, A. K. *Govind Narayan Madgaonkar: Vyakti va Vangmaya*. Mumbai: Marathi Sanshodhan Mandal, Mumbai Marathi Granth Sangrahalya, 1965.

Sharma, Ganesh. *'Kailasvasi Govind Narayan Madgaonkar.'* *Lokamitra* 18 (12 May 1909): pp. 73–80.

'Shenoy Goembab' Varde Valaulicar. *'Govind Narayan Shennoy Madgaonkar'*, *Swayamsevak* 3, Nos. 8–12, (August–December 1922): pp. 161–66, 182–88, 203–06, and 219–24. Also published with additional material in Shenoy Goembab. *Kaanhi Marathi Lekh*. Mumbai: Gomantak Chhapkhana, 1945. pp. 100–239.

Notes

1. Stocqueler, J. H., *Memoirs of a Journalist*. Bombay: Times of India Press, 1873.
2. A brief review of this development is provided in Deshpande, Kusumawati and Rajadhyaksha, M. V., *A History of Marathi Literature*. New Delhi: Sahitya Akademi, 1988. A detailed account is available in Marathi in Jog, R. S. (ed.) *Marathi vangmayacha itihas*. 6 Second edition Vol. Pune: Maharashtra Sahitya Parishad Prakashan, 1973.
3. Parulekar, R. V. (ed.) *Selections from Educational Records (Bombay). 1815–1840*. Bombay: Asia Publishing House, 1955.
4. Kulkarni, K. B. *Adhunik Marathi Gadyachi Utkranti*, Mumbai: Mumbai Marathi Granth Sangrahalya, 1956. p. 53.
5. Kulkarni,1956. p. 57.

6. A scholarly analysis of the development of an intellectual climate in Mumbai in the mid-nineteenth century is provided in Dobbin, Christine. *Urban leadership in western India: Politics and Communities in Bombay City, 1840–1885.* London: Oxford University Press, 1972.

7. Priolkar, A. K. *The Printing Press in India: Its Beginnings and Early Development.* Mumbai: Marathi Samshodhana Mandala, 1958.

8. Jambhekar, G. G. (ed), *Memoirs and Writings of Acharya Bal Gangadhar Shastri Jambhekar (1812–1846).* 3 Vol. Puna: 1950.

9. For more details see Naik, J. V., *The Seed Period of Bombay's Intellectual Life, 1822–1857.* pp. 61–75, in Patel, Sujata and Thorner, Alice (eds.) *Bombay: Mosaic of Modern Culture.* Bombay: Oxford University Press, 1995.

10. The Mumbai of the early nineteenth century was centred around the Fort (though the ramparts were demolished in the 1860s, the area continues to retain the name) with both residential and commercial sections – the Europeans towards the South and the Indians towards the North. The Esplanade provided an open space (originally intended to provide a clear range of fire from the Fort) all around the Fort beyond which and towards the North were the gardens and fields. In 1803, the area North of the Esplanade was settled to accommodate the local population which was affected by a major fire; it came to be known as the Native Town or 'Black Town' in contrast to the 'European Town' around the Fort. The rest of Mumbai, which came to include the entire island was largely rural for most of the nineteenth century.

11. Priolkar, A. K., *Doctor Bhau Daji: Vyakti Kal va Kartrutva,* Mumbai: Mumbai Marathi Sahitya Sangh, 1971. p. 12.

12. Priolkar, 1971. p. 14.

13. Priolkar, A. K., *Govind Narayan Madgaonkar: Vyakti va Vangmaya.* Mumbai: Marathi Samshodhan Mandal, Mumbai Marathi Granth Sangrahalya, 1965. p. 5.

14. Priolkar, 1971. p. 15.

15. David, M. D. *John Wilson and his Institution.* Bombay: John Wilson Education Society, 1975.

16. *Oriental Christian Spectator* 8 (1st series), 1838. *Second Annual Examination of the General Assembly's Institution in Bombay.* pp. 520–25.

17. *Oriental Christian Spectator* 9 (1st series), 1839. *Third Annual Examination of the General Assembly's Institution in Bombay.* pp. 5–11.

18. *Oriental Christian Spectator* 4 (3rd series), 1853.

19. Wilson, John, *Vakyavali – Engrezi ani Marathi* [Idiomatic Exercises], Second edition, Mumbai: 1839. Cover.

20. Priolkar, A. K. *Paramahansa Sabha va tyache Adhyaksh Ramachandra Balkrishna*, Mumbai: Mumbai Marathi Granth Sangrahalaya, 1966. p. 5.

21. *Oriental Christian Spectator* 8 (1st series), 1838.

22. Bhate, G. C., *History of Modern Marathi Literature 1800–1938*. Mahad, District Kolaba: 1939.

23. Madgaonkar, Govind Narayan. *Madgaonkaranche Sankalit Vangmaya: Khand Teesra*. Malshe, S. G. and Chunekar, S. R. (eds.) *Mumbai: Marathi Samshodhan Mandal*, Mumbai Marathi Granth Sangrahalaya, 1970. p. 102.

24. The 17 books referred to here included three books which had been translated from Marathi into Gujarati and perhaps alluded to a list of Govind Narayan's works (numbering 17) published at the end of the first edition of *Mumbaiche Varnan;* see Bibliography for details.

25. Deo, B. N., '*Govind Narayan Madgaonkar*', *Vividhdnyanavistaar* 49, No. 5, September 1918. p. 111; Speech delivered by Dr. Wilson on the occasion of a felicitation ceremony organized to mark Govind Narayan's retirement from public life on 28 January 1864.

26. *Oriental Christian Spectator* 1 (3rd series), September 1850. pp. 382–83.

27. *Oriental Christian Spectator* 2 (3rd series), May–June 1851. p. 232.

28. *Journal of the Bombay Branch of the Royal Asiatic Society* 3, No. XV. *Extracts from the Proceedings of the Society for the year 1850–51: Presents to Library.* p. 136.

29. Deo 1918. p. 113.

30. Department of Archives, Government of Maharashtra, Mumbai: Dakshina Prize Committee, Poona. Vol. 5. Minutes 1851–59. *Meeting of the Dakshina Prize Committee held on 22 December 1854.*

31. Kulkarni 1956. p. 68.

32. Kulkarni 1956. p. 259.

33. Priolkar 1965. p. 14.

34. Department of Archives, Government of Maharashtra, Mumbai: Dakshina Prize Committee, Poona. Vol. 5. Minutes 1851–59. *Memo No. 2 of 1857.*

35. Department of Archives, Government of Maharashtra, Mumbai: Bombay Government, Education Department, 1859–60, *Return of Periodicals and Publications subscribed by the Director of Public Instruction from May 1858 to 31st January 1859* dated 17 February 1859.

36. Priolkar 1965. p. 7.

37. Pathak, N. R., *Vishnushastri Chiplunkar*, *Vividhadnyanavistaar*, Vol. 61, Nos. 2 and 3, p. 55.

38. *The 'Times of India' Calendar and Directory for 1864*. p. 521.

39. Bhate 1939. p. 581.

40. For more details on the magazine, see Kulkarni, V. L. *Marathi Dnyanaprasarak: itihas va vangmayavichar.* Mumbai: Popular Prakashan, 1965 and Kulkarni, V. D. (ed.) *Marathi niyatkalikancha vangmayin abhyas. Khand ek: 1832–1882.* Pune: Mumbai Vidyapeeth Marathi Vibhag and Shrividya Prakashan, 1987.

41. Kulkarni 1956. p. 260.

42. Palande, Bhaskar Damodar, *Lahan Mulankarita Pahile Pustak* [First Book for Small Children], Mumbai, 1857.

43. Kulkarni 1956. p. 187.

44. Kulkarni 1956. p. 189.

45. Kulkarni 1956. p. 189.

46. Kulkarni 1956. p. 346.

47. Kulkarni 1956. p. 373.

48. Padmanji, Baba. *Arunodaya.* Third edition. Mumbai: Bombay Book Tract and Book Society, 1968.

49. *Oriental Christian Spectator* 1 (3rd series), 1850. pp. 382–83.

50. Deo 1918. p. 111; Speech delivered by Dr. Wilson on the occasion of a felicitation ceremony organized to mark Govind Narayan's retirement from public life on 28 January 1864.

51. There is some confusion regarding the exact amount. In his biography, Deo mentions a sum of rupees two thousand initially but changes it to six thousand in a later section. Priolkar quotes the lower sum while Khanolkar indicates an amount of rupees six thousand and also mentions that Govind Narayan used this money to buy a house in Jambulwadi, near Dhobi Talao. If the latter is true, the sum of Rupees Six Thousand seems closer to the truth.

52. Deo 1918. pp. 109–21.

53. 'Shenoy Goembab' Varde Valaulicar, *Govind Narayan Shenoy Madgaonkar,* Swayamsevak, Vol. 3, Nos. 8–12, August–December 1922. pp. 161–66, 182–88, 203–06 and 219–24, Ponda, Gomantak. Also published with additional material in Shenoy Goembab, *Kaanhi Marathi Lekh* [Selected Writings in Marathi]. Mumbai: Gomantak Chhapkhana, 1945. pp. 100–239.

54. Karve, C. G., *Marathi Sahityatil Upekshit Mankari* [Forgotten Notables of Marathi Literature], Pune: Venus Prakashan, 1957. pp. 15–22.

55. Khanolkar, G. D., *Arvachin Marathi Vangmayasevak: Pancham Khand* [Architects of Modern Marathi Literature: Volume 5], Pune: Venus Prakashan, 1962. pp. 122–35.

56. Priolkar, 1965.

57. Notices and reviews of the following books appeared in the *Marathi Dnyanaprasarak: Vrikshavarnan* (Vol. 8, No. 2, May 1857), *Lokhandi Sadakache Chamatkar* (Vol. 8, No. 12, March 1858), *Bhojanbandhu Pantambaku* (Vol. 11, No. 7, October 1860), and *Mumbaiche Varnan* (Vol. 14, No. 5, May 1863, pp. 151–57).

58. Kosambi, Meera, *British Mumbai and Marathi Mumbai*, pp. 1–24 in Patel, Sujata and Thorner, Alice (eds.) *Bombay: Mosaic of Modern Culture.* Bombay: Oxford University Press, 1995.

Govind Narayan's Mumbai

PREFACE

In order to successfully complete the task of narrating the history of a region, a man must be healthy, wealthy, intelligent, impartial, in possession of an independent spirit, be acquainted with the aged, associated with the scholarly, and equipped with a range of information about the region. Furthermore, he should have personal experience of the region extending to at least thirty to forty years, have visited most of the places in the region, and possess a thorough knowledge of the language in which the narrative is to be written. Once these requirements have been met, the author should, in an equitable and factual manner, ensure that his narrative provides his readers with information on a variety of topics, thus increasing their knowledge. However, in the event that one who desires to write a historical narrative about a particular region is not in the possession of all these qualities, he should not lose confidence but continue to work industriously. For, as a local proverb goes, 'strife begets success'.

While a desire had been present, for many days past, to write a comprehensive narrative of Mumbai, a city which has attained fame and grandeur, its undertaking was prevented by the sense that the requirements listed above remained unfulfilled. However, as time passed the realization dawned that it would be impossible to meet these requirements even if a lifetime was dedicated to their cultivation; one cannot hope to increase one's small fund of tales to any great degree by waiting listlessly as the years rush by. Once this was realized, all the material which was at hand was complied to the best of one's abilities to create this narrative. Though the rich may spend thousands in building their magnificent castles, the poor man should not put off building his thatched hut. A king might sleep soundly in his magnificent palace, on a sandalwood bed beneath an exquisite shawl, but the poor man who sleeps on a grass mat under a rough blanket is just as satisfied by slumber. Only once this truth was comprehended could this work commence.

The initial desire to write a history of our country would have meant travelling to many of its numerous regions and researching the plethora of books written on this subject. To successfully complete this task, the prospective writer must have vast funds of health, wealth, and intelligence at his disposal. In the case of an individual deficient in these resources, it is doubtful that he would be able to produce a work of acceptable quality. Thus the pursuit of this venture was inhibited by a fear of public ridicule. Our elders say, 'Cut your cloth according to your measure' and as we are closely rooted to the soil of this land, we have no option but to heed them. One has to make do with less and therefore this attempt at a modest narrative is made in lieu of grander schemes. Its successful completion, however, depends on that *Supreme Giver of Intelligence* without whose blessings even a pen will not write, let alone a book emerge.

Secondly, it is exceedingly rare for any book that has been written in Marathi, or in any of our other languages, to be published without the help of the English people. What a sorry state of affairs! If one writes a book either for the welfare of the nation or for one's personal interests, one has to seek help from rich Englishmen, Parsis or Mussalmans to get it published. All you learned people of this land! If a man writes a book, even if it is not up to your high standards, you should at least recognize his efforts, so as to encourage further endeavour. If nothing else, study his output to highlight the shortcomings of his work. You can then consider yourself as having worked for the betterment of the nation. If you set your heart on it, you can accomplish anything with ease, and ultimately to the benefit of the nation. Your many charitable deeds are all well and good – however, unless people are motivated to write books and read them, all your other efforts will be futile. Even if the writer makes a profit of five to ten thousand rupees by publishing a book with the help of foreigners, he will not be fully satisfied. It is neither about making money nor demonstrating scholarship. Only if our people read the books which have been specifically composed with them in mind, are enthused by them and are eagerly willing to encourage the author to continue writing, will the satisfaction gained by the venture be truly unparalleled, regardless of whether the publication is profitable or not.

Some days ago, a learned and philanthropic Englishman delivered a spirited speech at a gathering, in which he said the following with a view to bettering the lot of our people. 'In England, all activities relating to education, business or even the wellbeing of the nation are initiated by the people themselves; they establish innumerable societies for these purposes, and spend crores of rupees to found schools and publish books. They do not ask for the help of government in these activities. However once they have achieved a measure of success, they invite the government to inspect it. This is the reason for their independence and happiness, and only when, like them, your people are willing to invest both time and money in the research and gathering of knowledge, will you achieve true happiness.'

To the best of abilities, this description of Mumbai has been written with a view to benefit the nation. Through either personal observation or by studying books written about this famous city, a wealth of material on the places, government, state of the people and other related matters of Mumbai has been included in this book. As far as is possible, the history of this city and its current state of affairs have been described in a simple and straightforward style. No attempt has been made to employ florid language or esoteric words in order to make this book accessible to everybody. To go beyond one's natural capabilities in any task is, in any case, improper and, in the process, the reader may experience difficulties in trying to understand the real message of the author.

It is hoped that, after having taken in this meagre effort, the learned men of this city, will, in a healthy spirit of competition, write far superior histories of Mumbai; perhaps some will even be enthused to attempt a history of Hindustan after having traversed across its many lands. To do so, one must not forget the necessary endowments of health and wealth. But, by the grace of god, there are yet many such individuals amongst us. When it comes to the history of a country, it is best written by its offspring. If there are those who feel that Marathi is not an appropriate language for history, they are free to write in English; it will be welcomed by both the Englishmen and the locals. However, this is not to imply that Marathi is a defective language in any way. Marathi could achieve the refinement of Sanskrit if only scholars were inclined to cultivate it. In order to do so, it is necessary for many books on various subjects to be written and many new words created. Languages such as Sanskrit, Greek, Hebrew, Latin, Arabic, and Persian have the scholars who devoted their lives' energies to them to thank for their classical status. In contrast, the Europeans consider us as having a dull intellect, borrowed ideas, and enslaved minds, dismissing our book-making efforts as puerile and accusing us of self-aggrandizement based on the research and scholarship of others. This book has been written in the hope that the current generation of scholars will free us from these slurs.

A learned man appreciates the purpose served in learning many languages and becoming a scholar. He knows that it is certainly better to improve one's own language, by introducing new words and ideas from other cultures, than to become a scholar in languages that are of no benefit to the common people. Just as the son of poor parents achieves success through his industry and sustained effort to bring credit to his family, so too should scholars strive to bring credit to their own language; if however the son disowns his parents after becoming successful, he is termed an ingrate, and so too will such scholars be that reject their mother tongue. Men such as

Vyas, Valmiki, and Panini have become immortal because they contributed to the development of their own language.

Since poets such as Dnyaneshwar, Vaman, Mukteshwar, Tukaram, Moropant, Ramdas, Mukundraj, Shridhar, Sopanadev and Eknath began composing poetry in the language of the people, Marathi has achieved a measure of prominence and has begun to be accepted as a literary language. The common people have also acquired a taste for various kinds of metrical verse, the *arya*, *shloka*, *abhang*, *ovi* and *dindi* for instance. If they had not undertaken these efforts, the Marathi language would have died out long ago. As there have been no prose compositions in Marathi on the various fields of classical learning or *shastra*, the language has been overlooked by intellectuals. However, if a language proves itself capable of composing beautiful poetry, surely no man can call it worthless.

About three hundred years ago, the English language was fairly unrefined, and if any learned Englishman wanted to write something or make a speech, he would do so in Latin or French just as we write our letters, religious tracts, grocery lists, and even our marriage invitations in English. They were so ashamed of their own language that if a group of three or four people assembled they would converse half in English and half in Latin, just as we speak half in Marathi and half in English. As time passed, scholars such as Bacon, Newton, Milton, Pope, Shakespeare, Byron, Scott and Addison arrived on the scene and contributed to the growth of their language. Not only has English been accepted by one and all, but it has also achieved a status similar to that of the classical languages of Sanskrit, Latin, Arabic and Hebrew. Isn't it shameful indeed that scholars have come from England to prepare dictionaries and encyclopaedias in Sanskrit and other native languages for our use;[1] and that they rediscover books written in Marathi which we have carelessly lost? The German Professor Max Muller has interpreted the *Vedas* and published an annotated version for our benefit; while our students are examined in Marathi, Sanskrit, and Gujarati by English pundits such as Dr. Wilson, Dr. Mitchell, and Major Candy. Should we not be ashamed that teachers are imported from Germany to teach Sanskrit in Mumbai colleges?[2] In other words, this is the outcome of their love for their country and language and their sustained efforts towards improving themselves.

Some of you may ask why the fault lies with our people. When our forefathers could compose books such as the *Mahabharata, Bhagavad Gita, Ramayana,* and write vast tomes on subjects such as Astrology, Law, Logic, Grammar, and Medicine, why are we unable to do so? While one must accept that there have been many learned people in this country, including

Vyas, Valmiki, Gautam, Kalidas, and Panini, their knowledge has remained with them. It is of no use to us. One can benefit from knowledge, riches, good deeds, courage, health and happiness, only if we truly possess these things. When it comes to knowledge, only if one develops it can one possess it. One need not go far to realize that one's father's intelligence is no good to us. So why should we preen if our forefathers acquired a great amount of knowledge hundreds of years ago? Knowledge must be acquired through one's own efforts, or at the very least the knowledge acquired from one's ancestors must be properly conserved in order for it to be a credit to the current generation. Money earned through one's own efforts has a greater value than wealth inherited from one's father.

We can surmise from the foregoing discussion that in times past there were indeed great scholars amongst us, that their achievements have made us vain and that we have consequently become complacent. If there had been no scholars in our history, we might perhaps have undertaken greater efforts towards the acquisition of knowledge. The English had neither a history of scholarship nor any background in learning. They therefore sought knowledge from other countries, where they studied the various sciences only to glean the best from them, thus adding to their ever growing store of knowledge in order to rise in prominence.

The resources required by an author to compose a work of this calibre have already been described in detail. To the reader wondering which were available during the writing of this book, the author can only claim long years of residence in this city, acquaintance with a large number of scholars, both young and old, and a more than passing familiarity with our language. Despite the decidedly meagre foundation upon which this enterprise has been built, if the completed book is regarded by critical scholars as sound and well-written, the author will feel that he has accomplished the objectives of his endeavour. If, on the other hand, this book fails to meet their expectations, they are requested to read it carefully and identify its shortcomings, and to communicate the same either through the columns of a newspaper or a monthly magazine with the best interests of the author in mind in order that he might benefit from their criticism. The principal objective of this book is to consolidate the knowledge acquired over a lifetime and thus give meaning and fulfilment to this life. When our people start reading books with an inquiring mind and make known to the author the factual mistakes he has committed, only then will books of any appreciable quality be written in our language and our people enthused to read them. Scholars have still not accepted Marathi as a language of scholarship and research because many of its words have not been gathered together in a proper structure.[3] Only when dictionaries of our language are compiled and thousands of books of both prose and poetry are composed and critically reviewed will this language rank alongside that of Sanskrit.

I am grateful to Raosaheb Mahadev Govindshastri Kolhatkar, formerly Deputy Inspector in the Department of Education for the Pune and Satara districts and currently Curator of the Central Book Depot in Mumbai, who kindly read the manuscript of this book in great detail. Many other friends have helped in numerous ways to ensure that this book reached completion; I am indebted to all of them.

A glossary has been appended in which the words from various languages used in the book are listed along with their meanings.[4]

TABLE OF CONTENTS

The Current and Past Situation of Mumbai

Chapter 1

Layout of the city – People of numerous castes – Multitude of languages – Their dress – Famous places – Vehicles – Its earlier situation and fame – Grandeur of the Company Sarkar – Physical extent of the city – English Government – Arrival of people from various regions

While there are many large cities in India, it is widely accepted that Mumbai, though small in size, is the grandest of them all and home to the most outstanding things. It is certainly true that there is none so densely packed and unique. Having seen the magnificence of this city, many people have migrated from their native regions to settle here; perhaps this is the sole reason why such people have flocked to Mumbai. As you walk down any road, you are stunned by its enormous mansions, sprawling buildings, beautiful bungalows, and gardens. Many people are of the opinion that Mumbai is unique among all Indian cities for its broad, clean, straight, and well-planned roads. And just as plentiful are the methods invented to sprinkle water on these roads! The government incurs an annual expenditure of over twenty-five thousand rupees simply to keep them clean and in good repair. It is said that even the paved roads of Pune do not match up to the ordinary roads of Mumbai. Even the Sanyasis, Gosavis, and Bairagis who roam the streets of Mumbai use utensils and glasses. If you walk down the Bhuleshwar Road, you may come across one of these Bairagis with matted hair, caked in white ash from top to toe with a thick rope around his waist, carrying one of these expensive utensils under his arm as he wanders around. In many of their ashrams, you can even see these Sanyasis and Bairagis being served with glasses and utensils.

A local proverb talks about a land with "fifty-six languages and eighteen castes with different head-dresses". However in Mumbai, one is unable to fathom the number of languages which are current usage nor the number of castes which reside here. The Marathi language alone has between thirty to forty variations; one can only imagine the variations among the other languages in use. Then let us try and estimate the number of castes in

Mumbai. Among the Hindus there are over a hundred castes – Marwadi, Multani, Bhatia, Vani, Joshi, Brahmin (once again, approximately 25 to 30 castes of Brahmins can be encountered in this city), Kasar, Sutar, Jingar, Lohar, Kayastha Prabhu, Dhuru Prabhu, Ugra Prabhu, Shimpi, Khatri, Kantari, Jhare, Paanchkalashe, Shetye, Lavane, Kumbhar, Lingayat, Gawli, Ghati, Mang, Mahar, Chambar, Hajam, Teli, Mali, Koli, Dhobi, Kamathi, Telangi, Kannadi, Kongadi, Ghadshi, Purbhaiya, Bangali, Punjabi, *et cetera*. There is no end to the differences and variations within these castes. Moving on to the other castes – Parsi, Mussalman, Moghul, Yahudi, Israeli, Bohra, Khoja, Memon, Arab, Kandhari; these are the castes identified by the eighteen different head-dresses. And then come the hatted races,[1] including the English, Portuguese, French, Greek, Dutch, Turkish, German, Armenian and Chinese. Not only is one entertained by the variety of strange costumes worn by these tribes, but the sight of them inspires yet other thoughts in the mind.

If one happens to sit on the veranda for an hour or two, one can see hawkers selling many kinds of groceries and different types of cloth, and hear them cry out, each in a distinctive manner. The Hindu scriptures stipulate that prayers must be offered to god two hours prior to dawn; while the Portuguese have a similar custom of offering prayers in the morning, afternoon and evening. They are summoned to church thrice daily by the ringing of bells, which one can hear all over Mumbai.

At about four in the morning, before the ringing of these bells has begun, one can hear the cries of 'Mitto Neero Sakrya Neero', hawkers selling either sweet or salted *neera*. Over the next four hours, one will hear at least ten of these hawkers, and each of them will have a distinctive roll of the tongue as he advertises his wares. These hawkers sell *neera* on the roads from four o'clock until sunrise and again from sunset until ten at night.

Neera is the sap collected from the palmyra and date palms, palm and *mitto*, or sweetness, is its peculiar characteristic. It is not properly understood why this product is sold under the cloak of darkness, but it is said that it becomes sour after sunrise. Even though sweet *neera* is not very acidic, it produces some heat in the body, and thus certain people believe that its consumption may be harmful. One would not encounter any civilized person consuming it in public. The consumers of *neera* are mainly the English, Portuguese, Parsis or Mussalmans and occasionally some of the lower caste Hindus. Hardly anybody else drinks it. It does not behove the great city of Mumbai to find this product available day and night on every street. This outrage is proof enough that our island has been under the rule of the Firangis for too long a time.

In the hours that follow dawn, one can see a procession of hawkers each loudly proclaiming their wares. The ears are assaulted by a variety of sounds – Rice for *bhakri* – *chawli* peas – *chikki* jaggery – sugar – Rajapuri turmeric – green *hing* – coconuts from Mahim – mangoes – butter – chillies and coriander – garlic from Gogha – sugar cakes – rose and melon flavoured sweets – tur dal – hot ground nuts – red soil – raw nuts – *vaidya* for treating colds – *vaidya* for all ailments – Chinese bangles – jack fruit – locks and keys – oil – old silks – vegetables – *churans* from Hindustan – bottles – milk – cloth for blouses. About twenty years ago, an old Parsi would go door-to-door in the Portuguese areas with a large wooden container filled with a variety of pickles. He would make a variety of strange noises as he cried out the names of the different pickles in a foreign language. When he used to move about with his wares, a crowd of twenty-odd people would gather to listen to his cries, which went like this – Senor Caitan Mango Pickles, Senor Marian Mango Pickles, *et cetera*.

On any given day, over a hundred hawkers pass by every door from morning to evening proclaiming their wares in various languages. During the mango season, more than one hundred villagers, both men and women, can be seen carrying their wares either on baskets over their heads or in a sling-like contraption hung from a bamboo stick held across the shoulders. There are yet others who sell mangoes grown on grafts. If all their distinctive words were to be listed here, it would become a bulky book. These hawkers can be quite a pain. The old and the infirm are often troubled by the cacophony created by this unending stream of hawkers, and students are also distracted by the noise. Some years ago, unable to tolerate their harsh drone any longer, a friend retired to live in the silent area of Colaba.

In Mumbai, if one makes their judgements based solely on attire, it is almost impossible to distinguish between the rich and the poor. Isn't it surprising that the ordinary people of Mumbai are more fashionable in their costume than richest of the Calcutta babus? Even an ordinary milkman steps out of his shop wearing the finest of dhotis complete with large silk borders and a head-dress decorated in gold brocade. As he struts along the road in his soft vermilion slippers, with heavy studs swaying from his ears, one would assume that he was the scion of a prosperous business family.

In the year 1859, the Portuguese government started a museum in Goa, where some of the most exquisite objects from around the world were put on display. A friend sent them samples of the various kinds of head-dresses seen in Mumbai, and, even though it was only a sampling, the number of head-dresses amounted to over fifty. It is said that the people of Goa were astounded to realize the variety of people resident in Mumbai. You do not come across people of so many castes in any other city. One would not be wrong in terming it a melting pot for all cultures.

Clocks and watches are so common-place in Mumbai that it would be difficult to find even a third of their number in the rest of India. They come in many shapes and sizes, varying from that of a half-rupee coin to a large plate. Prices start at four rupees and increase up to a maximum of five thousand rupees. Some years back a local king commissioned a clock as big as a temple sanctum that plays tunes using a variety of instruments. To mark every hour, half-hour and quarter, figurines of soldiers emerge to spar with each other. A cockerel also appears and crows loudly. It is a truly marvellous clock, and cost five thousand rupees. Many of the rich people of this city have similar clocks in their houses. Small clocks are available from five rupees up to over one thousand rupees. They are often made of gold and studded with diamonds. The accompanying gold-plated chains are also very attractive. Even the ordinary people of Mumbai use clocks and watches, and in some areas, washermen and barbers can be seen sporting them. Any English gentleman would have a minimum of five clocks in his house and a couple of large watches at the least. The clocks are placed in the following places – one in the kitchen, one above the stairs, another in the reception area, one close to the dining table, one each in the study and drawing room, and yet one more in the bedroom. The Parsis, and other rich people, also place clocks in various places in their houses. One can see clocks in the stables from which animals are hired out, and occasionally one may see butlers and cooks walking around with watches dangling from golden chains. In public places such as temples, mosques, hospitals and offices, one can always hear clocks ticking, so that even the poor are conscious of the passage of time in all its divisions.

There are many shops selling a wide range of clocks both in the Fort and elsewhere in the city. They come from as far afield as England, America, France, and Geneva. Those from England are of the best quality. In every street, there are between five and ten establishments for the repair of clocks, which have been set up by Parsis and others. And whenever one peeps into these, one can see at least two gentlemen getting their watches repaired. Many of these watch repairers are quite shrewd and calculating in nature, and one can see baskets full of watches lying in their shops.

The Maratha people, delighted by the grand sights of this city, can be seen playing their tambourines and singing the praises of Mumbai at street corners and other prominent places. A few examples have been quoted below.

Lavani in Urdu

Surrounded by seas, blessed by nature
The Badshah in foreign lands rules this place.
Tellichery, Madras and the Calcutta of Bengal;
In all the big cities the fame of Mumbai has spread,
Not to mention the fine harbour of Damman
And the army on the seas, powerful everywhere.
The Sahib in Bengal rules all the cities,
The new docks in Mumbai receive goods from all countries,
Kashi and Gaya are now ruled by the Topiwalas,
Who supervise in Surat and have enlarged the city of Kochi.
The docks and wharves at Mahim and Mandvi are busy
With goods despatched to Karnatak, Muscat and China.
Prosperous is the city of Mumbai, Mumbadevi is her patroness.

The Fort is the symbol of the English rule,
Marvellous is Mumbai, this island of the South.
Shiv Shankar and Paigambar reside in this place,
None can compare to the clever people of this settlement.
Logs run on water with the help of wind,
Hundreds of pounds of flour are made by the windmill.*
The Navy grows legs and becomes the Army.
The clocks make a racket in the churches,
What an intricate mechanism they have designed!
Pumps attached to wells transport water into warships,
A fleet thousands-strong stand in the port,
Cranes lift cannons right into the fort.
Ships immense as mountains are built in the dockyard –
One man can do what hundred elephants cannot,
And transfer the ship from the yard into the sea.
Prosperous is the city of Mumbai, Mumbadevi her patroness.

How skilfully the Fort has been constructed!
A fort within a fort surrounded by a moat.
On the turrets, huge cannons are mounted,
The doors are always heavily guarded.

---

* The flour mill powered by wind was set up near Church Gate in 1725.

Inside the fort is the Sahib's Castle,
On it proudly flies the flag of the foreign Badshah;
Below the Fort is beautiful Colaba,
A huge light burns there to guide the ships.
On the other side is a fort upon a hillock
To keep watch over the entire city.
On Mazagaon Lake is Nawab Hunsha Sahib's bungalow.[†]
In Parel is a grand mansion which has no equal.
Adjoining Mumbai is Mahim which abounds in gardens,
Fairs everywhere, but Mahalaxmi is the one to see.
Prosperous is the city of Mumbai, Mumbadevi her patroness.

Traders and moneylenders have grown prosperous here,
Parsis, Gujaratis, Shenvi Prabhus run this place,
Mussulmans and other proud races have their base here;
Everybody is amazed by the general spectacle.
Twelve councillors meet every eighth day,
The Sahib dispenses justice by referring to a book.
Govindrao, Rana of Junnar, holidays here in style;
The Mallaris, inspired by their favourite idol, sing with great gusto.
Mother Mumbadevi, nothing happens without your grace,
Devotees sing your praise accompanied by drums.
Listen to my prayers like any other devotee,
I am a foreign bird, so grant me your blessings.
Prosperous is the city of Mumbai, Mumbadevi her patroness.

This composition in the Urdu language was created by a Southern Maratha named Malhari about seventy-five years ago. He then presented it to the Governor Sahib of the day who was very pleased with it and rewarded him with a sum of three hundred rupees from the government. This anecdote was related by an aged gentleman who also gave the peculiar explanation for this poet's exile as follows: The Governor was surprised that this man could, in so short a time, describe Mumbai in so felicitous a manner and suspected that, if allowed to stay, he might relay the secrets of the city's success to other kings. Such is the far-fetched imagination of our people!

[†]   The Moghul Badshah's representative, Hunsha Sahib used to stay in Mazagaon.

Whenever somebody visits Mumbai for the first time, they are most keen to see all of its famous sites including the Mint, the Docks, the Armoury, its cotton spinning machines and cloth looms, the Museum, telegraph machine, the metalled roads, the Observatory, its hospitals, the gunpowder works, the Town Hall, the Panjarapole – a home for destitute animals – the narrow strip of land at Colaba with the lighthouse at its very end, the mills, the Industrial School and others. Besides, many moneylenders have their counting-houses in the Fort, where one's eyes are dazzled by the heaps of freshly minted coins from the Mint. One is enthused by the constant ringing of the coins. There are shops run by Parsis, Englishmen and Mussalmans filled with exquisite crystal ware and other expensive objects. One can also see doctors, their shelves lined with potions of many colours; they look very impressive and one begins to feel that they might be real experts in the art of medicine. Similarly if one enters a merchant's house, one cannot help getting the feeling that one has entered the abode of Lord Kubera himself after looking at the opulent furniture, the grand vehicles, the demeanour of his servants and the obvious wealth visible throughout. There are bookshelves set against the walls, supporting thousands of neatly bound books on a myriad subjects, while pictures are displayed at various vantage points. In other words, wherever one goes, there is something to catch the eye. After five in the evening, attractive wagons decorated in a kaleidoscope of colours and drawn by Arabian horses can be seen along the road to the Camp. Their pomp and splendour left a man recently arrived from the Konkan momentarily dumbstruck. He exclaimed, 'Amazing! Your Mumbai is just like Paradise. If one doesn't visit Mumbai at least once in a lifetime, life is not worth having lived'.

In 1861, the mother of a Mod Brahmin arrived in Mumbai. Seeing the magnificence of Mumbai, she said, 'Your Mumbai really does take the biscuit. I have been soaking up the sights for over a month, but my eyes are still not satisfied. The roads are overflowing with vehicles; as you walk down the road, a vehicle is bound to nudge you from behind, and if you walk towards one side, a vehicle pushes you back from the other. God has been very kind to Mumbai'.

Some years ago, the renowned Sir Jamsetjee Jejeebhoy, Baronet presented a pair of the finest Arabian horses to her majesty Queen Victoria of England and India. It is rumoured that they cost over thirty thousand rupees. Thus we can assume that they were of a higher order even than the divine horses described in the *Puranas*.

When the Portuguese acquired Mumbai from the Mussalmans in 1530, it was nothing more than a wild and desolate village consisting of about 400 houses, both large and small, and with a population of between five and ten thousand made up of the Koli, Bhandari, and Panchkhalasi castes only. The land revenue paid to the government amounted to 700 *ashrafies*, that is, approximately three hundred and fifty rupees. The ground was not very productive and did not yield much grain, since it was rugged and rocky and susceptible to the sea's inundations. However, in spite of this the English traders had had their eye on it for a number of years. In the year 1654, the Company's Chief suggested to Oliver Cromwell, at that time the main officer of the Court,[2] that the island of Mumbai should be acquired from the Portuguese to further English trade in India and that if nothing else prevailed, it should be bought from them.[3] However, in a stroke of good fortune, they were shortly to acquire it gratis. In 1661, the King of Portugal gave his daughter in marriage to King Charles II, and included in her dowry the island of Mumbai. Even at that time, the revenue generated by this area was hardly worth mentioning, and the basic expenses of the city could only be met with great difficulty.

A Sutar, whose family have long been resident in Mumbai, is in possession of a marvellous composition, which gives details about the past state of affairs in Mumbai, when the English arrived, how the city achieved its prominence and how much of its land was reclaimed from the sea. This composition is written in the original form of the Marathi language spoken in Mumbai. The following two *shlokas* recount the original state of affairs in Mumbai:

*In *Samvat* 1720, the *Engrez* came from *Vilayat*
in the favourable month of *Jyesht* to Mumbai;
The *Firangis* gifted it to them as dowry
Since then the capable *Engrez* have prospered here.

Half of Mumbai was under the sea,
And there were hardly any settlements;
Dense forests and some farmland,
Small hamlets with huts and cottages.

In the year 1666,[4] administrative control of the island was handed over to the Company Sarkar,[5] by the King of England on the payment of a sum of hundred rupees, in gold coins, per annum. Since then, the city has slowly

---

* As it is presently *Samvat* 1919, it has been 199 years since this incident.

prospered, and people from other regions have migrated here. When Mumbai was handed over to the King of England, the gross value of all assets, houses, and government property in the city amounted to 28,340 rupees only. By the year 1688, it had increased to 64,960 rupees, and by 1812, it had increased to 13,260,000 rupees. In the year 1858, it was estimated that the sales of local merchants alone amounted to over fifty crore rupees. Besides this, one has to consider the personal assets of private individuals. In 1861, the Bombay Treasury had a balance of 31,255,230 rupees while the total amount held in all the treasuries of India amounted to 142,869,178 rupees. One can get a good idea of the extent of the Company Sarkar's influence from these statistics.

When people from other cities hear about the magnificence and splendour of Mumbai, they are under the impression that it must be a vast, sprawling city; however, it is no more than a small island situated on the Western coast of India at a latitude of 19°N. Not including Colaba, it extends around 4.5 *kos* in the North-South direction and about 1.5 *kos* from West to East at its widest point. All being told, the area is approximately 8 square *kos* and is shaped like a trapezium.[6] This is the total extent of the city, and is only achieved by joining three or four land masses. It is surprising indeed that this city, which was once in a very primitive state, has made such astounding progress. The sole thing of utility with which this island was already endowed was its harbour. It is said that there is no other place in all of India which has a harbour more amenable to trade and handling ships. In the Portuguese language, *'Bom'* means good and *'Bahia'* means harbour. It is commonly believed that *'Bombay'* was given as a descriptive name by the Portuguese because of this very same harbour. But unfortunately it is not possible to discover the earlier name of this island. Many other theories are given to explain why the island bears the name of Mumbai, but none are conclusive. They will be considered in a later chapter.

In India, Mumbai was the first place in which the English established a government, and for a long time Mumbai was the chief capital. Later, when Madras and Bengal were annexed, Calcutta was nominated as the chief capital and Mumbai was relegated to a subsidiary role. It is indeed astounding that a place where once there were only Kolis and Bhandaris, and where it was difficult to find a banker or trader, has now risen to dominate the entire Indian landmass! The English have made the local saying real – from a mustard seed may grow a great mountain. The origins of this success can be found in the factory at Surat and the government established in Mumbai. The Company Sarkar should be exclusively credited for the splendour of this city. It must be acknowledged that the secret to the success of the English lies in their remarkable industry and entrepreneurial cunning.

The kings, nobles, and rich men of this world spend thousands of rupees to come to Mumbai and marvel at its wonders, but the gentleman of Europe are, of course, in control of this city's fortunes. Amongst these, one can see kings and nobles of the Siddis who spend over six months of the year in this city. Famous business magnates and other notable persons come from America to descend on this city in their colossal ships, and one can daily spot the camps of the Indian Badshahs, kings, and other nobles. One day the King of Nepal, Jung Bahadur, will arrive; the Imam of Muscat on the next; the Amir of Sindh, the Diwansahib of Ajmer, the Elchi of Iran, the Thakur from Morbi on yet other days; Nawabs from Bengal, Shahzadas from Kabul, Babus from Calcutta; the Khanbahadur from Delhi; Subedars from the Carnatic, the Raja of Jhalewar, the Rana of Udaipur, the Mutsuddi of Arcot, the Vazir of Zanzibar and the Mansubdar of Porbandar; one of the Gaikwads, Holkars or Scindias, or possibly Pawar from Dhar, perhaps the caravan of Baijabai; traders from Indore; the Raja of Satara, the Maharaja of Kolhapur; today a Dhamdhere, tomorrow a Nimbalkar, the day after a Raste, followed by a Patwardhan, a Jamkhandikar, and a Kurundwadkar; today a Sardar of the first rank, tomorrow a Noble of the second rank. Everyday one can see these people in the street, accompanied by their entourage. Any visitor to this city is stunned by its opulence, and will spend over ten thousand rupees during his stay. A defining feature of this land is that even the most niggardly of men are converted to generosity upon arrival at Mumbai.

Just look! In this city of Mumbai, the poor and the infirm, the lame and the crippled, the deaf and the dumb, the blind and the maimed, the good and the bad, the thief and the scavenger, the fool and the fraud, whoever one may be, is deprived neither of food nor of clothing. Men who merely fold turbans to make *pagdis* can earn a rupee or two a day. If a rustic from Bankot can save up to fifty rupees within a year, it is barely worth mentioning that smart and industrious people are capable of earning hundreds of rupees in that time. Some years ago, a very old and blind Bairagi woman was carried around in the streets in a palanquin by two strong *Shudras*. At the end of the day, they would give her four or eight *annas* and keep the rest of the charitable donations. Thus it is not just the rich who flock to Mumbai; for even the blind, crippled, the aged and destitute, the infirm, the diseased, and a multitude of other beggars travel hundreds of miles to reach this city.

Chapter 2

A narrative of the ancient families settled in Mumbai – Reasons for surmising that before 1400 A.D. Mumbai was made of two to four islands – Original settlers – The earlier Mumbadevi and Kalbadevi temples – Vasai and other places – The coming of the Parsis

At this point in time, people of many races, castes, and tribes are resident in Mumbai, the differences between whom are clearly visible. A thorough investigation of the time of their arrival in Mumbai and their reasons for settling here will reveal the political and economic influences that transformed a small piece of barren land into this splendid city. When trade from Surat shifted to Mumbai, the former's fortunes took a turn for the worse. Consequently, many Parsis moved to Mumbai; just as many Brahmins and others from the South migrated here after the English conquered Pune. The flourishing trade in horses prompted the Arabs and the Kandharis to settle in this city. Similarly people from other countries also followed suit. When the English attacked Misar and other kingdoms, many noblemen and tradesmen from the Madras region came to Mumbai with their households. This led to the mushrooming of a Kamathi settlement in Mumbai. If one examines books written by Portuguese, Mussalman, and English authors on the subject of the settlement of Mumbai, one arrives at similar conclusions.

Similarly one can trace the antecedents of the original settlers of Mumbai by examining their language. Of the various kinds of Marathi spoken in Mumbai, that spoken by the Christians in Sashtee,[1] Mahim, Matunga, and Mazagaon is unique. One can therefore conclude that this dialect was spoken long before the Firangis converted these people from Hinduism to Christianity. It is most unlikely that the Portuguese taught them this strange tongue, as there is not a single word of Portuguese origin to be found in their diction. Furthermore, since they have been isolated from other Marathi speakers ever since their conversion to Christianity, there has been no opportunity for the other types of Marathi to influence their language. From this it is evident that prior to the advent of the Portuguese, the *lingua franca* of this island was that selfsame language currently spoken by the Christians of Mumbai. By extending this logic, one can assume that the castes which speak languages having a marked similarity or that bears a similar imprint to this distinctive dialect can be thought of as the descendants of this island's original inhabitants. Based on a study conducted on this premise, five castes emerge whose language can be linked to that of the Christians of Mumbai. An examination of the language of the ancient texts and fables of these castes also leads one to a similar conclusion, this being that they have been resident in the region of Mumbai since times immemorial, without any changes in their religious practices. The five castes are as follows: Koli, Bhongle Bhandari, Palshe Joshi, Pathare Prabhu, and Paanchkalashe – Vaadval – Sutar.

By extrapolating from this linguistic study, it can be concluded that these five castes were settled on this island prior to its acquisition by the Portuguese. We can further conclude that these castes were settled here prior to the arrival of the Mussalmans in the fourteenth century.

When the Mussalmans first attacked the Southern part of India in 1292, Allauddin defeated Ramdeo Jadhav, the Hindu King of Devagad, now known as Daulatabad, and established his rule in Mahim, Sashtee, the Konkan sea and various other ports. By the year 1318, when Mussalman rule extended unto the Konkan coast, Mubarak Badshah I defeated one Harpaldeo, killing him and sending his troops to defend the Konkan. A detailed account of these two incidents can be found in the ancient texts of the *Pathare Prabhus*.

The *Walkeshwar Mahatmaya*, a Sanskrit Purana describing the temple of Walkeshwar says that prior to the building of the Walkeshwar Temple, the Hindus were very much terrorized by the religious intolerance of Mubarak Badshah. This led to the arrival of Hindus of very high caste in Mumbai. If the population had consisted only of Kolis, they would neither have striven to build the Temple nor would they have been able to recognize the threat to their religion. Many of the Christians of Sashtee and Mumbai were originally Kolis and Bhandaris, and many of them retain their original surnames and languages. The key to establishing a connection between these five castes lies in their common language. While they speak the Marathi language, the Hindu and Christian Kolis have a distinctive enunciation, and use certain words, by which this dialect came to be known as the Koli language. Thus we understand that, since the earliest times, there were many Kolis in this island. The other four castes arrived thereafter, and after a long period of co-mingling with the Kolis, modified their pronunciation and vocabulary to adopt the peculiarities of their language. Kolis from other parts of the Konkan speak a similar language, but those of the lowest caste do not. Amongst the four castes, there is very little difference in dialect and, in recent years, hardly any noticeable difference exists between the languages of the Palshe Joshis, Prabhus and Paanchkalashes. The possible reasons for this include the migration to Mumbai of Brahmins from the South and the Konkan, as well as the introduction of a pure form of the Marathi language through the publication of books by *Elphinstone College*. Many of the educated people abandoned the language of their castes to speak in this pure Marathi diction, with a view to increasing the prestige of their respective castes. These are the three main reasons for the sweeping changes in spoken Marathi.

A simple way to identify the Bhandaris is their practice of playing the *bhongli*, or ceremonial drum. It is said that they took up this instrument after the arrival of the Firangis, to play on ceremonial occasions. In a letter written between 1672 and 1681, a resident gentleman mentions that the Bhandaris were the soldiers designated by the Firangi government to sound the salute, and even now, when the Court is in session, the Bhandaris hold the standard and blow the horn when the judge's vehicle nears the entrance. Given that this honour has been bestowed upon them, it is perhaps true that the Bhongle Sardars once acquired the kingdom at Mahim, as mentioned in several historical texts. At that time, the islands of Mumbai and Sashtee were within the kingdom of Mahim. From the aforementioned, we can conclude that the Bhongle Sardars were the ancestors of the Bhandaris – whose impoverished descendants continue to blow the horn for the government, albeit a new, foreign one. Many years ago, these people resided in Mahim, from which they governed Sashtee and a further few villages in the Konkan, under Raja Bhim. Other texts suggest that this King may have had two capitals – one at Mahim, and the other at Pratappuri, in Marol Subha of Sashtee. Prior to the advent of the Bhongle Sardars, Sashtee was ruled by the Nayaks. While in 1018, the reigning king claimed Tagar ancestry, copper plates found in Thane indicate that he may have belonged to the Nayak family. A stone inscription found in Sashtee records the grant of the village of Utan in Sashtee by King Keshideo in the year 1047. Further stone inscriptions evidence the grant of other villages, including Veur village, by a king called Harpaldeo between the years 1091 and 1100.

In connection with this, there is a further surviving account of the establishment of a kingdom at Mahim by Raja Bhim. This also describes the Pathare Prabhus and their fortunes, and, where relevant, discusses the other four castes.

When the Marathas conquered Vasai in 1739, one Janardhan Ganesh Mahimkar wrote a *bakhar*,[2] which he sent to one Anantkrishna at Mungipaithan; the relevant information from this document is described below.

In the year 1294, Allauddin defeated King Ramdeo in Paithan; but in spite of this defeat, Ramdeo restored himself to the throne and began to rule again. His son Keshavrao, undertook many heroic deeds with a view to preserving the kingdom of his father, some of which are described in this account. While this account has not been written in an accessible manner, one can conclude that King Ramdeo was originally from one of the lower castes, and that his surname was Jadhav. The account does not make any mention of this surname but instead suggests that it was Rane and that the King was a Suryavanshi Kshatriya. It also mentions that while he was still ruling, King Ramdeo promoted his second son, Bhimrao, to the kingship of Udaipur in Gujarat; but it is not clear as to where this realm was located. However, after the defeat of his father by Allauddin and the ascendancy of the Mussalmans in the South and the West, Raja Bhim was forced into exile in the year 1296, accompanied by 12 Suryavanshi Nobles, 64 clans of Noble Somvanshi Kshatriya families and a large army. He then moved to the South, where he defeated the Nayak King and conquered Chinchani-Tarapur, Asheri, Kelve-Mahim, Thal, Sashtee and Mahim one after the other to establish a kingdom. This kingdom comprised 444 villages, which were divided into 15 *mahaals* and allotted to the nobles accompanying the king. The account provides a detailed list of names of the Suryavanshi king and his nobles, their family names and the province they were each allotted. It also mentions that, at this time, Mahim was a barren island occupied solely by the Kolis. However, Raja Bhim believed that the place had prospects, and so sent many of his subjects to settle the island. He then built houses on it, and established gardens and farms. In due course, Mahim became the capital of a small kingdom, and is, in this *bakhar*, variously referred to as Mahim Island, Mahikavati, Prabhavati, and Bhimsthan. Many of the nobles stayed on in Mahim, while some of them were moved to places like Kelve-Mahim, Chaul, Vasai and other provinces; and eventually surnames linked to these places, such as Mahimkar, Kelvekar, Vasaikar, and Chaulkar, emerged.

After the death of Raja Bhim, he was succeeded by his son Pratapshah, who established a capital, called Pratappuri, in Marol, at Sashtee. In the later years of his reign, Pratapshah initiated a war with Nagarshah, the ruler of Chaul, who – although the account is unclear at this point – may have been his brother-in-law. After winning many battles, Nagarshah finally defeated Pratapshah and established his rule over Mahim. However, as he did not honour his promises of rewards to the nobles who aided him during his struggle against Pratapshah, they revolted against him, summoning the Mussalmans for support, who sent their armies to Sashtee and Mahim, killing Nagarshah established themselves as the new rulers of his kingdom. Nonetheless, since the Mussalmans were a minority at that point in time, the Bhongle Sardars gained power. They might well have been the ancestors of the Bhandaris, amongst whom the surname Bhongle is still prevalent. The fact that they continue to have the rights to blow the ceremonial horn, supports the contention that they might indeed have been in power at some point in time. The account goes on to say that the Mussalmans subsequently defeated the Bhongle Sardars and re-established their rule in Mahim and Sashtee.

It appears that, when the Portuguese arrived, the Bhandari people cooperated with them, which led to the restoration of their ancestral rights by the Portuguese rulers. After the defeat of the Bhongle Sardars, the Mussalmans gradually extended their reign over the Konkan region, and their leader, Bahadur Khan, gained control of the government at Vasai. When the Portuguese arrived, they bribed him to allow them to build a trading post. Soon after, they assembled a significant number of troops, and converted the trading post into a fort. Then, after a fierce battle, they acquired the islands of Sashtee and Mahim. This account then goes on to describe how the Portuguese gave Mumbai to the English, and how the Marathas gained ascendancy in the region and finally won control of the fort at Vasai in 1739 after fighting against the Portuguese for three years.

There is also another *bakhar*, composed from a collection of texts at Vasai. This also confirms the story that there was once a Raja Bhim, of low caste, who conquered Sashtee and some parts of the Konkan to establish his capital at Mahim.

From these historical records, we can conclude the following:

Prior to AD 1295, the Kolis were resident in Mumbai, and are the original inhabitants of this island.

In the year AD 1295, Raja Bhim, a Bhongle Sardar, acquired Mumbai, which led to the arrival of the Bhandaris, and planted many coconut trees there.

The king who succeeded Raja Bhim was defeated by the Chief of Chaul, who may not have been related to him but may have belonged to the Shetye caste.

The Chief of Chaul was in turn defeated by the Mussalmans. Mahim was later ruled by the Bhongle people, who were most probably ancestors of the Bhandaris. It is possible that they might have changed their family name from Bhandari to Bhongle after acquiring the kingdom The Bhandaris may have helped the Portuguese when they defeated the Mussalmans, leading to the granting of certain ceremonial rights, such as the bearing of the royal standard and playing of the ceremonial horn. In conclusion, the following sequence of groups held sway in Mumbai from the year AD 1290 onwards.

1. The Kolis
2. Raja Bhim and his descendants
3. The Sardar of Chaul, whose caste is unknown, but most certainly differed from that of the previous two rulers
4. The Mussalmans
5. The Bhandaris, otherwise known as Bhongles
6. The Mussalmans once again
7. The Bhandaris once again, although this is debatable
8. The Portuguese Firangi
9. The English

Furthermore, a reading of these two accounts also makes it clear that Mumbai and Mahim were two independent islands in 1295.

The above account has been extracted from a narrative written by Mr. Murphy, the former Chief Translator of the Supreme Court.[3]

The main evidence to suggest that the Kolis, Bhandaris, Paanchkalashe, Sutar, Vaadval, Prabhu, and Joshi were the earliest inhabitants of this island is their ancestral ownership of lands, farms and houses in Mumbai. To the South of Sion, there is a place known as the Palshe Hill, perhaps because the Palshes once resided here, while the Prabhadevi Temple at the border of Mahim lends credence to the belief that the Prabhus originally settled here. One can, of course, spot the sprawling estates of the Joshis and Prabhus across Mumbai, and also comes across mansions, houses, washing places, hillocks and other places owned by the Bhandaris and Kolis, many of whom are fairly prosperous. In the ancient districts of Girgaon, Kandewadi, Mazagaon, Parel, and Worli, one finds the houses of the Paanchkalashe, Sutar, and Vaadval castes, many of whom are rich, but choose not to flaunt their wealth as other people do. The majority of them continue to be dependent on their ancestral professions.

Kolbhaat, Koli Wadi, and Mugbhaat are common names for places in Mumbai. *Bhaat* is a word from the Goa region denoting a place, house or hereditary lands, and the Portuguese may have named these places by following this practice from the Goa region. Just as the traditional land revenue officials are known as Fazendar, Zamindar, and Vatandar in other regions, they are known as *Bhaatkar* in Goa. The land extending from the temple at Kalbadevi to the end of the Marine Lines is known as Kolbhaat, implying that it might have been the ancestral land of some Koli in the past. The sprawling lands behind the Atmaram Baba's Thakurdwar are known as Mugbhaat, and perhaps were once the property of a Koli by the name of Muga, since names such as Shimga, Posha, Bhoga, Manglya, Budhya, Jogya, and Muga are common amongst the Kolis.

This early account indicates that Mahim was a separate island at the time, and the capital of Raja Bhim's kingdom. Mumbai was another island, adjacent to Mahim. In addition to this, there were four to five other small islands adjoining Mumbai. These were Colaba, Mumbai (from the Fort to Pydhonie), Mahalaxmi, Worli, Mazagaon, and Sion. Many are of the opinion that there was a creek at Chowpatty which also separated Walkeshwar and Girgaon, but this claim cannot be substantiated. The areas which are said to have been creeks are presently low-lying, and no sweet water appears if a well is dug here. No fresh streams can be found at Pydhonie, Umarkhadi, Nal, and Bhendibazar, where the water is particularly bad. Many of the farms below Mahalaxmi used to be salt land; some of which still exist, and continue to be inundated by the sea during spring tide. The embankments at Worli and Colaba can be seen. In earlier times, one needed a boat to reach Mahalaxmi, which would pass through the area currently known as Kamatipura. Mr. Murphy has now proved that there was a creek extending from Kamatipura to Mahalaxmi, a conclusion supported by several others.

Many geologists, including Dr. Buist, are of the view that the five or six islands which currently make up Mumbai were once one large island that must have separated during a major earthquake or other catastrophe, leading to the current shape of Mumbai.[4]

Due to its fragmentation, this island had very few settlements, whose inhabitants were prevented from helping each other by natural barriers. Their lack of unity exposed them to many calamities; the island was infested with thieves and dacoits, who targeted the houses of the inhabitants; in addition to this, the chiefs of the neighbouring principalities would organize marauding trips to loot Mumbai. About forty to fifty years ago, so the old people say, an all-consuming fear of robbers would compel people to rush into their houses at sundown and securely lock themselves in. The dacoits had a run of the city during the night and would loot anyone unfortunate enough to cross their path, taking even the clothes from his body. When the English first arrived here, the situation was no different. At eight in the night, a cannon was fired to indicate that residents were not to step out of their houses; similarly at dawn, a cannon was fired at five in the morning to let people know that they were now free to roam the streets. This practice still continues, but although the cannons are fired at both dawn and dusk, people are not forbidden from roaming the streets. From evening until midnight, one can see people on the streets of Mumbai. However, if the police encounter anybody in the streets in the dead of the night, they are questioned about their identity and purpose, and only if an appropriate answer is given will they let them go. If the police meet somebody in the streets at night, the officer asks him in English – *'Who comes there?' to which the proper reply is 'Friend'. The police patrol the streets of Mumbai from ten in the night to five in the morning.

Within a radius of 20 to 25 *kos* of Mumbai, approximately 15 to 20 islands, both large and small, can be found. This entire collection can be called the Island of Mumbai. Towards the North, at a distance of 15 *kos*, is Vasai. South of Vasai, and larger than it, is Sashtee, also known as Thane. Adjacent to Sashtee are Chembur, Vesave, and Turbhe. A bridge has been built at the end of Turbhe to join Mumbai with Sashtee. To the South-East are Gharapuri, Divdive, Cheenalatekadi, and Khaneri-Unheri, and further down the island of Karanje, or Uran. To the west, a bridge has been built at Mahim to join Bandra with Mumbai. There are a couple of other islands which are too small to deserve a mention here. In previous eras, pirates and other marauders were based in Divdive, Cheenalatekadi, and Khaneri-Unheri, from where they were able to raid the neighbouring villages and loot ships.

In the adjoining villages of Turbhe, Vesave, Chembur, Kurla, Malad, Vasai, and Sashtee, there are settlements of the Paanchkalashe, Vaadval, and Sutar people, many of whom remain on their ancestral lands and farms. The majority of them are dependent on farming for their livelihood. While there are four to five different groups amongst these people, it is said that they have a common origin. Hari Keshavji, a scholarly gentleman of some renown, was from this caste. He was well-versed in the English language, knew Marathi well and had also studied the Sanskrit language. He translated seven or eight books from English into Marathi, both for use in schools and elsewhere, and was also a translator in the Sudder Adawlat. He died in 1858. After the study of certain ancient texts, he came to the conclusion that the Sutar and Paanchkalashe were Somavanshi Kshatriyas; ever since then these castes have referred to themselves as such. Perhaps

---

*   Since the police constable is not able to pronounce English properly, he says – "Hukumdar", and since the person who replies typically has similar skills in English, he replies – "Firang".

they were indeed one of the original races of this island, and may have ruled it for a while. However, one is unable to discover the basis for Keshavji's contention. Some people are of the opinion that the Paanchkalashe are descended from the Pandavas, hence the name; but again, no concrete evidence is forthcoming.

The Palshe Joshis are numerous in Vasai and Kelve-Mahim, where they own land and a number of farms.

While the Prabhus are now famous in the English courts, there is also evidence that they held positions of responsibility during the reign of Raja Bhim. After the arrival of the English, they learnt the English language and became clerks in government offices; that they also held other official posts is obvious from their current situation. For instance, a document exists which indicates that the construction of the embankment at Worli was entrusted to one Ramji Shivji, a Prabhu engineer. Even during the Portuguese rule, it is believed that this group learnt the Firangi language and had governmental responsibilities. In times past, many of the older men could speak the Firangi language and possessed documents written in it. Some years back, Dhakjee Dadajee, a Prabhu gentleman, achieved great fame in this city. He was the Diwan in the court of the Gaikwads for a while, then ran a trading business with England. There are many men amongst the Prabhus who hold positions of great responsibility in the government, and hardly one amongst them who has not learnt English.

The Shimpi people have been resident in Mumbai from the time of the Firangis, and certainly since the coming of the English. As the English started recruiting soldiers, allocating uniforms to the troops as per the English fashion, their numbers began to increase. The Shimpis used to dominate the tailoring profession, and many of them earned a lot of money in the process. One Atmaram Shimpi was well-known amongst them and considered a leading citizen. He had untold wealth and was also very generous. He built a large temple near Bhuleshwar and the permanent platform near it. Every morning, before sunrise, he would distribute two *pice* to every Brahmin, because the Hindus believe that an act of charity done in the early morning is a very meritorious act. Thus there would always be a great crowd of beggars at his doorstep in the wee hours of the night.

While one is unable to discover the original builder of the Mumbadevi Temple or to which caste he belonged to, it is said that it is at least four to five hundred years old. Many of the older gentlemen remember having heard that it had been built by a Koli which is highly probable, since the Kolis are the original inhabitants of this island and their presiding deity is Mumbadevi. Since there are female names like Munga, Shimgi, Mouna, and Bhongu amongst the Kolis, one can surmise that a Koli built this temple, and in the Hindu fashion, named it Mungadevi. This might have evolved into Mumbadevi over the course of time. Or perhaps a Brahmin replaced the 'Ga' with 'Ba' – a theory supported by Hindu tradition. When Dhakjee Dadajee built the temple at Mahalaxmi, the presiding deity of the temple was named Dhakleshwar. Installed close by is an idol of the goddess Rameshwari; thus named after Dhakjee Dadajee's wife. This lady was named Ramabai, from which the name Rameshwari is derived. Similarly, the idol installed by Mankoji at Parel is called Mankeshwar.

So be it. In earlier times, the Mumbadevi Temple was next to the Gallows Pond, located where the Camp Maidan now stands. Later, when the structures were being broken down to create the Camp Maidan, attempts were made to locate the owners of this temple, but nobody came forward. Since the Koli people had fallen into a degenerate state no enterprising individual took the responsibility upon himself. The government then estimated the value of the temple and gave permission for its reconstruction at the current site. The responsibility for running it was assigned to Pandushet Sonar, since he was an established trader in Mumbai, influential in court and was well regarded by the people. Thus he built the temple and thenceforth maintained it. Ever since, the temple has been run by his family. However, the tank at the present Mumbadevi Temple was built by one Shet Nagardas Navlakhia.

The temple at Kalbadevi is also very ancient, and one is unable to discover who built it. It is currently being managed by the Palshe Joshis. When the government widened the road at Kalbadevi, they issued instructions for setting back the temple. The original structure was demolished and the idol was installed in a new structure, the construction of which was financed by the government. The management of the temple was then handed over to the late Raghunath Joshi, a native of Mumbai and renowned personality in the city. The Joshis were traditionally the doctors of Mumbai, and even now many of them continue to practise this profession. They are also known to have officiated as priests in religious ceremonies at Mumbai.

An account of the history of the Mumbadevi Temple is extant in the Sanskrit language. There are no clues as to its authorship or when it was written. It says that in times past there was a very accomplished devil, Mumbarak, who lived on this island, and that the island was named after him. After much penance, he propitiated Lord Brahma and so pleased him that when Mumbarak asked him to grant the power of immortality and invincibility, Lord Brahma obliged! He then commenced terrorizing both the people on earth and the gods in heaven, who sought protection from Lord Vishnu and begged him to vanquish the evil Mumbarak. By combining their powers, Lord Vishnu and Lord Shiva created a Devi capable of killing the demon. The Devi defeated Mumbarak in battle and, as he lay dying, granted him a final favour. Extolling the virtues of the goddess, Mumbarak requested that she assume his name, so that it would become immortal and celebrated through the world. The goddess granted him this wish and named herself Mumbadevi. This account is attributed to the sage Suta.

Yet how can an inquiring mind truly believe this tale? This demon is only the first Mumbarak associated with the island. Perhaps Mubarak Badshah named this island after himself, as Mumbapur or Mubarakpur. Either may have been commonly referred to as Mumbai. Since the king was in opposition to the Hindus, the people of the island may have designated him a demon, and after his death, created a *Purana* from this tale.

It is not possible to clearly date the arrival of the Parsis in Mumbai, nor the initial number of families that arrived to settle permanently in Mumbai. It is certainly true that since around AD 1540, about ten years after the arrival of the Portuguese, there were a few Parsi families resident in Mumbai. Research indicates that they held office in the Portuguese Government. Their numbers increased sharply after the arrival of the English. When the English Company ran its factory in Surat, the Parsis were installed as their agents and chief officials, conducting all trade negotiations on behalf of the English. As the English evidently trusted the Parsi people, they invited them to settle in Mumbai once they obtained control of this island, and entrusted many sensitive assignments to them.

A Portuguese history reveals that, during their rule in Mumbai, a Parsi named Dorabji and his family resided in the city, and was responsible for government activities here. Furthermore, during the reign of the Company Sarkar, his descendants were officials in the government. Since the English had very little information about this island, they relied heavily on the Parsis. Initially, only the men would come to Mumbai, as nobody dared to bring their families because of its straitened circumstances. In 1672, Dr. Fryer visited Mumbai and wrote an account of it.[5] He does not directly mention the Parsis in this account, but does refer to the newly built Parsi Dokhma on the Babulnath Hill. We can thus conclude that at the time of his visit the Parsi settlement in Mumbai was recent and fairly small.

In 1692, there was an epidemic of plague in Mumbai, which wiped out most of the English army. The local people were also much affected. Sensing this opportunity, the Siddis from Janjira attacked Mumbai.[6] At this critical juncture, Dorabji's son, Rustom Dorab,[7] came to the aid of the English, organizing the Kolis into a standing force to patrol various strategic points in Mumbai. This honourable deed led to his being invested with the robes of the Patel of Mumbai, a title that was declared to be hereditary. He was also named the arbiter of disputes amongst the Kolis. Since then, this right has been exercised by his family. After the demise of Rustom Dorab, his son Cowasji Rustomji was invested with the robes of the Patel of Mumbai by Governor Hornby.[8] The Cowasji Patel Tank was built by this gentleman. He owned a lot of property in Mumbai, and was a man of great influence in the city due to the various critical assignments he undertook for the English. When the English defeated the Marathas and conquered Thane, he was instrumental to them in increasing the settlement and fortunes in that place, and established a colony of the Parsis there. Besides this, he was also a very accomplished trader.

In 1735, the Company's Shipmaster in Surat, Lowjee, was moved to Mumbai. He was very skilled in building ships. In the wake of his success, other important families moved to Mumbai and their numbers started increasing. They would take up all kinds of jobs, working hard both in trade and in the government, which led to their prosperity on this island.

The Parsis' native land is Iran. After the Mussalman revolution, they faced religious persecution and, in about the year 1200, left Iran to settle in Hindustan. They then moved to Diu in the province of Gujarat. Slowly but surely, their industry and dedication led to prosperity. When they first arrived in Mumbai, the Parsis had no houses or property and were practically destitute. From these desperate circumstances, they now own half of Mumbai – solely because of their industry and generosity. In the year 1854, there were 110,544 Parsis in India – men, women, and children, all told.

Chapter 3

Mumbai in the past — Reason for spread of many diseases — Worli embankment —
Pydhonie — Mahatarpakhdi — Umarkhadi — Colaba — Dongri — Chinch Bunder
— Masjid Bunder — Bori Bunder — Walkeshwar — Chowpatty — Shetodi —
Babulnath — A comparison of its earlier and current situation — Mahalaxmi —
Mama Hajani — And an old account of Worli

It is imperative for everybody to understand the original state of affairs in the city of Mumbai and its current situation because while one may not have a detailed knowledge of the affairs of the city, one should certainly have a passing familiarity with some of the major incidents relating to this city.

Nobody should conclude that the history of this city is useful only to the residents of Mumbai. It is useful both to the people of this region and to outsiders. Not only is it one of the capitals of the Company Sarkar, it is also one of the important centres of trade in the Indian territory. In any case, it is always useful to understand the historical narrative of any great city.

The old Mumbai was a small strip of land measuring about 1 *kos* in length and about half a *kos* in breadth. Dr. Fryer visited Hindustan from Europe in 1672 to undertake a journey across this country. About Mumbai, he says, 'A major part of this city, say 40,000 *bighas* of land is over-run by the sea and about 10,000 *bighas* of land can actually be counted as land proper. Mumbai is made up of five islands. As salt water creeks flow between them, the area is filled up with mud. During low tide, one can see these five islands distinctly. However, during high tide, water rushes in and the islands then number seven'. From this it is obvious that there is a big difference between the current and past state of the land in Mumbai. At that time there were no sprawling mansions and bungalows, which are common now. Instead of glass, the window panes were made from sea-shells. Till some years back, one could spot the houses of Christians which had window panes made of shell.

It was not that Mumbai was a wretched place because of its small size; but that the people fell prey to numerous diseases, and could not prosper. They had perforce to understand the reasons for spread of these diseases. At that time, though there were very few Englishmen, there were many amongst them with an inquiring mind and a willingness to pursue their tasks to completion. They set about investigating the causes favouring the rampant occurrence of these diseases. A theory was put forward that as there were many mud-swamps in Mumbai that were exposed during low tide, the vapours emanating from these swamps were the reason behind the spread of diseases. The Mumbai Sarkar decided that it would be very difficult to stay in Mumbai without eliminating these swamps. About 1685, it wrote to the main Company Sarkar in England that it would be impossible to encourage people to settle in Mumbai without first finding a solution to the problem and sought permission to fill in these swamps. Though this request was of an urgent nature, it took many years for a reply to arrive. Until 1685, the Chief of the Surat Factory was responsible for appointing the Deputy Governor and other officials as Mumbai was governed by the Surat Factory. From the year 1685 onwards, all powers were delegated to the Governor of Mumbai who was directly appointed in England.[1] It was not just the diseases that were a major source of dissatisfaction amongst those who had to move to Mumbai from Surat, but having come here, they had to struggle to find food and water. There was great resistance to coming to Mumbai. Even today, many of our people continue to be afraid of settling in Mumbai because they still hold on to the belief that the air in Mumbai is not good.

The presence of saline marshes all around Mumbai rendered the air cold and malarial, and led to all sorts of diseases amongst the residents. As the land was barren, not much grain could be grown here. Writing about the air in Mumbai, one of the first Englishmen to arrive here says, 'two monsoons are the age of a man'. And many called it the abode of death – Yamapuri. The atmosphere was really very bad in those days. But look how things have changed for the better! Many Englishmen now come to enjoy the air in Mumbai from other regions. The only reason why there might still be disease in the air currently is the crowd of people, not any inherent deficiency in its land or air. Is it not an astounding feat to recover the land from the sea and make it habitable and free of disease and earn lakhs of rupees in the process?

One of the main reasons for the spread of disease in Mumbai was the following. In those days, the fields and coconut groves were fertilized with a fish-based manure known as *kuta*. The fields and gardens used to emanate a stink when this *kuta* was used. As the people were inconvenienced, the government issued orders in 1720 banning the use of *kuta* in the fields. It was decided that cow dung would be used as manure instead of *kuta*. This led to many farmers and gardeners claiming that their livelihood had been taken away and they migrated to Sashtee and Thane. The Company Sarkar then had to write to the Court of Directors on this issue. The farmers and gardeners of places like Mahim and Worli submitted a joint petition to the Sarkar to let them continue their traditional practice of manuring their fields, in return for which they offered to pay the government a sum of ten thousand rupees. Their offer was refused by the government. Left with no other option, the people continued to farm their lands as in earlier times. Most people cannot look beyond personal gain, and ignore public good. The government however cannot afford to do the same.

In those times, a majority of the English officials and white soldiers gave way to their fancy in matters concerning eating, drinking, and lifestyle. This made them contract various diseases which inevitably ended in death, though there was an English doctor to minister to their needs. As they stayed in their respective houses, they would act in a wanton manner in relation to various indulgences and destroy their lives. It is a fact that if men are not careful about their eating habits, they shorten their lifespan. Keeping this in mind, the Chief of the Surat Factory instructed the Mumbai Governor in 1676 to build a small hospital in Mumbai. It was also indicated that the hospital should not cost more than four thousand rupees, should accommodate seventy patients and should not burden the government with a running cost of more than one thousand rupees per year. In the interim, the patients were to be accommodated in a suitable building within the Fort where a hospital was to be set up. In the following year, a hospital was constructed, and it is said that this indeed led to a reduction in the death rate of the white people.

In the year 1699, there were many internal skirmishes amongst the English people. An epidemic of cholera at the same time also killed many people. The natives were much affected by this epidemic. Of the white people, only seventy-six held on to their lives. To add to this grave misfortune, a cyclone hit Mumbai and left heavy destruction in its wake. Many farms, gardens, and houses were destroyed and grain was spoilt in large quantities. Countless ships foundered. The Governor of Mumbai, Sir John Gayer wrote a letter to the Chief of the Surat Factory in which he says, 'The people have no option but to walk. There is only one horse which can be ridden and just a pair of bullocks to yoke to a cart'. (This was a pair of large bullocks brought from Surat.) In those days, even the Governor and Councillors travelled in these bullock carts.

In 1700, when Sir Nicholas Waite arrived in Mumbai for the first time to take charge as Governor, commenting on the state of Mumbai, he wrote to the Chief at Surat that 'This island is in a very poor and impoverished state'. One can get an estimate of the state of Mumbai from the following.

A merchant representing the Badshah of Iran had arrived at the port of Mumbai with goods. He asked for permission to land but the English were hesitant to let him enter the city in case it betrayed the dire straits they were in. The Deputy Governor devised many stratagems to deny him permission to enter the city. The number of covenanted officers including the Councillors numbered just eight. They wrote a letter to the Court of Directors which said, 'If by the end of October, reinforcements do not arrive to relieve us, we will not be able to survive'.

Both the Moghul Sarkar and the Maratha kings were much feared by the English people in those days. They would hesitate to commit anything in writing about them openly. The Governor of Mumbai was hesitant to communicate the news of the death of Aurangzeb to the Court of Directors and wrote the following letter in code. This letter was written on 1 March 1707 and said that 'The sun has set on this side of the earth. As a star of the second order was near the sun, it has assumed its place; the star of the first order may be in another region but it is probable that he may also try to throw light'. What it meant was that Emperor Aurangzeb had died; his younger son Azim had assumed the throne, but his elder son Moazzim might arrive to stake his claim.

They were also in great terror of Shivaji. The news of Shivaji's death was sent by the Governor of Mumbai on 13 December 1680 to his counterpart in Bengal, who would not believe it. He felt that Shivaji was an immortal creature.

The Chief of Bengal wrote back to Mumbai, 'The news of Shivaji's death has made the rounds so many times, that people believe him to be immortal. Only when his brave deeds cease to occur, can we truly believe that he is dead. It is said that there is no one else similar in stature who can run the country'.[2]

While we are not able to trace any documents which clearly mention the start of the building of the embankment at Worli, the year in which it was completed, the number of years it took to build and the amount cost to built it, it is said that it was built between 1776 and 1780 during the tenure of Governor Hornby Sahib. In this respect, the extract from the *bakhar* only confirms the fact that it was built by the English. Some others say that since Hornby Sahib spent a lot of money in ineffectively trying to improve the fortunes of this useless island by building this embankment, he earned the displeasure of the (Court of Directors) Chief Company Sarkar. However this cannot be confirmed. This embankment is built with stone and is about a quarter *kos* in length. It is now famous as the Hornby Vellard. A contemporaneous Sutar had composed a few *shlokas* on Mumbai at that time; the following lines which confirm that the Company Sarkar built the embankment have been extracted from it.

They built a bridge in the sea like Shri Ram in Lanka,
Displayed great skill and spent crores of rupees;
Filled up the creek and made a smooth road,
And built the temple of Mahabhagavati Lakshmi.

The praises which have been heaped on the English people are well-deserved. The building of the embankment at Worli changed the fortunes of Mumbai. Isn't that amazing! In one stroke, the creek which swamped half of Mumbai was dammed and Mumbai was converted into a veritable Lanka. The island was under the Marathas, the Mussalmans, and the Portuguese for centuries; neither did this occur to any of them nor did anybody muster the courage to spend a fortune on this venture. Their only objective was to annex this territory and loot any wealth it may have had and use it for their own benefit. The general practice during these reigns was that the subjects had to eat any scraps the king threw at them, listen to him unquestioningly, stay where told, and gaze silently at his deeds.

An old Bhandari came up with a different version that a wealthy lady built this embankment. There is no proof to back up this contention. It is certainly true that many years back there was a wealthy lady named Madam Nesbit.[3] Regarding her wealth, it is said that she owned about one-fourth of the land in Mumbai and she built a large temple for the Portuguese people in Mazagaon. In both the Fort and Mazagaon, there are two roads named 'Nesbit Lane' which were built by her family. This probably indicates that this lady may have provided monetary assistance to the Company Sarkar to build this embankment.

Mahatarpakhdi, Umarkhadi, Mazagaon, and Mahim were distinct islands with narrow creeks flowing between them. There was a creek that flowed along the place known as Pydhonie and during high tide, the entire area from Bhendi Bazar to Chinch Bunder would be filled with water. The name 'Pydhonie' stuck because when people came from Mahim, Worli and Matunga to Mumbai they would wash (*dhonie*) their legs (*py*) at this point.

The embankment at Worli did not just stop the ingress of sea-water into Mumbai; drains were built along the original creeks so that rain-water and waste-water could flow from the city into the sea at Worli. These conduits are about as deep as the height of a man or a man and a half and were about four hands wide. They start from the Market, burrow under Dongri and pass along the middle of the road behind Bhendi Bazaar and then join the creek at Worli. Until some time back, the sewers behind the Market and Bhendi Bazaar were open drains, but since they inconvenienced people, they have been covered. This place has now been named as Null after the

pipes used to build the drains. While going to Mahalaxmi, one can clearly
see how this drain has been constructed through the fields all the way to
Worli. Since the drains have been built, water can flow freely during the
high tide and thus the embankment at Worli has endured. Else it would
have collapsed under the weight of the water at spring tide. At the extreme
end of the embankment where the sea-water meets the water from the city,
a terraced bridge has been built with limestone and below this bridge, gates
have been provided for the flow of water. During high tide, sea-water flows
in, and at low tide, water from the city flows into the sea. These gates have
been designed to open and close as desired. This operation cannot be
properly understood unless one personally sees it. In the last ten to fifteen
years, new drains have been dug across various roads in Mumbai so that water
from all parts of Mumbai flows into the main drain, but all these have been
covered. It will be very difficult to find another city like Mumbai with covered
drains. There are many places in Mumbai with smooth and beautiful roads, but
if you dig about a hand deep, you will find that they are as hollow as a tomb.

Colaba is a small desolate island at the Southern tip of Mumbai and was,
until recently, a grazing land with only a few Koli families living there. They
used to grow vegetables and sell fish to earn a living. There was a small ferry
which took you across the creek. In the year 1838, the Company Sarkar
built a bridge and reclaimed some land to unite this island with Mumbai.
Previously, the English used it as a hunting ground and deer were released
here. In the year 1728, the whole of Colaba was let out on the payment of
an annual rent of 130 rupees to the Sarkar.[4]

Since the land around Dongri and Chinch Bunder was completely filled
with sea-water and therefore useless, the government let the poor build their
huts in the upper reaches. However, their value has risen to such an extent
that they are now more valuable than gold. At the current price of a
thousand to fifteen hundred rupees per rod, land is very hard to find. A few
years back one of our friends bought a dilapidated house at Chinch Bunder
for five hundred rupees; traders are now willing to purchase it for five
thousand rupees, but he is unwilling to sell it. The principal area of
operations of the native traders extends from Masjid Bunder to Chinch
Bunder and Dongri. One can experience many unique sights and sounds in
these areas – a profusion of workshops – splendid shops – closely packed
houses – crowds – goods of all kinds being transported – the jangling of
pole-slings – noisy vehicles – shouts and screams of labourers – and a variety
of goods being transported in carts. One can see all of this if one just stands
here for a minute. The opulence of Mumbai and trade running into crores is
centered in this area. Kutchi, Mussalman, Israeli, Memon, Khoja, Lavane

and other traders mainly populate the area between Bori Bunder and Dongri. The settlements of the Dakshini people are fairly sparse. Many Kolis are also resident in this area; some of them are fairly prosperous and have built large houses for themselves. It is estimated that there are about ten thousand Kolis in Mumbai. Their ancient homesteads lend credence to the claim that they are the original settlers of this place.

At the South-Western tip of the island of Mumbai, there is a small hillock known as Walkeshwar. Many are of the opinion that even this was a distinct island in the past. This hill was also desolate and many government officials and rich people were allotted parts of this hill for grazing their animals at no cost. From official records, we can glean that in 1728, the entire hill was farmed out by government at an annual rent of 130 rupees. A part of this hill was rented out to the Kharvi people who grew vegetables like cucumbers, brinjals, a variety of beans, and corn cobs; the produce of this entire hill could hardly have been more than three hundred rupees. The area was so desolate in those days that common folk used to fear venturing into Walkeshwar even during the day. The extreme tip of Walkeshwar is known as Dandi and the official residence of the Governor is located there.[5] The ancient temple of Walkeshwar was located right next to the Governor's residence. This temple is said to have been built about six hundred years ago by a Maratha Sardar named Kebaji Rana; no evidence is forthcoming to support this claim. This Sardar might have been a contemporary of Raja Bhim. Some years back, the foundation of this temple was exposed. The foundations have now been dug up and a bastion is being built in its place. The present temple of Walkeshwar and another ten odd temples are located on the small level area about a hundred odd hands away from Dandi. There are over fifty *dharamshalas* in the vicinity of these temples. There is also a Brahmin settlement and in the centre there is a large tank called Banganga. People of all castes can use water from this tank. The Mahajans of Mumbai built this tank with public subscription. In the year 1832, it was decided to clean this tank and remove the mud and sedimentation accumulated in this tank. The Sarkar hired over 300 labourers and installed two hand-pumps. This team toiled for over a month but could not remove the water and mud from the tank. Finally, unseasonal rains washed all the mud and water back into the tank rendering the entire exercise futile.

Some years back the *Dnyanodaya* published the following account on Walkeshwar. If one undertakes any research on any ancient happenings in our country, one is bound to come across the most extraordinary accounts; this has prevented the writing of a proper historical account of India. Therefore one does not believe that the following account has any factual basis.

'Walkeshwar is properly pronounced as Walukeshwar which means god of Sand, shaped in the form of a *lingam*. It is believed that this *lingam* was installed by Lord Rama and not by mere mortals as in the case of other *lingams*. When Rama was on his way to Lanka with his brother Lakshmana, he reached the seashore at Dandi in Walukeshwar. It was Lord Rama's practice that everyday he would worship a *lingam* brought by Lakshmana from Kashi, but on that particular day, as Lakshmana did not arrive on time, Lord Rama made a *lingam* out of sand and worshipped it. Just as he finished installing the *lingam*, Lakshmana arrived with a *lingam* from Kashi. The *lingam* which Lakshmana brought from Kashi was then installed at Walukeshwar; therefore what is currently known as Walukeshwar is actually Lakshmaneshwar. The site of the real Walukeshwar is at Dandi in Walukeshwar. However the *lingam* that Lord Rama installed is no longer there and there must be a good reason for its absence. There is an unsubstantiated rumour that when the Firangis started ruling this place, the *lingam*, tired of the rule of the Mleccha kings, disappeared and has not been heard of since. Some people forward a more probable version that the Firangis broke the idol and demolished the large temple. One can still see the massive rectangular base of this temple; the size of the base indicates that it must have been a very big temple. After the destruction of this temple, the Lakshmaneshwar was referred to as the Walukeshwar. It is said, at that spot, Lord Rama felt thirsty and shot an arrow into the ground and produced a spring of water, with which he slaked his thirst. As an arrow or *ban* produced it, it is known as Banganga. After resting here for a while, Lord Rama proceeded to Lanka.' This extract has been taken from an ancient account of the temple known as *Walukeshwar Mahatmaya;* it also contains many other fantastic stories about the advent of the sage, Gautam Rishi and the installation of the *lingam*. It does not mention the time period in which these events happened and in general, has rendered itself useless for any research.

The present temple of Walkeshwar was built by a Shenvi gentleman, Ramaji Kamat about one hundred and fifty years ago. Ramaji Kamat died in the year 1728. This temple must have been built about fifteen to twenty years before he died. It is also rumoured that this gentleman got the land at Walkeshwar as a grant from the Sarkar. There is no doubt that he was a renowned person of his times. In the year 1718, the English consecrated their large cathedral in the Fort at Mumbai and the Rev. Mr. Cobbe sent an account of the event to the Governor at Surat in which he mentions that Ramaji and many other members of his caste had attended the event.[6] Ramaji Kamat was the chief of the native troops of those times. Shenvis are mostly from the Gomantak Province. After the Firangis established their rule in the province of Vasai and the island of Mumbai, the Shenvis arrived in large numbers in Sashtee and Vasai in search of employment or for trade. Some of them settled in Vasai during the rule of the Peshwas. The Shenvis have been traders in Mumbai for a long time and in Goa, Shenvis are currently synonymous with traders. They trade with countries like Portugal and China. Traders of the second rank operate in places like Karnatak, Rajapur, Mumbai, and Daman and also conduct trade within the province. When they dominated trade in Mumbai and held influential positions in the government, they built many temples in Mumbai. When they were on the ascendancy in Mumbai, they built the temples at Walkeshwar and Bhuleshwar, the Thakurdwar at Mahim and the Venkatesh Temple at Fort.

There is an official bungalow at Dandi in Walkeshwar. The Governor stays there occasionally. There is a permanent guard stationed here and people are not allowed to visit the place without official permission. The rich visit Walkeshwar during the summer to stay in the *dharamshalas* or almshouses. Some of them stay here through the year because of the clean air. On all sides of Walkeshwar, many of the prominent castes like Vani, Bhatia, Prabhu, Sonar, Shenvi, Brahmin and other Hindus have built multi-storied *dharamshalas*. While they are referred to as *dharamshalas*, they are actually not that. They are just bungalows where one can live the good life. The poor are not allowed to stay in these places. These places are always shuttered and well-protected. If anybody wants to stay here for a month or two for reasons of health, then he has to make repeated requests to the owner, and not everybody manages to get permission. He has to be well acquainted with the owner and should be fairly rich. The moneyed build *dharamshalas* only in name, as only they go to enjoy in these places. A *dharamshala* should, by definition, be open to everybody. The devout build houses for the poor and wayfarers and these houses are known as *dharamshalas*. They are always kept open. The only right that the rich builder has over this house is the right to repair it periodically. As per the scriptures, the builder of the *dharamshala* should not stay in it even for one night.

About thirty years back, a gentleman wanted to dispose of a small piece of land on the hill at Walkeshwar for around five hundred rupees but could not find any takers at that price. But the same piece of land is now not available for even thirty thousand rupees. Where only grass grew, there are now luxurious bungalows costing thousands and lakhs of rupees surrounded by beautiful gardens in which the best quality mangoes, custard apples, pomegranates, figs, and guavas are grown. The air here is better than anywhere else in Mumbai. Most of the English stay here. This small hillock yields an annual revenue of 159,965 rupees. There is not a single empty spot on the Walkeshwar hillock. It is held that the air and water in this place is as good as Mahabaleshwar.[7] A place that was abandoned for the poor, is now the choice place of residence for the richest in the city. Each of the different parts of the Walkeshwar Hill has distinct names – Cumbala, Tankerville, and the extreme tip of Dandi is called Shirgundi.

Chowpatty and Girgaon were also very sparsely populated places and abounded in coconut trees. Shetodi, a place where the Parsis have built five and six storied buildings and large, airy bungalows in the English style to rent to the English, was basically farm land which used to be mucky all the twelve months of the year, where extremely poor people would do some light farming. This place was considered to be totally useless, but if the rich man who used to own it about a hundred years ago visits the place today, he would feel that he has reached Delhi or the city of London.

Chowpatty, formerly a forested tract, is now populated with beautiful houses and gardens; a new spinning mill is being erected near by and a number of new bungalows are being constructed. Many warehouses have been built adjacent to the sea for storing wood; lakhs of *khandis* of wood have been neatly arranged in such large piles that ones eyes can't take all the sights in at once. There are about seven to eight warehouses in this place. Further ahead of Chowpatty and towards its right is the small hillock known as Babulnath. The Mahadeo temple here has been built by Panduseth Sonar. It is felt that the Sonar people have been on this island since the time of the Portuguese. Though they are called Sonars, they rarely do the work of goldsmiths. They have traditionally been businessmen and traders. Presently, many of them have learnt English and have taken up jobs in government and trading houses. Shankarsheth was a renowned person of this caste. The water at Babulnath is very good. One can see many Bairagis and Gosavis under the influence of *ganja* and *bhang* at Babulnath; many people addicted to *bhang* come here, and under the guise of accepting the Lord's *prasad*, brazenly partake of *ganja* and *bhang* with gay abandon.

Between Chowpatty and Girgaon lies the large mansion and garden of the renowned Vani gentleman, Seth Mangaldas Nathubai. This mansion has four entrances, with the rear entrance opening on to the road leading to Shetodi, so vast is its scale. There are many kinds of trees in the garden, and pathways have been created using sand from the sea-shore. The garden has been designed in the English fashion and Seth Mangaldas frequently resides in the mansion. The house is filled with many priceless objects. This notable businessman is one of the Hindu Mahajans and is also very religious and generous. He has built a clocktower at the Mumbadevi crossroads at a cost of thousand rupees for the benefit of the public. He has established a school for girls and donated twenty thousand rupees to the Industrial School. This gentleman spends a lot of money for public good. The garden is so captivating that if one spends a few hours in the garden, one is transported into a world that knows no hunger or thirst.

As has already been said, there was hardly any production of grain in earlier times in Mumbai as the land was infertile; however after the construction of the embankment at Worli and the closure of the creek at Mahim, a lot of rice is being grown in areas like Mahalaxmi, Worli, Parel, Mahim, and Matunga. The people say that this grain should suffice for about a day's consumption for the entire population of Mumbai. They also grow various kinds of fruits and vegetables in these areas.

On the Western side of the island, about two *kos* from the Fort lies Mahalaxmi. At the very edge of the sea, on a small hillock is the temple of Mahalaxmi and adjacent to it is the temple constructed by the late Dhakjee Dadajee, the renowned Prabhu gentleman. He spent about 80,000 rupees to construct this temple. Besides, there are numerous small temples and *dharamshalas* built by rich Hindus. At a distance of 50 hands from the temple, is a beautiful water tank paved with stone. It was built in the year 1824 by Tulsidas Gopaldas at a cost of 40,000 rupees and is shaped like a ship. People come to stay here in the hot season, and the sick come here for a change of air because of the purity of both water and air in this place. During Navratri, many people ritually visit the temple for all the nine days, both in the morning and evening to pay their respects to Mahalaxmi. They get up early in the morning, take a dip in the tank, visit the temple and are back in Mumbai by sunrise, while many others stay in their respective *dharamshalas*. The rich send for water from Mahalaxmi for their daily use; they all have built *dharamshalas* commensurate with their stature and visit whenever they feel like it. Some stay in their *dharamshalas* for months on end.

It is an indisputable fact that the temple at Mahalaxmi was built after the construction of the embankment at Worli. This has been mentioned in a *bakhar* possessed by a long-time Prabhu resident of this place. It says that when the English Sarkar was building the embankment at Worli, it collapsed twice during construction and led to a waste of labour and expenses. The Prabhu engineer who was supervising the construction had a dream in which the goddess Mahalaxmi appeared and told him that unless her idol which lay in the Worli creek was removed and installed in a temple, the construction of the embankment could not be completed! This gentleman retrieved the idol from the sea and installed it. After the construction of the embankment, he acquired the land as a present from the government and built the temple. These incidents extracted from this *bakhar* are truly mind-boggling. Our people have this tendency of grafting incredible stories onto any great deed some years after it has been done. They do not let one conclude which of these stories are true and which of them are imaginary. Any account of a temple or the building of a fort is bound to have some fantastic stories attached to it. It is therefore very difficult to trace the factual history of any city.

A *Shudra* has this to say about the fort at Malvan – when Shivaji Maharaj intended to build this fort, he had no money with him. However since he was a divine *avatar*, he could build many forts. He had engaged thousands of labourers for the construction of this fort. At the end of the day, he would distribute shoots of grass to the labourers as wages; when the labourers touched the grass, it would turn into gold! An even more astonishing twist to the tale was that those who worked whole-heartedly at their jobs received gold proportionate to their labour; similarly in the case of those who were lazy and shirked work, the shoots would turn into gold only to the extent of their labours!

While this *bakhar* does throw light on many relevant facts, it does not provide any proof or information on the issues that needed clarification and for which one exerted a lot of effort to source this *bakhar*. The writings of our people are typically incomplete. It is not clear whether they did this by design. To conclude, one can obtain the most incredible stories about the embankment at Worli and the temple at Mahalaxmi from this *bakhar*. While this *bakhar* has been written like a *Purana*, one can glean some useful facts from it. The facts are that there was a Prabhu engineer, proficient in English, who was entrusted by the Company Sarkar with the responsibility of building the embankment and that he built the temple at Mahalaxmi after constructing the embankment at Worli. The following extract has been copied from the *bakhar*.

'At some distant point of time, the English Sarkar Company Bahadur desired to build an embankment across the creek which flowed between Mumbai and the village of Worli so that vehicles could ply freely; even though the sea was very rough. After a lot of labour and toil, the embankment was completed and the land was made productive; the *ryot* was happy, and vehicles and people could pass freely. This can be considered as an act of *dharma* or religious duty. Everybody has free use of the road – this is the way of religion. Even though they are *mlechha*, they have been able to gain religious merit. Jealousy is causing the Hindus to ignore their religious injunctions and thus come to grief. This is the effect of the Kali Yug.

'When the English Sarkar made up their mind to build the Worli embankment, they exerted a lot of effort. Stones were brought in ships and dumped in the sea but the road could not be completed. They continued to strive for many days, and it then occurred to Shri Mahalaxmi, Mahakali, and Mahasaraswati that if the "milk is separated from the sea" the city of Mumbai whould prosper. The task could not come into fruition because these goddesses occupied the place. They then appeared in a vision to the Sarkar's engineer, Ramji Shivji Prabhu and asked him to retrieve them from the bed of the sea and install them in a temple on the hillock. They would then be amenable to the building of the embankment and ensure that he was able to build it. He should then approach the Sarkar and undertake to build the embankment, if they commanded him to do so. Then he should cast nets in the creek and they would emerge from the sea via the nets. Thus the vision of the goddesses ended.

Following the instructions of the goddesses, Ramji Shivji approached the Sarkar and offered to build the embankment on their behalf. The Sarkar then permitted him to build the embankment as per his designs. After he received the instructions, he then cast nets in the creek as desired by the Goddesses. And true to their word, the three stone idols of Mahakali, Mahalaxmi, and Mahasaraswati came into the nets! It was a miracle that such heavy stone idols were caught in such a fine and delicate net, and the net did not give way. The idols were then transported to the hillock where they are currently present. The hillock and the place were then taken as gifts from the government, a temple was built and the idols installed. They have been there ever since. The hillock is in the possession of the goddess and she rules it to the exclusion of everybody else. The extent of her rule is from the hillock and then through Worli along the sea up to where the Kalika Devi Temple has been built. Later Govindji Muga built a *dharamshala*. Sonar Shetye also built a *dharamshala*. And even Manki Kolni.'

At the extreme end of the Worli embankment, there is a small hillock on the West and near it is a small place about 100–200 hands wide and broad; it is known as Mama Hajani. In the creek between Mahalaxmi and Worli, about midway, there is a rocky platform known as Haji Ali. During high tide, it is surrounded by water on all sides but the water does not reach the higher areas. There is a tomb of a Mussalman fakir in Haji Ali. A small hut has been constructed atop the tomb. There are a few houses nearby. About fifty people stay in these houses, both Hindus and Mussalmans. During low tide, one can walk across the stones to the lower reaches of Mahalaxmi but during high tide one has to use a boat.

The tomb is worshipped by fakirs with *sabja* seeds. Many credulous Hindu women come here with their menfolk and children to fulfil their vows. They pray very devoutly at the tomb, and make offerings to the fakirs. Many Hindus and Mussalmans believe that this Pir is very efficacious and all their wishes will be fulfilled! Some say that once this Pir began to favour Sir Jamsetjee Jejeebhoy, his wealth multiplied many times over!

A Mussalman fakir relates the following story about the fame of this Pir and the reason for its being named Mama Hajani. In earlier times, a wealthy Mussalman named Haji Ali or Mama used to stay here. His sister also stayed with him. The siblings were extremely god-fearing and ascetic and there was a lot of affection between them. He distributed all his wealth amongst the poor and went to Mecca for the Haj. On his return from Haj, he renounced the world and became a fakir. He then stayed on the rock in the sea. As his sister was also similarly inclined, he told her to stay on the opposite hill in a saintly fashion, while he prayed to god on the rock. When asked why he preferred to meditate in that particular place, he replied that goddess Mahalaxmi was friendly with the siblings; as they conversed frequently, this place was most suitable. In this way, fakirs marry the Hindu and Mussalman religions and try to inveigle the simple Hindu folk towards their religion. After a few years, the duo expired, and following their wishes, the brother was entombed on the stone in the sea while the sister's grave was on the opposite hillock. Their graves are venerated and they continue to be worshipped. This saint is a real light in the world! If somebody does any religious deed in his name, the saint makes him or her happy! In this manner, wherever any research is undertaken, one comes across such extra-ordinary tales. To further prove his divinity, the fakir also said that however high the tide may be the sea water will never rise above the grave. It would come up to his feet, and then recede! The following is the reason why this place is known as Mama Hajani. Just as among the Hindus, somebody who returns from a pilgrimage to Kashi is known as 'Kashikar', among the Mussalmans, a person returning from Mecca after performing the Haj is referred to as 'Hajani'. As Mama Hajani stayed in this place, it was referred to by his name. In order to find out when this fakir stayed here and how many years have elapsed since his death, enquiries were made to an elderly fakir, who answered in Urdu, 'Toba! Toba! How do I tell you about him? That Pir has been staying in Mumbai for a long time. god knows how long it has been since he arrived here. But as far as I know, it has been a thousand years or two. The Pir Sahib would sit here, listen to requests from people, and present it before god. Coming from him, god would be kindly disposed to these requests.' This is an illustration of the nature of their devotion.

Perhaps, even if they know the facts, they are not willing to know the truth. This might be a stratagem to make the common people believe that this has been a holy place from times immemorial. Just as the *sadhus* of Pandharpur beg in the name of Tukaram, many Mussalman fakirs in Mumbai wander around asking for money in the name of Mama Hajani – 'May Mama Hajani shower his blessing on you' – they go around blessing the common folk.

A short account of Worli was obtained from a *bakhar* in the possession of an old Prabhu gentleman who has been settled here for a long time. The following extract is from this *bakhar*.

'The holy Raja Bhim Maharaj gave the village of Worli as *inam* to his Patil. He issued a *sunnud* in the favour of the Patil proclaiming that he and his descendants are to enjoy the produce of the farms, lands, hills, and the coconut and date palms in this village. Afterwards, the Firangis continued the same practice and confirmed the *inam* on him. Afterwards, the English, without any force or terror, also let the *inam* continue in the Patil's family. The Patil's family was big and after a while their fortunes took a downturn; the family members separated from each other and the assets of the Worli village were divided amongst them. Because their fortunes had rapidly declined, some of them started selling their shares. In this manner, much of the land was sold. Manohardas Roopji, Nasserwanji Modi, and Sokaji Raghunathji bought some of these lands, and the grove known as Badamchi Bhaat was bought by Bhikaji Mankoji, and a small part of the land was bought by Rustomji Burjorji. In the year 1753, when the English Sarkar apprehended an attack on Mumbai by the French, they communicated their intention to dig a moat around the Fort of Mumbai to the moneyed gentlemen and traders and asked them to financially assist the government. The *ryot* of Mumbai pleaded that while they did not have any money to come to the aid of the government, the government could, however impose a tax on immovable property and acquire a part of the produce annually. Once the present troubles ended, they could return the money. The Company Sarkar agreed to this and a tax was levied. Previously, there was no levy imposed on the lands at Worli as these lands were *inam* lands given to the Patils. In the other villages of Mahim, Parel and Mumbai, a pension tax had to be paid. From the year 1753, the Company Sarkar decided to impose a tax on Worli village.'

Chapter 4

Byculla – Mazagaon – Ghodapdeo – Sewri's fort and garden – Salt pans – Parel – Mandvi Bunder – Arthur Bunder – Apollo Bunder – Colaba in present times – Bori Bunder – Koli Bunder – Carnac Bunder – Masjid Bunder – Chinch Bunder – Clare Bunder – Kolse Bunder – Mahim – Matunga – Sion – Rewa Fort – Worli in present times – Sonapur

It is indeed true that there is hardly any city in this world that has been prosperous and famous from the start of its existence. Even the greatest of cities like Rome that have reached the pinnacle of glory were at some point desolate and barren places. Remember Pune before the advent of the Peshwas? It was just a hilly area with Pindari villages; however the Peshwas built a great city which has since prospered. As it did not have any water, they brought water from a distance of almost twenty-five *kos* through a pipeline. At least the land in Pune is very fertile with many trees; there are rivers and streams nearby and there are other cities close by. If one investigates the history of any great city, one comes across similar stories. However, Mumbai's case is very different and truly unique. In the first instance, it did not have the very land required for settling and erecting a city. It abounded in creeks flooded with sea-water and there was mud and mire all around. The only refuge from this mire was the sea itself. It was certainly no ordinary task to bring this place to a state where lakhs of people could happily reside in it and make a living. The value of land depends on the use it is put to. Just as the esteem of a lady increases if she gets a good husband, similarly if any land obtains a good overlord, it ascends to many glories. If one looks at the earliest maps of Mumbai, and notes the fragmented state of its land, one can imagine the obstacles that have been overcome to bring it to its present state.

The fortunes of Mumbai can be compared to that of an extremely poverty-stricken man who, either by the dint of his efforts or with the help of a rich man, achieves a state of prosperity. Places like Nagpada and Byculla were only remembered for being totally unproductive. They were desolate places where shepherds and herded cattle lived. It has now become the choice place of residence for the rich. If one visits this area, one can hear the relentless din of construction of new bungalows and buildings. The current fashion is to build structures resembling forts. Huge workshops have been built for the railway works at many places and various kinds of machines can be seen lying around.

Beyond Bhendi Bazaar is the Babula Tank. On one side of this lake is Nagpada and beyond that the Hospital – at a short distance lies Seth Cursetjee's Tank. This tank was constructed by father of Manekjee Cursetjee, presently the Third Magistrate in the Small Causes Court. During his lifetime, the people of Byculla faced a great shortage of water and after this philanthropic gentleman built the tank, people have been greatly benefited. The government is now of the opinion that this tank should be filled up and the land sold for erecting buildings. To propagate the memory of the kind-hearted soul who built this tank, it is proposed that a water-fountain be built opposite Sir Jamsetjee's hospital and named after him. Further ahead is the huge masjid built by David Sassoon. Adjacent to it is a school built by him for his co-religionists. Both these buildings have been constructed in a beautiful manner. At a distance of about twenty-five hands from these buildings are two schools built for the sons and daughters of soldiers. This school has been running since 1719 and is under the protection of the government. It was earlier located in the barracks at Fort. About 1838, the present building was constructed and the school shifted here. Children of soldiers and other ordinary Englishmen are enrolled here. This school was started by the Rev. Mr. Cobbe, the first bishop at the large English church in the Fort. He was an industrious person striving for public good and education. In the September of 1719 he preached at the pulpit and with the force of his words convinced the resident English population of the island of the need to establish a school for teaching English. Subscriptions amounting to 6,190 rupees were raised on the spot. A few days later, this school was started. Before this school started, there were no facilities for the education of English children. At that time, the Englishmen were amazed at the collection of over six thousand rupees for this cause, but currently, if a *khalasi* is shipwrecked and needs aid, a single Parsi gentleman will alone forward a thousand rupees. The *Government Press* and an English church are located next to this school. At a distance and across the road is the railway station and office. Just below it is the temple built by Ranmull Lakha, a wealthy Vani businessman of the Lavana caste. It is said that the temple was built at a cost of over fifty thousand rupees.

As we go along all the way to Mazagaon, there are bungalows of wealthy Parsi, Moghul, Mussalman, Vani, and English people each costing thousands of rupees. The beauty of each of these bungalows, the bewitching gardens and the sweet fountains is indescribable. Some of them have beautiful water tanks while in some cold water is stored in jars and pots. It has been pointed out that Mahatarpakhdi, Umarkhadi, and Pydhonie were creeks earlier, but if one visits these places now, one is unable to realize it because the innumerable gardens and bungalows erected there have changed the face of these places completely. All roads reveal new and astonishing sights.

At the very end of Byculla is the amazing temple built by Khemchand Motichand, a Shravak Vani. Our Dakshini people are not supposed to visit the temples of the Shravak Vanis and hence these temples are not much visited, but this one is certainly worth seeing. A lakh of rupees was spent on this temple; while the walls are sculpted, they are in the Marwadi style and completely bereft of any taste. The Marwadi people come here to pay their respects. At the entrance are two huge wooden elephants which have been colourfully painted. Many idols have been installed all over the temple, and mirrors have been installed inside.

The small hill near Tank Bunder, above Mazagaon, and the area around it is known as Ghodapdeo.[1] A large boulder sticks out of the hill; this has been anointed with oil and vermilion to convert it into an idol of a god. It is not known when this god was installed. However as this name is very well known in the Sarkar Durbar, it must have been installed a long time ago. Most of the servants of this temple are Kunbis, Malis, and Kolis; however ladies of other castes also worship here and undertake vows. This god is famous for granting sons! Barren ladies or those whose children die at infancy frequent this temple, and offer cradles and baby-danglers to the god. The temple is just an ordinary hut; one can see cradles and danglers hanging all over the place. People offer cradles and strollers costing about a rupee or a half and anoint the God with betel nut soaked in water.

There is a small fort at Sewri and a salt pan at the very end, where salt is produced.[2] The process of making salt is as follows. The flat land adjoining a sea-creek is cleaned as is similar to farm land, channels are dug and about a *hand* of water is let in which is covered with mud. As the sun shines, the water evaporates and a white milk-like sap is formed which hardens after about fifteen days. After a certain number of days, the upper layer is skimmed off which is the salt. The sea-water is let in again to restart the process.

There is a large government garden at Sewri.[3] It was established in the year 1830 and contains flowering and fruiting plants obtained from many countries. It is certainly a place worth visiting. The place abounds in gardens in all directions, similar to Sir Jamsetjee's exquisite garden and bungalow at Mazagaon.

Parel is famous for its government House and grounds.[4] This place has been in existence for many years. Besides bungalows and gardens of the rich and wealthy are packed into this area. The original inhabitants of this place are the Paanchkalashe, Sutar, Koli, Bhandari, and Christians. However it has now been overrun by the rich who flock here for the clean air. There is a small market here. Many of the original residents like Sutars and Bhandaris are also rich and have their large houses here. The water and air at Parel is very good. Parel is about one and a half *kos* from the Fort towards the North. Sewri is about half a *kos* towards the East. Mazagaon and Chinchpokhli are situated along the way to these places.

The Palo Bunder is next to the Camp Maidan near the Colaba bridge. It does not see too much traffic of goods. It is a point of debarkation when people arrive in steamships or other ships. As this Bunder is open on all four sides, a pleasant breeze blows throughout the day. The rich English folk drive down in their vehicles in the evening to enjoy the air; and so do our people. Work is currently in progress to build a bigger jetty and the old jetty has been demolished.

As we proceed down the docks, Mandvi Bunder is situated below Palo Bunder and is described later. Arthur Bunder is further up from Palo Bunder.

It has already been mentioned that Colaba was a desolate place. Considering the place to be totally useless, the government auctioned it off at a cheap price some years back. The land that was sold off at five hundred rupees now yields a monthly produce of a thousand rupees.

The creek towards the North-West of Colaba has been filled up and is used to store bales of cotton and piles of wood. A few warehouses have been built here and it is felt that in a while, bungalows will come up in this place. Colaba has been divided into three imaginary parts – Little Colaba from Arthur Bunder to the Gun Carriage, Middle Colaba reaching up to the Kabul Church, and further ahead is Upper Colaba extending to the very tip of the land or the Dandi.

At the head of Little Colaba is Arthur Bunder. On the jetty stands the Grant Building; behind it are two very large mills. There are many warehouses for storing cotton. Sir Jamsetjee Jejeebhoy and his partners have built a wharf for unloading their goods at an expense of around one and a half lakh rupees. They have a large factory here in which are installed eight machines that run on steam. Many other businessmen have their offices here. On one side is the Telegraph Office, and just opposite is the workshop of the Gun Carriage Office which was started in 1823. In this factory, cannons and cannon balls are produced; besides, many other iron and brass items are cast. There are many machines that run on steam and work goes on at a hectic pace. In one corner, woodwork is being carried out; in another, one can see big pipes being cast; and numerous other amazing things. Hundreds labour in this factory. One cannot take ones eyes away from these monstrous machines. One cannot understand the process unless it is properly explained. A visit to the mechanized workshops of the English people leaves one literally confounded and dumbstruck. The monthly expense of this factory is over ten thousand rupees. If one were to provide a complete description of the activities of a factory of this scale, one would have to spend at least a fortnight and understand the activity of each worker and his machine and the nature of their output. To conclude, only a visit to the factory itself can bring some understanding of its operations and structure.

The houses of the white regiments, the Hospital, and the Portuguese and English churches are situated in Middle Colaba. In the year 1848, a church was built in memory of the soldiers who fell in the battle at Kabul and is called the Kabul Church.[5] It is estimated that 80,000 rupees were spent on this church. Further ahead are the military training grounds, then the Kolse Bunder, many houses and a small market. Near the market is a building known as Kanji House, a dark mansion in which offending soldiers are punished.

Moving on to Upper Colaba, one first passes the bungalows of the Sahibs and then the Observatory, which should be certainly visited by all students. There are many instruments here and one can observe the movements of the wind. The instruments include barometers and thermometers. The employees of the observatory have to keep these instruments running all through the day and night. Further ahead is the tip of Colaba. There is a madhouse to confine lunatics. At the very end is a small fortress on which two cannons have been mounted. There is an English cemetery at the far end of the fortress where many English tombs have been built. The three parts of Colaba amount to one *Kos*. Upper Colaba is slightly hilly and is the Southern-most tip of Mumbai.

Right outside the walls of the Fort and near the Camp Maidan is Bori Bunder.[6] This port had limited landing facilities for those who came by boat. As the area was rocky, the passengers had to hop from one stone to another to reach land. It was quite awkward. There were hardly any facilities for landing goods or any approach for vehicles. Since there was a small hillock nearby with a lot of stones, it was a real scramble if ten or more people had to land at once. Though the area was very rocky, the Sarkar never considered improving the conditions. However, because of the passage of time, and the paucity of space, the Sarkar has been forced to spend thousands of rupees to improve this place. From about the year 1852, the hillocks and rocks have been demolished and a massive wharf has been built; it can handle about five thousand people and thousands of *khandis* of material can be stored easily. All the machines and paraphernalia required for the railways and large water pipes are unloaded here. As compared to the other ports, this Bunder has become the most convenient. On visiting this place, one feels like spending a couple of hours. As the port faces east,a pleasant breeze greets one in the evening and the islands of Kanheri-Huneri, Chinaltekdi, and Gharapuri can be seen in the distance.

As one proceeds from Bori Bunder towards Mazagaon, one passes the other docks – all arranged next to each other – Carnac Bunder, Masjid Bunder, Chinch Bunder, Elphinstone Bunder and Wadi Bunder. The Carnac and Clare Bunders have been built by the late Lakshman Harishchandraji Bhau, a renowned Prabhu gentleman. It is said that about eight to nine lakh rupees were spent on the construction. As the Clare Bunder was built during the tenure of the Earl of Clare, Governor Sahib, it was named after him. The Carnac Bunder is named after Sir James Rivett-Carnac as it was built during his tenure as Governor. Grains, fruits, vegetables, wood, grass and many other kinds of materials are unloaded in both these docks. The place abounds in warehouses, which have been designed in the most intelligent manner. The annual revenue generated from the rent of the warehouses and the landing rights fees is well over a lakh of rupees. Lakshman Harishchandraji, a wealthy man was both shrewd and scholarly. For many years, he held the tobacco farm and the garbage collection contract from the government. He would take large contracts with the value exceeding lakhs of rupees from government. It is said that when he had the contract for garbage collection, all the garbage was dumped into the creek adjoining these docks to fill them up. He could thus finish the job of filling up the sea cheaply; else the cost of constructing these two docks might well have gone up to between fifteen and twenty lakhs.

Chinch Bunder is used to unload various kinds of grains and other sundries. There is a Customs House with a Commissioner of Customs stationed here. On one side of the dock are about twenty odd tobacco warehouses. All the tobacco consumed in Mumbai is stored here. A fee of three rupees per *man* and the customs duty has to be paid by the retailers who purchase the tobacco from the warehouse keepers. Only those who have a government licence can buy the tobacco, a minimum quantity of one *man*.

Further ahead of the Clare Bunder is a hillock called Naoroji Hill.[7] A new dock called Elphinstone Dock is being built below this hill. An estimated five lakh rupees will be spent on this venture. This dock has been built on a grand scale and the facilities for the storage and handling of goods is very good. A lot of businessmen have come together to complete this venture. The partners are seventy-two in number and include both English and native businessmen. There are one hundred and fifty shares. These gentleman have divided these shares amongst themselves. The area of this Bunder is about 105,000 *vaar*. As the whole area was a creek, it had to be filled up at a cost of 167,000 rupees; it came to about 1.10 rupees per *vaar*. It is said that the garbage generated by all of Mumbai was dumped here, and this led to a significant reduction in cost; else it might have cost upwards of two lakh rupees. As this Bunder was first built in 1858 when Lord Elphinstone was Governor, it was named after him. Though it is not yet complete, it already generates an income of two thousand rupees for its owners. It is therefore felt that its income will rise further. The owners are trying to encourage the establishment of a number of mills and workshops in the vicinity of the docks. This is an example of how the rulers and the ruled have come together to increase the prestige of Mumbai; this is the reason for the all-round progress of this city. Not only do these ventures add to the strength and beauty of the city, they also improve the fortunes of the Sarkar and the *ryot*. If these people also had hidden their wealth under the ground like their forefathers, who would have benefited? After the coming of English rule, the people are no longer afraid of flaunting their wealth. They are also putting it to use, lakhs of rupees are given out on interest, huge factories are being built and wharfs and jetties erected. This has resulted in the flow of money within the city, the common folk have managed to get employment and developed an interest in living better, the rich are becoming richer, there is happiness all around, and new ideas are gaining ground.

In this dock, cotton, coal and other materials are handled. Steam-powered cotton mills are being built on the docks – about three are ready. Ten warehouses are scheduled to operate in just this dock. One is left spellbound by the machines, the immense wheels and other intricate mechanisms. Each of these mills has cost about ten thousand rupees. Steam-powered machines run in these workshops. A tank is constructed over them using sheets of iron and is filled with water. On the turning of a mechanism, the water is released down. This one tank contains hundreds of *handis* of water. It will cost one approximately two lakh rupees to build one of these factories. If one is to describe each of the bunders completely, a separate book will have to be written.

All the cultured people of this city of Mumbai should make a point of visiting these docks and factories with their families, at least once a year. Instead of just wandering about during festival days and wasting one's life, one is better advised to see these places and increase one's fund of knowledge. Students should certainly visit these places twice a year; perhaps they will be inspired to emulate these feats.

Moving further ahead, there are no buildings at Wadi Bunder. A few warehouses are scattered on the mire. Wood of various kinds – blackwood, teak wood, jack and others – is piled in neat heaps. Each of the logs is about thirty *guz* long and about three *guz* in diameter. Some of these logs can cost over three hundred rupees. Teak of the best quality comes from Kalikota and is used for building ships and houses. After the advent of metalled roads, the price of teak has doubled. Blackwood and jack wood are used for fine articles like cupboards, boxes, and beds. In addition, other building material like bamboos, planks, beams, and spars are also available here.

Masjid Bunder got its name from its location just below the Masjid. Many ordinary commodities are landed here and the clerks and soldiers of the Customs Commissioner patrol it. As there is a Bunder, there is bound to be a *chowki* for the police and the customs.

The Koli Bunder is a small jetty at the end of Bori Bunder and next to the Carnac Bunder. There is a Koli settlement near this Bunder and fish is landed here; nets are strewn all over the place. If one attempts to reach the place, one is assaulted by the smell of rotten fish at a distance of about fifty hands. One can spot people drying fish, and a few others are filling baskets with the dried fish. One can see the fishing boats of the Kolis bobbing in the sea. Of the five or six landing spots for fish, this is, by far the most important. In the vicinity of Sonapur, on the shore known as Back Bay, there are a couple of places where fish is brought in. They are however, not used regularly. A commonly found fish in Mumbai is the *bombil*. This fish is available only in the sea between Mumbai and Surat and nowhere else.[8] Thousands of *khandies* of dried *bombil* are consumed in Mumbai annually. The Kolis take their boats to fish in the sea around Mumbai up to a distance of around sixty *kos*. They use large nets. The Sarkar has allotted them different fishing areas. In these areas, they drive in long poles to hold their nets. These nets can be as long as two hundred hands and about as broad. If a boatman is caught unaware, his boat could well get entangled in these nets and be destroyed. In the history books, one comes across the story of a Portuguese ship which was destroyed near Chaul after getting entangled in these nets. The Kolis have to pay a tax to the Sarkar for catching fish and driving the poles into the sea. If their nets are destroyed or some other boat breaks their poles, the Sarkar collects a fine from the offender and pays the Kolis some compensation. The pole is known as *khunt* and the net as *doli*. No duty is levied on fresh fish brought into port, but dried fish from other regions is taxed.

Adjacent to the Koli Bunder is a place for butchering animals. It is known as Khatki Bazar. The Khatkis or butchers stay behind the market and this area is known as Kasai Wada. Many different types of animals are slaughtered here.

There is a jail for cattle just near the Koli Bunder and it is known as the Pound. Any horse, cow, sheep or goat found wandering in the streets is captured and sent to the Pound; the owners have to pay a fine to retrieve their animals. If a cow or a buffalo spends a night here, the owner has to pay a fine of a rupee and a quarter. The fine increases in proportion to the number of nights the animal spends in the Pound.

Further up from Ghodapdeo is the Tank Bunder. It does not have many facilities for the unloading of goods. There are docks in Sewri and Mazagaon. Logs, wooden planks, and bamboo are occasionally unloaded by ships at the Mazagaon dock. The dock serves as a refuge for ships during storms. Besides, there are another five to six minor wharves guarded by a solitary soldier.

The Kolsa Bunder is situated midway between Middle Colaba and Upper Colaba. It has just come into use. An increase in the number of steamboats, trains, and other steam-powered machines has led to the consumption of thousands of *khandies* of imported coal. As it was inconvenient to unload the coal at other places, the Sarkar identified this free spot which is now exclusively used to handle coal. Huge heaps of coal are piled here.

There is a large settlement at Mazagaon. There are many bungalows of rich people like Vanis, Parsis, and Mussalmans and a big Christian church; the Christians have a very large settlement here. There is a dock for repairing steamboats in Mazagaon. Further ahead is a factory for making gunpowder. There are many bungalows and gardens in Chinchpokhli, Parel and Naigaon that are mainly populated by the Parsis and the English; there are not many Hindus other than the Paanchkalashe, Sutar, and Bhandari. Rice fields border the metalled road that leads to Mahim and Sion.

Mahim is a small village to the North-West of Mumbai located at a distance of about three *kos* from the Fort. There are many coconut trees here. Only the Bazaar has some settlements, mainly those of the Paanchkalashe, Vaadval, Sutar, Bhandari, Kansar, Sonar, Koli, Mussalman, and Christian. Coconuts are produced in large quantities here; and as it is of the best quality, it is highly priced. The large estates are owned by the Vaadval who take care of the coconut and other trees. There are a few Portuguese churches and Hindu temples, one school and a large masjid which contains the tomb of a Pir named Mukdoom Baba. The *urus* of this Mukdoom Sahib is held in the month of *Margshirsha* and lasts for five to six days. Many traders set up shops and it is one of the more famous fairs of

Mumbai. People of all classes visit the fair. The Hindus lead the others in worshipping at the place. There is a Customs-House at the end and adjacent to it is the railway station. The Bandra Bridge starts here. The bridge was built by Sir Jamsetjee Jejeebhoy at a cost of 155,000 rupees in the year 1843 to benefit the public. His wife spent a sum of 22,000 rupees to build the big road leading to it.[9] There is a large gate at the point where the limits of Mahim are located. The Bhandari people are commonly found here; they tap the juice of the coconut tree and use it to make alcohol and jaggery. There is a small fort at Mahim which is quite ordinary. The port is mainly used to unload fish which is said to be of the best quality.

In Chapter 2, mention was made of Prabhadevi. The real name of this goddess is Prabhavati but it is commonly referred to as Prabhadevi. This goddess seems to have been installed in ancient times, during the reign of Raja Bhim. At that time Mahim was also known as Prabhavati, perhaps after the goddess. As the old temple had collapsed, the entire Prabhu community contributed towards the rebuilding of the temple in the year 1714. It is however, unlikely that the entire Prabhu community would have united to install a new idol. On the inner walls of the temple is an inscription which runs thus:

Shree

'The temple of Mother Prabhavati
built by the entire Pathare Prabhu
community on Vaisakh Shudh
11 Yeka. Samvat 1771
Vikramadi.'

One does not learn much from this inscription except the nature of written and spoken Marathi about one hundred and fifty years ago.

Earlier there used to be a military camp in Matunga and most of the military personnel stayed there. As the worm in the water infected the soldiers, they were moved to Pune. There are now many Christian settlements here. They grow vegetables and sell it in Mumbai. There are very few gardens and bungalows here. Further ahead is Sion, where there are Vaadval settlements and some gardens. Finally there is the official checkpost. Right opposite it is a hill on which is the Sion Fort.[10] An English Sardar and some soldiers are stationed here. There are no other settlements in the fort. Just below this fort is another small fort at ground level which is known as Rewa Fort.[11] There are many salt pans at Sion and Matunga which produce a lot of salt. Most of the residents are fairly poor. At the end is the checkpost manned by a clerk and soldier from the Customs

Department. There is a large tank and temple nearby. The Sion Bridge connects Mumbai and Kurla. At the borders of Sion, there is a large gate with a police station. This gate is closed once the cannon is fired at eight in the night and opens once the cannon is heard in the morning. The bridge at Sion was built in 1797 during the reign of the Governor Duncan Sahib and cost 50,575 rupees.[12] With a view to recovering this sum of money from the *ryot*, a scheme was devised by which a tax was levied on all vehicles, horses, and palanquins which used the bridge in the following manner: Bullock cart – half an anna, Horse – four *annas*, vehicle drawn by one horse – half a rupee, and a vehicle drawn by two horses – one rupee. The bridge would be contracted out every year and the government would earn about ten to twenty thousand rupees from this farm. In about 1831 when the Sarkar realized that the money spent on the bridge had been collected, on the suggestion of a philanthropic English official, the tax was withdrawn. How generous of the Sarkar! No other government would have let go of this income.

In the year that this bridge was built, a very severe famine swept across Hindustan. Thousands of labourers and others came to Mumbai from Gujarat and the Ghats; it was difficult to obtain even three to four *paylee* of parboiled rice for a rupee. These labourers would toil all day on the building of the bridge as long as they were provided with enough to eat. Thousands would queue up to do this kind of work. This is the reason why this bridge could be built at such a low cost. If it had to be constructed in recent times, it would have cost not less than a lakh. It is said that during the famine many philanthropic Parsis arranged to have thousands of *khandies* of rice transported from Bengal and distributed it amongst the poor. They are now reaping the benefits of this kind deed. An old Bhandari said that a Parsi named Dadiseth donated a lot of food during the famine.

North of Mahalaxmi lies Worli. It is a small hilly village; at the very end is a fort atop a hillock. The Koli, Paanchkalashe, Vaadval, Sutar, Bhandari, and Christians make up the population. There are about three to four hundred houses in Worli. In the recent past, many rich people have erected their bungalows and gardens here. In the upper quarter just below the fort is the colony of the Kolis. It is divided into three Pakhdis – upper, middle, and lower. The Middle Pakhdi is also known as the Shambu Mahadeo Pakhdi. This is a small village with most of its people in dire straits. Some of the Kolis are prosperous. There are many fish processing factories. There are a couple of Hindu temples. As the number of English who are settling here has increased, there is an increase in the production of fruits and vegetables. Mahim is about a *kos* away from Worli and Sion is about a *kos* and a half away from Mahim.

Towards the West of the city and adjacent to the Camp Maidan on the coast is Sonapur where the cemeteries of the Hindus, Mussalmans, and English are located. Besides, the Portuguese people have four to five cemeteries at various places. The richer English and Portuguese are buried inside their churches. Similar burial ceremonies are conducted in the big church in the Fort. In this church, beautiful graves of the rich and famous have been built into the walls, the threshold, the floor and other places. Their names and deeds are described on plaques installed on the graves. In a similar fashion, graves of various important people have been built in the courtyard. A lot of money has to be paid to be interred here.

The final resting ground of the Parsis is on the hill adjacent to Babulnath. These people neither burn the corpse nor bury it. They have spent thousands of rupees to dig huge wells in which they deposit the corpses which are placed upon large stones that are sited in various locations. Vultures and other meat-eating birds devour these corpses. The Parsis call these wells 'Dokhmas'. There are five dokhmas on Babulnath Hill. People of other castes are not allowed to enter this place.

The English have built a burial ground adjacent to Sonapur behind Jugonnath Sankarsett's house. There is another one in Marine Lines. This is a clean and peaceful place. Mausoleums of various kinds have been built here; some are triangular while some others are rectangular. They write the name of the dead person and describe his deeds. This place is certainly worth visiting. One can get an idea of the number of Englishmen who died, their identities and their major deeds. When one visits this place, it dawns on us, perhaps fleetingly, that this world is but a temporary abode and one will follow in the footsteps of great people who have left the world. Admittedly this is only a momentary feeling induced by the atmosphere of the cemetery, but those who live in their imaginary world, should step out of it, and contemplate the words on these graves. A famous English poet named Hervey has written an excellent book titled 'Meditations among the Tombs'.[13] A reading of this book will throw some light on the knowledge which dawns on us when we visit such places.

About two thousand people die in Mumbai every month, and about the same are born.

Chapter 5

*Architecture of the main and subsidiary forts – Docks and shipbuilding –
Established of judicial department – Armada of the Dutch and their plans to gain
Mumbai – Keigwin's revolt – Armoury – Strength of the army – Problems relating
to settling the city – Yakut Khan's attack – Mumbai becomes the main capital of
the English Sarkar in India – Mint – Raids on houses – Deeds of earlier
government officials – Colonies on the camp – Treasury notes – Enmity between
the English and Portuguese people – Colaba Dandi – Gunpowder factory*

Man has to be foresighted, intelligent, and courageous to accomplish a deed
which can provide benefits for a very long time. The earliest migrants into
Mumbai must have been very disheartened by this small island with its
innumerable difficulties. To make matters worse, enemies surrounded it on
all four sides. Traders used to fear for their lives all the time. Occasionally,
the Angrias and the Habshees would seize ships right inside the harbour.[1]
The Portuguese were of course next door, always looking for an
opportunity. The Court of Directors were hesitant to spend money on
Mumbai because of these reasons. Unmindful of these persistent problems,
Sir Joshua Child finally decided to commence construction of the fort. This
ultimately led to the island becoming prosperous. Though the construction
of the fort was not completed during his tenure, he should be credited with
the initiative that led to the completion of the fort. Sir Joshua Child was the
principal official of the Court of Directors and was the Governor of all the
Chiefs of the various factories in Hindustan. He was a practical man and
very shrewd in matters of trade, and on his recommendation the work on
the fort was started.

To combat the increasing aggression of Kanhoji Angria, the Habshees
and the Marathis, the Court of Directors sent instructions in 1710 that all
the trees within a distance of half a *kos* from the Fort be cut and the Fort
itself be further strengthened. The land tax exacted from the people was
increased. With a view to contribute to the cost of construction of the Fort,
the traders in the city and other notables suggested that an extra two percent

customs duty be levied on goods entering the city. A man-of-war maintained at the port to combat the menace of pirates patrolled the entire bay through the day and night. In the year 1716, the Portuguese commissioned officers in the Mumbai army and agreed to pay a sum of 15 thousand *ashrafies* or about seven thousand five hundred rupees for the defence of the Fort. The Portuguese officers played the role of landlords and they were additionally entrusted with the property of those who died without an heir and of orphaned children. They were known as *Variaodors*. When the moat around the Fort was dug, the *ryot* of Mumbai made a voluntary contribution of thirty thousand rupees to the government; this led to the citizens of Mumbai being exempted from compulsory conscription in the army. Thirty thousand rupees must have been equivalent to over thirty lakhs of rupees for the government of the day. Hundreds of people helped in digging the moat. The army personnel in the Lines were also commanded to help in this task. These soldiers, armed with shovels and pickaxes, would work for four to five hours. And if necessary, would then don their uniforms and act as soldiers.

The walls of the Fort and the Palo Gate were completed on 1 June 1716 during the reign of Charles Boone, as evidenced by a stone fixed on the walls of the Palo Gate. The English had intended to build a fort since 1669, and it took them 47 years to fulfil their wish. The earlier fort was fairly ordinary. It proved very costly to dig a moat and then to create the Camp Maidan around this fort. This work was started in 1753. The rich and noble people of Mumbai used to stay in the Camp Maidan in earlier times. They had their houses, estates, gardens, bungalows, temples, and masjids in this area; these were acquired by paying appropriate prices and then demolished. This proved to be an expensive process. It is said that it cost the Sarkar a sum of thirty thousand rupees to prepare the Camp Maidan, which was about 100 hands square. Between the years 1838 and 1860, all the three old Gates of the Fort were demolished and the area enlarged at an expense of three to four lakhs of rupees. The entire Fort and the Camp Maidan is estimated to have cost the Sarkar a crore of rupees.

In the year 1670, in addition to the main Fort at Mumbai, small forts of an ordinary kind were built at Mazagaon, Sewri, Sion, Mahim, and Worli, to augment the security of the city.

In 1670, during the tenure of Sir George Oxenden, the Company Sarkar constructed a dock to build ships. When the English people had to build ships, they had to ask permission of the Portuguese Durbar to build them at Vasai or Daman. In 1636, permission had been obtained from the Chief of the Portuguese Sarkar for building two small ships at both Daman and Vasai. They therefore gave priority to the building of this dock.

In the same year, the Company Sarkar sent an engineer named Wardwick Peat from the city of London. He built a few ships. This task was entrusted in 1735 to Seth Lowjee Nusserwanji Wadia. This famous Parsi gentleman used to build small ships for the Company department at Surat. This gentleman exhibited a great level of intelligence and practicality in constructing the most intricately designed ships. This work continues to be entrusted to his family. In those days, this was a small dock which was further enlarged in a few years. In the year 1810, a warship with 74 mounted guns named *Meanee* was built in this dock. It took ten years to build this ship at a cost of seven lakh rupees. Two battle ships named *Nerbudda* and *Jumna* were also built here. The Parsis built all these ships without any assistance from the English. The ships are so elaborately designed that even the pomp of Aurangzeb's Durbar cannot compare with their grandeur. There are numerous rooms filled with articles like canopied beds, chairs, couches, vessels, tassels and cupboards. Some years back an American ship named *Minnesota* had sailed into Mumbai port. It was five-storied and more palatial than many royal palaces. It even had a library. Over sixty guns were mounted on this ship. Thousands of people flocked to see this sight. A similar ship had called a couple of years back which was gilded internally, and was said to have been presented to the Queen.

A total of fifty three military ships and eighty two commercial ships have been built at Mumbai. Recently, two steam engines have been commissioned in this department, one with twenty horsepower and another with ten. These machines are used to split logs and also to produce a variety of copper and iron articles like nails, screws, and knives. If one spends a few minutes in this factory, one gets the impression that all the skilled workers and labourers are in a rush and there is a great deal of activity. Various kinds of sounds can be heard – *Dhun Dhun!!! Khat Khat!!! Thok Thok!!! Ghar Ghar!!!* This dock was expanded in 1816 and was named after the then Governor and called Duncan Docks. It was constructed at a cost of fourteen lakhs of rupees. It was further expanded in 1845 and 1852.

In the year 1843, commanded by the Sarkar, a rich and famous Moghul named Aga Mohammad Rahim built a dock at Mazagaon Bunder at a cost of eight to nine lakhs of rupees. It took five to six years to complete it. As the water was quite deep in this area, it was quite a task to remove the water and build the docks. This gentleman however did not lose hope and managed to complete the task. A beautiful bungalow has also been built which houses the office. There is a warehouse and a place for storing various machines. It is a very good and breezy place. Till some years back, ships and boats were built in this dock but this practice has been discontinued currently. The 'Peninsular and Oriental Steam Navigation Company', a large company based in England, operates ships on routes to Mumbai, Calcutta, China, Australia and other countries. On the establishment of their office in Mumbai in 1843, the Mumbai Sarkar has engaged its ships to transport all official mail and other goods to and from the European continent. Their revenue is worth lakhs of rupees. This company has rented these docks from its owner on an annual rent of twenty thousand rupees and uses it to overhaul their ships.

In 1862, a rumour spread that the Sarkar was planning to sell all the government docks and their associated workshops for a price of one crore and fifty lakhs. However, it is felt that the government will not take such a sudden decision as they own forty nine steamships and many other ships besides. If ever these need to be repaired or overhauled, the docks will be required but the newspapers are rife with rumours that the Government intends to completely separate the steamship division from itself as per the directions of the Chief Government. This department is known as the 'Indian Navy'.

The Company Sarkar established a department in 1670 to dispense justice. The Deputy Governor and Councillors functioned as the Chief Magistrates in the Court which was established at that time. A bench of two judges handled ordinary cases; one was an English employee of the factory and the other was a native gentleman. They dispensed justice in most of the cases. It is certainly gladdening to note that about two hundred years back a local person was nominated as a judge in the English courts. In 1671, the Governor of Mumbai requested the Company Sarkar in England to send a judge well versed in English law, but this request was denied. The proffered reason was that the Company had to bear a loss of thirty lakhs of rupees since it took over the island. They were of the opinion that this island was totally non-productive and unprofitable; therefore they did not make any effort to improve its fortunes. After many struggles, an English judge named St. John arrived in Mumbai on 9 August 1683.[2] He was given two servants, accorded the rank of Deputy Governor and was paid an annual salary of two thousand rupees. His jurisdiction did not extend to cases involving the military personnel and sailors. On the instructions of the Chief Sarkar in England, a Mayor's Court was established in Mumbai on 10 February 1728. A judge and a jury of nine men would dispense justice. The Chief Judge was paid an annual salary of 625 rupees. His rights were similar to that of a *munsif*, but he was empowered to decide on regular civil and criminal cases. The court of appeal was the Governor and his Council. This proclamation was read out by the Governor himself to a gathering of the *ryot* and *mahajan* of Mumbai at the Palo Bunder.

For many years, that is until the establishment of the Supreme Court, the quality of justice being dispensed was dubious. The Company servants were themselves the judges, and if one of them pressed a civil case, it was also investigated by one of their own. As their rule was recently established, the law had not yet been properly formulated. There were situations in which the plaintiff assumed the role of the judge and examined the defendant. If in some cases, the evidence was not adequate and if the judge desired to find the accused guilty, they would rake up some filth and sentence him. This was the kind of justice dispensed all over Hindustan. Since their rule was new, and as a number of years are needed to effectively consolidate one's power over the land, this kind of anarchy prevailed for a while. It took the Company a very long time to establish proper courts of justice. It was not that the English favoured their own people and discriminated against the natives. In those times, the form of justice dispensed to all kinds of people was the same, and the local people were treated better than they are currently. There was a lot of infighting amongst the English, more a sign of the times than a fault of that nation. The English historians roundly condemn the behaviour of their countrymen in those days. If an accused did not plead guilty or adequate evidence was not brought forward to prove his guilt, he would be tortured to extract a confession. This practice had already been discontinued in England many years previously. There were many schemers and speculators in Mumbai in those days who, unable to bear the good fortune of their competitors, would file false cases to destroy them. As there were no laws, no lawyers to plead their cases, and no barristers and newspapers to argue out legal niceties, many an innocent would come to grief. Examples of some of the civil cases have been extracted from the records preserved in the Government Archives and presented below.[3]

On the 24 of March 1720, a very important criminal case came up for hearing in front of the Council which was much talked about in Mumbai.

Ramaji Kamat was a respectable gentleman and a trusted servant of the English for many number of years. He was the chief of the native regiments and would attack the ships of Kanhoji Angria and others located in the islands of Kaneri-Huneri, Uran and Gharapuri. He was a courageous man of many skills but if there is a reversal in one's fortunes, nothing goes your way and from the status of a king, one is hurled onto the streets. He was very rich, quite powerful, and possessed a lot of immovable property in Mumbai. Of course he had also made many enemies. History reveals that they schemed to plot his downfall.

He was accused as a traitor and the following charges were laid against him:

1. In December 1717, Ramaji Kamat wrote a letter to Kanhoji Angria and told him not to release the English ship "*Success*" without extracting a huge sum as ransom from the English.
2. He wrote to him in October 1718 informing him to be on his guard since the English were planning to attack Kaneri. He was asked to keep his troops ready.
3. In the same year, he did not forward a letter written by the Portuguese Chief to the Governor of Mumbai offering aid to the English against Kanhoji Angria.
4. To facilitate an attack on Mumbai, Ramaji Kamat sent a map of Mumbai to Kanhoji Angria.
5. He secretly conducted trade with Angria.
6. He instructed the people under his command not to fight with the Angria by spreading terror and disheartening them.
7. Aware of the terrible consequences if his crimes were discovered, he hid fourteen boxes containing his private papers in Thane and other places.

The Governor Mr. Boone and the other councillors examined the charges laid against him. Ramaji Kamat was informed that these seven charges had been brought against him and based on the evidence given in Court and the letter written to Kanhoji Angria by him, the charges had been proved. The trial went on for many days. Many efforts were made to make the charges stick, but they could not produce any evidence to prove him a traitor. The Council finally decided that this man was guilty of certain misdeeds and he was imprisoned. His property was confiscated by the government.

After some years, Ramaji Kamat died in prison. Before his death, he wrote a letter protesting his innocence and appealed to the Court of Directors for justice, but he received no reply. A few years after his death a new Governor was appointed to Mumbai who realized that Ramaji Kamat had been the victim of a devious plot. The letter bearing Ramaji Kamat's seal which was purported to have been sent by him to Angria was found to be a fabrication – a fact which was confirmed by further investigation. He then wrote to the Court of Directors that 'Though the then Governor and his Council may have felt that they were doing the right thing, based on the evidence presented by our people and the people of Mumbai, one can conclude that gross injustice was done to Ramaji Kamat'. On the instructions of the Court of Directors, an annual allowance of four thousand rupees was sanctioned to his son for the upkeep of the family. However the confiscated property was not returned on certain grounds. It is also said that the Portuguese Chief was also involved in the conspiracy against Ramaji Kamat. At any rate, this was inevitable because of the unstable system of justice prevalent in those days. In our times, the English system of justice can be termed as the best in the world. This is because of the Supreme Court and its laws. The judges strive very hard to dispense justice in accordance with the crimes. Even the poorest of the poor have many opportunities to seek justice. If any poor man is unable to engage a lawyer, he can ask to be represented by the government lawyer for free. If somebody is charged in the mofussil courts, the First Magistrate examines him. The case then proceeds to the Sessions Judge who is assisted by a jury. The Chief Magistrate in the Sur Adalat then decides it. This system ensures that justice is dispensed.

In the year 1840, Sant Aluparu was accused of crimes of a heinous nature and sentenced to be exiled. The Sarkar confiscated all his assets. His son appealed to the government in England, that since his father had been exiled, he should inherit his assets as his rightful heir. Alternatively, the Sarkar could confiscate all his assets and release his father. After a legal fight, he could finally recover the property. Thus the English law took its course! These laws are certainly praise-worthy.

In another extraordinary case of those early days, Mr. Bradyll, the Councillor and his wife were strolling down the road in the evening. A horse-rider suddenly rode into them and this led to Mr. Bradyll's raising his voice against him. To this the rider replied, 'If I had had a gun with me, I would really have taught you a lesson!' Mr. Bradyll said, 'Really?' to which he retorted, 'Do you have any doubts?' and rode away. The following day, the whereabouts or identity of the rider could not be discovered. Suspecting a person named Matthew Bogle, a case was launched against him in which the plaintiff was also the judge! How was the accused to prove his innocence? In due course he was held guilty and sentenced to be tied to a pole in the market and whipped forty times. He was also asked to labour on the Company ships for as long a period as the Governor desired. Such was the spirit of those times!

Another incident will illustrate the anarchy of the times. One evening Rev. Mr. Spensser (a preacher) was invited to dinner where many people were gathered, including a youth and a girl of marriageable age. They felt a sudden desire to get married on the spot and requested this priest to marry them and declare them man and wife. Mr. Spenser was taken aback by this request and thought it a joke. He then told them that if they truly intended to marry, he would conduct the ceremony the following morning. This did not go down well with the youth and the next day he complained to the

Governor that Mr. Spenser had not discharged his duties as a priest. The charges were pressed but the outcome of this case is not known. This has been extracted from a letter written by the Mumbai Governor to the Surat Chief dated 15 January 1687.

Even the great Rev. Mr. Cobbe who strove ceaselessly to build the big church in the Fort and established a free Charity School for the English children was also embroiled in a case. How could any one else expect to fare better? He was a very frank speaker, proud of the Christian religion and very scrupulous about the discharging of all religious obligations. Mr. Bradyll was the Councillor in those days. He had started some repairs on his bungalow in the months of April and May and would get work done by the labourers even on Sundays. One Sunday, Mr. Cobbe happened to visit his residence and heard the din of the labourers; he roundly flayed Mr. Bradyll for getting work done on a Sunday when the scriptures prescribe a rest on that day. Bradyll apologized and explained that as the monsoons were approaching, he had to call the labourers on a Sunday to complete the work. This did not however satisfy the extremely orthodox priest. He condemned Bradyll from the pulpit in front of all the churchgoers and termed him irreligious. This and a few other similar cases led to complaints against him which led the Council to dismiss him from his post.

A female exorcist was dealt with similarly. She was a poor woman who would minister to the needs of the ill, tie magical threads on their arms, feed them rice which had been prayed upon to invest them with supernatural powers, and smear ash on them. She was accused of black magic and on 24 July 1724, the Sarkar ruled that as she had not exercised her magical powers to harm anyone, she be administered 11 lashes in front of the temple. She was whipped and then set free. It was also proclaimed that anyone practising black magic would be similarly dealt with.

An Englishman named Jenkinson was robbed of fifteen guineas[*] from his cupboard by his slave and his horse-driver. They were found guilty and sentenced to death. In the same year, a woman, at the insistence of her paramour, murdered her husband; she was sentenced to be burnt to death for this heinous crime.[†]

Are not the current laws in the true interest of the *ryot*! In the year 1855 a case was heard in the Supreme Court which captured the attention of the

---

[*]   A guinea is an English coin worth ten and a half rupees.

[†]   Extracted from the government records of February and July 1728.

city. An Englishman named Mr. Meason engaged the services of a tailor named Vithoba Malhari, but as he was not paid his monthly salary regularly, the tailor stopped work and pressed charges for the payment of his accumulated salary. In reply, Mr. Meason wrote to Major Baines, the then Police Master and asked him to arrest the tailor as he had ceased work without informing Mr. Meason, and that he be fittingly punished. Based on the letter, Major Baines arrested the tailor, imprisoned him for a night and the following morning, presented him before the Senior Magistrate, Mr. Garfield. Mr. Meason had also written to Mr. Garfield in a similar fashion and requested that the tailor be punished. Relying on this letter, Mr. Garfield did not conduct a proper examination of the case, held the tailor guilty of running away from domestic service without the permission of his master, and sentenced him to 21 days of hard labour in the new prison. After his release from the prison, the tailor petitioned the Supreme Court that he had been wrongly sentenced to imprisonment by the Senior Magistrate, Mr. Garfield and demanded an apology and a compensation of rupees six hundred for the loss suffered. The case came up for hearing on 16 June 1855 in the Supreme Court before the Chief Justice Sir William Yardley and Sir Charles Jackson, Junior Magistrate. The case was heard for seven consecutive days. The case attracted a lot of public attention with English officials and other gentlemen thronging the court to hear the arguments of the respective lawyers. The judgement delivered on the 25 June held Mr. Garfield guilty of wrongly punishing the tailor, Vithoba Malhari. He was ordered to pay a sum of five hundred and one rupees to the tailor. Mr. Garfield was then transferred to another department. In those times, such impartial justice was common.[4]

The Mumbadevi Tank was located at the place where the washermen wash their laundry near the Camp Maidan. Adjacent to it is the place where criminals were punished. This place was chosen as it is opposite to the Bazaar Gate which is normally very crowded. In former times, it was the popular opinion that all punishments had to be administered in full public view to strike terror in the hearts of any prospective criminals. Our people are also of the view that any punishment be administered in the public square. Based on the nature of the crime, the accused was pelted with cow-dung or eggshells. He could also be caged and taken on a procession or tied to a pole and flogged. He could be made to sit on a donkey with half his head tonsured, his forehead smeared red with vermilion, his face painted black, a garland of onions around his neck, and the most outlandish costumes to make him as grotesque as possible. He might also be made to sit with his front facing the donkey's tail and taken around the streets at the head of procession with a cacophony of music. Around fifty raucous boys hurling dust or dung would make up the tail of the troupe. The Sarkar would spend quite a lot of money in administering this punishment. Next to the pond was the place where murderers were hanged and hence the pond came to be known as the Gallows Pond. There was a wooden contraption that threw dung at the criminals; and right next to it was a cage in which a prisoner was rotated for an hour or a half until he fainted. In this small stretch of land, they had made arrangements for administering five different kinds of punishment. As these kinds of punishments have been stopped, these instruments of torture have been removed. The gallows have been shifted behind the old jail. Any corporeal punishment is limited to hard labour, and very rarely, flogging.

The English had built small forts at various places and garrisoned them with a minimal number of soldiers. On the 20 of February 1673, the Dutch Admiral Rijckloff van Goens attacked the island of Mumbai with a force of six thousand people. The then Governor of Mumbai, General Aungier was a very shrewd and capable man. He marshalled his forces intelligently and spread them out to defend the city. He had an army comprising three hundred Whites, four hundred Christians, three hundred Bhandaris, and a regiment of five hundred Portuguese commanded by an English general. He also had sixty guns. These were mounted on the wall and five hundred people were assigned to the Mumbai Fort. At this, the Dutch Admiral changed directions and proceeded to Mahim to land there. When Aungier Sahib realized this move, he sent three hundred Bhandari people to the Mahim Fort armed with cudgels and prevented the landing. Besides, there were three strong warships in the Harbour with thirty guns each and five French ships which had promised to help the English. Observing the nature of these defences, the Dutch admiral retreated.[5] In those days, the standing troops consisted mainly of Bhandaris, as the Bhandaris and Kolis were the largest in number.

In the year 1683 of the Christian era, during the tenure of Mr. Ward, the Company Sarkar was faced with a major problem, and English rule was suspended in the island of Mumbai for almost a year. When Captain Keigwin was named as the Chief of the armed forces of the island, he was granted permission to take meals at the table of the Deputy Governor, in addition to his salary. In a move to reduce the costs of the city, the meals were suspended. Captain Keigwin wrote to the Deputy Governor that he be paid expenses related to his meals, and it was agreed with the Court of Directors that he would be paid an additional twenty rupees per month for his food expenses. As these were not paid, on 26 December 1683, Captain

Keigwin mutinied. He arrested Mr. Ward and expelled the other officials. He then assumed control of the affairs of the island as a representative of the King of England and allotted duties to his co-conspirators. The employees of the Company at Surat made many efforts to recover the island, but to no avail. Captain Keigwin ruled Mumbai for almost a year until the news could be communicated to the Chief Sarkar at England. The King sent his representative Sir Thomas Grantham, an Admiral and a man-of-war with 70 mounted guns. Under his seal, the King sent orders which read, 'On receipt of this letter, restore the island of Mumbai to its previous state and hand it over to the Company.' Captain Keigwin came back to his senses after he saw the letter and agreed to leave the island. He however asked Sir Grantham to forgive his crimes, who agreed and the island was surrendered to him on 12 November 1684. Mr. Ward was released and the island was handed over to the Company, as per former times.[6]

Despite Keigwin's mutiny, he was quite a shrewd and capable person, and well-versed in political affairs. Though he had assumed complete control of the island, he did not run the island under his own name but acted as the representative of the King of England and ruled the island in a proper manner. He did not try to accumulate personal wealth. He continued to uphold the prestige of the English Sarkar and tried to increase the Company's trade. He continued to maintain the supremacy of the English over the Siddis and other local chieftains. This trait of the English helped them to consolidate their rule in the coming years.

In those years, though the English Sarkar was very careful in limiting its expenses, it discharged its political responsibilities very diligently. When they took over the island of Mumbai, the local army had a total of 125 men including the English, French, Portuguese, and the Blacks.

In 1686, the Court of Directors sent a regiment to the island of Mumbai under Captain Clifton.[7] It was decided to pay him a salary of three hundred rupees annually. The regiment had both White and Black troops. By 1777, the strength had increased to six thousand troops. In that year, the Company Sarkar introduced a rule under which traders and rich people of Mumbai had to learn military manoeuvres so that they could be mobilized, if necessary. About a hundred odd Vani and Brahmin gentlemen refused to take up arms, and paid a certain sum of money to get themselves released from this obligation. In 1794, the total strength of the Mumbai army was 15,801 including 3,273 Whites and 12,528 Blacks and the total expense incurred by this Department was 4,720,760 rupees. By 1807, Whites numbered 5,000 and Blacks were 23,450 with the total being 28,450 and their expense was over a crore and a half. In 1847, 11,210 Whites and

65,845 Blacks accounted for 77,055 troops and the Sarkar incurred an expense of three to four crores on their behalf. In 1861, the number of military personnel in Mumbai was estimated to be around seventy five thousand. Besides there were armies under the Madras and Bengal Presidencies. This gives us an idea about the rapid progress the Company Sarkar made in these years. Just as a water-body is very small at its source and then becomes a large river, Mumbai has proved to be a similar case for the Company Sarkar. One hardly comes across a parallel in history where a race has established its rule in a foreign country thousands of miles from its native land. Truly amazing! Starting with thirty five troops they have now swelled their ranks to over a lakh, and from the small factory at Surat have managed to extend their rule over the whole of India. What can be more amazing than this fact! Our locals believe that if 1 becomes 21, it is truly amazing. But if 1 becomes 1000 and much more, how does one compare? This Company has over three lakh troops based in Mumbai, Madras, Calcutta and other smaller places and all the kings and nobles are under their overlordship. There is not a single king in India who can go against the writ of the Company Sarkar. This is the result of their shrewdness.

As in 1861, when many traders, officials and other English gentlemen volunteered to join the army and started training, designating themselves as captain or colonel or general and were in general prepared for battle, a similar enthusiasm could be seen amongst the Englishmen in 1798. The reason for this was that the English and French had fallen out with each other and it was feared that the French might attack the island of Mumbai; another reason was that Hyder Ali and the other kings of Hindustan were looking for an opportunity to drive the English out of India. When the Court of Directors got to know of this threat, they wrote to Duncan Sahib, the then Governor to keep the army ready for battle. In October 1798, Duncan Sahib read out the orders of the Chief Sarkar at a public meeting held in the theatre at the Fort, and himself made a very reasoned speech about the necessity of this move. He urged all the government employees and other men present in the gathering to volunteer for military services and prepare themselves for battle. All the men including the Governor pledged their services to this cause. As money had to be raised for this venture, a subscription was called for during the meeting and Duncan Sahib himself contributed 25,000 rupees and General Stuart contributed 30,000 rupees. Others contributed sums ranging between 10,000 and 1,000 rupees depending on their capacity and stature. The total sum collected was 300,000 rupees. Of this, a sum of 127,673 rupees was retained by the Mumbai Sarkar and the remaining amount was sent to the Secretary of the

English Government to aid the Military Department. Lord Nelson had just returned after emerging victorious in Egypt. A public demonstration proved the fealty of the Mumbai *ryot*. This military detachment was retained for a few years and then broken up. These military troops were known as 'Volunteer Corps'.[8]

It was proving very difficult for the Company Sarkar to increase the population of this island. Shivaji's son, Sambhaji had an eye on this island and occasionally amassed troops on the islands of Gharapuri and Kaneri-Huneri. The traders and other people who frequented Mumbai were routinely harassed by the Angrias of Alibaug, the Siddis of Habsan, the pirates from Janjira, the Savant of Wadi and Dhulap of Vijaydurg. Sometimes very large ships were captured. They would loot the ship, and either arrest or kill people. From 1672, Yakut Khan would periodically amass up to ten thousand people and camp at Mazagaon. He would raid the neighbouring villages or those in the Maratha kingdom. As he was fighting with Shivaji, he would use that as an excuse to set up a base here. This led to a lot of problems for the Hindu *ryot* of Mumbai. His army would resort to a variety of terror tactics. For a couple of years, the Portuguese and Sambhaji enforced an embargo on the transport of grain from their territories into Mumbai and this really created a grave situation in Mumbai. Every year, the English had to face problems of a similar nature.

On 22 February 1689, the Siddi of Habsan, Yakut Khan arrived with a force of twenty thousand, landed at Sewri and commandeered the Sewri Fort. He entered the city at midday and at about one in the morning of the following day, the English fired three cannons from the Fort to signal a foreign invasion, and that the people should move to safer places. What was to happen? This led to uncoordinated chaos with people running helter-skelter. But where could they go? All the escape routes had been sealed by the Siddi's army. They attacked the fort at Mazagaon the following day and drove away the sentries. All the guns and gunpowder and about ten boxes of money fell into their hands. They sent a body of troops to the Mahim fort to conquer it and spread terror in the neighbourhood. They set up cannons on the fort at Dongri and targeted the Fort of Mumbai, which was the only fort in the hands of the English. Most of Mumbai was under their control and they had amassed a troop of over forty thousand. Yakut Khan stayed for over a year in Mumbai and finally left on the 8 June 1690 after burning down the fort at Mazagaon. Sir John Child was the Governor of Mumbai and most historians believe that he had provoked the attack through his thoughtlessness. After his departure, an epidemic of plague swept across Mumbai and caused many deaths and led to a famine. Of the English army, only thirty five White soldiers survived the plague.[9]

Sir John Child found it very difficult to negotiate for peace with Yakut Khan. He sent two English ambassadors to the Emperor at Delhi to persuade Yakut Khan to lift the siege in Mumbai. These ambassadors were able to convince Aurangzeb and Yakut Khan had to make peace with the English. Aurangzeb had a very low opinion of Sir John Child because of his rough behaviour. Many of the clauses in the peace treaty were insulting to the English but they had no choice except to accept them. One of the clauses stipulated that Sir John Child leave Hindustan within a period of nine months; however he died a couple of months before the expiry of the deadline. As the English were very submissive on this occasion, orders were sent to the Siddis to lift the siege. This encounter with the Siddis caused the Company Sarkar a loss of 4,160,000 rupees as they had to pay Yakut Khan all the expenses he had incurred to mount the siege on Mumbai. Many are of the opinion that if Sir John Child had behaved sensibly on this occasion, he would not have exposed Mumbai to this sudden attack. Given that he had the use of two English men-of-war anchored in the harbour, many English historians believe that if he had stoutly defended the island and fought against Yakut Khan, he would not have been reduced to such a disadvantageous position. However, this gentleman did not issue any orders to attack the invaders and this encouraged the Moghuls to attack Mumbai. He had first initiated the idea of extending the political domination of the English, but did not rise to the occasion during this attack and put the people of Mumbai in a very precarious position.

The ambassadors who had been sent from Mumbai received a *firman* from Aurangzeb. This has been translated into English and published by Bruce in his history. It has been reproduced below.

'Dated February 27th, 1689–90, in the 33rd year of a most glorious reign:

'All the English having made a most humble submissive petition, that the crimes they have done may be pardoned, and requested another Phirmaund, to make their being forgiven manifest, and sent their Vakkeels to the heavenly palace, the most illustrious in the world, to get the royal favour: and Ettimaund Caun, the Governor of Suratt's petition to the famous Court, equal to the skie, being arrived, that they would present the great King with a fine of 150,000 rupees, to his most noble treasury, resembling the sun, and would restore the merchants' goods they had taken away, to the owners of them, and would walk by the ancient customs of the port, and behave themselves for the future no more in such a shameful manner; therefore his Majesty, according to his favor due to all people of the world, hath pardoned their faults, mercifully forgiven them, and out of his princely condescension agrees,

that the present be put into the treasury of the port, the merchants'
goods be returned, the town flourish, and they follow their trade as in
former times, and Mr. Child, who did the disgrace, be turned out and
expelled. This order is irreversible.'[10]

In 1681, the Company Sarkar received permission from the Chief Sarkar in
England to mint coins under its name; an ordinary mint was erected in
Mumbai and coins of various denominations like *Mohurs, Paanchi, Rupiya,
Pavlaya, Chavlaya* and copper *paisas* were brought into circulation. They had
started minting coins from as far back as 1670; these were minted under the
name of the Emperor of Delhi and had Persian lettering which created
problems in the Moghul Court. After receiving this permission, they started
minting coins under their own name. From that time on, the goddess of
Wealth, Lakshmi seems to have blessed the English; coins were accepted in
many other countries and this increased their prestige, and consequently the
trade in Mumbai. Hundreds of braziers and goldsmiths used to work in the
mint – they have now been replaced by a steam-powered machine. Major
Hawkins built the present mint in 1825 and all the machines were designed
by him. All the steps are automatically done by the steam-powered
machines – melting of the metal, casting them into bars, rolling the bars into
sheets, cutting out blanks from sheets and then forming the blanks into
coins. The process must be seen to be believed. There are three steam-
powered machines – the largest can generate 40 horsepower while the other
two can generate 24 and 10 horsepower respectively. Such is their speed
that these machines can produce 150,000 coins of assorted variety in one
day. These machines run only on the power of steam. The machines were
put into operation in 1830 and since then only these coins have been in
circulation in this Presidency. If anybody is keen on expanding his
knowledge, he should certainly visit such factories. One needs to obtain
permission from the Mint Master to visit this place. The mint can be visited
only on Fridays. In 1681, the Court of Directors sent one Mr. Smith to assay
the coins produced by the mint. His annual salary was 600 rupees while the
current Mint Master gets a monthly salary of 2,000 rupees. He has about
four assistants and their salaries range from 500 to 600 rupees.

In 1687, Mumbai was declared the chief capital of all the territories which
were under the English in India and all the administration was overseen
from this place.

In 1688, under instructions from the Chief Company Sarkar, it was
decided to impose a tax on houses in Mumbai. Prior to this imposition, the
Company Sarkar had not levied any new tax in Mumbai.

The Portuguese have been associated with Hindustan for over three and hundred fifty years; in this period they have not paid the least attention to the culture of the people of India, the various religions, the numerous languages which are spoken here, and the reasons behind the importance of their religious centres. The only thing they did was to break the idols of the Hindus and treat them with contempt. They did not realize that they had to learn the language of the people over whom they ruled and never bothered to learn the secrets of their languages. One rarely came across a Firangi from Portugal who had learnt Marathi or Urdu. Their only achievement was the forcible conversion of Hindus and the destruction of their idols. Many Portuguese families have been resident in India for over five to six generations; however they have no knowledge of the Hindu religion and do not understand one word of Marathi.

It is said that some years back the Governor of the Portuguese people in Goa had to understand the religion of the Hindus for a specific reason. A resident Shenvi gentleman explained the religion to him in the most simple and straightforward manner. He took along with him a lump of white clay known as *Gopi Chand* and a *lota* of water. He wet the lump and inscribed a mark on the forehead and said that this was the teaching of the Hindu religion. It is further said that this royal personage actually believed he had obtained an understanding of the Hindu religion through this demonstration.

Compare this with the shrewd behaviour of the English! When they first established their factories in India at Surat, Khambaiat, and Kochi, they learnt the language of the country on the orders of the Court of Directors. They were also given an allowance to learn the language. Their foresight can be gauged from the fact that a pundit was named to manage the affairs of the Surat Factory. Captain Gary, who was the Deputy Governor in 1667, knew two or three languages. Besides, he learnt Arabic and wrote a small book in the language and presented it to the Governor at Goa.

Though the islands of Gharapuri, Divdive, and Kaneri-Huneri are just about two to three *kos* away from Mumbai, they were not easily accessible because the Angrias had a base here and the neighbouring seas were pirate infested. Overcoming these difficulties, Captain Pyke managed to visit these islands in 1712 and saw the caves and idols on these islands and sent drawings of these statues to England.[11] These caves had not been discovered by any of the earlier visitors as their location was not clear and it was believed that they were the handiwork of Alexander.[12] Some felt that they were Chinese in origin, but it is now agreed that they are Hindu in origin. The Portuguese destroyed a large part of the work by firing cannons at the statues. In 1718, an employee of the Company Sarkar, Mr. Boucher sent a copy of a Parsi scripture named *Vendidad Sadi* to England. However it languished there for a long while as nobody could read it. Now, they have not only read the Vendidad, but also the *Vedas* of the Hindus and translated them into English, and have commented on them in Sanskrit. There are many Englishmen in Mumbai and all over India who can speak languages like Sanskrit, Marathi, Gujarati, Urdu, Tamil, and Persian. How deserving of praise is this trait! Governor Charles Boone examined the caves at Gharapuri in 1715, and wrote an account of his visit and drew pictures of the caves. Recently, a book has been published on these caves with a number of illustrations. The point behind this anecdote is that the English have been undertaking such investigations ever since they came here, and they continue to do so. New theories are being formulated and new conclusions are being drawn. They might have spent thousands of rupees in these ventures. Gazetted officers have to learn a local language like Marathi, Urdu, Gujarati, Kannadi, Tulvi or some other language before they could be promoted to senior positions like Collector. It is certainly good political sense, that one learns the language of the ruled if one is to administer properly.

English scholars have prepared large dictionaries in languages like Sanskrit, Arabic, Urdu, Marathi, and Gujarati. Some years back, an English official named General Vans Kennedy[13] who was posted in Mumbai knew over five native languages very well and was an expert in the English language. If anybody was to be hired by the Sarkar as a pundit or *Shastri*, he was first examined by this Sahib. Many of our Pundits, *Shastris*, and *Puraniks* approached him to clarify any doubts they might have had about the meaning of a certain *Shloka*. In 1824, he published a Marathi to English and an English to Marathi dictionary. He had a huge collection of books in Sanskrit and other local languages. He died about 1840 at the age of ninety five. In spite of his great age, he continued his studies in Sanskrit and other languages. He was a pure soul with boundless generosity, and was very compassionate towards the interests of the people of this country.

In 1720, Mumbai had forty gazetted officials, but their salary was fairly low. The Governor's annual salary was three thousand rupees, the Deputy-Governor was paid one thousand rupees, the Councillor of the third rank was paid seven hundred rupees and so on down the hierarchy. They were also paid food and other allowances. They would also get an annual bonus. The salaries in the military department was even lower, and they were paid only once in six months. The two doctors in Mumbai were paid three hundred and fifty rupees each. The padre was paid five hundred rupees annually and a bonus of five hundred rupees besides. He was the only clergyman in the island at that time. The government discontinued the practice of maintaining dining tables, and gazetted officials were paid an additional sum of twenty five rupees per month. In 1739, the gazetted officials wrote to the Governor, Honourable Stephen Law, Esquire that this sum was grossly inadequate to meet the rising expenses of food articles and other items in Mumbai and that they were incurring an expense of fifty two rupees per month, and therefore the food allowance be increased to at least fifty two rupees per month.

In 1700, the Company Sarkar wrote to the Mumbai Governor that as the expenses in the island of Mumbai had increased beyond control, the salary of the Deputy Governor be reduced to one hundred rupees per month and the entire expenses of Mumbai city be limited to seventy thousand rupees per annum including the Revenue, Military, and Ecclesiastical Departments. The annual income of the government amounted to ninety four thousand two hundred rupees which was derived by levying customs duty and land revenue.

Such was the state of affairs in India in those days. A quick review of the current state of affairs reveals that the earlier annual limit of seventy thousand rupees would not suffice for a day's expense currently. The then monthly salary of the Governor has now become his daily salary. Isn't this truly amazing? The government spends over ten lakhs of rupees in just building new roads, maintaining and watering existing roads, keeping the city clean and supplying water to the city. One can imagine the scale of other expenses from this example.

Before 1768, most of the rich and important people of the island of Mumbai stayed on the Camp Maidan where they had their palatial mansions and temples. The choice place of residence in Mumbai extended from the gates of the Fort to Masjid Bunder. The ancient Mumbadevi and other temples were located on the Camp Maidan at the location where the *dhobis* wash their laundry. There was also a Portuguese church adjacent to these temples and further ahead was the Jumma Masjid. These were all demolished by the Company Sarkar and moved to the present locations at their own expense. The Camp Maidan was thus created. When the Fort was being built and a moat dug around it, the houses and lands were acquired by the government and demolished. The householders and owners of other immovable property numbered around nine hundred including one hundred Brahmins and Vanis.

As the expenses of government increased and revenue decreased, the English Sarkar issued orders in 1720 that money be borrowed from the *ryot* at four or five per cent interest and the funds of the treasury augmented; a note signed by the Governor General was issued to the depositors and interest paid to them every six months. The practice of issuing Treasury Notes at four or five per cent has remained since then.

In the same year, increasing differences between the Portuguese and the English led to the breaking of transport links between Bandra and Mumbai; the English issued a proclamation that all residents of Mumbai should relocate themselves to Mahim within a period of twenty one days. However, this proved to be unnecessary as the tension was quickly defused.

In the year 1775, the Dandi or Point was built at Upper Colaba and the Mumbai Fort was strengthened at an expense of one crore of rupees. The reason for building the Colaba Point was to get a clearer view of any approaching enemy ships. A lighthouse was also built at this point so that ships arriving at night would be able to see the rocks in the sea. Thirdly, as the captains of ships arriving from foreign lands were unfamiliar with the layout of the harbour, they could possibly make a wrong approach thus damaging their ships. These stray ships could be spotted at a distance with a telescope and a guide-boat would be sent out to lead the way. These were the various reasons for the building of this Point which has saved many ships from destruction, thousands of lives from being lost and goods worth lakhs of rupees from being destroyed.

The newly constructed lighthouse has been built on land seventy feet above sea level and it has a height of eighty-nine feet, giving a total height of one hundred and fifity-nine feet above sea level. The circumference of its base is approximately seventy hands. Previously there was only large lamp; from 1847 however, a mechanism has been introduced by which the lamp rotates and casts its light in all four directions. The lighthouse consumes about one and half *man* of oil every day. It can be seen from a distance of twelve *kos*. Nobody should miss out on a visit to this place.

While one is not able to make a clear estimate when the factory for making gunpowder was started, it must not have been later than five to ten years after the Company Sarkar obtained possession of the land. It was earlier in Lower Colaba. In 1728, Lieutenant Archibald Campbell was employed as an engineer on the ship *Princess Carolina*. The English Sarkar had not nominated any engineer on the island as it was very expensive to maintain the position. He built the first factory for making gunpowder in Colaba and devised a waterwheel that ran on wind power and ground the powder. This had to be shut down because the people could not operate the machine. They instead built twenty-four grinding mills to prepare the gunpowder. After a while they realized that the place was not suitable for this operation and sold the mills for a song. They built a new factory on the Camp near the Palo Gate. It was then moved to Kamathipura. As the density of population increased in Kamathipura, there were a couple of accidents; this led to the gunpowder factory being moved to Mazagaon in

1790 as it had a low density of population. However, the settlements were on the increase even in Mazagaon.[14] Every year about 900 *pimps* or 69,000 *rattals* of gunpowder is produced. Nobody else is allowed to produce gunpowder in Mumbai. This factory employs about a hundred to hundred and fifty people. The sale of gunpowder is also restricted and all those who desire to buy it have to show proper reasons before they can do so.

Chapter 6

There are about eighteen bazaars in the city of Mumbai – some big and some small. The main bazaar is the one situated in the central part of the city near the Jumma Masjid. It is commonly referred to as the Market. It has been very intelligently designed. In earlier times, Mumbai was sparsely populated; there were hardly any traders, and retailers would spread their wares wherever they felt like it. It is said that the land where the Market is located actually belonged to a Vani businessman. This philanthropic gentleman donated this land for the bazaar and requested the vegetable and fruit vendors to do their business there. It took a few years for the Market to gain acceptance. The Hindus believe that building a public market is as worthy of blessings as building a food-shelter or a water-fountain or digging a well or erecting a tank. Based on this belief, he donated this land for the Market. A few years later in 1809, during the tenure of Duncan Sahib, the Sarkar built a wide open square to comfortably accommodate the vendors. Permanent positions were however not allotted and nobody could lay claim to any particular place. The policy followed was first come, first served, and the sooner one came in the morning, one could choose a place with more vantage. Though nobody had any permanent rights on a particular place, the vendors placed their benches and would occupy the same position every day. The Market was not as accessible as it is these days. During the rains, it was covered in knee-deep mud and stones were placed at short intervals for people to jump on as they made their way through the market. It was very inconvenient to visit the market on such days. In 1838, the Sarkar reconstructed the Market and the current layout was implemented. It is not possible to obtain an account of the earlier condition of this Market. Anyone can sell vegetables in the Market without paying the Sarkar any fees. As the sale of fish and other related products is banned in the Market, it is clean and odourless. This is certainly an excellent arrangement.

On a beam in the Market near where the fruits are sold, a notice has been hung on which the following is written in English and Gujarati.

'Market for the sale of vegetables and fruits.
The Honourable Jonathon Duncan, Esq.
Public Notice

"This market has been built for the sale of vegetables, fruits, leaves, etc. People of all castes and races are free to sell their wares here. No tax, fees or levies will be levied on the sale of goods.'"

Passing by Kalbadevi, one first comes across the shops of Ramdas, Ramlal, and other prominent businessmen and moneylenders; walk a few steps ahead, and Bhuleshwar Bazaar is to the West and Bhendi Bazaar to the North. There are rows of shops of braziers and grinders. All the way to Sir Jamsetjee's hospital, the whole place is like a bazaar. Somebody is selling sweets, someone else cloth, there is an oil mill here, a stable there and inns all over the place. Further ahead are shops selling Chinese and local bangles and other trinkets made of shellac and shops of cobblers from Surat. There is a large stable of the Arabs, which houses over a thousand Arabian horses. Recently, a horse of the most exquisite breed was sold for a price of over five thousand rupees. Most of the rich buy their horses from this stable. There are three to four such stables, but this is, by far, the largest. Up ahead is Byculla where a market is set up early every morning; and gardeners from Bandra, Mahim, Worli, Parel, Matunga, Mazagaon, Kurla, Sion and other places bring various kinds of garden-produce for sale in the small hours of the morning. The retail vendors of Mumbai buy their goods here and sell it at various locations. This bazaar lasts only for an hour or two and by daybreak, the whole place is deserted. In this manner, each road of this city has a market of some kind. Wherever one goes, there are workshops with workers milling about. Here is a soda-water factory, somebody is extracting oil there; vehicles are being painted or somebody is producing gold brocade from silk.

If one turn towards the East at Mumbadevi square, one comes across the counting-houses of the big moneylenders. They sit on pristine white cushions and recline on huge bolsters, while their servants bustle about in the front of the shop. There are over fifty such shops. Just a little ahead are the opium traders, mainly Marwadi and other kinds of Gujars, who conduct their noisy and boisterous trade on the streets. Just behind the Mumbadevi Temple is a line of shops selling shawls. There are shawls hanging everywhere. If a bundle is opened, one can see priceless Amritsari and Kashmiri shawls of various colours and silken borders. One is amazed at their beauty! A little ahead are bright shops selling pearls, diamonds, and rubies. A few more steps and one comes across shops selling copperware. Numerous varieties of newly forged utensils are arranged from top to bottom in these shops. Here and there are also shops selling broadcloth, goldsmiths, and gold assayers. Leaving them behind, a few steps will bring you to the sweetmeat vendors! Rows and rows of benches with red, yellow, and green-coloured sweets neatly arranged in baskets – one gets satisfaction by just looking at them. Adjacent to them are the *Gandhis,* with extracts from flowers and other medicinal plants, and many of them making small packets of these extracts. At various points, one will come across Gujarati Brahmins dressed in a *dhoti* and rags selling plates and cups made of leaves. In this small area, you will find a number of these Gujarati Brahmins packed in all corners. Further are the shops of the grain-dealers. Various types of grains are filled in baskets and tins and the Marwadi proprietors eagerly await their customers in the fashion of Bakasura. And if somebody ventures into their shops, they try to cheat him in many ways. If one gets into their clutches, one is bound to emerge with hardly a hair on one's head. Imagine the state of affairs if one takes goods on credit! You are just asking for more for the same! Further on there are shops selling *ghee*, sugar, oil, and coconuts. Adjacent to the Maruti temple is the new Market for selling foreign cloth and if one turns eastwards, the Market can be seen. Many exquisite things can be seen in the markets. Both sides of the Jumma Masjid are lined with shops selling spices. Next to them are shops selling gold jewellery and further ahead, one can buy fragrances like *attar, gulab, abir,* and *udkadi*. Spread on the road are spices like cloves, cardamom, mace, nutmeg, and others. Behind them in the next row are over twenty shops selling Muscati products like almonds, raisins and dates. The next row consists of shops selling fruits and next to them those selling vegetables. As we go further eastwards beyond the Null, the Bazaar still continues. In a long row, there are shops owned by the Bohras selling gold jewellery, silk brocade and other similar items. Various kinds of artists are working in these shops and crowds of Mussalmans and Kutchis are milling around a multitude of eateries. There are many places where clay utensils are sold. It is estimated that this city buys locally made clay utensils worth 24,000 rupees. On one side there are many shops selling boxes and chests of many shapes and sizes. Similarly, there are shops where one can buy beds and mattresses. Not an inch of space is available and all the people seem extremely busy. Most of them are from the Gujarat Province.

If one enters the market and looks around, one sees heaps of sugarcane bundles, mountains of flowers, piles of lemons, and a thousand other products stacked everywhere. Various kinds of vegetables, fruits, heaps of pineapples, baskets of pomegranates from Muscat, juicy figs, bunches of red and yellow plantains, bunches of red and green grapes neatly arranged in baskets, and mangoes, jack fruits, guavas, and a multitude of other colourful fruits can be seen in all corners. It is true that seasonal fruits are always available in large quantities, but in Mumbai most fruits are available twelve months of the year; of course, the prices are outrageous. During the mango season, this place becomes so bright and pretty, that many people come here just to have a look at the mangoes. During the mango season, one can easily see fifty different kinds of mangoes in as many colours here. One can get whatever one wants as long as one has got the money. The prices can be so steep that for a rupee one can get only two mangoes, or four pomegranates, or eight figs, or about ten bananas. On the far side of the Null are the shops of the Bohras where one can buy goods from Vilayat, China and other countries. In the neighbourhood are carders, turners, and shops selling bangles and other jewellery made of shellac; the dyers stay nearby. Shops selling candles, pots, glasses and many other articles of household use are also there. In a space approximately half a *kos* square, there are a multitude of shops extending all the way from Masjid Bunder to Dongri. The bazaar starts early in the morning and closes at about ten at night; the vegetable vendors wind up a little earlier.

If one leaves the market and moves southwards, that is towards the Camp, one first comes across shops selling dry fruits like dates, dried coconut, almonds, and raisins. Most of the shopkeepers selling trifling and miscellaneous articles are arrogant and couldn't care less. They are not courteous even to the most distinguished of shoppers. Those who sell chillies, coriander and other trifles behave similarly. They ask an anna for what is worth a paisa, and also add – 'Take it or leave it!' – so arrogant are they! Further ahead is the cloth market with a hundred odd shops. Goods of the highest quality including cloth from Vilayat, Dhanwadi textiles, and gold and silver brocade are sold here. The shops are darkened with thick curtains, and a couple of Bhatias are perched stylishly on benches watching intently for an unsuspecting customer to venture into their clutches. One can see this happening quite openly. A piece of cloth costing one rupee is sold for five rupees to the customer, and as if that were not enough, sub-standard or used goods are passed off. A customer who tries to complain is treated to waved fists and punches. About twenty-five years back, these Bhatias and other cloth-sellers would openly cheat the poor. Since Mr. Forjett joined the Police Department, things have improved quite a lot. The cloth-sellers are not the only rogues. Vendors of gold jewellery practise various kinds of dishonesty. The shopkeepers feel that it is their right to cheat the customers. It is certainly very sad that in a great city like Mumbai, there is no honesty in the bazaars. Given this state of affairs, it is heartening to note that many of the bigger traders, moneylenders, and most of the wholesalers are honest and can be relied upon. The dishonest traders are mostly retail vendors and those selling trifles. Just talking about honesty can be so very pleasing, and to witness honesty in action is many times so! Honesty adds majesty to the trader and is his true capital.

At the end of the market, towards the west is Lohar Chawl. The ironmongers have their workshops and iron goods can be bought in shops here. If you turn southwards, you arrive at the Camp Maidan. Towards one corner are parked vehicles available for hire, and at the other corner, at about five in the evening, a bazaar of *mochis* or cobblers assemble. At that time, about twenty odd cobblers display footwear of various types and colours. There are large buildings behind the Lohar Chawl and in front of the Camp Maidan. Many shopkeepers have their shops here and many more huge buildings are currently being built. Right ahead is the Free Church and next to it is a very large building known as the Sailors' Home which was built at an expense of over one lakh rupees.

Then come the buildings housing the Elphinstone School, the Small Causes Court, the Bible Society, and the Money School which brings one to Dhobi Talao. On the upper side of the Lohar Chawl is an open space where a market for the sale of old clothes is held. Twenty odd Mussalmans have their shops which are full of old and torn clothes. One can buy clothes worn by people of various castes and classes. Skirts worn by the madams, trousers worn by Sahibs, the Parsi vest or *sadra*, the loose pants worn by the Mussalmans known as *tumani*, and various kinds of clothes worn by the Hindus like *pagoti, angarkha, bandya, dhotar, lugdi, shawl, choli* and other old clothes can be bought at prices ranging from an anna to a couple of rupees. They also sell items like broken shoes, torn sandals, and crushed suitcases. This bazaar sits during the afternoon and evening. It is referred to as the Chor Bazaar as the thieves of Mumbai sell their stolen goods here. There are five to six such bazaars in Mumbai. There is also a Bhikar Bazaar on the Null where, in the evening, the beggars of Mumbai sell the grains and other articles that they have collected during the day. There is hardly a place in this city that does not have shops, not to mention the hawkers who roam with their goods from morning till night. It would not be wrong to say that Mumbai is the bazaar of Western India. Except for gold and silver, everything else can be bought at one's doorstep. Jewellers visit the homes of the rich carrying expensive rings set with diamonds, pearls, and rubies. Similarly the sellers of shawls visit these houses carrying bundles of the most exquisite shawls.

The open space below the Lohar Chawl at the end of the cloth bazaar, admeasuring about half a *kos* square is known as the Camp Maidan. Up ahead is the Gallows Pond or Faansi Talao where the *dhobis* wash their laundry. This is where the railroad starts and this is the main station for the railway. To the left and right of this Maidan are living quarters of the Black Troops. The open space in the middle is dotted with wells full of sweet water and military drills are conducted here. In the open space towards the left, the officers of the military regiments pitch their tents in November and stay there until about April. At the far end, near the seashore, there are permanent tents set in beautiful gardens planted with shade-giving trees. These tents are more regal than our royal palaces. They are festooned and decorated with many costly articles arranged inside. On both sides of these tents are military hospitals where the sick can be admitted; they are very clean and neat and have all the comforts which the ailing need. Finally, opposite the Bazaar Gate, the Gawli folk bring their buffaloes and sell their milk every morning and evening; vehicles for hire are parked here. Up ahead is the Fort of Mumbai. This is a very strong fort and worth visiting. A moat has been dug around the Fort which is filled with sea water that can be let in or drained as desired. During the rains, some of the drains conducting rainwater from the city open into the moat. During this period, the water is sweet. At various places, the Fort has one, two or three walls as the case may be. There are three gates which open to the North and one towards the West. Towards the South, the sea skirts the Fort. Cannons and guns are mounted on the walls. The gates are named Baazar Gate, Sali Gate, Churchgate, and *Palo Gate.[1] Sali Gate is a small one and horses and vehicles cannot pass through; only water is transported through this gate and many people use this route to pass through. Churchgate was earlier known as the Windmill Gate or Pawanchakki Darwaja because the Sarkar had built a mill for grinding wheat right opposite this gate which was powered by wind. A large waterwheel was built to which were attached oars

---

* Its actual name is Apollo Gate. Apollo is the name of a Greek god.

in a fan-like structure. This was connected to a mill built inside and the whole mechanism was powered by wind. This grinding mill was dismantled a few years ago. The Gujaratis refer to this mill as Pawanchakki. It is said that wheat was ground in the mill and supplied to the Military Department. On the roads leading from both the Churchgate and Bazaar Gate to the Camp Maidan, at a distance of eight to ten hands, poles have been fixed to which are attached lanterns which are lit in the evenings at the expense of government. On both sides of the road and in between the lanterns, shade-giving trees have been planted. The Sarkar must have spent thousands of rupees on this account. All four gates are patrolled by guards. To enter through the Bazaar Gate, one has to pass through three doors. The first thing one sees is shops selling broadcloth of various colours and qualities. And then one sees five- and six-storey buildings in which big businessmen have their offices. The Bohras have shops selling crystal ware and adjacent to it is the Market. This was built under the instructions of Admiral Sir Edward Hughes Sahib in 1792, and has been burned down twice since. It was then rebuilt with a subscription collected by native gentlemen. One can buy fruits, vegetables, and other goods here. There are many shops run by the Bohras where one can buy crystal from Europe, China and other places; one also finds blades, knives, scissors, weighing balances, saws, cups, saucers, glasses, *et cetera*. Further ahead is an enormous building known as the Barracks where the English military personnel used to stay, but is now used to house government offices. Thousands of rupees were spent on the construction of this building which was built during the tenure of Duncan Sahib in 1809. Then comes the Mint and the Black Fort or Kala Killa where various kinds of instruments of warfare like swords, spears, pikes, and daggers are neatly arranged. Official permission has to be sought to see this collection. Adjacent to it is the Treasury or the Jamadarkhana containing lakhs of rupees. This has one of the strongest doors in the Fort and is patrolled by soldiers. The safe house and the armoury are also patrolled round the clock. There are always some soldiers at the gate of this fort and cannons and guns are also at hand.

The part of the Fort behind the Treasury is known as the Bombay Castle or Kala Killa and the English standard is always fluttering atop this building. This is the national flag of England. The flag is hoisted in the morning and lowered in the evening. When it is hoisted in the morning, the troops patrolling the station at the Marine Lines on the Camp Maidan salute the flag and for about a quarter hour, a band plays music in the English fashion to mark this occasion. The flag is lowered in a similar manner. There are three other flags flying at Parel, Tardeo (on the hill at

Mahalaxmi), and the tip at Walkeshwar, but similar ceremonies are not conducted there. If a steamship arrives from England, a standard is hoisted above this flag to broadcast its arrival to the public. It is also hoisted when other important ships call at Mumbai. Each country has standards of different colours and with different signs; when a ship from a particular country arrives, the appropriate flag is hoisted. If one is not aware of these symbols, one cannot understand anything. Details about such standards can be found in a large book.

The Town Hall is situated near by and towards the North is the fire station. It is equipped with water pumps and other apparatus for extinguishing fires. Nowhere else are there facilities to protect the *ryot* from fire, in an almost divine fashion. There are five fire stations in Mumbai and this department has over fifty salaried employees. They have to be always ready for any emergency. When time is of essence and the situation critical, even senior English employees do not hesitate to help in extinguishing fires. Pipes have been laid so that water is readily available at various places. During a fire, the water can be tapped by turning a screw, and one can get on with the business. In the firestation at the Fort, there are nine pumps, the Police Master has got seven, there is one at the Governor's residence at Parel, and all the military Lines have one each amounting to a total of thirty two pumps in Mumbai.

Just next to it is the ancient theatre which was built about a hundred or hundred and fifty years ago by the government with contributions from the public. It was auctioned off by the government a few years ago. It was purchased by Seth Bomanji Hormuzji Wadia and converted into his offices. In the front is an open space about five hundred hands square known as the 'Bombay Green'. Our people refer to it as the Chowk. In the centre of the Chowk, a small temple-like structure has been built and a statue of Lord Cornwallis, the Governor General has been installed there. This Sahib was very compassionate and a true well-wisher of India. To perpetuate his memory, the residents of Mumbai got this statue made in England. This Sahib was the Governor General at Calcutta till 1805 and he cast his kind eye on all matters. This statue was installed here in 1822. There is a small courtyard surrounding the statue and trees have been planted on all four sides of the courtyard; a heavy iron chain is looped through poles of teakwood stuck in the ground to cordon off the area. The achievements of this prominent man have been inscribed on the base of the statue.[2]

Many of the labourers and the poor used to worship this statue, and place coconuts and other offerings in front of it. Recently the government has put a stop to this craziness. Our people are hopeless! Truly naive! If they see any shape in a stone, they bring a coconut and fold their hands in respect. They do not bother to think.

In May 1862 the government bought many houses surrounding the Bombay Green. In many other places, government property was sold off. A completely new and brilliant layout has been planned for this area.[3] The houses of Seth Bomanji Hormuzji Wadia have been purchased by the government for six lakh rupees; a few years back, they had sold it to him for fifty thousand rupees. An open ground and garden will be created here and a five-metal statue of Queen Victoria will be placed in the centre; David Sassoon has undertaken to donate fifty thousand rupees for this venture according to newspaper reports.[4]

In a similar fashion, a statue of General Wellesley has been installed at Churchgate. This famous warrior had convincingly defeated the Marathas in 1803. This battle was fought at Assaye where the English suffered major losses; however this Sardar courageously led them to victory. The army of the Marathas consisted of thirty thousand cavalry and ten thousand infantry. In spite of the English army being about one-fifth this size, this great warrior led them to victory. The Sarkar at Calcutta presented him with a beautiful sword worth 10,000 rupees as a mark of their appreciation. The commanders of the army in India presented him with a gold plaque with the details of the Battle of Assaye inscribed on it. They also presented him a silver dining set.

This famed fighter occupied the post of Governor General in 1798 and was known for his foresight. He was very sympathetic to the needs of the natives, and trade multiplied during his tenure; consequently the businessmen of Mumbai contributed towards the installation of a statue in 1814 which was ordered from England. The statue has been sculpted very artistically – Wellesley Sahib is sitting on a throne with a purse in his hands; a Maratha *pahelwan* stands in front of him and Wellesley Sahib's hands are poised to gift him the purse. Next to him is a statue of a lady. On her left hand is a plaque on which are inscribed the words – 'Wisdom, Energy, Integrity'. The Battle of Assaye is depicted at the base of these three statues. Sculptures of a lion and a lioness have been carved at the rear. One's heart is extremely gladdened at the sight of this exquisite sculpture and its grand concept. The people of Mumbai refer to it as the *pahelwan's* statue. All the public work undertaken by the traders of Mumbai are regal in stature and are examples of their generosity.[5]

When this statue was installed, many of the Maratha simpletons of Mumbai were very delighted as they felt that the Company Sarkar had very kindly imported an English god for their worship. And what ensued? There was no limit to their happiness and they started worshipping this statue. For many years thereafter, they would offer coconuts to the idol, conduct *pooja*, and take vows. When the Sarkar realized that this was inappropriate, they put an end to this practice. An iron fence has been constructed and entry has been prohibited. If somebody tries to worship the statue, the watchman appointed by government restricts him.

At the end, behind the Customs-House are situated many mills which employ hundreds of workers who create quite a racket. Next is the Customs-House in the Fort; if one climbs to the top of this building and spends an hour or half, one can take in all the restless activity going on below. If one turns to the South, the entire bay is visible packed with steamships, *taarve*, *botello*, boats, *fattemar*, *kote*, *dol*; and fishermen unloading and shifting their catch. It seems as if the entire harbour is dancing. If one looks at the wharf, horses are being landed, piles of copper plates are stacked, iron rods are piled up high, boxes of opium are stacked one on top of the other and many other types of goods are lying around; government officials are opening boxes to inspect the goods and are generally bullying the poor people. If one goes upstairs into the office, one sees about fifty odd clerks and English officials concentrating on their jobs and businessmen, clutching receipts in their hands entreating the clerks. On one side is the *shroff* with three money boxes, his assistants tallying accounts nearby. A pile of coins and a stack of notes lie in front of him; thus one can see numerous trades. Down below are the weighing machines for about ten different types of goods. About ten employees are discharging their duties; each of them is allocated a specific responsibility; so the office does not get very crowded.

Gujarati people like Vani, Parsi, and Bohra, especially the Parsis, mainly occupy the stretch between Bazaar Gate and Churchgate. From Churchgate to Palo Gate, one sees both government and other business offices and some residences of the English and the Parsis. This area is known as the Ingrez Bazaar. The dock is near the Palo Gate and on its far side is the Post Office. 77,689 people stay within the Fort, giving a very high density of 314 people per acre. If one counts more carefully, one can add another ten thousand to this number; it will certainly not be less.

Though most of the settlements in Mumbai are fairly mixed, most people prefer to stay close to members of their own caste. If some ten Parsis stay in an area, a Hindu would not prefer staying there. And where there may be twenty houses of the Dakshini people, a couple of Gujaratis will not take up residence there. The Parsis, Mussalmans, Bohras, Christians, and others behave in a similar fashion. Only the English are not bothered to stay amongst their own people. If the area is clean and the air is good, they take up residence in any place. The population of this city in 1816 was 161,750. In 1844, a census was conducted by Major Baines, the Police Master (the city's *kotwal*) in which 275,190 men and 248,931 women and children were counted. The total population was 524,121. It is estimated that the current population is over eight lakhs. In the year 1850 there were 6,936 Brahmins in this city, and 288,995 Hindus of other castes, 1,902 Jains, 124,155 Mussalman, 114,698 Parsi, 1,172 Jews, 7,456 mixed Portuguese and Christian, 1,333 Anglo-Indians, 5,417 local Portuguese, 5,088 English, 889 Siddis, 7,118 of the other miscellaneous races;[6] but in the last ten years, the population of all these castes seem to have increased by over fifty per cent. Isn't it amazing! The speed at which the wealth and population of Mumbai has increased is breathtaking. In 1851, the population of the various areas is as follows:

Colaba	7,030
Fort	77,689
Camp	4,000
Market	25,624
Mandvi	69,470
Umarkhadi	87,394
Dhobi Talao	104,921
Bhuleshwar	31,809
Khara Talao	17,951
Girgaum	10,888
Chowpatty	2,142
Walkeshwar	3,768
Mahalaxmi	1,492
Mazagaon	6,170
Tad Wadi	4,957
Kamathipura	26,231
Parel	5,150
Sewri	2,262
Worli	11,483
Mahim	9,452
Sion	4,830

Not counting minors	514,713

The Dakshini people mainly live in Dhobi Talao, Kalbadevi, Girgaon, Cawaji Patel Tank, Mazagaon, Parel, Matunga, Mahim, Worli, and Sion. The settlements of the Bhatia, Vani, Parsi, Mussalmans, Khoja, Memon, and Kutchi are mainly at Fort, Masjid Bunder, Chinch Bunder, Dongri, Mumbadevi, Bhuleshwar, and Bhendi Bazaar. One can also find Dakshinis like Maratha, Ghati, Koli and artisans from other castes. When there was a major fire in the Fort in 1802,[7] many of the richer Gujaratis moved to Bhuleshwar, Bhoiwada, and Mumbadevi. They then built mansions for themselves and permanently settled there. The population of Shetodi, Kumbharwada, Matunga, Duncan Road, and Nagpada is heterogeneous and at the far end, there are settlements of the Dhed, Mahar, Mang, Chambhar, *et cetera.*

This city has many markets for selling fish, but it is worth mentioning that the market places for selling fish and meat are distinct, and are mostly not located in open places. When people buy these products, they ensure that they are properly covered and hidden from sight. The vegetable markets are separated from these markets and selling of fish and meat is prohibited on the roads. Hundreds of varieties of fish can be seen in Mumbai and each of them has its own name. They can be very costly. If a fish of good quality is around two *viti* long, it can fetch over a rupee. The trade in fish in Mumbai is around five to six lakhs of rupees annually. Fish are mostly sold by the Kolis, and the Kasais sell meat. On the far side of the Market is an area known as Khatki Bazaar where most of these Kasais stay. It is prohibited to kill animals at any place. There is a separate bazaar for fowls where chickens, ducks, and eggs are sold.

It is said that about seventy thousand rupees worth of *bombil* is sold in Mumbai annually, mostly in the dried form. It is exported to many countries including England. It looks like a small stick about a *vit* long. The locals refer to dried *bombil as kaadya*, and the wet bombil is called *gallu* or *gatgatay*. It is very popular among fish-eaters. It is cheap and available throughout the year. In the residences of the Kolis, bundles of *bombil* are stored. The *bombil* available in the bay of Mumbai is the best and the reason it is not available in any other part of the sea is explained as follows. When Lord Rama was building a bridge across the sea to get to Lanka, all the fish except the *bombil* helped him. This enraged Lord Rama who twisted it in his hands and tossed it away. It fell in the Mumbai bay. From that time on, its bones have been crushed and it has become soft. Devoid of a backbone, it is as soft as cotton when fresh!!! Simpletons can weave such outlandish stories like the proverbial Sheikh Chilli.

In the last eleven years, there has been a tremendous increase in the population.

The *bombil* are dried on the sand on the sea-shore. The dried *bombil* lasts for more than a year. In earlier times, most of the Koli stayed in Mazagaon and fish was transported to Mumbai from that place. Therefore it was known as Macchi Gaon. This was then corrupted to 'Mazagaon' and is now in common usage; so says a Portuguese writer. Perhaps the original name of Mazagaon was indeed Macchi Gaon.

There have been two great fires in the Fort at Mumbai which caused a lot of destruction. The first was in 1802 when it started suddenly near Bazaar Gate where the Vani, Bhatia, Parsi, and Bohri people stay.[8] A description of the devastating fire was obtained from a member of one the ancient families of Mumbai. It describes the fire in detail and seems to have been written by a religious-minded person. It mentions that over half of Mumbai was burnt down and this is certainly true. At that time the area from the Fort to Mumbadevi was considered as Mumbai. In this composition, the poet has far exceeded his poetic licence. He says that this fire frightened the Gods and that the poet himself was in communication with the gods, Vishnu and Lakshmi. This is a gross exaggeration, and there are other mistakes of metre and composition in the poem but it does provide an example of old poetry as composed in Mumbai.

The cause of the fire could not be found but many strange theories have been propounded. Some say that when a woman was frying *wadas* on the third floor of a building, water suddenly fell into the frying pan leading to sudden outburst of flame which set the roof on fire. There is another account which says that this fire raged for ten days and consumed all the houses and property of the residents, destroying the entire assets of hundreds of people. The fire continued to smoulder for a period of six months after it was extinguished. A ninety-year old Bhandari woman who actually saw the fire still lives in the city and she gives two reasons for the fire. That year, there was wedding in the house of a Parsi gentleman, Ardeshir Dadyseth[9] and he spent over fifty thousand rupees to erect the most beautiful marquee, such as had not been seen since the Pandavas ascended to heaven. He spent thousands of rupees to get workers from various countries to build this marquee. When the Pandavas in heaven saw it, they were furious that they were in danger of being outdone in their splendour and would therefore be forgotten by the people! Their fury caused the fire!

The second reason concerns a Bairagi who had recently come to Mumbai. He continued to beg door-to-door for ten consecutive days but nobody was honourable enough to give him anything. This incensed him and he cursed the city and this caused so much destruction in the city! A Vani named Seth Ramdas was the only one who attended to his needs and sent him some food. He blessed him and advised him to abandon his residence and transfer all his property out of the Fort within two days. He then disappeared! There are many older people in Mumbai who believe in such nonsensical stories.

In 1822, bales of cotton stored behind the big church in the Fort caught fire and wreaked havoc in the city. In both these fires, Mumbai suffered a loss of over one crore rupees.

On 15 June 1837, a mighty storm raged over Mumbai. All the government offices and factories were closed in Mumbai. For a whole day, nothing functioned normally in the city. It rained incessantly and a strong wind blew away many houses, uprooted many trees, and hundreds of ships were rent asunder. Many boats were washed ashore. Quite a number of people lost their lives. Goods worth lakhs of rupees were lying in the waters around Mumbai. In the Fort and other places, there was knee-deep water. Mumbai really drowned on that day. It is said that the losses on this day amounted to thirty lakhs of rupees. A similar storm hit Mumbai on 1 November 1854 and was described in the Marathi newspaper *Chandrika*.

In this storm about two hundred people drowned in the harbour and about two hundred ships were destroyed along with their cargo. The loss has been estimated at thirty lakh rupees. There were further losses because of the loss of goods in the city. Thousands of coconut trees fell down, houses crumbled, and many warehouses were waterlogged. Perhaps the total losses in Mumbai must have been in excess of half a crore. Goods were floating in the water around Mumbai. The poor people would fill up baskets full of rice, wheat, millet and other grains, rotting coconut and cotton and spread them out to dry in the sun.

Every year there are fires in houses and markets, mishaps with boats in the harbour and similar calamities which cause a loss of around ten lakhs of rupees every year. By the grace of god, there is no permanent diminution in Mumbai's wealth. In fact, the losses are made up by more than ten times. In the year 1851, there were fifty fires.

In the fire of 1802, Sir Jamsetjee Jejeebhoy suffered great losses in property and wealth, so it is said. This reminds one of a puerile saying among the Kunbis: 'If fire destroys your house, your wealth multiplies, and if a tiger eats you, you become a king'. So be it. It is certainly true that in the city of Mumbai, the Parsis, and indeed all the traders, are prospering beyond measure. During the days of Deepawali, they spend a lakh or two in offering *pooja* and for charity without much thought. It is obvious that nobody would spend so much money at one go unless they have immense financial strength.

The people of Mumbai are very generous in some matters. More often than not, the Parsi people spend a lot of money on charity. In 1862, a Parsi gentleman conducted the *sadra* ceremony for his son; on this occasion, he kept aside one and a half lakh rupees for charity and his wife donated some ten thousand rupees on that day. In the previous year (1861), a meeting of the European and native residents of Mumbai was held in the Town Hall to discuss schemes to help assuage the suffering caused by the famine in the North-West Provinces. The military chief of Mumbai presided over the function. The relevant point is that within a period of fifteen days, a sum of one lakh rupees was collected for this humane task. Isn't this amazing! A Parsi gentleman offered 90,000 rupees as an interest-free loan to start the task of comforting the poor immediately and also contributed 1,000 rupees. In the entire province of Mumbai, a sum of over two lakhs of rupees was collected within three to four months. About six lakhs of rupees was received from England. The total money collected was rupees 851,838-3-11. A point to be noted here is that, unless prompted by the English, our people do not display qualities of compassion, munificence, and liberality. Among the Hindus, munificence is at a low ebb these days. And in direct proportion, their wealth is also being whittled away. There is a saying that goes, 'Be generous, be wealthy'. The generosity of the Parsis is worth describing. At a distance of about six *kos* from Mumbai, there is a village called Chembur in the Thane district. There is a small creek near this village which greatly inconvenienced the poor people and prevented them from moving easily in the neighbourhood. On hearing this, Dhanbai, the wife of the late Dhunjibhoy Nusserwanji Cama donated 15,000 rupees for filling up this creek and building a bridge with connecting roads. One can find hundreds of similar examples amongst these people. Seth Cursetjee Nusserwanji Cama spends hundreds of rupees every month to help poor students and other needy people in every way. In May 1862, news arrived from England of a famine in the district of Lancashire. A sum of 75,000 rupees was collected within fifteen days to alleviate their misery. The Parsis donated most of the larger amounts. On an average, about ten such subscriptions are made by the rich and generous every year on various accounts.

The Parsi community decided in 1862 that only those who had been educated according to their religious texts would be allowed to officiate in the positions of *andharu* and *dastur*. It was decided to establish a school to teach the scriptures, and once the children graduate from this school, they would be ordained as *dasturs*. It is said that Sir Jamsetjee Jejeebhoy's wife donated thirty seven thousand rupees for this venture.

Chapter 7

Order to kill dogs – Parsi Riot – Robbers and conmen – Gangs in the harbour – Mussalman Riots – Revolt of the army in Bengal in 1857 – Prayers – Prayer of the Mumbai people during England's war with Russia – Queen's Proclamation of 1858

An old government rule ordered the culling of stray dogs in the city every three to four months. Pursuant to this rule, notices would be stuck in all corners of the city or a general announcement would be made. Policemen and specialized dog killers would then roam the streets and kill any dog on which they could lay their hands to obtain a reward of eight *annas* per dog. This practice had been going on for many years. It is not possible to determine when this rule was enforced and why. All those who were asked were of the opinion that it had been in force for many years. A sixty-year-old man said that the rule was still new when he was fifteen years old. This means that the rule is about forty-five years old.

It is said that some years back a senior English Government official died after a dog-bite. On his deathbed, he gave a substantial sum of money to the government so that the interest on this sum be utilized every year to kill stray dogs which roamed the streets of Mumbai, terrorized the public, and attacked the passers-by. This practice has been going on for a long while. The dog squad would kill the dogs and show the carcasses to the Police Master to obtain their reward of half a rupee per dog. In this manner, about a cartload of dogs were killed daily. They would then be buried. Sometimes they were left on the roads to be removed by the garbage van after a couple of days. After a while, the Police Master ordered that once the dogs were killed, only the tails needed to be submitted to the government to obtain the normal reward, but this allowance was much abused. If a dog was encountered on the streets, they would cut off its tail and let it go. This led to reverting to the earlier practice. In 1830, Sir Jamsetjee Jejeebhoy, Seth Motichand Khemchand, Seth Devidas Manmohandas and many other Parsi and Dakshini *mahajan* approached the Sarkar jointly to request them not to kill dogs in this manner. It was suggested that they instead be captured and released elsewhere. This request was accepted for a few years. Dogs were captured and kept in a warehouse hired for the purpose. When the opportunity arose, they were loaded on to ships and sent away. This went on for a while. The dog squad would capture all the available dogs to obtain their half-rupee reward. They would forcibly enter gardens and courtyards of houses to take the dogs away. They had the government's orders, a police escort and the incentive of a reward. This was bound to happen! But the government's orders were clear; they were to capture only those dogs which had no owners and were roaming freely in the roads and lanes, and not those which were in gardens or houses.

The Vani and other Gujar people believe it to be an act of charity to take care of dogs and give them food and water. They were very upset to see dogs being treated in such a manner. They could not do anything because of the government. Amongst the Parsis, the dog is considered a holy animal, and it is required during the final rites. Just as a crow has to touch the offerings during a Hindu funeral, a dog is offered food during a Parsi funeral. They have a lot of devotion for dogs. They were very sad that the dog squad was capturing dogs right from the doorsteps of houses.

On the 7 June 1832, the Parsis called a strike in Mumbai and rioted. The reason given is that the previous day, the dog squad had entered the houses of many Parsis and had taken away their dogs. The Parsis entreated them not to do so, as it was against government rules, and asked them to release the captured dogs. The dog squad did not listen to them and walked away with the dogs. There were some skirmishes between the Parsis and the dog squad. It was then decided in a meeting of a hundred odd Parsis that all the food and grain shops would be closed on the 7 June, food supply to the English stopped, and a general strike be called. They indicated their programme to the shops inside the Fort and the bazaar outside the Fort. The only positive aspect was that the rich Parsis were not with them and were in fact unaware of their plans. Most of the rioters were of the lower class like cooks and water-carriers; there were also some middle-class gentlemen. On that day, they closed the shops, and stopped the supply of *roti* and bread which was being sent for the soldiers at Colaba. Many of the Khatki people did not support the strike; when they were transporting meat, they were beaten up and the meat was thrown into the moat surrounding the Fort. The Portuguese Christians, who supplied bread to the English regiments, were intimidated and their produce spoilt. In this manner, they continued till about ten in the morning. Their actions spread terror amongst the English. The Magistrate wrote to the Town Major asking him to send some troops as the Parsis were rioting. He however did not respond for a long time. The white regiment in Colaba did not receive the bread they were supposed to on that day. The English who were going to their offices were waylaid and many offices to open. They obstructed the vehicle of Sir John Awdry, the Chief Justice of the Supreme Court and threw some garbage and a dead goose into his vehicle. This was the kind of anarchy they perpetrated. The Magistrate arrested many of them and appealed to Sir Jamsetjee Jejeebhoy and other prominent Parsi gentlemen to control the situation. They tried to find ways to control the situation, but the rioters were so excited that they did not come to their senses. At about three in the afternoon, white troops from Colaba were stationed in the Fort with instructions to shoot if the incidents of the morning were repeated. The Parsi gangs were disheartened at the sight of the white troops; they dispersed and ran away. Many of them were strong and powerful but could do nothing against a regiment of white troops. Many of them were captured and jailed; some of them were sentenced for two to three years. The only bright aspect of these Parsi Riots was that there were no murders. These riots led to the Englishmen distrusting the Parsis for many years. This was resolved only when the English Sarkar was convinced that the upper class Parsis did not support the rioters, and were in fact, much against them. The Sarkar began to favour them in the old fashion and perhaps favoured them even more.

Currently, bullock carts with iron cages have been provided for the capture of stray dogs. They are then kept in the Panjarapole.

After the commencement of English rule in Mumbai, dacoity and banditry, and such other looting gradually stopped. But ordinary theft and crimes continued for many years. It is said that after nightfall, people would lock themselves into their houses out of fear of robbers and thieves. As they made their way back home in the evening, many were deprived of their *turbans*, and their jewellery would be snatched after they were beaten up. Not only did the pickpockets and scoundrels in the markets scheme to loot the poor, they would cause trouble for anyone who tried to stop them. Gangs of Memons and Khojas would roam around the Camp Maidan, Dongri and Khatki Bazaar trying to seduce people into gambling. They would proceed to cheat them in the process. Those protesting would be beaten up before the gangs made their getaway. Many a trader was robbed by rogues posing as cheap suppliers who snatched their money and scrambled away after terrorizing them. Many people even lost their lives. There was a gang which exclusively looted goods from warehouses at the dead of night. The story goes that the *mukadam* of this gang had around four hundred different keys;

at nightfall he would wear thirty odd golden rings on all his fingers, gather his gang, and step out with the bunch of keys hanging from his waistband. Using his keys, he would open whichever warehouse was full of valuable goods and loot it. If somebody tried to raise an alarm, he would silence them by dropping a couple of gold rings into their hands. He would then continue his looting without any fear.

About thirty-five years ago, a very strange and dangerous gang used to operate in this city which used to steal thousands of rupees from traders in broad daylight.

They operated in the following fashion. About ten to fifteen of them would rent a bungalow for around hundred rupees. One of them would pose as an English trader, but would not be seen in public. Others would pose as clerks, treasurers, and agents. They would invite businessmen to their lodgings and buy pearls, shawls, gold, coral and such other readily saleable materials on credit. If necessary, they would sell it cheap to some other trader and convert it back to money or distribute it amongst themselves. They would then sell the chairs, tables and other office paraphernalia at half price to some old furniture dealer and then disappear overnight. They would all vanish before the expiry of the credit period when the traders would arrive to recover their dues. Sometimes, they would pose as a Moghul, Nawab, or Raja and stay in a large estate. They would buy goods worth thousands of rupees under his name and then disappear in a similar fashion. There was no telling what their next criminal deception would be. These kinds of incidents have decreased of late, but there are still many scoundrels in operation. 'Where there is a village, there is a Maharwada'.

Another well organized mob of scoundrels who operated in Mumbai was known as the 'Bunder Gang'. It consisted of Khojas, Memons, Lavanes, Bhatias and people of other castes and numbered around three hundred people. Many of them were very rich and were otherwise considered reputable citizens. Their horses, vehicles and mansions were the very proof of their status. Many of them also owned large ships. They had employed many fishermen to carry on their underhand dealings. All their trade was conducted at night. They would unload tobacco and other goods bought from various places and would bring them into the city without paying customs duty. To ensure the smooth flow of operations, they had contracted a monthly sum with many constables, *havildars*, and many soldiers of the Police and Customs Departments. It is said that just as the government paid a monthly wage, they had a list of names to whom the salaries were regularly delivered every month. And at an opportune moment, they would steal goods from the docks. They would not spare boats either. They had spread a reign of terror in the Mumbai harbour, but for many years, there was no trace of them. The richest amongst them did not have to venture out of their houses; they would just get their cut of thousands of rupees every year. Any black deed, however stealthily done, is exposed in due course of time and God punishes the perpetrators sooner or later. Providentially, their operations were finally halted in 1843 when Captain Burroughs was the Chief of the Police Department. Many of them ran away and quite a few were arrested and sentenced to *Kala Pani*, exile in a distant island.

Every year or two, large ships laden with goods would suddenly burn down in the Mumbai harbour; however no cause could ever be ascertained. After a while, by the grace of god, the mystery was solved. The above mentioned gang would hire a large ship on the pretext of shipping expensive goods like opium and cotton to China or England. The ship would be insured for these goods and then they would load it with boxes of sand, mud, rubbish, nails, stones, rags and anything else they could lay their hands on. They would then insure it for a large sum like five or seven lakhs. After the anchors were hauled in and the ship had sailed some distance from the harbour, they would either try to burn or sink the ship. If it was successful, they would claim lakhs of rupees from the insurance company. They would take the Captain of the ship into confidence when they planned such activities. They would also corrupt many of the sailors under him and get the work done by them.

They were discovered in the following manner. In October 1842, many of the gangsters booked space in the ship named *Belvedere*, and as was their normal practice, loaded bales of rubbish on the ship which was insured for seven and a half lakh rupees. They bribed the Captain of the ship heavily to burn the ship at sea. When they got the news that the ship had burnt down en route to Singapore, they pressed their claims with the insurance company. However when the money was split between the gangsters, there was some disagreement and one or two of them went to the government and revealed the deception. When this came into the open, many of the gangsters ran away. The government rigorously pursued and arrested them and in October 1844 produced them before the Sessions Court. The trial went on for three days. Aluparu was sentenced to life imprisonment in exile, Shivaji Amal was sentenced to ten years, and Haji Bhogabhai was sentenced to one and half years hard labour in the new jail.

On 17 October 1851, the Mussalmans of Mumbai rioted at ten in the morning. The reason was as follows. A newspaper named *Chitradyanadarpan* was published by a Parsi; every issue contained a write-up of famous people with illustrations. In one of the issues, he wrote a small profile of the Prophet

Muhammad and published a drawing along with it. The picture of Muhammad was shoddily executed and a drop of ink on one of his eyes seemed to have blinded him in one eye. This picture was stuck on the door of the Jumma Masjid one Friday morning by a trouble-maker. When the Mussalmans emerged from the mosque after their Namaz around eleven in the morning, they were incensed by this caricature of their prophet. Believing that a Parsi wanted to insult their prophet, they decided to exact revenge. Hundreds of Mussalmans, screaming 'Deen Deen', rushed with clubs in their hands to wreak havoc on the Parsis. If they saw a Parsi on the roads, they clubbed him besides injuring many other bystanders. A couple of Portuguese were injured in the Camp Maidan. They could not be controlled by the policemen. Looting broke out in the Bazaar and shopkeepers shut their shops and ran helter-skelter. The Parsis were very frightened and many of them ran into their houses and bolted their doors. Gangs of Mussalman rioters roamed the streets. The city's *kotwal* tried to stop the riots but things did not cool down. The army was called in and stationed at various places and the number of police personnel was increased. On the Chowk near the Market, a small body of troops was stationed for a month. The rioting and destruction went on for over a month. In those days, children and women feared to venture out. The Parsis were much affected.

The hostility between the Parsi and Mussalman communities continued for over a year. It was not that there were scuffles and riots through the year but the Parsis were afraid to venture into the Mussalman *mohallas*. In the second year, the Police Commissioner, Secretary Lumsden, and other important government officials organized a meeting of the Mussalman and Parsi communities. The Kazi of the Mussalmans and other personages participated in the meeting. This facilitated in removing any misunderstanding between the two communities. The publisher of the picture was made to apologize and he admitted his folly and said that the incident was due to a lack of understanding. This ended the quarrel and the two communities have been united since then. On the day the reconciliatory meeting between the Mussalmans and Parsis was held, many prominent Parsi and Mussalman gentlemen drove in their carriages through the major streets and Mussalman *mohallas*. In each carriage were a couple of Parsis, two Mussalmans, and an English official. The *Dnyanodaya* had the following report on this incident.

The Gujarati magazine *Chitradnyanadarpan* published an article on the Prophet Muhammad along with a drawing of him pinned up by somebody near the Mussalman's masjid. Some ignorant Muslims felt that the Parsis had started abusing their prophet, and vented their ire on the Parsis. There has been an uproar during the last fifteen days, and there have been a few skirmishes between the Parsis and Mussalmans. It is not the fault of the publisher of *Chitradnyanadarpan*. He had extracted Muhammad's profile and the offending picture from an English book. He has the right to do this; if he had mischievously concocted the tale himself, he is liable to punishment but that does not seem to be the case. It is improper to use abusive language which may offend the religious feelings of people, and those who do so must be punished, but to indulge in rioting on that account is very unjust. If somebody has any grievances on any topic, he can appeal to the government which will investigate the matter and come to an appropriate conclusion. It is not that those who indulge in rioting will get away; they are going to get into deep trouble, and the government will punish them heavily.

It is worth contemplating the fate of the Parsis and others, if there had been a Muslim government in power. We should thank god that the present government is impartial and extend all support to the government.

The mutiny of the Bengal army in 1857 resulted in great losses to the *ryot* of Hindustan and the Company Sarkar. Most of the Black Troops in the Bengal Province rebelled causing considerable unrest. There were disturbances in Delhi, Lucknow, Ujjain and other places. Battles ensued in these places leading to the death of many English officials and hundreds of soldiers. The mutineers attacked English settlements and needlessly killed English women and children. These kinds of atrocities terrorized the whole of Hindustan. Even the people of Mumbai were reduced to a similar state. By god's grace, the troops in the Mumbai Province did not revolt and the residents of Mumbai were not in the least harmed. The Mumbai Sarkar controlled the situation in Mumbai very shrewdly. Though this mutiny had its origin in the Bengal Province, all of Hindustan had to bear the brunt.

The Sarkar had to spend over two crores of rupees to bring the mutiny, which extended over two years under control. Two individuals in the Mumbai armed forces were accused of conspiring with the mutineers; they were blown from the mouths of cannons in front of the entire troops at Camp Maidan. From the onset of this calamity till the time it ended, members of all communities offered prayers in their respective temples on three occasions to seek victory for the English, that their rule continue unharmed, and that they suffer no further setbacks. Once the mutiny was brought under control and English rule was established in various places, the businessmen of

Mumbai and the government declared a holiday in their respective establishments to express their happiness over the turn of events, and gathered in various places and temples to praise god and thank him for his kindness.

There was a battle between the English and Russian armies in Turkistan.[1] On this occasion, the government ordered that Sunday, 16 July 1854 be observed as a day of fast and prayer all across the Indian region to pray for the victory of the English army. In Mumbai, traders and *mahajans* from various communities like Prabhu, Parsi, and Shenvi prayed in their respective fashions. The participants in this prayer were those who considered themselves reformed. Though the Brahmins were not involved, the Prabhus and other communities invited *shastris* for prayers. Invocations in the form of poems to the formless god were composed and published.

During these prayers, *kirtans* were sung at Thakurdwar and Bhuleshwar, a *homa* was conducted at Mumbadevi, and similar events were held at other temples. Hindus even participated in the prayers of the Christians in their churches. Most importantly, a large number of Parsis collected outside their *agiaries* in a burst of enthusiasm and passion. They took the lead in showing that the Natives could out-pray the Europeans on this occasion. The prayers of the Parsis were mainly in the Avestan language but the meaning of one of their Gujarati prayers has been explained below.

O Almighty God! We pray to you that the Queen of this country be granted an honourable victory in the present fighting. The King of Kings should grant her army and navy special strength and wisdom, bless the Queen with a long life, and ensure the prosperity of her empire. God destroy her enemies and bless her fully. O God, please pay attention to all these matters and ensure their fulfilment and take the side of the Queen's armies in the battlefield to ensure their victory. We therefore pray to you sincerely to ensure the continuity of the just and generous rule of the Queen and that her fame continues for generations hereafter. We also pray that she continues to retain her status and majesty.

Though the Mussalmans did not do anything special on this day, they did not seem to have utterly forgotten Turkistan and England.

The prayers of the Jews was published in the *Vartamandeepika*.

'As per the instructions of the government, people of many communities prayed to God for the victory of the English Sarkar over the Russian Sarkar; the Israelis of Mumbai did the same.'

After the prayers were recited, all the Israelis responded by saying 'Amen'.

In the year 1855, the *ryot* of Mumbai celebrated the victory of the English people over the Russians and thanked God for the same.[2]

After the revolt had been suppressed and peace had been restored to all parts of the country, on 1 November 1858, the Queen issued a proclamation notifying that the government of Hindustan had been transferred from the Company Sarkar to the direct rule of the Queen. There was a lot of excitement in Mumbai and a huge meeting was held at the Town Hall. The proclamation was read out to the important people of Mumbai on that occasion. It was as follows.

PROCLAMATION BY THE QUEEN IN COUNCIL

ALLAHABAD, *Monday, 1st November 1858.*

The Right Honorable the GOVERNOR GENERAL has received the Commands of HER MAJESTY THE QUEEN to make known the following Gracious Proclamation of Her MAJESTY to the Princes, the Chiefs and the PEOPLE OF INDIA.

PROCLAMATION

BY THE QUEEN IN COUNCIL TO THE PRINCES, the CHIEFS and the PEOPLE of INDIA.

VICTORIA, by the Grace of God, of the United Kingdom of GREAT BRITAIN AND IRELAND, and of the COLONIES and DEPENDENCIES thereof in EUROPE, ASIA, AFRICA, AMERICA, and AUSTRALASIA, QUEEN, DEFENDER OF THE FAITH.

WHEREAS, for divers weighty reasons, We have resolved, by and with the advice and consent of the Lords Spiritual and Temporal, and Commons in Parliament assembled, to take upon OURSELVES the Government of the Territories in INDIA, heretofore administered in trust for Us by the HONOURABLE EAST INDIA COMPANY.

NOW therefore, WE do by these Presents notify and declare that, by the advice and consent aforesaid, We have taken upon OURSELVES the said Government, and We hereby call upon all OUR Subjects within the said Territories to be faithful and to bear true allegiance to Us, Our Heirs and Successors, and to submit themselves to the authority of those whom We may hereafter from time to time see fit to appoint to administer the Government of OUR said Territories, in OUR name and on OUR behalf.

And WE, reposing especial trust and confidence in the loyalty, ability, and judgment of OUR right trusty and well-beloved Cousin and

Councillor, CHARLES JOHN VISCOUNT CANNING, to be Our First Viceroy and Governor General in and over Our said Territories, and to administer the Government thereof in Our name, and generally to act in Our name and on our behalf, subject to such orders and regulations as he shall, from time to time, receive from Us through one of OUR Principal Secretaries of State.

And WE do hereby confirm in their several Offices, Civil and Military, all persons now employed in the Service of the Honorable East India Company, subject to OUR future pleasure, and to such laws and regulations as may hereafter be enacted.

WE hereby announce to the NATIVE PRINCES OF INDIA that all Treaties and Engagements made with them by or under the authority of the Honorable East India Company are by Us accepted, and will be scrupulously maintained; and WE look for the like observance on their part.

WE desire no extension of OUR present territorial possessions; and while We will permit no aggression upon OUR Dominions or OUR Rights to be attempted with impunity, WE shall sanction no encroachment on those of others. We shall respect the Rights, dignity, and Honour of Native Princes as OUR own; and WE desire that they, as well as OUR own Subjects, should enjoy that prosperity and that social advancement which can only be secured by internal Peace and Goods Government.

WE hold OURSELVES bound to the NATIVES OF OUR INDIAN TERRITORIES by the same obligations of duty which bind Us to all OUR other Subjects; and those obligations, by the blessing of ALMIGHTY God, WE shall faithfully and conscientiously fulfil.

Firmly relying OURSELVES on the truth of CHRISTIANITY, and acknowledging with gratitude the solace of Religion, We disclaim alike the right and the desire to impose OUR convictions on any of Our Subjects. WE declare it to be OUR Royal Will and Pleasure that none be in anywise favoured, none molested or disquieted, by reason of their religious faith or observances, but that ALL shall alike enjoy the equal and impartial protection of the Law; and WE do strictly charge and enjoin all those who may be in authority under Us, that they abstain from all interference with the Religious Belief or Worship of any of OUR Subjects, on pain of OUR highest displeasure.

And it is OUR further will that, so far as may be, OUR Subjects, of whatsoever Race or Creed, be finely and impartially admitted to Offices in OUR Service, the duties of which they may be qualified, by their education, ability, and integrity, duly to discharge.

WE know and respect the feelings of attachment with which the NATIVES of INDIA regard the lands inherited by them from their ancestors, and WE desire to protect them in all rights connected there with, subject to the equitable demands of the State; and WE will that generally, in framing and administering the Law, due regard be paid to the ancient Rights, Usages, and Customs of India.

WE deeply lament the evils and misery which have been brought upon India by the acts of ambitious men who have deceived their countrymen by false reports, and led them into open rebellion. OUR Power has been shown by the Suppression of that Rebellion in the Field, we desire to show OUR Mercy by pardoning the offences of those who have been thus misled but who desire to return to the path of duty.

Already, in one Province, with a view to stop the further effusion of blood, and to hasten the pacification of OUR INDIAN DOMINIONS, OUR Viceroy and Governor General has held out the expectation of pardon, on certain terms, to the great majority of those who in the late unhappy disturbances have been guilty of offences against OUR Government, and has declared the punishment which will be inflicted on those whose crimes place them beyond the reach of forgiveness. We approve and confirm the said act of OUR Viceroy and Governor General, and do further announce and proclaim as follows:-

Our clemency will be extended to all offenders, save and except those who have been or shall be convicted of having directly taken part in the murder of British subjects. With regard to such the demands of justice forbid the exercise of mercy.

To those who have willingly given asylum to murderers, knowing them to be such or who may have acted as leaders or instigators in revolt their lives alone can be guaranteed; but, in apportioning the penalty due to such persons, full consideration will be given to the circumstances under which they have been induced to throw off their allegiance, and large indulgence will be shown to those whose crimes may appear to have originated in a too credulous acceptance of the false reports circulated by designing men.

To all others in arms against the Government, WE hereby promise unconditional Pardon, Amnesty, and Oblivion of all Offences against OURSELVES, OUR Crown and Dignity on their return to their homes and peaceful pursuits.

It is Our Royal Pleasure that these terms of Grace and Amnesty should be extended to all those who comply with their condition before the FIRST Day of JANUARY next.

When, by the blessing of PROVIDENCE, internal tranquility shall be restored, it is OUR earnest desire to stimulate the peaceful industry of India, to promote works of public utility and improvement, and to administer its Government for the benefit of all OUR Subjects resident therein. In their prosperity will be OUR strength, in their contentment OUR security, and in their gratitude OUR best reward. And may the God of all Power grant to Us, and to those in Authority under Us, strength to carry out these OUR wishes for the good of OUR people.

The said proclamation was read out by the Oriental Translator Mr. Vinayakrao Vasudeoji. It was greeted with tumultuous applause.

The *ryot* of Mumbai greeted this proclamation with a festival of lights and by hanging festoons at various places. The Sarkar had declared a holiday for two consecutive days for these celebrations which were fully utilized by the public. About four to five lakh rupees must have been spent on this occasion in Mumbai. About seventy thousand rupees worth of coconut oil was burnt on that day. Lamps had become so expensive that many of the richer men had to rent them at the rate of ten rupees per hundred; large chandeliers were hung on the roads.

The English had fought at Mysore, Assaye, Bharatpur, Kabul and other places in connection with the Mumbai Province, and had emerged victorious in all, but this kind of excitement had not been seen before. It compared with the celebrations held in London when Lord Nelson returned home after winning the Battle of the Nile.

The Kabul War started in 1839.[3] The Company Sarkar suffered huge losses in this war. Many of their war heroes were killed. In the same war, Sir W. H. Macnaghten was killed in 1841. When this gentleman was in Kabul, he had been nominated for the post of the Governor of Mumbai, and he was about to leave to join his post when he was killed by the Afghans. When the English captured Kabul in 1842, they brought Dost Mohammed Khan's son, King of Kabul to Mumbai along with the booty of gold, silver, and gems worth around twenty lakhs of rupees; this was exhibited in the Town

Hall for over a month. Thousands of people thronged the place every day to see the jewellery. Each ring was studded with gems weighing over Five *tolas* and was worth over a thousand rupees. All the jewellery was auctioned off. When the silver door of the Somnath Temple, which was ransacked by Mohammed during his attack on Gujarat in A.D. 1024 and taken away to Ghazni and installed in his masjid, was finally brought back to Hindustan, it sadly did not generate this kind of enthusiasm in Mumbai.

In 1858, during the mutiny, a lot of jewellery, pearl necklaces and other ornaments of the royal family were brought to Mumbai and exhibited in the Town Hall for the benefit of the public. The collection included diamond necklaces, each of which was said to be worth over thirty thousand rupees. All of this was also auctioned off.

Chapter 8

Governors and their deeds – Efforts to increase trade – The Number of traders –
Establishments – Brief history of the famous businessmen Sir Charles Forbes and
Sir Jamsetjee Jejeebhoy – Government revenue from the city – Number of houses
and revenue therefrom – New taxes and the reasons for levying them – New notes –
Government order rescinding license tax

In 1661, Mumbai was transferred by treaty to Queen Infanta Catherine, wife of Charles the Second, King of England. In the same year, the Earl of Marlborough arrived as the representative of the King in a fleet of ships under the command of Sir Andrew Shipman to stake claim on the island; they arrived in the harbour on the 17 September of that year.[1] They had an order from the Portuguese Government addressed to the Chief of the Portuguese Sarkar in Mumbai commanding him to hand over possession of the island to the English. Accompanying them was a Portuguese noble who was to convey the same instructions orally. The Portuguese stationed in Mumbai wanted to retain control of this island and raised a few objections to the transfer; only Mumbai would be transferred and Sashtee would be retained by them. The Earl of Marlborough indicated that, as per the original treaty, Sashtee was also part of the transfer along with Mumbai. The second objection was that as the order issued by the Portuguese King was not in order as per custom, they were unable to hand over the island to the English. This prompted the Earl of Marlborough to find a harbour where he could drop anchor. Sir Andrew Shipman, also referred to as Sir Abraham Shipman, was nominated as the first Governor of the island, but that was not fated to happen.

As the five hundred white sailors on the fleet were beginning to suffer, Sir Andrew Shipman landed on the island of Anjediva (Adyadeep), about fifteen *kos* distant from Sadashivgad near Goa. This was a small island where they camped. Leaving Sir Andrew Shipman and the troops here, the Earl of Marlborough took the ships back with him to England. Not having proper houses to protect themselves from the elements, the marooned troops suffered a lot during the monsoon and also became prone to diseases. About three hundred of the troops including Sir Andrew Shipman died here.

When the news of the death of Sir Andrew Shipman reached England, the King of England nominated Humphrey Cooke as the Governor of the island, and ordered him to take possession of the island with the help of the remaining troops.[2] He came here in February 1665 and took possession of the island. He however had to accept various conditions stipulated by the Portuguese Chief, but he ensured that he took possession of the island and established his government here. Humphrey Cooke was soon after accused of furthering his private interests and had to resign. Sir Gervase Lucas who was named in his stead assumed command of the island on 5 November 1666. After his demise, his Second Captain, Henry Gary took over the position of Governor on 21 May 1667. He was the last Governor to be the representative of the King of England. Believing the island to be of not much use, the King handed over the island to the Company and since then, the Company has nominated the Governor.

To administer the island of Mumbai, nay the entire Mumbai Province, the English Sarkar nominates a Governor from the city of London. To run the government, employees civil, judicial, and military also come from the same place. The Governor is named by the main government in England for a period of five years. He gets an annual salary of one lakh twenty thousand rupees, besides twenty-five thousand rupees for other expenses. He has two official residences, one at Parel and other at Walkeshwar. He also has a retinue of servants, a chariot drawn by four horses, and an escort of horse-riders provided by the government. His gates are always patrolled. He stays for a few months each at Walkeshwar and at Parel, and in Poona during the monsoon season of four months. From there, he proceeds to Satara and Ahmednagar for a few days each, and comes back to Mumbai in November. He is assisted by two or three others in his administrative activities. The Chief of the military, who is nominated in England, gets an annual salary of fifty thousand rupees. His chariot is escorted by a team of horse-riders and sentries are posted to patrol his house. A lot of money is set aside as travel expenses.

While the military Chief's command extends only to the armed forces, he is the second-in-command after the Governor in the Council. Though he does not have any civil responsibilities, the post draws an annual salary of sixty thousand rupees, and a rental allowance of three thousand six hundred rupees. Two other people, with many years of experience and well-versed in civil administration are nominated by the Governor to the Council and are known as Councillors. They receive an annual salary of sixty thousand rupees each and have men patrolling their houses. These officials get together to deliberate on matters of government. Officials are named to the revenue, army, law, health, ecclesiastical and education departments and they receive salaries ranging from five hundred to three thousand rupees. Non-gazetted officers are also named by them. The Governor can also take over the responsibilities of the Commander-in-Chief. A few years ago, these four met in a Durbar every Thursday afternoon in the Town Hall for consultations on matters of government. This is known as the Council where the Secretaries present official papers for consideration. The practice of meeting in the Town Hall has stopped for the last ten years. The meeting used to be conducted in the Governor's residence for a few years. Papers relating to matters under discussion and any decisions to be taken are circulated amongst each other.

A list of the names of the Governors nominated by the King of England and the Company Sarkar since they took possession of the island of Mumbai is given below.[3] In the last two hundred years of political administration, fifty individuals have discharged this function. Many of them have been very kind to us, and we should remember them for that.

Appointed directly by the King of England

Humphrey Cooke	1665
Sir Gervase Lucas	1666
Captain Henry Gary	1667

Nominated by the Company Sarkar[4]

Sir George Oxenden	1668	Richard Bouchier	1750
Gerald Aungier	1669	Thomas Hodges	1767
Sir John Child, Baronet	1680	William Hornby	1776
John Hawks	1690	Rawson Hart-Boddam	1784
Bartholomew Harris	1690	Andrew Ramsay	1788
Bartholomew Ansil	1692	Sir William Meadows, K.B.	1790
Sir John Gayer	1698	Sir Robert Abercrombie, K.B.	1790
Sir Nicholas Waite	1702	George Dick	1794
Sir Henry Oxenden, Baronet	1707	John Griffiths	1795
William Aislabie	1709	Jonathon Duncan	1795
Charles Boone	1724	George Brown	1811
William Phipps	1731	Sir Evan Napean, Baronet	1812
Robert Cowan	1734	The Honourable Mountstuart	
John Horne	1734	Elphinstone	1815
Stephen Law	1739	Sir John Malcolm, K.C.B.	1827
William Wake	1742	Sir T.S. Bakewith, K.C.B.	1830
John Gicki	1742	John Romer	1831

Sir Robert Grant, G.C.H.	1835	The Honourable Lestock Robert	
James Farish	1838	Reed	1846
Sir James Rivett-Carnac,		George Russell Clark	1846
Baronet	1839	Lord Viscount Falkland,	
Sir W.H. Macnaghten,		G.C.H.	1848
Baronet	1841	The Right Honourable John Lord	
Honourable George William		Elphinstone, G.C.H.	1853
Anderson	1841	Sir George Russell Clark,	
Sir George Arthur, Baronet	1842	K.C.B.	1860
		Sir Henry Bartle Edward Frere	1862

Sir George Russell Clark handed over the post of Governor on 24 April 1862 and left for England. Sir Henry Bartle Edward Frere, earlier a member of the Council at Calcutta, was nominated to this position. He came to Mumbai from Calcutta on 22 April 1862 by ship. The nomination of Sir Bartle Frere to the post of Governor of Mumbai Province was welcomed by the *ryot* of Mumbai as he was known to further the interests of the *ryot* and had spent many years in the Administrative Department in Mumbai Province. During his earlier tenure, he had shown many examples of his generosity and compassion. When the Governor first alights from his craft at Palo Bunder, he is accorded a seventeen gun salute. The road from Palo Bunder to Churchgate is lined with both black and white troops to welcome the Governor. The top officials from both the civil and military departments and important traders of the city are presented to him. This Governor landed at Palo Bunder at around two in the afternoon; as it was very hot at that time of the day, the kind Governor called off the parade of the military and went to the Walkeshwar residence of his brother W. E Frere, Councillor.

On the appointment of Sir Bartle Frere as Governor of Mumbai, an Englishman under the name 'Well-wisher' published a poem in the English *Guardian* newspaper in praise of the Governor.

Prior to the Honourable Mountstuart Elphinstone, many of the Governors did much for the welfare of Mumbai city; but they were all overshadowed by the improvements undertaken by Elphinstone Sahib. Only Duncan and Hornby Sahibs still manage to shine out from amongst the rest.

As the embankment at Worli was built during the administration of Hornby Sahib, it has been named Hornby Vellard. The huge building in front of the docks which houses the Supreme Court was built by him.[5] This is his private property and is huge and brings in a monthly rent of 1,800 rupees. It has been named as the Hornby House. A road in the Fort has been named after him. It has been difficult to determine the builder of the official building in the Fort which houses the Secretarial offices, but many say that it was built by the Portuguese Sarkar. The Governor used to stay in this enormous building earlier. When Duncan Sahib built the Governor's residence at Parel, this building was vacated. During the tenure of Mountstuart Elphinstone, the Secretarial offices were located here. The building at Parel is also vast and sprawling. It was originally built by the Portuguese as a residence for the holy men of their religion, according to popular opinion. At any rate, it came into prominence during the reign of Mountstuart Elphinstone. It has been refurbished completely to bring it up to date. The facilities inside the building are worth seeing. The residence at Walkeshwar was also built by Mountstuart Elphinstone Sahib. This building is not a very big one, but has an excellent location.

The harbour, the houses for the military at Colaba and Fort, Bellasis Road, the new road to Mahalaxmi, now known as Duncan Road, and the embankment at Sion were all built during the tenure of Duncan Sahib. He also undertook many other works for public good. He tried to put an end to the practice of infanticide prevalent among the Rajputs. He had a great affection for the natives, and as he was very devoted to the Brahmins, he has been referred to by Sir James Mackintosh as the Brahminised Duncan on some occasion. Sir Evan Napean was the Governor in 1812. While it is said that he did a lot of work for the benefit of the people, he is not very famous. A possible reason for his obscurity can be related to the fact that the people of Mumbai were not very appreciative of the deeds of the English in those days unlike now. Mumbai was in its heyday during the tenure of Mountstuart Elphinstone and all the tasks that he undertook have ensured that he will remain immortal. He laid a very strong foundation for the kingdom and most of the Governors who have come after him have modelled themselves on similar lines, and have perforce adhered to the style set by him. Sir John Malcolm continued in the same pattern as Elphinstone Sahib. In his speeches made at various gatherings, he had this to say. 'It is indeed very harmful to the English to work against the interests of the natives. No English official is to believe that since he is an Englishman and has a position in government, and as the English are in power, there is a vast difference between him and the natives, and that he need not be amicable with them. Nobody is to carry this impression. They should interact with each other with a clear conscience.' On one occasion he mentioned that he was once so proud of his position that he felt it beneath his station to associate with the rich natives; but experience had taught him that it was profitable to maintain equitable relations with the native people. It is best for the ruler and the ruled to deal with each other with an open mind so as to engender confidence and affection in each other. He made many such advisory speeches.

When the English first took possession of this island, the threat of the Marathas prevented many people from settling here. But the English did not trouble anybody on matters of religion and allowed everybody to practise their religion freely. This only led to an increase in the population of the impoverished, scoundrel and good-for-nothing sort, with no increase in the revenue. The Governors of those times therefore had to devise plans to attract the rich folk and businessmen to come and settle in the island. They negotiated with the rich and skilled people of Goa and other provinces and agreed to their conditions to make them settle in Mumbai. Christians from Goa would come here to make socks which were purchased and sent to the Court of Directors in England. They devised many such schemes. They got a prominent Vani trader from Daman named Nima Parakh to come and settle in Mumbai, on the condition that a separate area would be demarcated for the settlement of Vanis, that no Mussalmans and Christians would be allowed to reside in their neighbourhood, and that their religious practices would not be hampered.[6] In a similar fashion, many other prominent people were induced to settle on the island. From that time, separate places must have been demarcated for the sale of fish and meat, and traffic of fish, alcohol and similar items was prohibited through the Bazaar Gate as Vani, Bhatia and Marwadi traders used to reside there. This practice is still continuing. The law relating to the prohibition of transporting fish and meat in an uncovered manner through the city must also have been enacted at that time. Even today if these products are carried around, they have to be wrapped in cloth or paper.

Bearing in mind that to increase the number of traders, trade on the island had to increase, Bartholomew Harris wrote in 1690 to the Company Sarkar in England that if prominent traders are to be attracted to Mumbai, customs must not be levied on certain goods, and at concessional rates on some others and the security of their goods must be ensured. Certain concessions were therefore made. For the first two or three years, customs duty on certain goods was waived for traders. There were other reasons for the population of Mumbai not increasing. The Siddis of Janjira, the Angrias of Alibag and Sawants of Wadi used to regularly attack the island. They would camp on the islands of Kaneri-Huneri and Chinaltekdi and if an opportunity offered itself they would raid the ships in Mumbai harbour and loot whatever was available. They would also enter Mumbai and rob the residents. Shivaji also mounted attacks occasionally. These sudden raids made rich people hesitate to settle with their property and children in Mumbai. When Charles Boone became Governor in 1724,[7] he strengthened the Fort and set up patrols against the Siddis of Janjira and other pirates. From that time on, traders, businessmen and other rich men slowly started flocking to Mumbai. The first to arrive were the Parsis from Surat. They were followed by the Vani, Bhatia, Lavane, Khoja, Memon, Bohra, Kutchi, Marwadi, Arabs and traders from the Southern provinces who came to conduct business transactions in Mumbai. Earlier, the employees of the Company Sarkar traded on their personal account and this deterred the other traders from entering the market. To combat this problem, it was decided that government employees should not trade on any account. The first English traders to establish offices in Mumbai were Forbes, Leckie, and Remington.

Sir Charles Forbes was the principal owner of Forbes & Company. Not only was he very shrewd and well-versed in business, he also worked for the welfare of the natives and held them in high esteem. The establishment of his office in Mumbai was very beneficial to the traders of Mumbai and other people. His wealth was legendary and it was said that his business turned over crores of rupees every year and his treasury held lakhs of rupees. He used his influence in the English Sarkar, for the benefit of the natives. The advancement of many natives can be traced to his arrival in Hindustan. He treated all the clerks and workers in his establishment very well and kept them happy. He died in November 1849. In conclusion, this Sahib was generous, kind, wise and behaved in an impartial manner. At the time of his death, he willed a large part of his wealth to all his employees and when he was alive, he would send them annual gifts of watches, pens, silver snuff boxes, or exquisite pieces of cloth. Including the clerks and others, the total number of employees in his office exceeded a hundred. He started the practice of paying his retired employees a pension, which continued to be given to their wives after their death; this has been continued by his heirs and partners to this day. This philanthropic gentleman gave a sum of twenty-five thousand rupees to the Court of Directors to help them find a solution to the problem of water scarcity faced by the residents of Mumbai. He also donated a similar sum for the building of a home for the poor. This has been described at the appropriate point. His statue has been placed next to the statue of Malcolm Sahib and on his seat it says the following.

SIR CHARLES FORBES, BARONET

The Disinterested Benefactor
of the native inhabitants of this island,
and the tried and trusted friend
of the people of India.

Erected
In Token of Esteem and Gratitude
By
The native inhabitants of Bombay.

1841

The offices of the more important English traders number fifty one, that of the Yahudis twenty, the Mussalmans thirty nine, the Parsis fifty eight, and the Hindus, Gujar, and Dakshini people number two hundred and nine. Of the Dakshini people, the most famous establishments are those of Baba Sahib Diwanji (Angre), Gopalrao Mairal, and Daji Sahib, a trader from Indore. Traders of the medium range, *shroffs*, shopkeepers, agents, moneylenders, artisans and the like number seven hundred and twenty five, comprising people from all castes, especially Parsis and Vanis. Shopkeepers, traders, and artisans of the ordinary sort number over eight to ten thousand.

In most of the offices, Parsis function as agents and earn commissions worth lakhs of rupees every year. Amongst the traders, there are many Parsis, Khojas, Memons, Bhatias, and Vanis. One rarely comes across a Dakshini Hindu trader. In recent years, Khojas and Memons have become substantial traders in Mumbai with business running into lakhs of rupees. Only amongst the Dakshinis, the desire and ability to do business has been steadily declining. Amongst the native traders, Sir Jamsetjee Jejeebhoy is clearly the shining star. He has been to China five times. He has also visited Calcutta and Sinhaldweep (Sri Lanka). This famous gentleman has earned lakhs of rupees through trade by his own efforts. The brief biography of this philanthropist which follows has been taken from another book.

This prominent Parsi was born on 15 July 1783 in a village called Maleshwar situated in Navsari Mahal of Gujarat Province. Sir Jamsetjee's father's name was Jejeebhoy Chanjeebhoy and his mother's name was Jivanji. Though he was poor, Jejeebhoy was highly respected in Maleshwar. In his sixteenth year, he lost both his father and mother in the span of less than a year. His parents sent him to Mumbai when he was still a child; he stayed at the residence of his father-in-law Seth Framji Nusserwanji Batliwala. At that time, Nusserwanji had set up a small shop for selling bottles in the Fort in which he was assisted by Jamsetjee. Jamsetjee picked up the Gujarati and English languages and script along the way. In the year 1799, he worked under his maternal cousin Meherwanji Manikji Seth to learn the ropes of the business. As the above-mentioned gentleman traded with China, he had to go there frequently. Jamsetjee went to China for the first time with Meherwanji Seth in 1799. After his second visit, he acquired enough knowledge of business to start a business in partnership with his father-in-law, Framji Nusserwanji Seth. Though they did not have more than two thousand rupees, he managed to accumulate a capital of over thirty five thousand rupees due to his business acumen and the help provided by his father-in-law.

While his father-in-law was stationed in Mumbai, Jamsetjee made frequent trips to China. Once while returning from China, he rescued men who were fighting the French from a battleship owned by the East India Company. A battle ensued between the English and the French on his ship in which the English were victorious, much to the relief of Jamsetjee. During the big fire of 1802 in Mumbai, Jamsetjee lost some of his goods, which caused him some distress.

Jamsetjee made a total of five trips to China and the last one was in 1807. He did not travel thereafter. With Mumbai as his headquarters, he conducted trade with China, Calcutta, Singapore, Siam and other countries. Others could hardly be expected to match his prowess in trade. Between 1807 and 1842, he earned a tremendous amount of wealth, and his fame spread across many countries.

In 1822, Jamsetjee paid off the debts of many poor people in Mumbai and freed them from the debtors prison; this was his first act of benevolence. From then on to the present day, his generosity flows like a stream, and just as the river is very small near its source, but increases in size along the course of its run, his generosity seems to know no bounds with each succeeding year. We do not have the full details of his philanthropic activities, but it has been estimated that he has spent 3,500,000 rupees on charity in his lifetime. His good deeds and desire to improve the lot of his native country led the former Governor Sir James Rivett-Carnac to recommend him to Her Majesty Rani Sahiba who conferred the knighthood on him in 1842, which gave him the title of 'Sir'. In 1843, the Queen presented him with a plate studded with gems. In 1858, he was awarded the title of Baronet, which is hereditary in his family. This prominent man died on 15 April 1859 at the age of seventy six. There was hardly a person who could match him in a population of 250,000,000 in an area extending from the coast of Arabia to China.

As is the practice amongst English nobles, his eldest son has inherited the name and the title from his father and has therefore been named Jamsetjee Jejeebhoy, Bart.

On this topic, the *Dnyanaprakash* from Poona has published the following article.

Sir Jamsetjee Jejeebhoy, Knight

Sir Jamsetjee Jejeebhoy, Knight who has been most generous and kind, worked for the welfare of his countrymen and has been ever ready to solve their problems. He has, in his old age, devoted himself entirely to do deeds for the benefit of the public. It is appropriate that we think of ways in which the memory of this 'Friend of the World' can be perpetuated. This thought occurring to many of the reputed citizens of Mumbai, a meeting was called for on 24 June 1856 at the Town Hall.[8] The assembly included the Governor of Mumbai, all senior government employees, prominent traders and other Hindus and Parsis. The kind Elphinstone Sahib was in the Chair. The government Secretary, Anderson Sahib and Jagannath Shankarseth made speeches reviewing the charitable deeds of this gentleman and paid the most glowing tributes in an entertaining and appropriate manner. After listening to their speeches, a collection was mobilized and 25,000 rupees were collected. It was decided that the amount collected would be used to erect a marble statue of this gentleman in a proper place. This statue was commissioned in England in 1860 and is presently installed at the Town Hall.

The bank in 1720

The English had managed to collect traders and businessmen of various castes from numerous places. These included the *shroffs* and *nanavatis*. The *shroffs* would charge exorbitant rates for bills of exchange and if somebody was unable to discharge their obligations they were charged five rupees per hundred, besides a very high rate of interest. This led the employees of the government to call for a meeting on 25 July 1720 of all the English and native traders in the city to establish a bank. The bank was entrusted to two gentlemen named Mr. Brown and Mr. Philip, a capital of one lakh rupees was collected, and all arrangements for the functioning of the bank were made. This pleased the businessmen of the day. They also agreed to pay an extra tax of one percent on their assets to ensure the security of this establishment. Its scope of activities included accepting and providing bills of exchange, and providing mortgages on houses, estates and other movable and immovable property. The Governor and two members of the Council were designated as the presiding authorities of the bank. It was decided to pay an interest of two *pice* per day per hundred rupees on sums deposited with the bank. On the 12 December 1720, a public proclamation was made with drums to announce the establishment of the bank. However, as it was not properly managed, money was lent without any security and could not be recovered leading to substantial losses. The immovable property which had been procured as security also turned out to be unremunerative and this led to the closure of the bank in about four to five years.

In 1840, the Bombay Bank was established. It was initially capitalized at 5,225,000 rupees but it now has over three crores of rupees at its disposal. There are seven such establishments in Mumbai. Besides, the government, in a spirit of public welfare, has established a savings bank to encourage the poor to save money, to ensure the security of their savings, and their prosperity. Sums ranging from one rupee to fifteen hundred rupees can be deposited here. An interest of four per cent is paid annually. Deposits can be withdrawn at any point of time. People have deposited thousands of rupees in this establishment.

If one wants to get a feel for the rate at which trade in Mumbai has prospered, a study of the following figures will be useful. In 1814, goods worth 926,980 rupees arrived in the port of Mumbai from other countries while in 1862 it was 218,556,797 rupees and goods worth 212,999,605 rupees were exported. Opium itself accounted for a third of the exports. In 1678, the customs duty on all goods was about thirty thousand *ashrafies* and tobacco, snuff, marijuana yielded twenty thousand ashrafies, amounting to a total of around 24,000 rupees.[9] In 1860, collections worth 28,516,143 rupees were made. In 1859, the yield from all the houses and lands in the island of Mumbai was 5,413,465 rupees. The government stamp duty was five per cent leading to a collection of 270,673 rupees. The rateable value was 6,119,210 rupees in 1860 yielding a stamp duty of 359,600 rupees. Thus the yield in 1860 was 35,000 rupees higher than that in 1859. The output from all other activities has also increased in the same proportion. The government earns an income of two lakhs of rupees from just tobacco, snuff, and marijuana. In 1860, horses worth 1,599,000 rupees were imported from Iran, and the value of dates, almonds, pistachios and other dry fruits was 717,315 rupees. 7,556 vessels, both large and small, called on the port at Mumbai and 6,066 vessels embarked from Mumbai.

The income of the railway company from the railroad after accounting for all expenses was rupees 363,299-12-11 for a six month period. The weekly revenue from the transport of people and the movement of goods is about 48,000 rupees. In this fashion, the monthly revenues, since regular services have started is about two lakhs of rupees.

In this minuscule island of Mumbai, there are 16,941 buildings including palatial mansions and five-storied buildings known as *chawls* in which fifty odd families can stay. The practice of levying stamp duty on houses was started in Mumbai in 1688 by the Company Sarkar. The income to owners of immovable property from just the Walkeshwar area is 159,965 rupees annually. Prior to 1800, many of the large mansions in the Fort and outside it were built of wood.

The number of two-wheeled and four-wheeled vehicles owned by the English and the natives, and registered with the government is 2,668. 532 vehicles are available for hire and there are 30,508 horses. There are 640 bullock-carts and 6,551 hand-carts for transporting goods. The total number of vehicles are 10,361. The total number of *palkhis*, both personal and available on rental, is 400. The government earns a stamp duty of 156,730 rupees annually on these vehicles. All these figures relate to the year 1860.

Licence fee for selling alcohol – 59,922

Licence given by the police to sell alcohol – 7,859

Issuing public proclamations with drums on behalf of people – 3,202

Stamp duty on weights – 934

Tickets issued to hand-carts – 1,608

Fees for issuing licence numbers to vehicles – 191. All these figures are for 1860.

The Municipal Commissioner and other departments collect revenue for the management of the city and deposit it every three months. In 1860, between January and March, a sum of rupees 609,063-15-7 was collected and for the period from April to 17 July, the collection was rupees 582,311-14-3. During this six month period, a sum of rupees 726,567-3-10 was spent on the upkeep of the city by this establishment.

In 1860, the English Sarkar introduced two new taxes. It has been indicated that one of them will be in force for five years. Anybody having an annual income ranging from two hundred to five hundred rupees will have to pay a sum of two rupees per hundred and those having an annual income in excess of five hundred rupees will have to pay a sum of four rupees per hundred to the government every year. It is not possible to estimate the revenue which the government will generate from this 'Income Tax'. Perhaps the sum will be in the region of 2,000,000 rupees from Mumbai alone. The sum from all the territories of the Company Sarkar in Hindustan is estimated to be 19,100,000 rupees. It has also been estimated that the government will have to spend a sum of seven to eight rupees per hundred to recover this tax. The second tax known as the Stamp Act was introduced in the month of October; documents relating to any transactions, bills of exchanges, *et cetera* with a value ranging from ten to fifty rupees will have to be affixed with a stamp of half an anna, and for transactions exceeding hundred rupees, a stamp of one anna will have to be affixed and the documents will be legally valid once the signature has been made over the stamp. Somebody has said that the businessmen of Mumbai bought stamps worth thirty five thousand rupees on the very first day. It has been estimated that this tax will generate an income of around thirty to forty lakhs of rupees from this city. Many have got licences from the government to sell stamp paper and stamps. They have established shops at various places to sell the stamp paper and stamps.

A third new tax called the Licence Tax was introduced in 1861 which was applicable only to those who did not pay Income Tax. It was decided to levy a tax on all ordinary traders, artisans, and workers who had the capacity of earning less than two hundred rupees annually at the rate of 3, 2 or 1 rupees depending on his earning capacity. It was indicated that this tax would be levied for five years. It was however suspended within the year in 1862.

'People are requested to pay their taxes to ensure that those who toil to keep you trouble-free become debt-free and the Sarkar will recognize your gratefulness and loyalty and this will enthuse them to work for your eternal well-being.' *Vartmandeepika.*

The following article on the necessity of paying tax has been taken from the *Dnyanaprasarak.*

There seems to be a lot of misunderstanding amongst the ignorant about the tax to be paid by us to the government. They are under the impression that the government is oppressing them by levying this tax and the tax or levy paid to the government is a waste. We do not apparently get anything in return for the payment of taxes which are paid only under threat from government. We have no connection with the government and it is just a tyrannical burden which has been imposed on us. This is certainly a grave mistake. The government has neither meant it as a burden nor an imposition but as something which is absolutely necessary. In return for the taxes paid to the government, what we get back in return is certainly worth a lot more. Spare a thought to those lands which have no government and one realizes the benefits of having one. In certain parts of Arabia and in some countries of Africa there is no governmental authority. All men have to be permanently armed in these places as they are infested with robbers and dacoits. One never knows when one is going to be robbed or an attempt made on one's life. In such countries, a farmer has to take an armed companion to work his fields, else he may be robbed off his seeds, or his bulls taken away, and perhaps he may lose his life. In other words, two men are required to do the work of one – one to work the fields and the other to defend him from robbers. And even this may not be enough to protect him. Gangs of marauders may attack both the farmer and his guard and take away all their belongings. In an island called New Zealand groups of four or five people build small cabins in remote and inaccessible places and plant stakes all around to protect themselves from marauders. This has not prevented such incidents from occurring. In such countries, there is strife all around. Peace and happiness are available to none, and there are a thousand obstacles to work. Nobody is sure that their labour will yield fruit, and whether they will be able to enjoy the fruit of their labour. It is more likely that the opposite will happen. This leads to very few industries and most people are deprived of an opportunity to enjoy worldly pleasures. Most of the land is fallow and the population is very small. People belonging to better classes have to struggle for food and clothing while those in a very wild state also have to suffer similarly. The reason for their troubles is man's ignorance and the insecurity of property.

The solution for providing means of security to men and property is called government. Government is that which maintains order amongst the people and protects them from each other and foreigners and this obviously implies that they have some rights over the people. The prime function of government is the protection of the land and its people giving rise to the Sanskrit saying which goes 'Protector of the land is the King of the people'. This shows that from ancient times our people have had a very good understanding of the role of the government. Alas! Our contemporary Hindu Kings have completely forgotten this fact!

To discharge its responsibilities, the government employs servants (and in certain cases, maintains an army) to protect the land and its people from foreign enemies; and maintains a police and legal system to protect people from each other and thieves. They also have to maintain many other employees.

The expenses which are incurred in maintaining these employees are financed by collections from the public, and this is a fair arrangement as these employees are maintained for the welfare of the people. People therefore pay tax and land revenue to the government.

We are not doing anything particularly excessive, but just reimbursing the government for expenses incurred by them in our service and for protecting us. This is similar to us paying any person in our employment or paying for any goods that we have purchased. In case we do not discharge our obligations to the government, and they are unable to protect us, the country will be reduced to a wild state like some of the other countries mentioned before and each farmer will have to make his own arrangements for security, which is not only very inconvenient but also very expensive. Half of our income will be spent on security, an amount far larger than what we currently contribute to the government. That this security will be inadequate and transient is obvious from the situation of the wild people mentioned earlier. It is certainly true that not all kings protect their subjects in a similar manner. There have been many kings, who instead of protecting their subjects, indulge in various acts of tyranny and kill thousands of people. However, it is better to have such kings than be ungoverned. Even the most excessive regimes in the history of this earth or the worst which can be imagined are a thousand times better than a state of anarchy. While the people in such states may well be in a state of peril, they are certainly more secure than those in a wild state. There have also been many other governments which exact more money from the people than is spent on their welfare and spend it in a dissolute manner. Even these governments extract far less money from the people than what they would have spent in an ungoverned state. They may have to pay a fifth of their income to the government, which is still five times less than the expense they may have incurred (as mentioned earlier) if there had been no government at all. This government may be a source of trouble and loss to the people but these troubles are nothing compared to those the people have to suffer when there is no government.

Those who are grumbling about the payment of money to the government can now understand the necessity and usefulness of having governments. The government renders service to us in return for money collected. In case the government does not render these services, how are we to stay in this country? If there is no police to catch thieves and rogues, and no judges to try them and pronounce sentences, there will be a spate of robberies in every village. If there is no army to protect the country, foreign enemies will invade the country and destroy it. For these reasons, we, the *ryot* of this country should not grumble about paying taxes to the government. It is working for our own good. The people should monitor the usage of the money given to government and if it is not used appropriately, they should (if possible) take the matter up with government. To do this, the people should possess wisdom, strength and patriotism. It is not possible by the ordinary man. People of merit discharge this function in the European continent.

Many governments exact excessive taxes from their *ryot*, while some tax them very lightly. It is not as if those who levy more taxes are governed better, neither is it that the *ryot* which pays higher taxes becomes impoverished. As a government establishes methods for the security and protection of the *ryot*, and gives more attention to the people, their expenses increase. And governments have different policies. The population in Hindustan is five times that of England, but the income of the government in England is twice that of Hindustan. We can conclude that an individual in England is taxed ten times more than an individual in Hindustan. However nobody can conclude, that the regime in England is unnecessarily harsh or that the people of England are more impoverished than the people in India. On the other hand, the government in England is a lot more compassionate than the one in India, and there is no doubt that the people in England are a thousand times richer than the people in India. As there is a higher volume of general activity, including trade, art, and culture amongst the people of England, their government has to employ more people for their security, and as the people are very industrious, they can afford to pay the higher taxes. The taxes we had to pay during the earlier Maratha regime may well have been more than the taxes we pay under the current English regime. In spite of that, everybody will have to accept that the security of life and property was far less then than it is now. There were many raids and robberies, leading to a huge loss of life and destruction of grains and property. Things have changed now. And unlike the earlier government, the present government is paying a lot of attention to the education needs of the *ryot*. But obviously, this government will need more money for its activities. The salaries of the English employees in Hindustan is very high, possibly the highest among all countries, and most of this money is sent out of the country, which is certainly a grave loss to us. It is not the fault of the English Sarkar as these employees come from foreign countries, and return home after their term of employment. This is because the English people behave as visitors and the English Sarkar has no other option until our people are ready to take on bigger responsibilities.

We are ourselves responsible for the levy of the three new taxes on us. If the revolt had not happened in 1858, these taxes would not have even occurred in our dreams. It has to be said that the teaching of the wise that our troubles are the results of our own actions is certainly true word-for-word.

In 1862, the Sarkar introduced money in the form of notes. These notes are in denominations of ten, twenty, fifty, hundred, five hundred and, thousand rupees. These were printed in Vilayat. Earlier, only banks issued notes and they could perform business transactions exchanging lakhs of rupees. This duty has been taken over by government. The government has introduced notes worth a total of four crores and ten lakhs in all the three provinces of Mumbai, Calcutta, and Madras. These are like credit notes payable to the bearer and have the same currency as coins in all areas under the English flag. From 1862, the government has entrusted the management of the treasury and the management of notes in Mumbai to the Bombay Bank.

Between 1859–60, the total income to government from the Mumbai Province was 72,776,640 rupees and it spent 95,690,110 rupees, leading to a deficit of 22,319,470 rupees in the accounts of the government. The government has had to introduce these new taxes to balance deficits that have been increasing every year.

Between 1861–62, the revenue earned by the government from Income Tax and Stamp Duty in the Mumbai Province excepting Sindh, Nagpur, Mewad, and Baroda was as follows.

Income Tax	rupees 4,235,108
Stamp Duty	rupees 2,945,686

Duty on salt, tobacco, opium and other materials amounted to 37,897,259 rupees and the expenses of this department was 1,359,236 rupees. In the year 1862, there was increase of around ten crores in the volume of trade just in the city of Mumbai. The trade in this city has been rapidly increasing.

There are about 137 offices in Mumbai to run the affairs of the civil, military and other departments. They are mainly managed by gazetted English officials. Below them are about five thousand clerks educated in English and workers who earn anything between ten to eight hundred rupees a month. These include Brahmins, Shenvis, Prabhus, Sutars, Vanis, Parsis and people from almost all castes. All the transactions in these offices are conducted in the English language and script.

After the arrival of the English, there has been an onset of the competitive spirit in business, a spread of education, an increase in knowledge, a propensity towards generosity, and a desire to do charitable works.

The English possess many territories in the Asian and other continents. But there is no other place like Mumbai which has benefited from their government and has reached the pinnacle of trade and prosperity. Perhaps, the island of Mumbai is the origin for the fame and success of the English in all other countries, and they are duty-bound to ensure its proper protection and security. The English will not be much affected by the loss or destruction of other cities, but any disaster in Mumbai will certainly affect the grandeur of the English in India. Most of the people in Mumbai desire from their deepest hearts that the English rule be permanent here, and if god ensures their supremacy forever, they will be happy.

As there was an increase in the government's revenue, the Licence Tax was abolished by government in 1862 in the light of the difficulties experienced by the people.

The former Governor General of India and the Queen's Viceroy, Charles John, Viscount Canning Sahib took the initiative to exempt the *ryot* of India from the Licence Tax. This Sahib was a well-wisher of the natives and undertook many projects for their welfare; after concluding this final task, he resigned his position and left for England in 1862. He died within a few months of reaching England. The news of his death was received sadly by the people of Hindustan. In order to perpetuate his memory in this country, the people of Calcutta have decided to collect money for the installation of his statue at a prominent place.

Chapter 9

*Supreme Court and other courts – Legislative Council and High Court –
Marwadi, Doctor, Gandhi, Vaidya, et cetera – Learned Brahmins, Vaidic et
cetera – Balgangadhar Shastri – Dispensaries – Hospitals – Dharamshalas –
Water – Establishment of post – Steamships – Telegraph – Establishment of the
Elphinstone School and other education departments – Newspapers – School for
girls – School at Poona – Desire to learn English*

Given the large population of Mumbai, it is but natural that one should
wonder about the administration of law in this city and by whom it is
implemented. There are four courts in Mumbai – a High Court, a Small
Causes Court and two Magistrates.

The Supreme Court hears civil cases above five hundred rupees and
criminal cases of all types. A session is held every three months when a
bench of two judges pronounces verdicts on criminal cases. The Chief Judge
is paid sixty thousand rupees annually, while his deputy gets fifty thousand
rupees. This department has many other employees. The Supreme Court
was established in 1830. Until some years ago, three judges were nominated
to this Court. Between 1806 and 1830, the judging authority was known as
the Recorder's Court while the one which operated from 1775 to 1805 was
referred to as the Mayor's Court. The Small Causes Court has three judges
and hears only civil cases ranging from one rupee up to five hundred rupees.[1]

It has been decided that the judge of the Supreme Court should reside in
Mumbai for seven years. After completing his tenure, he returns to England
and receives an annual pension of ten thousand rupees. If he leaves about a
year or two earlier for any reason, his pension is reduced to seven thousand
rupees. A junior judge on the expiry of his term receives a pension of seven
thousand rupees. If the Chief Justice expires within six months of his arrival
in Hindustan, his family receives a compensation of one lakh rupees, and if
death occurs within twelve months, they receive fifty thousand rupees. The
Queen's Government nominates this judge and therefore the court is known
as the Royal Court.

As mentioned earlier, there are three Magistrates in the Small Causes Court and the division of work amongst them is as follows. The Chief Magistrate has his office in the Fort. Two Magistrates sit in this office while the third one has his office in Mazagaon. Minor criminal offences are heard and sentenced in this court. Serious offences like murders are given an initial hearing and evidence is recorded and forwarded to the Supreme Court for the verdict. When the session is held, a jury of twenty-four individuals comprising *mahajan* from all castes examines all the evidence which has been collected regarding the criminal cases. After considering all the evidence, they decide whether a particular case can be decided or needs to be investigated further during the session. The *mahajans* are known as the Grand Jury. After examining the cases, a judge and a jury of twelve people pronounce their decision on them. They are known as the Petty Jury. The police commissioner, who is known as the Police Master, heads the Police Department. There are about seventy-five English constables to assist him and manage the force comprising of mounted police, police constables, and *ramoshies* totally numbering one thousand and eighty two. The Sarkar spends a sum of 228,382 rupees annually for their expenses. Besides, there are a thousand other *ramoshies* on loan from the police force who are posted at the houses of the English and rich native gentleman. They have to be paid seven rupees every month, while the Sarkar is to be paid half a rupee every month. Police inspectors and constables have been posted at various places and *chowkis* have been established at road corners. The police patrol the streets throughout the day and night. Mounted police roam the streets during the day. If somebody is spotted indulging in mischief, his hands are bound behind his back and he is led away.

The Company Sarkar has established a court called the *Sudder Adawlat* in the island of Mumbai but this hears cases from the mofussil districts of the Mumbai Province. The Company Sarkar has named three judges to this court, a Councillor being one of them. In this department, fifty to sixty thousand civil and criminal cases are heard every year. In 1860, fifty thousand cases were examined.

The Sheriff maintains his offices in the Supreme Court at Mumbai. He has constables and English officers working under him and all the prisoners in criminal and civil cases are entrusted to him. They are dealt with further depending on the sentence. A fee has to be paid to the Sheriff for civil cases.

There are two Sheriffs – the Chief and his Deputy. The post of the Deputy Sheriff is a permanent one with a salary of three hundred rupees per month. The Chief Sheriff is named on the first of January every year at the pleasure of the Governor. He is paid an honorarium of three hundred and fifty rupees per month, in addition to his fees. The post of the Sheriff is mostly conferred on English people. In the fifty odd years since Sheriffs have been nominated, Parsis have been nominated only twice; firstly Seth Bomanji Hormuzji Wadia and then Manekjee Cursetjee.[2] He does get a payment from the Sarkar, but from the fees to be paid to the government in civil cases, he can retain two rupees per hundred. As the number of cases in the court increases, the income of the Sheriff goes up. In earlier times, he could retain five rupees per hundred. However, after Sir Erskine Perry, in 1850, increased the limit of the cases that could be heard by the Small Causes Court from hundred rupees to five hundred rupees, the income of the Sheriff's office has drastically shrunk.

In the period from 1840 to 1850, the income of those who assumed the Sheriff's office was 114,284 rupees. The Deputy does all the work in this office, while the Chief Sheriff enjoys a sinecure. He has to be present only when the court is in session or for some very urgent work. The Governor has been given powers to nominate persons of his acquaintance at his sole pleasure. Between 1840 and 1850, Mr. Rivett was the Sheriff thrice and earned 41,310 rupees during this period; one can estimate the number of civil cases that are heard by the Supreme Court by just this figure. There are lawyers and barristers in this court; all cases have to be initiated through them and these worthies charge mind-boggling fees. If the case is complicated, it may drag along for ten or twenty years and the fees may run into thousands of rupees. Many have become bankrupt in the process. There were ten barristers and twenty lawyers in this court in 1862.

A few years back the Supreme Court was hearing a dispute between two brothers. As this case dragged on for many years, one of the brothers had to put up surety for over one lakh of rupees towards fees for lawyers and barristers and other expenses. He finally died a sorry death as a debtor, but the case continued to drag on. Filing cases over minor domestic quarrels in the Supreme Court has destroyed many families. At least on this count, our people should be very careful and ensure that such quarrels remain within the house. Two Moghuls have been fighting a suit in the Supreme Court concerning a business transaction; it has been about fifteen to twenty years since this case has been filed and it is said that both parties have spent over ten lakhs of rupees in the process; the case is still in the preliminary stages and nobody can guess when it will reach its conclusion.

In 1861, there was a case in the Supreme Court concerning a Maharaja from Gujarat.[3] In a Gujarati newspaper edited by Karsandas Mulji, an article was published finding fault with the Maharaja's behaviour in a certain matter. The Maharaja, Jadunathji, alleged that Karsandas had falsely accused him and this had caused a consequential loss of over fifty thousand rupees; he filed a case in the Supreme Court accusing Karsandas of slander and asked him to produce proof of his accusation. This case created a furore amongst the Bhatia and Lavane people for quite a while. There were many reputed Vanis and Bhatias who supported the defendant, but the supporters of the Maharaja conspired to call for a meeting in which it was decided that none would bear witness against the Maharaja, and if anybody did so, he would be treated as an outcaste. As the details of the Maharaja's thoughtless behaviour were publicized through this case, many of the Vanis and Bhatias were disgusted by the facts. The defendant, Karsandas filed an appeal with the Magistrate in the criminal court that the conspirators were preventing people from giving evidence in a case being heard in the Supreme Court, and asked for redress. This case was examined by the Police Department and sent to the Supreme Court for the verdict. The result was in favour of the plaintiff and all those who were guilty were fined sums ranging from five hundred to a thousand rupees.

The Maharaja's case was heard in the Supreme Court in February 1862. Both parties presented reputable men from the Vani, Bhatia, Brahman, Shastri, Prabhu, Parsi, Shenvi and other castes as witnesses. The case was heard in the Supreme Court for twenty-two days. There were over fifty witnesses for the plaintiff and the defendant. People thronged the Court to hear the case and there was no standing space. For a couple of days, the doors had to be closed before the case could be heard. Fearing possible riots by the Vani and Bhatia supporters of the Maharaja, English officers patrolled the place. The bench consisted of both the judges. Both the plaintiff and the defendant had engaged two lawyers and barristers each. They would present their arguments and ask the witnesses various questions relating to the practice of religion. Occasionally, a barrister would speak for six hours at a stretch to present his client's case. The audience was eager to hear these speeches and the legal agreements. It is certainly very profitable to listen to these orators. One should, of course, have a good knowledge of English. It is said that the parties spent over fifty thousand rupees during the hearing. When the case was being heard, the defendant had to pay the court fees of three hundred rupees per day.

The hearing ended after twenty-two days. However the judgement was not delivered until two months after the hearing. The population of Mumbai, perhaps all of Western Hindustan, from all castes like Brahman, Kshatriya, Vaishya, *Shudra*, Parsi, Mussalman, Yahudi, and English were eager to hear the outcome of this case. For a couple of months, this case was the talk of the town in Mumbai and exposed the Hindu religion to public scrutiny.

The judgement of this case was delivered on 22 April 1862 by a bench consisting of both the judges. Crowds thronged the Court to hear the judgement. The Chief justice first read out his opinion; and just said that as Karsandas could not back up a few of his statements, he pay five rupees as compensation to the Maharaja. The rest of the case was decided in favour of the defendant. The junior judge completely favoured the defendant. He sang the praises of Karsandas's deeds from the judge's seat for over two hours. His oratory, his legal mind and his gravitas impressed all the worthy people assembled there. After the conclusion of his speech, the barristers and other prominent people congratulated Karsandas Mulji. The Maharaja's party distinctly paled. It is said that the Maharaja had to incur an expense of over fifty thousand rupees in this case. The following article was published in the newspaper *Dhumketu* on 25 April 1862.

'In our earlier issue, we had indicated that this case will conclude on the 22nd of the current month. The two judges of the Queen's Court read out the judgement on that very day. People had gathered in the court since eight in the morning, and by eleven, there was an unprecedented crowd in the Court. The crowd consisted of people from all castes and religions – Hindus, English,and Parsis, with Bhatias accounting for a large proportion. Our readers already know that in this case, Karsandas Mulji, the proprietor of *Satya Prakash* had in his paper accused the Maharaja of bad and immoral behaviour. The Maharaja filed a case of slander against the defendant Karsandas. Of the eight points of complaint referred to, he could prove four of them; however the Maharaja was ordered to bear the expenses of Karsandas. As he could not prove the remaining four statements, the defendant Karsandas was fined five rupees.'

A fee of twelve rupees per hundred had to be paid for cases filed in the Small Causes Court, but that has been reduced since July 1861. The revenue from this department was huge and as a huge surplus had accumulated with the Sarkar, they reduced the fees. This is certainly a very praiseworthy decision. In 1860–1, 17,673 cases were decided in this Court and the total fees collected and remitted to the Sarkar's treasury was 115,061-8-10 rupees. The income of this department has rapidly increased. The annual expense of the Court including the salary of the judges and other expenses is eighty thousand rupees. It is not necessary to hire a lawyer or a barrister to file a case in this Court. However, if the case is complicated, some people hire a lawyer for about a hundred rupees. The use of a lawyer is entirely optional and depends on the party. The surplus generated from this department after deducting all expenses in 1861 was 32,830-12-3 rupees.

On Thursdays, the Petty Session is held in the office of the Senior Magistrate by a bench comprising the Senior Magistrate, an English Justice of the Peace and one of the Native Justices of the Peace. They hear ordinary criminal cases and are empowered to hear cases relating to theft of sums less than twenty rupees and can award sentences ranging from six months hard labour to a fine of up to a hundred rupees. Judgements on simple cases are delivered every day by all the three Magistrates, and more serious cases are sent to the High Court for further examination.

There are two hundred and fifty Justices of the Peace, both English and native. The Sarkar in England confers this title on wealthy and reputable people. Their powers are limited to maintaining order in the city. They are expected to monitor the funds spent by the government in maintaining the city and listen to any complaints received from the *ryot*. They are the representatives of the Queen monitoring the affairs of the city. No compensation is received from the Sarkar for their services. They have to ensure the happiness of the *ryot* and ensure that the dispensation of justice is fair. In sum, they have to strive for cleanliness and order in the city. Native people have been awarded this honour for the past thirty years. They can assume the title of Esquire upon being designated as a Justice of the Peace.

In 1858, the total number of cases relating to murder, robbery and other criminal cases decided in the courts of the three Magistrates of the Police Department was 15,873, and the total number of people convicted in these cases was 27,142. A total amount of money stolen in various incidents was 171,203-8-10 rupees; and sums worth 73,747-2-6 rupees were returned to the owner after the robber was caught. The fines levied on the accused amount to over thirty thousand per year. In October 1860, the total fines levied on criminals in the Magistrates' office amounted to 3,730 rupees.

In 1860, 21,906 cases were examined in the Magistrates' court of the Police Department and of these 6,386 men were released as their cases could not be proved. The others were convicted and various punishments were awarded. The cases from people of various castes was as follows:

Hindu	13,174
Mussalman	5,643
Parsi	983
Native Christians of various castes	962
European	934
Mixed castes of various types	210
Total	**21,906**

Amongst the Hindus are 1,130 women who have been criminally charged. There are women from other castes too, but not as many. The women in this city are a brazen lot and as there are no proper laws to restrain them, they behave in a rampantly shameless manner. This is a major shortcoming of the English law.

At the end of May 1862, 382 people of various castes had been jailed for criminal cases, both at the Old Jail and the New Jail, many of them sentenced to hard labour, while some have been sentenced to simple imprisonment. There are people who have been sentenced to periods ranging from fifteen days to two or three years and there are prisoners who have been sentenced to *Kala Pani*. If there is an increase in the number of prisoners, and there is a shortage of space, they are sent to jails in the districts of Thane, Poona, and Ratnagiri. Hard labour is exacted from them and they are made to work on building roads. They are also used to transport stones and to pound lime for use in the construction of government buildings.

Before the establishment of the Recorder's Court, if anybody had to be sentenced heavily, a public proclamation would be made in the city, and he would be exiled and dropped off at places like Panvel, Alibaug or Uran. This was the *Kala Pani* of those days![4]

In 1861, 16,200 people died on this island. These included 8,949 men, 6,914 women, and 337 children who died at birth. Of these 10,559 were buried, 4,736 were cremated and 905 were consigned to the *dokhma*, these being Parsis. In the same year, 11,000 children were born.

Every year, new laws are introduced by the English Sarkar in the city of Mumbai and in all other territories in the Indian subcontinent that are under the English flag to maintain law and order. The administration is done according to these laws. These laws are made at Calcutta. A separate committee of eleven people has been designated for making laws. Of these, there are three Englishmen from each of the provinces of Mumbai, Calcutta and Madras who have been in the service of the government for many years and are familiar with the modes and traditions of the people of these provinces. Each of these gentlemen is paid five thousand rupees monthly and they jointly make new laws. They act as representatives of these provinces. If a new rule has to be enacted in a particular area, the representative of that province prepares the first draft, which is then examined and finalized by the committee. It is then presented to the Governor General for his approval after which it is published in the Government newspaper or Gazette along with translations in the local languages to publicize it amongst the people. It is implemented three months after the publication. A copy of the new law has to be sent to the

Parliament for its approval. Even if a minor law is to be introduced in the Mumbai Province, it has to be first approved by the Calcutta Sarkar before it can be implemented. The approving committee consists of the Governor General, the Chief Justice and the Commander-in-Chief of the Bombay Army.

The Panchayat of the Parsi people has drafted a set of laws relating to the settlement of domestic disputes among the Parsi people and has sent it to Calcutta through the offices of the Mumbai Sarkar. The committee has approved these rules. The Parsis have been very shrewd in drafting these laws, and as the Governor General has approved them, they have to be considered as good. A committee consisting Sir Joseph Arnold, Seth Rustomji Jamsetjee Jejeebhoy and five other prominent people has been set up to further examine these laws.[5]

It has been the desire of the people for many years that the law making committee include educated and scholarly native gentlemen to ensure that the new laws are acceptable to the people. The English Sarkar has recently fulfilled this desire of the people. The committee for making laws for the Mumbai Province met in the Fort on 22 January 1862. The committee consisted of the following gentlemen – the Governor of Mumbai and the President of the Council; the army Chief of Mumbai and Second- in-command in the Council, Sir William Mansfield; M. R. Westropp, Esquire, Government lawyer in the Supreme Court, Meherban Abdul Dulerkhan Abdul Kherkhan, Nawab of Savanur; Shrimant Madhavrao Vittal Vinchurkar; the famous Seth Rustomji Jamsetjee Jejeebhoy; the Honourable H. W. Reeves, third in command in the Council; the Honourable W. B. Tristram, Esquire; and Shrimant Jagannath Shankarseth, merchant of Mumbai. The new members have been given the title, Honourable.

It is hoped that this committee will work for the welfare of the country and the respect of the native people will be restored. Our people have to show their abilities and pay attention to the welfare of the common public in the belief that the public's welfare is their welfare; but many of our people are of the opinion that their personal welfare amounts to the welfare of others. Only if this does not happen will the *ryot* benefit. An article was published in the *Dnyanodaya* on this subject and most of it has been reproduced below.

Some time back, the Parliament in Vilayat felt that the different provinces of Hindustan should have councils that are law-making bodies and these should include representatives of the *ryot*. Among the subjects of the Hindustan Sarkar, the businessmen, landlords and other white people are to be represented by the Sahibs, and the native people are to be represented by the native gentlemen to form the Council and all the laws that are required to administer Hindustan are to be framed with their consent. Based on this guidance, our celebrated Governor General Lord Canning Sahib made proposals that have been recently implemented. These councils have been started in places like Calcutta and Mumbai and its members consist of European and native gentlemen.

This is certainly an epoch-making event in the history of Hindustan. It would not be wrong to say that no law-making body had been established until now in this country. In the earliest times, hardly any king framed rules for governance and administration of the country; they therefore descended into despotism, tyranny, and misrule as a natural consequence, and their subjects had to bear the brunt of this oppression. There have been quite a few kings who have been wise, thoughtful, kind, philanthropic, and well-mannered; and they have undertaken many tasks for the welfare of their subjects. And even if the king was stolid or careless, if his minister or chief was wise, kind, and of proper deportment, the subjects have lived in a state of happiness and prosperity. It was however unlikely that any laws were framed for the administration of the kingdom. How then could law-framing bodies come into existence? Many kings seem to have governed by some codes of governance; not ones framed by themselves but those laws, codes, and rules framed by Manu, Vidur and other legends. It is not the purpose of the present book to evaluate the appropriateness or lack thereof of these rules and codes. The only point to be made is that the ancient rulers of this land did not have law-making bodies.

It hardly requires mentioning that the recent Maratha and Mussalman kingdoms also did not have any law-making bodies. The Emperor at Delhi, Akbar Badshah had many scholarly and talented people in his court. They however did not have any administrative responsibilities. A group of nine wise men at his disposal were known as the Navratna or Nine Gems. He did not get them to frame laws but consulted them on various delicate and critical issues. He and his ancestor, Timur have written books pertaining to law but these are not laws made by committees, but by themselves. The Raja of Satara had eight ministers who were referred to as the Ashta Pradhan.

'Pradhan, Amatya, Sachiv, Mantri,
Sumant, Nyayadhish, Nyayashastri,
Senapati, the chief among them;
Ashta Pradhan valued most by the King.'

These eight ministers do not seem to have made laws, else these laws would have been famous among the people. History would have recorded these laws but that does not seem to be the case. These eight ministers were allotted eight different portfolios.

It has been the practice of the advanced races of Europe to appoint law-making committees. This practice was, to some extent, followed in the ancient states of Greece and Rome, but it was very common in the German countries even prior to the Christian era. In course of time, England adopted this practice. If representatives of the *ryot* are present in the court and if laws are made with their assent, it is likely that the *ryot* will be happy as these representatives will take care of their interests. The people of England, with a view to protect their freedom and happiness, confronted the government and won a hard-fought right to elect their own representatives. It was then noticed by the king that the people accepted the laws enacted with the support of these representatives and the taxes levied with their assent. Experience had taught them that administering the country with the help of these elected representatives was not only beneficial to the *ryot*, but also useful to the government. In the country of the United States in America, this committee runs the administration on the most proper lines and their people are very satisfied. In many countries of the European continent, this mode of governance is being put into practice. But many countries still have no idea of the benefits of this practice. While the populace of many other countries continue to fight with their governments, sometimes putting their lives at stake for this right, it is certainly the good fortune of Hindustan that due to the generosity of the Parliament in Vilayat, and without any effort on the part of the people, the representatives of the people will become members of law-making bodies, which was not the case before.

While it is certainly beneficial for both parties to obtain the assent of representatives while framing new laws or levying fresh taxes, it is imperative that these representatives be elected by the people and they should have the freedom to express their views on what is beneficial to both parties. If this is not the case, it does not matter if this committee exists or not.

We also feel that each class or caste of people should have one representative in this Council, that is one representing whites who are not employees of government, and one each for the Hindus, Mussalmans, Parsis, Israelis, Portuguese, and native Christians. This will be most proper.

In 1862, the government of England decided to merge the *Sudder Adawlat* and the Supreme Court to establish one higher legal authority to be named the 'High Court'. These courts have been established at Calcutta, Madras, and Mumbai. It started in the month of July in Calcutta. While fifteen judges can be appointed to this court according to the law, thirteen English and one native gentleman have been named. The court was established here in Mumbai on 14 August 1862 and seven judges have been appointed. If one of those nominated belongs to our race, it will be miraculous. The salaries of the judges named to the Calcutta High Court are as follows. The Chief Justice get seventy-two thousand rupees per month while the other judges get fifty thousand rupees per month. If the Chief Justice is appointed in England, he gets relocation expenses of ten thousand rupees while the other judges get 8,000 rupees per month.

Given the density of the population in Mumbai, it is natural that one wonders about the arrangements made for the medical treatment of so many people. The wise people have said that if proper arrangements for treatment are not made in a place, it is not worth staying. There is a Sanskrit *shloka* on this subject which advises a friend not to stay in a place which does not have *shroffs*, *vaidyas*, learned Brahmins and a river with sweet water.

All these four factors are present in Mumbai from the most inferior grades to the most superior. Not only are there many rich and generous *shroffs* in Mumbai, there are many minor roving Marwadi *sawakars* who number over one thousand five hundred and who roam from door-to-door with their books. These Marwadis lend amounts ranging from eight *annas* to over ten to fifteen thousand rupees to people. They seem to have a facility and the courage to lend money. However poor, down-and-out or bankrupt one may be, they are willing to lend some amount of money. In return they expect a ten for a one or maybe a twenty-five for a five. There have been instances where a sum of four rupees has been lent, made up to five rupees using their *sawai* practice of adding a quarter to the principal, and four different bonds are issued. If the money is returned in five days, then five rupees have to be given, twenty-five if returned after a month, fifty after two months, seventy-five after three months, and hundred after four months. In this manner, bonds worth two hundred and fifty-five rupees are issued for a four-rupee loan and there are takers on these terms. Sometimes, they try to enforce all these four bonds and try to cash them and if there is any life left in the debtor, he is squeezed out completely while they extract their money.

The Marwadi people have come to this city from Marwar. When they first came here, they did not bring any money, capital or goods with them. The only possessions they carried with them were about a rupee for travelling expenses, a brass bowl, a vessel of dried white gourd known as *tumba*, a white shawl or woollen blanket and a stick in their hands. A Marwadi man having absolutely no acquaintances in Mumbai takes on a menial job in a shop for an annual payment of fifty rupees. After working for a couple of years, and once he has accumulated around fifty odd rupees, he rents a small shop in some narrow lane for a couple of rupees a month and arranges his baskets full of goods there. In some cases, he initially buys grains or jaggery worth a rupee or half and roams the streets of the city to sell it. In the evening, when the lamps are being lit, he hawks coconut or groundnut oil. Some of them sell spices and *masala* in the morning rounds and oil in the evening rounds. They thus accumulate about a hundred rupees by hawking goods like onions, garlic, turmeric and anything else they can lay their hands on. They then lend sums of five to ten rupees on terms varying from one-and-a quarter, one-and-a-half and double interest rates. They build a network of acquaintances through the money-lending business. People begin to treat him with respect and address him with deference as Thakarji, Jethaji or Motiji. He then sets up a larger shop with about a *sher* or two each of rice, wheat, *moong, urad* dals, *et cetera* and a few jars filled with oil, *ghee*, sugar and such like. He also sets up a small wooden box on a piece of *khadi* cloth on which are arranged loose change worth a couple of rupees. He thus runs two businesses from the same shop – selling grocery and lending money. And as his capital increases, he builds up the stock in his shop. He gets a partner, lends money on interest and then there is no stopping him.

Within a couple of years, he has accumulated a capital of over five thousand rupees. If he runs his business smoothly for about ten years, he easily becomes a wealthy man worth twenty thousand rupees or more. And then all sorts of freeloaders and low life flock to him and sing his praises. They borrow money from him at one-and-a-half and double rates. If a piece of jewellery is worth five rupees, he offers two rupees as loan against it. If one's clothes were in tatters, he would only give a loan of three rupees against a security worth ten rupees and charge excessive interest besides. And if these goods are not redeemed within the agreed period, they are immediately sold for cash.

They live in the most frugal manner and they exercise excessive economy in matters of food and clothing. A couple of white *dhoties* or *panchas* would suffice for a year or two; a piece of cloth about ten hands long could easily serve as a *turban* for about ten years; and if it gets dyed once in a few years, that is quite a bonus. A thick, coarse vest will serve to cover the body for over two years, and it most likely would have about ten patches with oil stains and dust all over. He hardly needs the services of a *dhobi,* maybe a couple of times in a year. When it comes to food, vegetables worth a couple of *pice* would suffice for five people. They are really a careful lot. One hardly comes across a Marwadi shopkeeper with clean clothes. Very few of them are squanderers or gluttons. They do cheat people in various ways while transacting business, but very few of them are unprincipled or robbers. They are hardly literate and start trading with just a minimal command over the alphabets. They also maintain accounts with this minuscule knowledge of letters, but are very good at it. While they may swindle others, they are very friendly and helpful to each other. If a Marwadi works in a shop, he toils very honestly. Not only are they extremely frugal in food, clothing and other matters, they even use water, which is freely available, most economically. They may bathe once a week with a moderate quantity of water. If they need to wash their hands, they will use a small glass of water and consume about a couple of handfuls. They may use a bucket or two to wash a few clothes. In sum, these people use a very small quantity of water. It is however certainly true that the lives of many people in Mumbai depend on these Marwadis.

It is a commonly held belief that once people go to Mumbai, they put on airs and become spendthrifts. However, the Marwadis continue to behave in a miserly manner even if they leave Mumbai and go to Vilayat. Expensive vehicles and fashionable dress do not in the least excite any desire in their hearts to emulate their fellow citizens. Admittedly, some of the richer bankers now maintain horses and vehicles, but they continue to spend niggardly sums on their clothing.

They are also very industrious people. From morn to midnight, they are engaged in hundreds of tasks. Before the sun rises, with their books tucked securely under their shoulders, they visit their debtors' houses to extract collections. Some of the debtors may have cases filed against them while some may have had their goods confiscated. They roam the streets of Mumbai in the morning to complete their various tasks. The debt-ridden fear them as they would fear tigers.

There are many English doctors educated in England, doctors who have graduated with degrees from the *Grant Medical School* or *Vaidya Shaala* and numerous *vaidyas* who have been educated in the *Sanskrit Vaidya Shastra* from various regions who administer potions and powders to earn their livelihood. Then there are those who treat ailments of the ear and eye roaming in the streets with their trays full of bottles of medicine, shouting out their calls – *Ras-sindur Vaidya, Lohabhasma Vaidya.* Their manner of prescribing medicines is as follows. If somebody has a stomach-ache and approaches one of them for medicine, he lets a cup or two of blood from his back. They indulge in very strange practices and are happy with even half an *anna*. When they have given some medicines to somebody, they make sure they don't cross their path again.

The only real doctors in Mumbai are the English doctors and about a hundred learned natives. Between 1850 and 1861, fifty-six natives have graduated from the *Grant Medical School*. Many of them are posted in places outside Mumbai to run government Hospitals at hundred rupees a month. Some of them are employed in hospitals in Mumbai while a few of them have established their own practices. There are others who dispense native medicines from plants and chemicals. In some places, the *gandhis* themselves act as *vaidyas* and dispense medicine. There has never been an instance where a *gandhi* has refused anyone medicine; they are not particularly bothered about the efficacy of the medicine; they just give them some random powder. To personally examine their behaviour, one gentleman sent a boy with a few *pice* to one of them to get an *anushtubhchand*; on being approached by the boy, the *gandhi* was unfazed and wrapped a radish in a leaf and gave it to the boy. This is the normal practice amongst these *gandhis*. Even if one asks them for thunder, they will certainly give you something in exchange for a pie or two.

The number of learned Brahmins and other gentlemen has been increasing at a rapid rate in this city. Pundits from Kashi to Rameshwaram are always camped here. There are many other learned men including the Kazis, Mullas, and Hakims of the Mussalmans, the Rabbis of the Yahudis and the Dasturs of the Parsis. There are many professors and religious scholars from Europe in this city. It is very easy to obtain explanations or clarification on any topic. There are also numerous pundits of lesser merit. Anybody who can read the *Laguhitopadesa* calls himself a pundit. And if you know the first four pages of the *Rupawali* by heart, you become a *shastri*. If you can pronounce 'Lambodarashvavikato' properly, you are qualified as *vaidic* and if you can read the *Pandav* and *Pratap*, you are a *puranik*. One comes across such scholars in every house. Some years back a *Saptaah* function was held here to which such *shastris*, *vaidics*, and *puraniks* flocked. They arrange books like *Vidurniti*, *Ramdasi Shloka*, and *Esapniti* in front of them, cover their hands with a *gaumukh* and tell the beads in a posture of meditation. During the *Saptaah*, a hundred and eight *puraniks* sit in a large tent for seven days and recite the *Bhagavad Gita*. A minimum of ten thousand rupees is required to conduct this function and in the last thirty odd years, seven or eight such functions have been held. Numerous exorcists, palmists, and chiromancers walk the streets. A few years back an *Ashtaavdhani Baba* had come to Mumbai who could do eight tasks simultaneously. He would have a book in one hand, read and expound its meaning, make a move in chess, cast the dice for draughts with his right hand, count seeds thrown at his back, and such other tasks at the same time. In 1862, the Guru of the *Madhvamatanuyayi Vaishnavs* came to Mumbai. He is said to be a great scholar and as part of the austerities, his disciples have to brand themselves. His name is *Poorna Pragyatirth* and his greatness has been recognized by the *Vidvajan Brahmavrund* at Kashi.

In the Mumbai Province, there are about fifty to sixty English priests and the Sarkar spends about two to three lakhs of rupees on their account annually. The head priest of all the churches in the Mumbai Province is called the Bishop and is paid a sum of twenty-five thousand six hundred rupees annually. A travelling allowance of thousand rupees has also been provided to visit the inner districts. The priests under him are paid monthly salaries ranging from five hundred rupees to one thousand five hundred rupees. The Bishop is ranked at the same level as the Chief Justice.

Bal Gangadharshastri Jambhekar died at a very young age just as he was beginning to achieve fame and fortune. He was very well-versed with the Sanskrit, Marathi, and English languages. Besides, he also knew the Urdu, Kannada, and Gujarati languages. He was a gem amongst all the native scholars in Western India. Sadashiv Kashinath Chhatre, Principal of the *Elphinstone School* was his *guru*. Recognizing his sharp brain and great ability, he brought Jambhekar to Mumbai, maintained him at his residence, and asked him to undertake studies in English. It is said about him that he had infinite powers of absorption and could learn anything at the first reading. He was the first among the natives to be eligible as a professor in an English college. His untimely death saddened the people of Mumbai. He was equally endowed with knowledge and grace. A short history of this gentleman appeared in the *Dnyanodaya*; a short summary of the article has been reproduced below.

He was recognized as a great scholar by both the native people and the Sahibs. He was the most educated amongst all the native people of Maharashtra and it was his desire to spread the light of education amongst his brethren, and he acted out this desire through the years. Many of his students have benefitted from his teachings; we hope that his association would have generated a love for learning amongst a few of them and that they will devote themselves to the spread of education like he did.

The late Balgangadhar Shastri Jambhekar is much lamented by the people. He was born in 1810 in the village of Pongurle near Rajapur in the South Konkan district. In 1829, he became a teacher in the Society's school, now referred to as the *Elphinstone Institution* and since then he has been influential in its running. He has written many books useful for children in their studies. He ran two papers by name *Digdurshan* and *Durpun* for a few years but people did not patronize it as they did not recognize its worth. It was very obvious from these papers that he was not in the common state of darkness which envelops most other people. He was engaged in writing a book on *manasvidya* after Abercrombie and a history of Hindustan based on the work of Elphinstone Sahib. He also contributed a few articles to the Bombay Geographical Society and the Asiatic Society. He died on 17 May 1846 afflicted by fever.

Just as they have made arrangements in other areas for the welfare of the *ryot*, the English Sarkar has created facilities for the ill and the diseased. This practice was set in motion way back in 1676. Separate hospitals have been set up for the English and the natives. The most excellent doctors have been appointed in these hospitals. Many years back, the Sarkar built the European General Hospital just below Sir Jamsetjee's house in the Fort. This was sold to Rustomji Jamsetjee Jejeebhoy for three lakh rupees in 1861. A new hospital will be built for these people elsewhere. There is a large hospital in Byculla named after the late Sir Jamsetjee Jejeebhoy. The ill who have been abandoned can stay here and all arrangements for their care including food, water, clothing and, medicines have been made; a couple of doctors have also been appointed. The students at the Medical School are required to administer the medicines, and patients have been allotted to them. The hospital was built at a cost of two lakh rupees of which Sir Jamsetjee Jejeebhoy donated one lakh seventy thousand rupees while the Sarkar spent thirty thousand rupees. The total annual expenses on this account is thirty-three thousand rupees; the sums donated by Sir Jamsetjee Jejeebhoy to its expenses yield an interest of four thousand rupees per annum while the rest of the expense is borne by the Sarkar. It is not only the poor and sick destitutes who utilize the services of this hospital; even the middle class uses this hospital. As there are many learned doctors in this hospital, even diseases like black leprosy can be treated here.[6]

In 1861, 3,867 men and 1,038 women were admitted to this hospital for treatment, while the number of patients who were carried forward from the previous year was 217. Of these 614 men and 203 women died, while 4,135 patients returned to their daily lives after recovering. In this year there were a total of 5,152 patients in this hospital and in 1860–61, over a period of eighteen months, the total expenses to government were 36,365 rupees. Besides medicines were provided by the hospital daily to 200 patients, including men, women and, children.

Lying-in chambers are located just next to the *Grant Medical School*. Arrangements have been made for poor and other pregnant women for the delivery of children. No compromise is made in their care. Numerous philanthropic people have contributed 31,385 rupees for this venture. As Sir Jamsetjee Jejeebhoy contributed fifteen thousand rupees of this amount, besides donating the land, these chambers bear his name. To ensure its continuous operation, it has been handed over to the Sarkar. Of the balance of twelve thousand rupees, the interest goes towards salaries for the midwives and others.

It is the practice in this country, that a pregnant woman calls a midwife during the delivery of a child but this midwife is generally not trained. This leads to complications during childbirth. Even if the woman survives, she has no strength and her health remains in a delicate condition for many days. This delivery home has been made for this purpose. All the medicines and nutrition required after delivery are available here and as the poor do not have to pay for it, it is best they go there for delivering children. This generous venture has been possible through the efforts of Dr. Morehead Sahib and Sir Jamsetjee Jejeebhoy and we have to be grateful to them. It is heard that Sir Jamsetjee Jejeebhoy donated thirty thousand rupees for this venture.

Opposite the hospital is a medical school. Around ten doctors graduate every year with certificates. The Sarkar spends thousands of rupees on this account. This is known as the *Grant Medical College*, built in the memory of Sir Robert Grant. It was built at a cost of ninety thousand rupees and was started in 1845.

A large five-metalled statue of Sir Jamsetjee Jejeebhoy was installed opposite the medical school in 1862 by his son and his wife, Ratanbai. It was sculpted in England.[7]

Further ahead on the road to Mahalaxmi from Byculla, a *dharamshala* has been built for which Sir Jamsetjee Jejeebhoy donated a sum of fifty thousand rupees while the Sarkar provided twenty-five thousand rupees. To meet the expenses of this establishment, this philanthropic gentleman has provided a sum of three hundred rupees per month. It was established in 1847. In this *dharamshala*, the blind, lame, crippled, old, and infirm are provided with food, clothing, and shelter. If somebody does not want to stay here, they are provided an amount between three and ten rupees every month. This monthly stipend is provided only for the completely destitute. The following account of the *dharamshala* has been extracted from the *Dnyanodaya*.

Sir Jamsetjee Jejeebhoy has built a beautiful *dharamshala* at Byculla near Kamatipura at a cost of 80,000 rupees for the use of the poor and destitute and handed it over to the District Benevolent Society of the Sarkar to ensure that it is run smoothly. He has also deposited a sum of 50,000 rupees with the Sarkar so that the interest of 300 rupees is used for the running of this institution. The *Times* newspaper has said that Sir Charles Forbes has sent 30,000 rupees for this *dharamshala* and Lady Jamsetjee, that is Jamsetjee's wife has promised to give 20,000 rupees. The extra 50,000 rupees will yield an additional interest of 300 rupees for its expenses. We are gratified to publicize such news. It is certainly more appropriate to do such charitable works than to toss away one's money. It will help those who are truly poor and destitute. There are many lame, crippled and blind people and it is appropriate that the rich and generous people send money to this institution for their care.

The annual report of this *dharamshala* has come to our hands. We understand that currently there are three hundred and twenty four residents in this *dharamshala*, including sixty-one blind, eighty-five lepers, one hundred and nineteen lame, crippled and old and fifty-nine girls of whom fourteen are orphans. If one looks at the accounts of this institution, the total income is 17,142 rupees while the total expenses are 11,030 rupees indicating a surplus of 6,112 rupees. Of these 3,600 rupees are donated by the Seth. In these days, the number of beggars who roam the streets of Mumbai and beg door-to-door has increased considerably. As people give them money on the roads, these beggars are flocking here. Prudent people are requested not to give any money to beggars on the roads this year and instead donate it to the *dharamshala* where it can be put to proper use and the nuisance on the roads can be stopped.

In this city, a lot of children fell prey to smallpox, the curse of the Devi Durga. This led the Company Sarkar to establish a department for the treatment of smallpox in 1816–17. It was first located near Kalbadevi. Though this curse of the *Devi* wrought a trail of destruction, our people did not particularly like this new method of saving lives. As they were under the impression that they may contract the disease if they were vaccinated, many of our simple folk therefore hesitated to get their children vaccinated. If they saw a worker from this office, they hid their children away. Some of them moved to other places. At any rate, the Sarkar has very forbearingly continued this venture keeping in mind the welfare of the people. If the children are very poor, they reward their mothers with a few *annas*.

When this department was started, an English doctor was assisted by a *joshi* (a *vaidya* from Mumbai), two clerks and eight peons. They would administer the smallpox vaccine every Monday. At that point, the rich folk absolutely refused to let their children be inoculated. The workers would forcibly fetch children from the houses of poor people. It was very difficult to find even twenty-five children every Monday. The wives of the *shudra* folk would start wailing and shouting if the workers took their children away. They would try everything within their means to get their children back from the workers. Only recently have people begun to realize that vaccination is beneficial for them, and most people voluntarily get their children inoculated. Dr. Anant Chandroba is currently posted in this department. Seven workers and three others assist him. They visit different places every day to administer the vaccine. The rich get the vaccination done at their residences. This vaccination has protected thousands of lives and has saved them from the scars of smallpox. The curse of the *Devi* leaves some people blind, paralyses legs, shrivels hands, takes away their speech or sometimes scars their faces very badly; the vaccine has saved people from such distressing conditions. In 1861, 8,861 people were administered this vaccine just on the island of Mumbai while in the entire Mumbai Province including Sindh a total of 274,433 individuals were inoculated by the Sarkar in 1860. Any praise of the English Sarkar in this regard is insufficient.

The traditional treatment of smallpox in Hindustan is demonic in nature, but it is certainly amazing that our people are not afraid of this treatment. An incision is made on the hand of the infected person at a distance of about a *viti* from the wrist; the scabs of the pox which have fallen off his person are powdered and placed on the incision and it is tightly bandaged. He is fed parched rice mixed with jaggery and other flatulent substances. The patient develops a fever after a couple of days and starts writhing as if possessed by the *Devi*. Many people lose their lives in the process. The treatment is done by devotees of the *Devi* who are offered presents. Either he or his wife is invested with the afflatus of the *Devi* and worshipped as the *Devi* herself. The introduction of vaccination has begun to put an end to this madness. When the *Devi* is said to possess the body, they behave in the craziest fashion. Is this not terrifying and demoniacal? The present method is mild and moderate. This English mode of treatment can be safely administered to a fifteen-day-old baby and it will never ever be afflicted with this disease.

Shrimant Jagannath Shankarseth has established a charitable dispensary in Girgaon. Patients are examined in the morning and evening and free medicines are given. Every month, this dispensary supplies medicines to approximately three hundred patients. A doctor educated in the *Grant Medical College* prescribes the medicines in this dispensary. There are about four to five charitable dispensaries established by rich people while government dispensaries are located at various places.

Water is easily available in many places on this island. If one digs about twenty hands deep, one strikes water. However the water is not sweet in all places, and is in fact salty in a majority of places. One can get sweet water at the Camp Maidan and Girgaon. It is not sweet at Masjid Bunder, Dongri, Chinch Bunder and Bhendi Bazar but if it rains properly, there is no scarcity of water anywhere. There are wells in every house and the city of Mumbai including Mahim, Sion, Worli, Mazagaon, and Parel has between seventy-five and eighty tanks. There has been an abundance of water in recent years. Pipelines have been constructed for transporting water to various places. It is as if the Bhagirathi has overflowed into Mumbai. These kinds of facilities are leading to a daily increase in the population of this city.

When the English first came to Bharat Khand, apart from trading they also annexed a few small territories. As there was no proper system of post in this country, they were much inconvenienced in maintaining correspondence with each other. The English staying in Mumbai did not hear from home (England) for over six months to a year, and if they had to write a letter urgently to a friend in some other part of Bharat Khand, they had to send a special messenger. The ordinary folk had no way of sending letters to each other. One had to spend up to fifty rupees to get one letter delivered. With the passage of time, the island of Mumbai had been under the control of the English for many years. As the Marathas dominated most of the countries of Bharat Khand, no postal system could be developed. The English experienced great difficulties in communicating with each other on matters of state. After the defeat of the Maratha Sarkar and the unfurling of the English flag over Bharat Khand, a regular postal system was established. In Mumbai, the post office was first established around 1694 under orders from the Company Sarkar, but from 1818 onwards branches of this post office spread to all the villages and other regions. During the regime of the Peshwas, restrictions were imposed on the establishment of post offices in the Maratha territory. When Elphinstone Sahib was stationed in Poona and had to send sealed official letters to Mumbai and other places, sending the letters to Mumbai took a considerable amount of time. After a while, a regular post arrived from England and letters could be delivered all over Hindustan, though the postage was quite exorbitant. The Hindu courts did not understand the meaning of post and its system of administration. Needless to say, our people must have been amazed by this prompt delivery of letters.

Until 1828, steamships called at Mumbai occasionally. In March 1831, the Earl of Clare, Governor of Mumbai arrived in a steamship named *Lindsay*. He was the first Governor to come in a steamship while the earlier Governors came by ships with masts. The practice of bringing the post had not yet started. A proposal to start a monthly postal service to Bharat Khand with special postal boats was under consideration in Parliament since 1825. The Court of Directors estimated the additional annual expense required to maintain this service just for the Mumbai Province at twelve lakhs of rupees. This led to the proposal being kept in a state of suspension for a few years. After a few years, the steamship *Lindsay*, as it had a full load of passengers and other arrangements had been made, carried a post of 3,463 letters and newspapers and arrived in Mumbai on 28 April 1837. It could not reach Mumbai in exactly a month because of some turbulence in the sea and took an additional five days. When our people witnessed for the first time that the post and passengers had arrived in a month's time, they were amazed. While it took old ships with masts almost six months to make this journey, the steamship took only a month and its speed led many of the simple folk to believe that its Captain must be the son of the god of Winds, Vayu. Currently, there are two steamships which shuttle between Mumbai and England carrying post and passengers every month. In 1858, the Sarkar earned a revenue of 464,846 rupees from the post. In August 1862, the steamship came from Vilayat in nineteen days.

It costs half an *anna* per quarter *tola* to send letters to any part of Bharat Khand from Kashi to Rameshwaram, and it takes from a day to a maximum of ten days to reach its destination depending on the distance between the two places. One can also send books and other material through the post.

In 1858, a faster method was discovered to send messages from one country to another. This is a truly remarkable method. This is, of course, the telegraph by which messages are transmitted through wires across countries within a couple of hours and replies received in about the same time. The *Dnyanodaya* had published the following article on this subject in 1852.

In order to obtain an estimate of the costs of laying telegraph lines, a line of about 82 miles was laid in Bengal which cost 30,000 rupees. Assuming a cost of 350 rupees per mile, it will cost 900,000 lakhs of rupees to lay a line from Mumbai to Calcutta. It will certainly be very useful. This service was made available to the public from 1855. This department generates an annual revenue of over a lakh of rupees. This excellent means of communication has been very useful to businessmen, traders, and other people of this city. This and other methods have contributed to reduce the fear of losses amongst businessmen. The value of this method must be considered priceless.

The report of the Postal Commissioner for 1861 says that a total of 914 post offices in all of Hindustan and 43,551 miles of roads are ready. Post was transported over 1,016 miles of railway and over 574 miles by vehicles, and 26,785 miles by postal steamships and ordinary ships. The total number of articles handled included 4,707,010 letters and 4,242,684 newspapers. The volume of letters and newspapers has increased compared to the past three years and one can assume that the revenue of the Postal Department must have increased substantially. New post offices are being established in various regions. Besides, the telegraph seems to have spanned all the nine continents. How can one not be stunned by the manner of the English people in running their empire!

As man accumulates wealth, power and fame, man normally tends to ignore the poor and destitute, and perhaps also begins to neglect his duties. This did not happen during the reign of the generous Mountstuart Elphinstone Sahib. The foundation of the English empire is built on such stones. As their power and wealth increased, they introduced more facilities for the *ryot*. Raids by dacoits, *pindaries* and other predators frequently bothered villages; the English first put an end to these happenings and ensured the security of their lives and property. *Bhils, Thugs, Ramoshies* and other robbers used to attack travellers, pilgrims and other solitary wayfarers all across Bharat Khand; order was restored by exterminating them. They built roads and established checkposts at various points to ensure the security of wayfarers. Now one can wear gold and walk all the way from the tip of Rameshwaram to the Himalayan peaks without any fear.

In 1821, the Honourable Mountstuart Elphinstone Sahib felt that while all possible arrangements had been made in other matters, unless facilities were created for the people of this country to obtain complete knowledge of their own languages and study English, they would not be able to ensure the continued prosperity of the country. It was decided that the government would establish a school in Mumbai, where besides native languages like Sanskrit, Marathi, Gujarati, and Urdu, the English language would also be studied; this would expose the students to various branches of learning current in the European continent and increase their abilities and skills thus ensuring the prosperity of the coming generations. They would then be thankful to their respective gods for having been provided this opportunity. With this in mind, he called for a meeting of the prominent businessmen and other reputed residents of Mumbai and explained his noble intentions. He also undertook to contribute a substantial amount for this venture on his own account. The other gentlemen contributed sums ranging from one to five thousand, according to their means. It is said that the generosity and enthusiasm exhibited by our people on that occasion has never been exceeded since. This ensured a collection from the residents of Mumbai but this philanthropic gentleman did not stop at that. He wrote letters to all the royal families in the Mumbai Province explaining his intentions and asked for their help in completing this task; they responded generously to his request. After adequate funds were collected, a large school under the name of the *Native Education Society* was established on 21 August 1822. A building was erected for this school in the Camp Maidan. The original small structure has since been enlarged.

A Marathi printing press was established for the production of books and other material. Captain Jervis was appointed to manage the work in this department who discharged his responsibilities in the most discriminating manner. Sadashiv Kashinath Chhatre and Jagannath Shastri were serially appointed to examine the work of the Marathi school. Many other *shastris* were appointed under their supervision to prepare books for use in schools. Sadashiv Kashinath Chattre prepared and printed beautiful books like the *Balmitra* and *Esapniti* for use in schools. Jervis Sahib himself prepared books on Mathematics, Geography, and Geometry. He also ensured that excellent books on Chemistry and Material Sciences were prepared. A learned scholar named Hari Keshavji, who was an excellent translator of English books into Marathi, also prepared a few books. These efforts provided a strong foundation for bringing out text-books in the Marathi language. Books on Marathi Grammar were compiled and Sanskrit books published. Marathi government schools were set up in a couple of places. This was the seed of all the schools in the Mumbai Province. There has been a rapid increase in the number of schools in the Mumbai Province with schools being established in every city, town, and village and new schools continue to be set up. This school has recently been named the *Elphinstone Institution* and associated with this is the *Elphinstone College*. Professors have been invited from England to teach here at salaries ranging from seven hundred to a thousand rupees per month. There are five to six such professors who teach very intricate and complex subjects. The Marathi and Sanskrit languages are also studied at the highest level. The establishment of this school has, to some extent, kindled a quest for knowledge amongst the general population and thousands of natives have become educated and very well qualified. The present Chief Director of the Education Department receives a salary of two thousand five hundred rupees per month. He is assisted by two other Sahibs and native scholars. The Sarkar incurs an expenditure of three to four lakhs of rupees every year on account of this department. An assembly of scholars known as the University has been established to provide an opportunity for native students to become experts in various subjects.[8] Students are expected to learn many subjects and they are certified as pundits once they have cleared their examinations. The Sarkar spent 352,730 rupees in the years 1856–57 on account of the Education Department in the Mumbai Province.

This school has been the main reason for the resurgence of the Marathi language. Marathi was earlier considered a vulgar and uncultivated language and nobody bothered to study it. As there were no Grammar books, dictionaries and works in prose and poetry in this language, any pundit, *shastri* or *puranik* who composed any work in this language was subjected to ridicule. However after this school was established, many works on grammar, dictionaries, and other books have been published in Marathi. This has opened the eyes of the people and they have come to feel that Marathi can be used for literary purposes.

The Chief of the Education Department, called the Director of Public Instruction, E. I. Howard Sahib strives very hard to create an interest in the native languages amongst children. He has published many books in prose and poetry in Marathi and Gujarati for use in schools. He has provided a lot of encouragement for the publication of extracts from ancient poetry, teaching them to students and encouraging them to compose verses in their own language. This has led to an increase in the prestige of the native languages and many new books are being published.

In 1848, the ex-students of the *Elphinstone Institution* and other schools got together to establish the Students' Literary and Scientific Society; the objective of this organization was to add to the fund of knowledge and spread it amongst our people. The members of the Society write essays in the English language and deliver speeches in turn. A Marathi and Gujarati school for girls has been established after collecting donations. The Marathi and Gujarati *Dnyanaprasarak Sabha* are branches of this Society. One of the members presents an essay in the Marathi language every fortnight under the aegis of the Marathi *Dnyanaprasarak Sabha*. These essays are printed in the monthly magazine, *Dnyanaprasarak*, published by the Sabha.

The Medical College and School of Law are branches of the above mentioned University. In 1838, the Governor of Mumbai Sir Robert Grant died in Dapoli and the Medical College was named after him. His friends collected a lot of money to establish the institute and the Company Sarkar contributed the rest. The government meets its expenses. When Sir Erskine Perry, the Chief Justice of Mumbai returned home in 1853, a collection was made to establish a School of Law as a mark of respect. The study of law is undertaken at the *Elphinstone Institution*, and an English legal scholar has been appointed. Dr. Reed Sahib teaches law in this department. Look! this is certainly a good progression. First, one learns the grammar of the native language properly. After about ten years, one studies the English language and acquires a thorough knowledge of the same; one then moves on to medical sciences, legal sciences, building sciences or any other subject that is of interest. If one is willing to strive hard in the city of Mumbai, one can easily turn from zero to hero. No other place can compare to Mumbai in terms of the facilities for education and learning. In spite of so many facilities for the pursuit of education that are available in Mumbai, the people of Mumbai do not seem to have a great enthusiasm for learning and there are very few among the original residents who have tried to benefit from this knowledge. The local people do not seem to have an iota of industry, competitive spirit, concentration and initiative and they do not seem to strive as hard as the Brahmins and other people who have come to this city.

There are around three hundred and fifty schools in the island which teach various languages like English, Marathi, Gujarati, Portuguese, Yahudi,[*] Persian, Urdu, and Arabic and approximately twenty-five thousand students of different castes study in them. There are about forty libraries, with books in many languages, which can be read on the payment of monthly subscriptions ranging from four *annas* to ten rupees. Remember – some years back, it was difficult to find even one English school and five old-style schools on this island! If anybody wanted to learn English, they went to the fort at Dongri and paid five rupees a month to one of the soldiers there who would teach them for an hour or so; hardly more than twenty people could be bothered to do this. Many children took tuitions from some gentleman who might have learnt a smattering of English; they would learn a few lessons for an year or two and then try to obtain a job in some office on the strength of a few phrases learned by rote. They would assume that their education was complete if they could count up to hundred and had learnt the alphabet. And if they reached up to seven-letter-words in the English spelling book, they considered themselves experts in the language. And now! There are hundreds of schools teaching many

---

[*] Hebrew, the language spoken by the Yahudis or Jews.

languages. There were hardly a hundred students learning English when the *Elphinstone School* was first established, and even they were assembled after a lot of effort. In those days, if a student exhibited some sign of intelligence, he was honoured with *pagotas,* shawls, brocades, and silver and expensive books were presented to him. In spite of such inducements, even the better sorts of people were hesitant to send their children to this school. Now even the poor are willing to pay fees every month to send their children to school. Thus the city is enthusiastic about education. About two thousand rupees are collected as fees from the government schools.

In order that the native folk develop a sense of the aesthetic and are able to produce pictures and diagrams of plants, trees, mountains, cities, villages, estates, bungalows, *et cetera* in the English fashion and develop a complete knowledge of the mechanics of art, Sir Jamsetjee Jejeebhoy, Baronet has established an art school as a department in the *Elphinstone Institution*. A couple of learned and skilled Englishmen teach in this school. They teach the art of drawing from seven to nine in the morning and it is free for everybody. Sir Jamsetjee has given twenty-five thousand rupees for this generous venture.

It was difficult to find even one school for girls in Mumbai. When boys could not read their lessons, who would bother to teach the girls to read and write. Besides, the Hindus believe that it is not proper to teach women to read and write. However in 1814, missionaries arrived from America and established schools for girls at various places and spent thousands of rupees on that account. They had to struggle a lot to set up these schools for girls. The rich absolutely refused to send their girls to these schools. They however managed to attract and bring girls from poor households by offering them inducements like skirts, blouses, saris and money. Many refused to rent their property for these schools even at twice the normal rent, but this did not deter them. This was how the schools for girls were first established and now there are twenty-five of them. The Students' Literary and Scientific Society runs five of these. In the Mumbai Province, 44,166 girls study in government-run schools and 91,330 girls study in village schools.

It has been forty years since the establishment of the *Elphinstone School* and many teachers have been appointed to this school. Mr. Murphy was the first teacher to be appointed to this school, followed by Mr. Mainwaring. After a few years, the Professors Bell and Henderson were appointed and since then the school has prospered. In 1833, the Honourable Mountstuart Elphinstone appointed Professor Orlebar and Dr. Harkness to this school. Dr. Harkness was named as the Chief Teacher of the school and he was entrusted with the management of the school. He received a salary of one thousand rupees per month. He has managed the school very astutely and has devoted his life by serving in this position for twenty-seven consecutive years and ensured that the tree of education showers many fruits on this land. This gentleman has provided us with the key to European knowledge. He was very kind towards the natives, especially the students, and was dedicated to teaching them. He would also give four or five rupees as pocket money to poor Brahmins and other orphan children, and take lessons for them.

A scholar named Hamilton has written a book on psychology in which he says that 'Man is the most important being in the world, and intelligence is most important for man'.[9] One can assume that this Sahib must have behaved in accordance with this maxim. His students are spread all across the world and many of them have reached positions of eminence. He deserves part of the credit for their success. Many of his students are now in various positions like Collector, Judge, Principal Sudder Ameen, professors, businessmen, writers, newspaper editors, lawyers in the Supreme Court, translators, doctors, engineers, and pundits. His generosity and large-heartedness has led him to strive hard to ensure that his students reach positions of responsibility and discharge their duties in a proper manner.

The University (school for pundits) was established in this province in 1857. From that time on, these philanthropic professors have worked hard to enthuse their students to obtain degrees in the English fashion. God has fulfilled their wishes. In March 1862, six students were examined in the Town Hall. Of these, four met the mark.

Ra. Mahadeo Govind   Ra. Ramakrishna Gopal
Ra. Bala Mangesh   Ra. Waman Abaji

On 1 May 1862, in a function held at the Town Hall, these people were awarded the pundit title of A. B. by Sir Henry Bartle Frere in the presence of English and native businessmen, government officials and other important people. The function was a grand affair. Sir Bartle Frere made a very appropriate speech on the occasion and reminded the awardees of the necessity to uphold the importance of the honour that had been bestowed upon them because of their excellent qualities and behaviour. He also indicated that they should strive hard to spread the knowledge obtained by them. He also briefly outlined the key problems faced by native students in the acquisition of English knowledge and which needed to be addressed.

Dr. Harkness, the chief teacher of the *Elphinstone College* resigned his office and prepared to leave for his native country, England on 12 May 1862. When the fact of his resignation and impending departure became known to his past students and those who were still studying in the school, they, with a view to perpetuate his memory and as a small token for all the favours he had rendered them, organized a collection as *Gurudakshina*, each contributing according to his means, and a sum of around sixteen thousand rupees was collected. A gathering was organized in the *Elphinstone School* on the Camp Maidan and a scroll extolling his achievements in the English language was presented to him. This was first read to the audience by Dr. Bhau Daji. It reviewed all the philanthropic activities undertaken by him and further requested him to accept, as a small token presented in grateful memory of all the favours showered by him, a *tulsipatra* (this bag containing ten thousand rupees). They also requested him to acquiesce to their desire, in order to perpetuate his memory, to place his statue in the proposed Framji Cowasji General Museum.[10] They further asked him to agree to their desire to pose for a photograph that could then be displayed in the houses of his students as a permanent memorial. Dr. Bhau Daji then handed over the scroll to Dr. Harkness. It had over a thousand signatures. Dr. Harkness then made a very moving speech in which he praised his students and the other gentleman, following which the gathering was dissolved. Shrimant Jugganath Shankarseth, Seth Sorabji Jamsetjee, Seth Bomanji Hormusji, Ra. Dadoba Pandurang and many others including the English attended the meeting. In his stead, Sir Alexander Grant has been named as the Principal of the *Elphinstone College*.

When the Honourable Elphinstone Sahib was the Governor, the Commissioner of the Southern Districts, Chaplin Sahib, established a Sanskrit College in October 1821.

Gurus were appointed for teaching subjects like *Nyayashastra, Vedant, Dharmashastra, Rigveda, Vyakaran, Yajurveda, Alankar,* and *Vaidya,* and about a hundred students were assembled. The famous pundit Raghavacharya was appointed as the Chief *Shastri*; he was also entrusted the subject of Nyayashastra. The Commissioner initially oversaw the functioning of the school and after that post was abolished the work was entrusted to the Collector. As these two gentlemen had numerous other responsibilities, they oversaw the school only in name. The affairs of the school devolved on the Chief *Shastri*, but as he had become increasingly lazy and indifferent, Major Candy was named as the Superintendent of the School in February 1837. The affairs of this school have been in order since then.

This school in Poona has been a big benefit to the schools and populace of Mumbai. Many of the *shastris* who graduated from this school have been appointed as teachers in Mumbai. Many of its students have come to study English in Mumbai, while many students from Mumbai have gone to Poona to learn Sanskrit and classical Marathi in this school. In association with this school, Candy Sahib compiled the English-Marathi dictionary, and Molesworth Sahib prepared his monumental Marathi-English dictionary. Though Molesworth Sahib was not in any way connected with this school, there were a large number of *shastris* in Pune because of the school and as many books were being prepared, a lively discussion on words was possible. These two Sahibs have prepared these two dictionaries and have done a big favour for the people residing in the Western parts of Bharat Khand. The people of Mumbai should remember their deeds very gratefully. As no standard Marathi language was current, it was very difficult to learn the English language and also to make appropriate translations. The coming of the railway and the establishment of the English college in Poona has led to the ties between schools at Mumbai and Poona to be further cemented.

Those who used to do odd jobs earlier are now learning English. Many have left their traditional trades to learn English and obtain employment. As jobs have become easily available, everybody wants to learn English and become a clerk. Nobody pays attention to the old saying that goes 'Farming is best, business is middling and a job the meanest'. These days even the children of Kolis, Malis, Ghatis, Mahars, Mangs, and Chambars are learning Marathi, Gujarati, and English. About thirty odd children of the butchers are paying fees of one rupee a month to learn English. This school has been established in their *mohalla*. The missionaries have established numerous schools for the education of the children of the Mahars.

Many orphan Brahmin children come to Mumbai every year to study English; they take up positions like *acharya* or *shagird* and whenever they get the time, they go to school. Some subsist on alms begged in the mornings and evenings and go to school to learn English during the intervening hours. Once they come here, the poor are able to somehow arrange for food and clothing. Many Parsis and others give these poor students a rupee or two and ensure that they are able to study. Isn't this a praiseworthy quality? One comes across many such students who have overcome these difficulties and are successful today. At some places, students from other castes as well as children of the rich spend about fifty rupees a month and come to Mumbai to study English.

Chapter 10

Khatris and the silk trade — Mills and the cotton trade — Silk — Industriousness of the Parsis — Presses — Ganpat Krishnaji — Newspapers — Quest for knowledge among the Parsis — Workshop for plating gold and silver — Workshop for producing pictures — Ice warehouses — Metalled railways — Ginning and cloth weaving factories — Artisans — Workshops for vehicles — Workshops for casting iron — Comparison with Ravana's legendary wealth — Intricate embroidery work — Workshops for paper and glass manufacture — Oil mills — Workshops for manufacturing soap — Design of gas lights — Liquor distilleries and taverns — Tobacco and shops selling paansupari — Opium trade and shops — Opium smoking dens — Sweets — Alchemists — Fire-crackers, Flowerpots, et cetera — Steamboats for short journeys — Jewellery

The Khatris are originally from Chaul. Their early origins cannot be traced from books, but as they claim to be descendants of Arjuna, one can assume that they are Kshatriyas. Their actual name was probably Kshartiya but most of the populace being agrarian with hardly any learned or accomplished person amongst them, they perhaps did not pay any attention to the difference between the words Kshatriya and Khatri. Molesworth Sahib is of the opinion that the Khatris are Kshatriyas. Their settlement in Chaul consisted of over eighteen hundred houses. Many families were forced to migrate from Chaul to save their lives from a disease called Goli that had turned into an epidemic.

There is still a Golika Devi Temple in Chaul. Later the settlement in Mumbai increased and it became a place of choice for traders. The Khatris came to stay here during the reign of the Portuguese around the year 1600.

The Khatris who came to Mumbai continued to carry on their ancestral business of silk and during the reign of the English, their numbers increased by leaps and bounds. About forty years back, they were in demand in all the houses of Mumbai. They used to make the most exquisite silk articles including the best-quality *pitambaris*, paithani sarees, silk *pagotis*, shawls known as *khes* and sell them. In order to increase the population of the city, the English urged artisans from various villages to settle in Mumbai and offered them many inducements. The English must have helped these people in many ways as many of them are now quite rich and have been owners of immovable property for many years. And as they were skilled in handicrafts, they could earn money by their labour. However, they have not built any temples or undertaken other philanthropic activities. After coming to this city, many of them have become tailors and some of them have become businessmen. They stitch excellent coats for the English gentlemen and gowns for the ladies. Many have made their money by these means. At present, they have however begun to abandon both the silk and tailoring professions and have taken to learning English and taking up jobs in government offices or trading houses. Ramachandra Keroji of this caste is a prominent gentleman. He was a translator in the Police Department for thirty-six years and was highly reputed in government circles. He was paid two hundred rupees per month.

Thousands of rupees' worth of silk arrives from China in this city and the silk traders include Parsis, Vani, Marwadi, and Bhatia. From Mumbai, it is sent to other regions. Many varieties of silk are being imported from other places and are being sold at cheap prices. This has forced the Khatris to abandon their ancestral profession.

There is a large trade of cotton in Mumbai. Cotton is imported from the hinterland and exported to the European continent and China. It is estimated that the cotton trading business started in this port from around 1750. The trade was earlier conducted in the port of Kalyan. Kalyan had been a large trading town for many centuries. About two crores rupees' worth of cotton is exported every year. When bales of cotton come from the hinterland, they are about five hands high and half as broad. As bales of this size took up a lot of space in the ships, they were slightly compressed in a simple device made of tamarind wood. In 1684, the Company Sarkar sent an iron cotton-press (cotton-screw) to Mumbai. It was however not used properly for many years. From 1792, these cotton-screws have been used extensively and thousands of bales of cotton are compressed every year. The Parsis first adopted this practice and Dadabhai Pestonji set up a workshop with six cotton-screws in the Fort. There are about 40 such cotton-screws operated by these people in the Fort and another 50 in Colaba. There is a large steam-powered cotton-screw in Colaba which is said to be unique. Hundreds of men were required to rotate the cotton-screw earlier, but it is mostly powered by steam these days. In Chinch Bunder, Motisha has a work-shop with six cotton-screws which are still operated manually. There are still many such ordinary screws in the Fort.

About fourteen *man* of cotton is put into these presses and compressed so that it becomes hard as stone and a compact bale about one and half hands high and two and half feet long is formed. Traders can save thousands of rupees of freight. Where three thousand bales used to be transported earlier, about six thousand such compressed bales are loaded on to ships. This has also increased the business of the shipping industry. The owner of the cotton-screw is paid one and half rupees for compressing each bale. In spite of this high cost, traders have profited by lakhs of rupees.

In 1800, the shipping family of Lowjees made an additional revenue of 32,000 rupees because of the loading of compressed bales. Other shipping lines also made similar profits. Many of the traders also saved amounts ranging from fifteen to twenty thousand rupees. There are over a 100 cotton-screws all over Mumbai and many people come to these workshops to observe how the cotton bales are compressed.

The businessmen of Mumbai have experienced a resurgence in the cotton trade. In the period 1860–62, many of them have become *lakhpatis*. The *Times of India*, an English newspaper writes that the profits made by the cotton traders of Mumbai in this year are unprecedented in any other place in any other trade and in all times past. The export of cotton from America to the European continent and China has stopped because of the hostilities between these nations; as a result cotton worth eighty rupees a *khandi* is now being sold at four to five hundred rupees per *khandi*. The huge increase in the price of cotton this year is completely unprecedented. Many ordinary people have emptied their personal bedding and mattresses and sold hundreds of *khandis* of cotton stuffed in them at the rate of eight to ten rupees per *man*. In 1862, many of the big traders in Mumbai have made profits ranging from ten to thirty to even seventy lakh rupees; so says the August 1862 issue of the *Guardian* newspaper. The manager of a Lavana who used to earn twenty five rupees a month made a profit of two lakhs of rupees in cotton trade in the last two years, that is 1860–62. In 1861, 717,821 bales of cotton were exported from Mumbai. The total trade of cotton in this city must have been around ten to fifteen crores of rupees in 1862.

Cotton arrives in Mumbai from places like Bhadoch, Surat, Jambusar, Dholera, Bhavnagar, Umravati, Barshi, Nagar, Mangalore, Kumthe, Dharwad, Khandesh, Veravali, Mahwa (Mhow), Porgaon, Akot, and Nagpur and is mostly unloaded at the docks in Colaba.

For many years, cotton worth lakhs of rupees used to be exported from America to England to feed hundreds of cotton spinning mills. Thousands of labourers and other employees depended on these mills for their livelihood. In 1861, because of differences between these two countries, fighting ensued, the planting of cotton was prohibited and the export of cotton to England was suspended.[1] People in the Lancashire district who had no means of livelihood were starving, and were in dire straits. It is said that they numbered around twenty-five to thirty thousand.

The cotton traders of Mumbai profited greatly from this prohibition. The price of cotton shot up from fifty to sixty rupees per *khandi* to five hundred to six hundred rupees per *khandi*. This led to a veritable shower of gold in the houses of these traders.

When business boomed, the traders and other affluent people in Mumbai were requested by the Governor of Mumbai and other prominent gentlemen to help people in the Lancashire district in their hour of distress. This led to a meeting in the Town Hall on 17 September 1862. About seven to eight hundred prominent residents of Mumbai attended this meeting and Sir Bartle Frere Sahib presided. Speeches were delivered by him, Sir Alexander Grant, Dr. Murray Mitchell, Dr. Bhau Daji and many others exhorting the audience to fulfil their duty of alleviating the misery of the people of Lancashire. A list was circulated inviting contributions and both Seth Rustomji Jamsetjee Jeejeebhoy and Cursetjee Fardunji donated twenty-five thousand rupees each. Others donated sums ranging from one to seven thousand rupees. This one meeting yielded a collection of 109,000 rupees and in a few days, the collection mounted to three lakhs of rupees.

Ropes and cords made from coir come to this city from Calicut, Malabar, Gomantak, Malvan and other places. Hawsers used in the shipping industry come mostly from the Malabar and Karnatak regions. Thousands of *khandies* of rope made from coconut fibres land in Mumbai though it is also made here. Strings are twisted out of the coir. Workshops to make the hawsers for ships are dotted here and there. Ropes as large as an elephant's foot and around four hundred hands long and weighing about four to five *khandies* made in these workshops, are referred to as *kaddori*. Such workshops are located behind the Panjarapole, and at Duncan Road, Chowpatty, Chinch Bunder, and Kamathipura. These workshops are about fifteen to twenty feet long and have some rudimentary wooden machines. Strings are twisted out of coir, fibres from hibiscus seeds and broadcloth. If one wants to see how large ropes are twisted, one has to visit these places. The hawsers are stronger than iron link-chains and are used to anchor the ships to the dock.

All kinds of materials related to shipping are sold in three to four shops run by Parsis in the Fort, and many shops run by Bhatias in Chinch Bunder. Hundreds of *mans* of these ropes are piled up in these shops. There are many kinds of workshops in Mumbai and if one sets about describing all of them, a book as big as the *Bharata* would be written.

1. *Temples at Walkeshwar with the Banganga tank in the foreground; the temple of Rameshwar Shiva (left) and Ganesh (right) with a devotee standing on the bathing ghats.*

2. *A view of the beach at Chowpatty with timber stacked in the foreground. It was beginning to be 'populated with beautiful houses and gardens' visible in the background.*

3. *The temple at Mahalaxmi.*

4. *The Mankeshwar temple built by Ranmull Lakha near the Byculla station.*

5. *A view of the bay from the hill at Mazagaon.*

6. The 'Cotton Green' at Colaba where new facilities for the handling of cotton had been built.

7. *Panoramic view from Malabar Hill overlooking the Back Bay and the island town.*

8. *The Jumma Masjid in Mumbai. The small shops selling various knick-knacks and spices which line the masjid walls are still there.*

9. *The road leading out of Churchgate with a part of the Fort ramparts. The Esplanade (populated by white tents) is in the background.*

10. *A close-up of the Cornwallis Monument on the Bombay Green with the Government House in the background. Note the iron railings used to cordon off the Monument.*

11. *A view over Bombay Green with the harbour in the background. The Town Hall is in the centre with the Mint towards the left. The Bombay Castle and the famous palmyra tree (visible in the centre) are behind the Town Hall. Note the well with a crowd of bullock-carts and horse-carriages in the foreground and the Cornwallis Monument on the right.*

12. *Looking South over the Bombay Green with the Custom House in the middleground. In the background is the Bombay Bay packed with a variety of boats.*

13. *The Sir Jamsetjee Jejeebhoy Hospital at Byculla with the Babula Tank in the foreground.*

14. *The Grant Medical College.*

15. *The Town Hall with a part of the Bombay Green.*

16. *The Cathedral at Mumbai and its clock-tower.*

The Parsis have largely taken the lead in installing machines and establishing factories. They were the first to set up workshops with cotton-screws and to start printing presses. They took up the job of building ships in the docks. The Chief Engineer of the docks is also a Parsi. They introduced cotton spinning and weaving machines and travelled to countries like China, England, and America to establish trade relations. In other words, they have been at the forefront of all initiatives related to trade and other important works. This is the reason why Lakshmi, the goddess of Wealth resides in their houses. This characteristic of theirs is not only worth emulating but also praiseworthy. Only when the Hindus make them their exemplar will they be able to attain the heights of prosperity and fame. There is no point in futilely complaining that Lakshmi has gone to reside in the abode of the foreigner because it is now the Kaliyug. Lakshmi behaves similarly in all ages and does not distinguish between caste, colour or creed. She is quite happy to stay in the house of the lowest *Shudra* and the highest Brahmin. She was as capricious in the Satyug as in the Kalyug. There has been no change in her behaviour. She has always been a slave of industry. It is clear that wherever there is industry, fairness, single-minded devotion and religion, Lakshmi will automatically be there. Kabir has this to say on this subject:

As worries dull the intellect, and ills the body
Do sins reduce wealth, so says Das Kabir

Lethargy is the abode of sin. As lethargy increases in a community, they are slowly impoverished. And if one becomes poor, one should assume that one has many shortcomings. As the English, Parsis, Mussalmans, and Vanis are strenuously exerting themselves, rivers of wealth flow in their houses. They are the wealthy people of Mumbai, and the Dakshinis are hardly comparable to them.

For many years, the people of Bharat Khand had no idea about types and printing. If they were told that letters could be pressed on to paper, they would be mighty surprised. A printed paper was looked at as if a planet had descended from the very heavens. In 1777, a Parsi gentleman named Rustomji Kersasji brought a printing press to Mumbai and published an English almanac in 1780.[2] In 1790, a printing press and newspaper by the name *Gazette* was started. After a couple of years, the *Courier* printing press and newspaper was started. Printing presses in Gujarati and Marathi were established in due course. The first types of the Marathi alphabet were produced at the *American Mission Press*. The missionaries have done many useful deeds in this city. These will be described later but it suffices to say that they also initiated printing in Marathi.

The American missionaries established a printing press in 1813 to produce books printed lithographically in the Marathi language on Christianity. In *Shaké* 1762, that is in the year 1840, the late Ganpat Krishnaji was inspired to establish a printing press for the publication of books on the Hindu religion and other subjects, in a similar vein. However, he did not have any apparatus for printing nor was it available in Mumbai at that time. He then built his own printing press by observing the one at the American Mission. This gentleman belonged to the Bhandari caste. He was very skilled, intelligent, far-sighted and had great faith in the Hindu religion. He first built a wooden machine with his own hands. He then obtained small stones from various places to see how the alphabets could be printed therefrom. He then went about researching the manufacture of inks. He initially produced a few types of inks with formulae of his own making. He finally mastered the whole process with a lot of effort and industry. As he slowly improved the process, his enthusiasm increased and he strived harder. He focused all his attention on the printing press and ultimately achieved the desired results. He then got an iron printing press manufactured here and bought large stones and started printing small books. In 1841, he himself compiled a Marathi *Panchanga* and printed it. Nobody had heard of printed almanacs earlier. Each copy of this almanac was sold for eight *annas*. Though the Brahmins of that time hesitated to touch any printed book, the beautiful print of this accurately prepared almanac enticed them enough to shell out the money and they used it to read the astrological forecasts for the coming year on the *Samvatsar Pratipada*. He showed some of his work to Dr. Wilson, Father Garrett and Father Allan. These Sahibs were delighted to see the books and praised Ganpat Krishnaji's intelligence. They also provided him with some printing work to promote his press. As the fame of his printing press spread, the flow of work increased.

In 1843, he undertook to manufacture the types himself. After many attempts, he made the punches of the alphabets and set up a workshop for casting types. He prepared a complete fount for all the alphabets and started a workshop for printing using types. In both these printing presses, he produced thousands of Gujarati and Marathi books. The works produced by other Marathi presses do not compare to the work produced by his press. He also did some work in English. He undertook the execution of pictures, maps, engravings, and carvings himself. His almanacs were of the best quality and were renowned everywhere. While other almanacs are available for an *anna* or half, his almanac was not priced below four *annas*; it was however purchased eagerly by the people. His printing press is now very big and does a lot of work for both government and business. This gentleman died in 1860. His son Rajashree Kanoba Ganpat, who is also blessed with the best qualities, now runs the press in the same fashion. He has also become a celebrity following in the footsteps of his father.

Many of our guileless and orthodox Brahmins are afraid to touch printed paper. There are many in Mumbai and other places who still do not touch any printed paper and do not read printed books. It is however certainly a happy circumstance that there are over forty presses currently in Mumbai, printing in English, Marathi, Hindustani, and Gujarati. There are seven English newspapers and four English monthlies, ten newspapers and five monthlies in Gujarati, five Marathi newspapers and six Marathi monthlies, and one newspaper each in Hindustani and Portuguese. Besides, every month thousands of text-books are printed in Marathi and Gujarati. Books on religion and many other subjects are also printed. Countless books are published in various languages every year by the priests and distributed all over the city. The bigger presses which are worth visiting are the *Education Society Press* at Byculla, the *Exchange Press* at Fort and *Ganpat Krishnaji's Press* at Dongri.

The printing of books has ignited a desire for knowledge amongst the Parsis. Even the poorest amongst them send their children to schools and are willing to expend money on this account. Earlier, the Parsis were known to indulge in sport and merriment, plays and dances. Once they had learnt a little Gujarati and knew how to sign in English, they set themselves up in business. The Hindus were proud that only they could speak and write in English and none could match up to them in Mathematics and Astrology. Now they have to swallow their false pride. The other Gujarati folk have also turned to education in a lesser or greater degree. As the Parsis have acquired a taste for reading, many Gujarati books are being written; the large number of schools opened for their community has enthused them. The Dakshini Hindu folk have not yet acquired the habit of reading newspapers or Marathi books. It is not that our people are too lazy to read Marathi books; they are not interested in reading English books either. Their minds are mainly engaged in sport and dancing and showing off. The only thing they know is to perpetuate practices which originated thousands of years back and believe that these should not be changed even though they may be harmful or inappropriate in the present time. The English are successful because they introduce new laws and practices every year, focus on their own welfare and apply their minds to the tasks in hand. The Parsis are also behaving on similar lines to some extent. The more educated the Hindu, the more backward he is. He does not think beyond received tradition. Even a Koli or Mali will see the futility of applying the laws of the Kretayug in this Kaliyug under the rule of the English.

New kinds of workshops are established in Mumbai practically every day. In the last few years, workshops have sprung up which plate silver on copper and brass utensils using a machine run on electricity. Practically everybody wants their utensils and the appurtenances of their vehicles cheaply plated. There are many such workshops all over the place. This process, which is known as 'Electroplating' or 'Gilding', produces a clean and smooth surface which lasts for a long time.

In recent days, workshops which use the power of sunlight to produce pictures are dotting the landscape. The machine that produces these pictures is known as the 'Camera'. One can produce pictures of men, animals, houses, and landscapes with this machine. The machine is placed in the sunlight and the face of the man whose image is to be captured is positioned for a few seconds in front of the machine; finally the glass or the paper on which the picture is to be produced is put into the machine. Hundreds of exact copies can be reproduced if required. This is a simple but wonderful process. One is left astounded while observing the process by which these pictures are produced. There are thirty to forty men who can produce such pictures. Many youths have mastered this process and have established workshops in their houses to capture the images of their near and dear ones. Among the Hindus, Dr. Narayan Daji and Harishchandra Chintaman have become experts. Ra. Harishchandra Chintaman has set up a large workshop in the Fort and has published a small Marathi book on this science. Mr. Johnson is famous among the English. He has produced pictures of Gharapuri, Kanheri, and other amazing places, buildings, temples, *et cetera*. He has also photographed men and women of all castes in this city and has taken them to present it to the Empress. He is much acclaimed for his work. Another speciality of this process is that once a picture has been made, hundreds of copies can be reproduced.

Ice is imported from America in the largest ships. Many of our people will surely be surprised when they hear this. About two thousand rupees of this frozen water that is referred to as ice is consumed everyday in this city. There are huge warehouses in the Fort filled with ice. This ice is as hard as stone and comes in blocks weighing about a *khandi*. It is crystal clear and is broken into pieces with an axe. It has to be stored very carefully because if it is exposed to air, it melts and become water. The warehouses where ice is stored are lined with plates of glass and are well secured to prevent air from getting in. It is sold by weight at the rate of ten *rattals* per rupee. It is very cold to touch. The English, Portuguese, Parsi, and Mussalmans are the main consumers. Hardly any Hindu consumes this product. If ice is brought home, it has to be wrapped in felt or wool, to prevent it from melting immediately. Look how the English have imported even water from another continent and turned it into money! Their deeds are truly unparallelled. Many unthinking folk are too lazy to see the amazing things that are present in Mumbai but are willing to travel hundreds of *kos* to see an ordinary dance or a fair. Visits to the numerous workshops of Mumbai will make them better people in all respects.

The diligence and research of the English people is indescribable and their deeds are amazing. In 1862, many of the English felt that transporting thousands of *khandies* of ice from America was too cumbersome and made the ice very costly, they decided to manufacture ice here in Mumbai. To manufacture ice which is naturally made according to divine laws is a remarkable idea! A huge structure has been erected at Girgaon and various machines have been installed to aid in the production of ice. This process confounds the human mind. Water from Vihar has been brought here through pipes. Water is converted into ice by using the power of steam. Water when passed through this machine comes out hard and crystalline. About two hundred *khandies* of ice are produced daily. It is sold at the rate of three-quarters of an *anna* for a *rattal.* From the day the factory commenced production, people have thronged in large numbers to see ice being manufactured.

In 1843, many Englishmen, government employees and private traders realized that the introduction of the steam-train had proved very beneficial for their country and its populace. They felt that the population of Bharat Khand should also partake of this benefit and devised plans to build metal railroads. A few public meetings to notify the public of their plans and invite monetary contributions from them for this act of public good were called. However, it was not well received and numerous objections were raised. It was argued that this was just a new method introduced by the English to collect wealth from this country. They tried to obstruct the plans by making many such objections. Many were afraid that the metalled railroads would destroy their businesses and impoverish them, while the poor would be left destitute. Not much support could therefore be drummed up for this project.

Mr. Chapman was entrusted with the responsibility for this task in 1844. He spent thousands of rupees in advertising the project and tried everything within his means to convince the people of the usefulness of building the metalled railroads. Even this failed to elicit handsome contributions from the people. Finally the Sarkar agreed to assume control over the finances of this company. Under their supervision more money started flowing in. The capital that had accumulated then was 15,000,000 rupees while the present capital of the company is 80,000,000 rupees.

While the metalled railroads were being built, many ignorant people spread the vilest rumours about them and tried to poison the minds of the people. Some said that as the railroad was being laid, a couple had to be sacrificed at periodic intervals. Another rumour was that a child had to be buried under the railroad before it could be properly built. These wild fancies dispirited the people. When the railroad was being built at Khopoli, it was said that a demon who resided in those parts demanded a sacrifice of twelve couples and that soldiers were capturing women and children for that purpose. These rumour-mongers however, quickly realized their foolishness. This shows the ignorance of our people. They spread such empty words since they are unaware of the English belief in the primacy of man's soul and body. They try their utmost to protect it, and have no belief in demons. On 16 April 1853, at five in the evening, the first steam-train left from Mumbai. A public holiday had been declared in all government and business offices. Thousands of people arrived in Mumbai from numerous places to witness this spectacle. Large crowds had gathered from Bori Bunder to Parel about three hours before the train left. The people were amazed to see the speed of the train and communicated their appreciation with loud applause.

Four hundred people including the Governor of Mumbai,[3] important government officials and other prominent traders took the first ride. The train was pulled by three steam engines and had about twenty carriages attached to it. The vehicle left Bori Bunder at five and reached Thana at around six in the evening. It left Thane at about eight in the night to return back to Mumbai. Many wise men are of the opinion that it is the beginning of the new age in Bharat Khand.

Efforts are currently being made to take the railroad over the Bhor Ghat and over thirty thousand people are labouring every day. It is said that to prepare this section of the railroad a sum of five to ten crores of rupees will be spent. Many labourers have been brought over from Europe to tunnel through the mountains and they are paid ten times the amount given to the local labourers. At present, trains travel on 438 miles of railway. In one week of May 1862, the total revenue generated from passenger and goods traffic was rupees 727,151-5-7.

There are two mills for spinning and weaving cloth in the foreign fashion on the road to Mahalaxmi near Tardeo. They have been operating for the last four to five years. The spinning mill was started about two years prior to the weaving mill. The machines and other apparatus in these mills are beyond description. The erection of the weaving mill cost about eleven lakhs of rupees. The construction cost about two lakhs of rupees but the machines cost a lot more. The spinning mill cost about a couple of lakhs lesser.

When we first went to see these machines, the most marvellous scenes came to light. Thick and thin threads were emerging from different machines while coils of thread were neatly stacked elsewhere. Cloth is woven and starch applied to it in quick succession. A second machine dries it while a third machine folds it automatically. These marvels compel us to praise the intelligence and industry of the English. More than a thousand people, including women and children work in each of these mills every day. Ignorant women and children are now able to do the work of skilled artisans. Amazing, isn't it? If one visits these mills, one can see women and children as young as seven or eight operating these machines and doing other jobs. After the opening of these mills, the Maratha women have become smart and diligent. They have lost their fear and have become courageous. All the machines in these mills are operated by the power of steam, and their speed at times can be frightening.

Everyone should visit the mill to observe how foreign cloth is woven, how the finished cloth is stacked, the number of threads being spun in each machine, how the machine automatically stops if even one of these threads snap and how it starts again once the link has been repaired. The designers of these machines must truly have extraordinary brains. Efforts are on to set up five to six similar mills.

The following article published in a Pune newspaper, *Dnyanaprakash*, provides a good description of these workshops. It has been reproduced verbatim below.

Cotton spinning mills in Mumbai

We visited Mumbai for personal reasons and while visiting the numerous workshops in Mumbai, we went to a cotton spinning mill near Tardeo. The astonishment that one felt on seeing the mill cannot be put into words. Where does one start? The structure was about four hundred hands long and about as broad. It is full of machines and wheels which are whirring incessantly. Men are not required to power these wheels, as they rotate automatically. At one place, the cotton is carded and cleaned and all the dirt is removed. In another place, this cotton is converted into hundreds of fine fibrils which are then spun into thick or thin threads in yet another place. While we were standing stunned after seeing these marvels, one of the owners of the mill approached us and asked us, 'Why are you standing here as if shell-shocked? Who are you and where are you from? It seems that you are interested in seeing the mill. Come with me and I will show you everything.' We were then reduced to a state similar to the proverbial 'blind man who asks for an eye and god gives him two'. As the gentleman took us around the factory, he realized that we were strangers to those parts, and explained the functioning of each machine in detail. I guess this mill must have cost anything between five to ten lakhs of rupees. The owner was a grand man but he welcomed this stranger without any arrogance and himself explained the entire operations of the mill with a clear mind. Isn't this marvellous? Only the truly deserving achieve success.

This gentleman first took us to a room which contained three huge iron vessels. Each of them must have been about fifteen hands long and about four hands wide. The water in them was converted to steam by the application of heat. The steam rotated a huge wooden wheel, about twenty hands in diameter, situated in the next room. The gentleman told us that the application of steam rotated the wheel at sixty horsepower.

When we were taken around the other parts of the factory, we saw that the power of this large wheel drove numerous other wheels that powered all the machines and the work was all done automatically. Men were required only at certain times.

In one room there was a big box for cleaning the cotton (fly machine). Bales of cotton are loaded on one side of the box which separates all the dirt and seeds and clean cotton emerges from the other side which is spooled onto a wooden stick. Once one spool is coiled, it is replaced with another stick. In this manner, hundreds of spools of clean cotton are produced every day.

These spools are taken to another large room which must be about sixty hands long. On one side of the room, numerous iron boxes are arranged in a single file and a spool is hung next to each box.

The cotton slowly enters this box and gets carded and comes out in the form of a rope about a finger thick and falls into an iron tube. When about fifty to sixty hands of rope fall into the tube, it gets filled up and is replaced by another one. Once eight such tubes are filled, they are taken to another machine. This machine is known as the Carding Machine. It can also be called a cotton-rope extracting machine.

Now the eight tubes filled with cotton-rope are brought to another machine. All these eight ropes are combined in this machine to form one big rope which gets elongated in some wheels and again comes out as a rope about one finger thick. The machine that elongates the rope is known as the 'Drawing Machine'. The ropes which emerged out of the earlier machine are not uniform in thickness so, this machine makes them uniformly thick. Now that the rope is ready, one can start spinning the thread. As it is difficult to obtain fine thread in one go, it is first twisted into thicker thread in a 'Roving Machine' which twists the rope.

This machine lengthens the rope and it is then twisted into thick thread. The thickness of this thread is about that of a pea. This thread is then wound on to a whirler which is about a span long. These wound threads are now taken to another machine to produce spun yarn. These thick threads enter the machine from one side, are lengthened and then wound on a spindle.

These spindles are then taken to another room where they are arranged next to a wheel which unwinds the thread from the spindles and it is bundled beside the wheel. Once about an *achher* of yarn is collected, it is sold to traders.

This was the wonder which the owner showed us. The most amazing machine was the one which spun the yarn. Sixteen hundred spindles were running simultaneously under the power of steam and approximately one thousand hand lengths of yarn are produced in each spindle every hour. This means that about sixteen lakhs hands of yarn are produced from all the spindles in one hour. These machines run for approximately six hours. This means that at least a crore hands of yarn are produced in this factory every day.

If a man is skilled in the art of spinning, he may produce five hundred hands of yarn every day. If this man sits for two days, he will produce a thousand hands of yarn and if he sits for two hundred days, he will produce one lakh hands of yarn. Two hundred days is almost seven months. Let us assume that this man produces one lakh hands of yarn in six months; he will need fifty years to produce one crore hands of yarn. If one thinks about it, these machines in Mumbai can produce in one day what a man needs fifty years to do. It is suggested that our readers ponder about the power of these machines.

All the machines had not yet been installed in this factory. Machines had been installed in about a fourth of the area. Workmen from England with assistance from our local workers were assembling the other machines. As one enters the workshop, Kamathi women are seen spinning the wheel to make bundles out of the yarn. Two women handled each wheel. Wherever men were required, children between the ages of fourteen and seventeen were seen to be working. When the yarn was being spun, these children attended to the breakages very nimbly. To ensure that the children concentrate on the job, a unique clock has been designed which tracks the amount of work done by each of them and displays it in figures. As they were paid according to the amount of work done per day, they stuck to their jobs assiduously. The native Hindus and Parsis of Mumbai have erected this mill. The machines and experts have been brought from Europe. This business company has collected a capital of five lakh rupees, as told to us by our friend. The work was initiated by Cowasji Nanabhoy Parsi. It is understood that another company has been formed and they are constructing a building near this factory.[4]

The number of workers in the city is increasing rapidly. Yarn and foreign cloth are manufactured here. The Mussalman and Salvi make dress articles like *lugdi, khann, pagoti, shela,* and *dhotarjoda* in this city. There are many skilled artisans among the Lohar, Kansar, Sonar, Sutar, and Kumbhar castes. Woodwork of superior quality not seen in Europe is done here. This may seem like an exaggeration. It is however certainly true that in 1851 when a glass museum was built in London to house artistic and precious objects from all countries of the world, the throne for the Queen was taken from Mumbai. The carvings on the throne were exquisite. A few years back when General Barr Sahib went back to England, he took two small ordinary chairs made from black-wood, which might have cost him around two hundred rupees. About fifteen years ago, a bed was commissioned by a king for his son-in-law and it was kept on public display in Vittalwadi. Thousands of people thronged the place. The work on the bed was very intricate and a lot of money had been spent on it. A similar bed was built for the Raja Bahadur Ganpatrao Gaikwad after a few years. Many people went to the Fort to see this bed too. About five years back, a Parsi ordered an exquisite palanquin for Baijabai which cost around five thousand rupees. It also attracted huge crowds. In 1856, a Parsi from a lane in Shetodi made two small chairs, in which he had put in his best efforts. He was quoting eight hundred rupees for these chairs. In 1861, a table was made for an Englishman, and a Parsi carpenter says that it cost five hundred rupees. Woodwork is mostly done by Parsis but they get the carvings done by Gujaratis. There are many who can produce exquisite wall murals and paintings with earthen colours. Two of the best painters of this type were Ramachandra Chinchankar and Ramachandra Jharya. Their pictures have been sent to England. They could earn a thousand rupees or two by producing a couple of pictures in a year. These famous painters died about fifteen years ago.

The Ghansaris grind stones of various colours at Mumbadevi. They grind stones for rings, pendants, rubies, emeralds, gems to be studded on the lids of snuffboxes, and other ornaments. In 1845, a stone worth 88,844 rupees named *akik* or cornelian was exported to other countries from Mumbai. This stone is brought from Khambayat.

The Multani people produce carved boxes of various sizes from sandalwood, ivory, and black-wood. The biggest of them would be about a hand long. These boxes are of the most wondrous colours. They inlay it with velvet. A few years back these boxes were sold from ten rupees to over two hundred rupees. However they are now currently available for as little as five rupees to around a hundred rupees. The English madams, who mostly buy these boxes, use them to keep their sewing articles and jewellery. It is said that such boxes are not made in Europe and many of them are sent to Europe.

There are many workshops which make new vehicles in this city. Vehicles of many types and superior quality similar to ones made in Europe are manufactured here and many are also imported from London city. One of these vehicles can cost five to six thousand rupees. They have many different names. They are also painted in many colours to a fine mirror finish so that one can see one's face as in a mirror. Cushions covered with many kinds of cloth are placed inside and the interiors are lined with velvet and other expensive types of cloth. The silk curtains and tassels and other appurtenances so enhance the beauty of the vehicle that one is amazed. English, Parsi, and Hindu gentlemen own these workshops. The vehicles have many names – buggy, *kareti*, daynight, phaeton, *rekda*, *shigram*, chariot, open chariot, curricle, brougham, cab, sociable; there are about fifty such different kinds of vehicles which can be seen in Mumbai. The *Puranas* talk about fourteen branches of learning and sixty-four branches of art, but their numbers in Mumbai are beyond counting.

In this city, there are numerous factories which produce a multitude of articles from iron, copper, brass, and tin. There is a large workshop for producing cast iron articles like huge pipes, railings, bars, wheels and anything else which is ordered. A similar workshop is in Nagpada. Braziers, blacksmiths, carpenters, and turners have their workshops in numerous places. Articles worth thousands of rupees are manufactured here. The import of English coal has made work easier for the owners. English coal is very useful in steam-trains, steamships, workshops in the Mint, docks, and gun carriage; and in carpentry workshops to power various machines. These workshops cannot do without this coal for even an hour. Lakhs of *khandies* of English coal are imported every year. Trade worth thousands of rupees is carried out on account of this product. This coal is not made by burning wood but is dug out of the ground like minerals.

Mussalmans and others in this city can produce the most exquisite and intricate designs from silk, *jari*, and brocade. If a rich man orders a vest for his son with some intricate designs, it may cost well over a hundred rupees. The Parsis and Vanis are very keen on embroidered dresses. A lot of embroidered sarees, blouses, shawls, skirts, and caps are made here. A Vani gentleman had produced an embroidered saree studded with pearls.

The poets of Bharat Khand have described the immense wealth of Ravana, King of Lanka. Lanka has been described as the City of Gold and the very gods used to work as his servants. Lord Brahma was his scribe; Varuna, the Lord of Water, his washerman; Vayu, the Lord of Wind, his cleaner; Agni, the Lord of Fire, his priest; Dhanvantri his doctor; Ganpati his cowherd; the king of gods, Indra was his gardener, the Lord of Death, Yama was his water-carrier, and the Lord of Wealth, Kubera himself was his storekeeper. These and other stories are from the *Puranas*. But in modern Mumbai, in the Durbar of the English Sarkar, these stories have come true. Just look! Agni and Varuna are doing strange deeds indeed. They are stamping coins in the Mint. They are running the steamships in the ocean and pulling carriages with thousands of passengers and lakhs of *khandies* of goods over land as fast as the wind. They weave numerous types of cloth and form various articles. They are doing such extraordinary deeds. The goddess Saraswati is at their doorstep at all hours of the day with her open books. The Lord of Industry, Udyog is bending his back to fill their treasuries with bags of silver. The goddess Lakshmi has opened her treasure-chest and urges them to fill their pockets. Vayu is transporting thousands of *khandies* of goods across the seas, besides powering their machines. Dhanvantri has concocted numerous kinds of medicines and chemicals and dispenses them from door-to-door. Kubera is depositing gold, diamonds, rubies and pearls from both the worlds into their houses. The Lord Surya with his chariot full of armaments exhorts them to conquer any country they fancy in all parts of the world. Vidyulata, the goddess of Lightning is willing to work for them as a messenger through their telegraph wires. How can Ravana's wealth compare with all this? In his Durbar, Agni was just a priest and Vayu a washerman; but here they are earning crores of rupees for the English. If Lanka was the City of Gold, there is no harm in terming Mumbai the City of the Philosopher's Stone. A medicine worth a farthing can be sold for hundreds of rupees in the city while somebody who makes sculptures from mud can easily earn a thousand rupees. How can gold retain its value in comparison to all this?

In a similar fashion, sewing is of a very high quality. It costs about twenty-five to thirty rupees to stitch a coat in the English style. If some fashionable person gets a coat stitched out of broadcloth, it would easily cost over ten rupees. A very high quality of needlework is also undertaken here.

There is a large trade in ivory here. It is exported to Europe and hundreds of *khandies* are also consumed locally. Tongue scrapers used by Vanis, toys for children, boxes, containers, caskets, dolls, combs and similar articles with a lot of carving are prepared from ivory. These ivory teeth are as long as five to six hands. An old gentleman remembers that about forty years back, an ivory tusk was landed at the wharf in the Fort which was around fifteen hands long and about one and a half *viti* in diameter.

Workshops to manufacture paper in the English fashion were set up about eight to ten years ago. They turned out to be an expensive proposition as the output was meagre and of low quality. This led to their closure. This activity has however been revived and a workshop has been established in Girgaon. The large machines and the huge wooden vessels for processing rags are worth a look. There is also a steam-powered machine. Thick paper in the Ahmedabadi fashion is also produced in Mumbai. There is also a paper factory in Mahim which produces ordinary paper of the English type.

Glass manufactured here turns out slightly greenish as the people are not familiar with the process. Utensils and other articles made of this glass are very fragile, and crack even if the weight is only slightly more than the norm or if it is over-exposed to the heat of the flame. The manufacture of this glass is sharply reduced because crystal from China and Europe is now cheaply available. Bangles of local design are made here or are obtained from the neighbouring villages.

There are many oil mills at Bhendi Bazaar and Dongri. The Mussalmans mostly do the work of extracting oil from coconut, sunflower, sesame, groundnut, castor-seed and many other seeds; they most frequently extract coconut oil. Ten *pucca sher* of water is added to three *mans* of dried coconut to obtain two *mans* of oil. The residue is used to feed cows, buffaloes, and goats. An Englishman has set up an oil mill at Moti. There is an oil mill at Mahim too. Besides thousands of *khandies* of oil arrives from all the villages around Mumbai. Coconut oil is exported to England in large quantities. It has been estimated that about a third of the oil coming into Mumbai is exported to England.

There are many workshops which produce soap and wax in the English fashion. The Goan Christians make wax-candles of the best quality. A couple of Englishmen have established huge workshops at Chinchpokhli and Mahim to produce soap in the English and Kaparvanji fashion. They also produce many types of wax-candles. A lot of candles are imported from Kochi and Gomantak. A few years back, there were many workshops producing Kaparvanji soap. The Hindus never used to touch soap earlier but some of them are doing so now. Many Brahmins and people of other castes actually took a bath to purify themselves if they touched a piece of soap. Many orthodox women were more nauseated on catching sight of a cake of soap in somebody's hands than when they saw rotten fish!

Liquor worth lakhs of rupees is imported into this city from Europe and many types of liquor are manufactured in this country. In Mumbai, alcohol is made from the sap of the coconut, palmyra palm, and date palm. There were many liquor stills in this place earlier, but they have moved to Uran though a few remain at Mahim. There are retail shops selling liquor run by the Parsis and Bhandaris all over the city at short distances from each other. Besides there are many warehouses owned by the Parsis and English where various wines are sold wholesale. A licence has to be obtained from the Sarkar for the retailing of liquor. The annual licence fee depends on the volume of sales and ranges from one hundred rupees to over five hundred rupees. It is said that the consumption of alcohol has increased since the inception of the English rule. While the English consume a lot of alcohol, they should restrict its sale. Akbar Badshah had banned the sale of alcohol in his empire, but when the English came to stay in Surat, he provided them with a special dispensation by which they could buy and consume alcohol because he believed that 'they are born in the element of wine, as fish are produced in that of water', 'and to prohibit them the use of it is to deprive them of life'. Such were his thoughts.[5]

In Mumbai, there are plans to introduce lights which are powered by gas just as in England. Mr. Forjett has taken this task upon himself and it seems that it will be accomplished fairly soon. Wow! The grand design of Mumbai will be complete with these lights.[6] There is no stopping the establishment of new factories in this city. Once it has been started, it is somehow turned into a success. As the people here are wealthy, no task is too difficult for them. Even as a new venture is being planned, a couple of lakhs of rupees are collected. It seems to be the Sarkar's desire that this project for lights in Mumbai be completed as it has written to the Justices of the Peace, who oversee the law and order in this city to set aside a sum of one and half lakhs of rupees for this project and give it the highest priority.

In Mumbai, the trade in opium runs into crores of rupees, and it is almost a gamble. There are many Marwadi, Vani, and Parsi traders who speculate in opium and gain or lose lakhs of rupees in this trade daily. Thousands of chests of opium are sent to China every year. In 1861, forty five thousand chests were sold in Mumbai. Each chest costs around fifteen hundred rupees and contains three and a half *man* of opium. The Customs Duty on opium runs into lakhs. The earlier rate was six hundred rupees per chest of opium but from October 1861 it has increased to seven hundred rupees. A licence has to be obtained from the Sarkar to retail opium at a cost of eighty rupees. There are forty-one such shops. Besides there are many opium smoking dens or *Chandolkhanas* established by the Chinese in practically every street. This is leading to the utter destruction of the people. Many young men have acquired this habit and their lives have been destroyed. The smoking of opium is known as *Chandol*. Once acquired, this habit cannot be thrown off and it completely destroys the body, mind, and soul. Parents have to guard their children against such addictions more carefully than death itself. Many are of the opinion that the consumption of alcohol has increased among the Hindus since the coming of the English people. It is certainly very sad to note that as enlightened a government as the English Sarkar is allowing the free consumption of such intoxicating substances. While there are many restrictions in the Hindu religion regarding the consumption of alcohol, the *Shudras* and other castes in Mumbai freely consume liquor. There are many who smoke marijuana and drink *bhang*. A licence has to be obtained from the Sarkar for the sale of tobacco, snuff, and marijuana. There are three hundred and fifty shops which sell tobacco in Mumbai, while there are shops in every street which sell *paan supari*. Local tobacco is procured from Bhadoch, Surat, Dharwad, Miraj, and Sindh. The tobacco from Miraj is considered to be the best among them. Snuff and tobacco of superior quality is imported from Europe and America. This tobacco comes in many forms – plaits, threads, cakes, and filaments; it is black in colour and soft to touch. The various types of snuff include Rafi, Mecoba, and Portuguese; Mecoba snuff is sold at the rate of ten to twelve rupees per *rattal*.

In Mumbai, there are *paan supari* shops at a distance of every few hands. If some rich gentleman or friend comes home visiting, some people first welcome them with *paan supari*. If somebody is keen on smoking tobacco, he is offered the hubble-bubble. Offering a pinch of snuff to friends is considered to be a great sign of friendship! If one meets somebody on the road and offers him an open box of snuff, it is considered to be a great honour! He may either use it or cast it away on the road, but he cannot refuse to take a pinch!

The practice of eating *paan supari* is widespread among the local population. One comes across people who eat *paan* worth four *annas* in a day. Previously, raw *paan* used to come in at Mandvi and was ripened here. The ripened leaves are sold at the rate of one per quarter *anna*. Betel nut is procured from many regions. It comes in many forms – *chikni, pandhri, bardi, bedi.* The *pandhri* or white *supari* from Shrivardhan is excellent and there are many who are skilled in cutting and cleaning it. It can be cut in three to four ways – as fine as a saffron filament, or a little thicker, or as thin as an onion peel. Ripened *paan* from Pune is most popular these days. *Paan* is also grown at Mahim. *Supari* is also grown there. The red *fulbardi supari* from Vasai is par excellence. Every year, *paan* worth more than a lakh of rupees is consumed here.

There are many shops which sell intoxicating substances of various types in Mumbai. Opium is sold in ten to fifteen different forms – *goli, madat, furmishun, chandol, kusumba, et cetera.* Other intoxicating substances include *majoom, bachnag, ludgee, bhang,* and *ganja.* There are *bairagis* who consume intoxicants made from arsenic. These intoxicants have burnt up many bodies and destroyed many minds.

While there are many wonderful places on this island, there are numerous hellholes full of vice too. It has been mentioned that there are *chandolkhanas* here, but to describe them fully will require the skills of a person who has been to hell and back. The Chinese, who are expert opium-eaters and can tolerate a high level of intoxication, manage these places. *Chandol* is opium processed into tablets. It is smoked through a *hookah.* These *hookahs* and hubble-bubbles are of a special type. They do not have any fire burning in them; instead a burning wick dipped in *ghee* is held in the right hand and held to the bowl where the tablet is kept and a deep breath is taken in. One has to lie down while smoking *chandol,* and there are various misshapen cots, beds, and benches scattered all around. Coarse bamboo mats are laid on them and opium addicts from practically all castes like Mussalman, Brahmin, Prabhu, Shenvi, Sonar, and Bhatia are sprawled on them. Somebody is glaring; someone is vomiting; flies cover a person's face; somebody is coughing, contorting his face or sucking on a piece of sugar cane; somebody is popping pomegranate seeds into his mouth; or eating bananas; and some lie sprawled unconscious. There is filth and refuse lying all around and it is altogether degrading. All those who have become opium addicts seem gaunt and horrible to look at. Once a healthy boy of sixteen starts smoking opium, he is reduced, within a period of six months, to a state of emaciation. The mask of death is on them. Their lips are dark and black. Their faces are listless. Many children in Mumbai have been lost to the world due to this addiction. If one just peeps into this place, it is enough to give one shivers of fright. One is reminded of the Puranic tales of Yama and his hell when one see these ghost-like bodies sprawled around in a haze of smoke. The only difference is that these people have come here voluntarily. Once a man wanders onto these paths, he seems to prefer the tortures of hell! Isn't this very strange! It is best if the English Sarkar puts an end to these activities.

It is true that there is no fear of *pindaries* and dacoits in Mumbai presently, but there is a constant dread of imposters, fraudsters, and tricksters. These people are even more dangerous than the *pindaries*. The *pindaries* grab what they can at one go but there are others who insidiously destroy one's wealth and mind. These are the alchemists who come in the form of *bairagis, gosavis, sanyasis,* and *fakirs*. They beguile people in various ways and convince them of their powers of alchemy. Once somebody is drawn into their clutches, it is impossible for him to back out. On occasion they have run away with a couple of thousand rupees. Often, they reside here in Mumbai and try to acquire wealth by perpetrating various frauds. Their alchemy is just a fraud. They con people by lighting a fire with a little bit of vegetable fat containing a small bit of gold and then claim that they have produced gold. Many rich people in this island have got entangled in their wiles and have been reduced to beggary. It is still amazing that people are not more careful. They are very cruel besides. Commenting on this craze for alchemy, the wise wife of a rich Parsi gentleman commented, 'How stupid can these people be! They want to turn copper into gold under the influence of alchemists. They do not come to their senses in spite of being cheated so often. Where is the power of alchemy? Alchemy is in industriousness. If man is industrious and hard-working enough, he is able to convert mud into gold; how can any form of alchemy exceed that?'

Sweetmeats pour into Mumbai from various countries, while numerous kinds of sweets are also made here. One can get any kind of sweet or delicacy – *burfi, peda, jilebi, mawa, maisur, basundi, malai, sakharpheni, boondi laddu, puri, paapad, bhaji*. One can also buy sweets prepared and sold by people of various castes. There are huge factories in the Fort and other places run by the English, Parsi, or Christians which produce English sweets, bread and biscuits. Huge quantities of these sweets are sold during Christmas and the New Year. One can get everything one wants in this city. About ten years back, somebody had served a meal with a thousand dishes – *burfis* and *puris* were included in the menu.

Numerous kinds of firecrackers are available in the market – sparklers, flowerpots, moonlights, rockets, fire-wheels, and so on – and are purchased by the people during Deepawali. Exquisite fireworks used to be made in Mumbai a few years ago but there is nothing worth describing these days. In the year the Honourable Mountstuart Elphinstone was to leave for home, the people of this island had held a reception. A grand function was organized in a huge marquee erected at the Camp Maidan near

Churchgate. The display of fireworks on this occasion was marvellous; people compared it to the burning of Lanka.

Thousands of rupees worth of fireworks are imported every year from China. Similarly thousands of rupees of this stuff is sent to other regions.

Everybody is allowed to travel freely by the landways and waterways. Railroads are currently being built which will facilitate travel from Kashi to Rameshwar. Small steamships are easily available to go to places like Karachi, Sindh, Khambayat, Surat, Karnatak, Goa, Vengurla, and Ratnagiri. They traverse along these routes two or three times in a month and ferry passengers. These steamships are built here in Mumbai. There is a separate company which runs this service known as 'The Oriental Steam Navigation Company'. The factories to make these steamships are mostly run by the Parsis. In this city one only needs wealth, health, and brains to achieve anything; if anyone wants to circumnavigate the world, he can do it quite easily and in a very short while.

This city is full of jewellers who make gold and silver ornaments and gem jewellery of the highest quality; studded rings and other jewellery made in Mumbai are exported to Europe. The English people do not have the desire to wear gold ornaments on their body. They may, perhaps, wear a diamond ring. Their ladies may, on occasion, wear a bracelet studded with gems. Their ornamentation is all in their clothes.

The jewellery worn by the Bhatia, Vani, Kutchi, and Mussalman women is huge and clumsy. The Bhatia women wear silver anklets weighing over ten *shers* and they are strange and squat-shaped. Ordinary and gold-plated ivory bracelets are common. Their gold jewellery is also clumsy and their nose-rings weigh around two to four *tolas*, the central portion is as thick as a child's little finger. The nose-ring is tied with silk threads to ensure that it does not break and fall off. Their entire appearance and ornamentation is just as clumsy. The Marwadi women are about the same.

The Parsi women also wear jewellery, but they are fairly coarse and do not have any delicacy about them. They seem to bother less with jewellery these days. Their nose-rings are very ordinary and many of them do not wear it. There is no compulsion amongst their women to wear chains, anklets and toe rings on their feet. The men do not wear any jewellery, save, perhaps, a diamond ring.

The jewellery worn by the Prabhu, Sonar, Shimpi, Sutar, Shenvi and Brahmin women are very similar, though there are a few differences. These people love to wear heavy jewellery. Hardly anybody prefers to wear delicate and well-crafted ornaments. They sport excessive jewellery on their hands including a wristlet weighing six *shers*, a *tod* of four *shers*, bangles weighing two *shers*, and and a bracelet weighing five *shers*. Most of the Hindus in Mumbai have an eye for heavy jewellery. The women of the *shudra* folk normally wear silver. The jewellery of the Koli, Kharvi, Ghanti, and Kumbhar are of different forms and styles. The jewellery of the Pardeshis is particularly obscene. The diameter of the nose-ring of these women is occasionally around half a *veet*. It has been observed that they pass their food through this ring and then into the mouth. If all the various kinds of ornaments and jewellery worn by the different castes and races of Mumbai are collected, the number could exceed five thousand.

Prominent gentlemen also wear a lot of jewellery including rings on their hands, chains around their neck, and pendant rings called *chowkda* in their ears. The *chowkda* is more commonly worn by the Gujar folk, but even they are giving up this practice gradually. Men of the Prabhu, Shenvi, and Sonar communities also wear rings, chains, and other trinkets. About eighty years back, even men used to strut around with pride wearing bracelets weighing four *shers* and chains weighing hundred *tolas* dangling from their necks. The famous Dhakjee Dadajee wore a bracelet for many years. A rich Prabhu gentleman named Sunderlahiri used to wear a lot of ornaments. It is the practice among many respectable people to present a child with a gold chain, ear-studs and a golden waist-thread on the sixth day after its birth. By the time the child is five years old, ornaments worth seven to eight thousand rupees adorn its body. This is the practice among the rich in Mumbai, and even the poor take loans and other burdens to continue this ancient practice. This practice of wearing jewellery has spelled doom for many children. Many women have lost their lives, and many have become bankrupt and gone into exile. Every year, there are at least five criminal cases before the Magistrate relating to attacks on children wearing jewellery. This has not stopped our people from indulging in this vice. The craze for jewellery has prevented us from elevating our children to the rank of the scholarly and the learned.

Many government employees, magistrates and scholars have talked about the ills of making children wear jewellery and have urged the people to drop this practice. They have not been very successful. Mr. Forjett wrote a small pamphlet on this subject in the Marathi language and distributed it all over the island. He has skilfully highlighted the risks which women and children run when they wear jewellery.

The desire to wear gold and silver jewellery is so strong amongst the populace of Mumbai that even the wife of an ordinary clerk with a salary of fifteen to twenty rupees will bedeck herself with about a *man* of gold, besides other kinds of ornaments, on festive occasions. These ornaments have normally been collected from around ten to twenty acquaintances; but her demeanour leads one to believe that she owns all of it. A few years back, the late Professor Henderson came across a procession on the Kalbadevi Road. Observing the ladies who were bedecked from head to toe, he commented, 'Even Queen Victoria's treasury has less gold than the house of a clerk in Mumbai'. The vain exhibition of wealth has become harmful to us Hindus.

Chapter 11

*Town Hall – Royal Asiatic Society – Geographical Society – Agri-Horticultural
Society – Bombay Association – Mechanics Institution – Board to make books in
the Southern languages – Native General Library and other libraries – Museum –
Victoria and Albert Museum – Victoria Garden*

The initiatives undertaken by the English people to erect buildings and
edifices to add grandeur to the city without any expense on the part of
Sarkar are very commendable. One is amazed and stunned by their ability
to collect money through various schemes. Just look at the scheme they
launched for building the Town Hall, an enormous and extremely useful
building. In 1811, Sir James Mackintosh was the President of an
organization known as the Literary and Scientific Society that worked
towards the acquisition of knowledge.[1] He was the one who conceived this
building based on feedback received from many citizens of Mumbai. Many
prominent citizens felt that a city like Mumbai should have a grand edifice
for gatherings of the scholarly and respectable people, the establishment of a
library, or for prominent public meetings for discussing various issues. As
this project required a lot of money, it was planned that the Sarkar would
float a lottery scheme, and any profits obtained from the sale of lottery
tickets would be used to fund the building. Everybody assented to his speech
and to his profitable scheme. Once the assent of the government was
obtained, the first lottery scheme was launched. The brisk sale of tickets led
to a good collection. Some of the tickets were unsold, and one of these
tickets won the grand prize of around fifty–sixty thousand rupees, besides
other smaller prizes. Thus a collection of over a lakh was made in the first
lottery scheme. This led them to believe that if two or three such lottery
schemes were to be floated, the money required to construct the building
could be raised. However the second lottery scheme was not successful as
very few tickets were sold because of some misunderstanding in the minds of
the people. In spite of this setback, a profit of thirty thousand rupees was
made. The lottery was abandoned thereafter.

In many lottery schemes that were launched earlier, fraud was rampant.
These lotteries had a variety of prizes including gold and silvery jewellery,

clothes with gold brocade, houses, estates, clocks, and money. People rushed into this business as money could be doubled quite easily. Occasionally, the Sarkar would launch a lottery scheme. These schemes led to numerous people bearing losses while just one person profited. The Sarkar has prohibited this trade as it is akin to gambling. This has led to the welfare of the people. Many have been utterly destroyed by their craze for gambling.

About twenty years back (around the year 1840), a poor Gujarati potter had subscribed hundred and twenty-five rupees to a lottery and won seventy-five thousand rupees. However as the man was thoughtless and profligate, he ran through the money in about a couple of years and went bankrupt. He then went to jail for a debt of twenty-five odd rupees. His distress ultimately led to his untimely death. Wealth obtained by such means, more often than not, leads to such an end. There is a proverb in English that goes thus. 'A man who becomes rich in one year is reduced to a beggarly state in six months.'

Another story about the lottery schemes has come within hearing. It is not possible to determine when this event exactly happened. A Bhangi won a prize of one lakh rupees in a lottery. When he went to collect the money in the Fort, he went hysterical with joy on seeing the moneybags and died on the spot. If one tries to become rich overnight, one ultimately meets with such experiences.

Once the Company Sarkar had allotted a place for building the Town Hall, designs were prepared for the building, and engineers were assembled to build it. The work was started even though the money was insufficient. The Company Sarkar made a contribution of ten thousand rupees and the work started in earnest in September 1821. Captain Hawkins was named as the Superintendent of this venture.

In 1823, the money ran out and though over two lakhs of rupees had been spent on the building, it was concluded from fresh estimates that this building could be completed at a cost of three lakhs of rupees. It was felt that the Company Sarkar should take over the responsibility of this project; the Company Sarkar in turn wrote to the main Court of Directors in London town. They wrote back saying that if a large part of the area was given over to government offices, the Company Sarkar could take over the responsibility of completing the building. Once this was agreed upon between the parties, the Company Sarkar took over the building, undertook to spend the necessary money, restarted the construction in 1826 and quickly completed the building. However the building was not constructed as per the original plan. It had some drawbacks. This building is 260 feet long and 100 feet wide and took over fifteen years for its completion. On the

Southern side of the principal hall of the building, a statue of Mountstuart Elphinstone Sahib has been installed, and towards the North are statues of Sir John Malcolm and the famous trader, Sir Charles Forbes. In the front is the statue of the illustrious, philanthropic, and famous businessmen Sir Jamsetjee Jejeebhoy. Statues of two other famous Englishmen have also been installed. A total of five lakh rupees were spent in the construction of this building. The Company Sarkar spent 386,165 rupees while the remaining was spent by the earlier team.

Meetings of the Council, Durbar, and those relating to government and trade are held here. Many government offices and various philanthropic organizations have their offices here. The skilled engineers, Colonel Cowper and Colonel Waddington, completed this building.

The offices of two famous organizations, the Agri-Horticultural Society and the Geographical Society are situated in the Town Hall.[2] The objectives of the Agri-Horticultural Society are to introduce improved methods of gardening and to procure and sell seeds of various new types of plants from the European continent and other nations. This has led to the planting of many European trees in India. Beautiful gardens are being created. This society sells seeds of European vegetables like cabbage, salad leaves, French beans, turnip, kohl, cauliflower, parsnip, and lucerne. They provide all kinds of encouragement to committed gardeners who plant new varieties of fruits and vegetables and take good care of them. They used to give awards to gardeners that ranged from a pair of bullocks, an English plough, an English blanket and other implements and tools. It is not known why this has been stopped in recent years.

The objective of the Geographical Society is to collect new information on various places in the Bharat Khand and describe the land and recount the discovery of new mineral deposits, plants and animals and present the findings in front of the Society. These accounts are filed at the Society's office and collected together and published in an annual publication. Various kinds of objects have been collected in the Society's offices. The members of the Society are Englishmen and quite a number of Parsis and Hindus. This Society has rendered a lot of help to the science of architecture and agriculture.

If one takes the stairs up from the Northern entrance of the Town Hall, one reaches the famous and extensive library of 'The Bombay Branch of the Royal Asiatic Society'. The joy one feels when one sees the various wonders of Mumbai are multiplied a thousand-fold when one sees this library. One should stand at the centre of this library and look in all the four directions – shelves upon shelves of books in various languages arranged from the floor to the ceiling. There is a huge collection of Sanskrit books towards one side. To the other side are thousands of books written in Marathi, Gujarati, Arabic, Hindustani, Kannada and other languages of Bharat Khand. Various ancient artefacts are kept in a separate chamber. A first-time visitor is bound to be astounded by the number of books in English. A team of five to ten people has been appointed to take care of this library. The members of this library have all sorts of facilities for study in the library.

Just imagine the extent of efforts undertaken by the authors of these books written on various subjects! How many nights must they have been awake? How many years of study must they have undertaken? For how many years did they forego the pleasures of worldly life? How much money must they have spent? Through what tortures did they have to put their body through? Nobody can answer these questions. A native poet has this to say.

How, in the sea, do the fish sleep?
Become one and go far into the deep.

One can obtain books on practically every subject one can imagine. It is not wrong to say that the knowledge scattered in various parts of the world has been gathered together at this one place. The mention of the one lakh books in the library leads one to think of those one lakh philanthropic scholars, endowed with skill and art. One begins to wonder about the nature of this assemblage of one lakh people, their habits and demeanour, and the various efforts they must have made to collect this knowledge. As one enters the portals of this place, one thinks of Vyasa, Valmiki, Parashar, Gautam, Manu, Panini, Patanjali, and Katyayana – the wise men of our land who shone the light of their knowledge on this world and have become immortal having drunk from the nectar of knowledge. One also thinks of foreign writers and scholars like Homer, Hesiod, Herodotus, Plato, Aristotle, Pythagoras, Virgil, Cicero, Seneca, Pliny, Bacon, Newton, Locke, Harvey, Milton, Shakespeare, and Baron. The thought itself is mind-boggling. If we had not been exposed to their fount of knowledge and wisdom, how could we have even thought of them? A place which can engender such ennobling thoughts can hardly be compared with any other place.

It is not the objective of the members of this library to collect huge tomes to decorate their shelves. The Society has taken upon itself the challenging task of collecting the ancient writings of this land in the form of stone inscriptions, copper plates and other writings on the arts and sciences and studying them thoroughly. There is also a huge collection of coins, seals and stamps to help in the study of kings and emperors of this ancient land and determine the period of their reign. Hundreds of rupees are spent on deciphering ancient scripts and their meanings are expounded in articles published in a book reviewing the yearly activities of the Society. This work has been entrusted to the famous scholar, Dr. Wilson who is assisted by a Pundit engaged at fifty rupees per month with the help of the Sarkar. The Sarkar has spent over thirty thousand rupees on this account. When scholarly Englishmen are posted in different parts of the country, they write essays on any new topic which they may encounter and send it to this Society. After the essay has been presented in the Society, it is published in a book. The library has been run in this manner without any obstacles since its establishment. A book in this library titled 'The Discovery of Asia' contains beautifully written essays on the kings and palaces of Bharat Khand, its temples and ancient scripts. One is often unable to track down factual accounts of many of our kings; the work of this charitable Society has enabled us to gain a better understanding. Have they not done us a big favour? This library publishes very useful books in this manner. Of the many excellent books published in England every year, five thousand rupees' worth of books are bought every year which the members can read in turn; it is the practice of this Society to maintain a collection of monthly and quarterly magazines and newspapers for the use of its members. See how their altruistic activities have advanced their own knowledge and kindled the desire for knowledge in others too. The number of books in this library is increasing rapidly. A few years after its establishment, it was decided to publish a catalogue of books in the Society; the late General Vans Kennedy undertook this task very diligently. This catalogue has been published in two huge volumes. This work could only have been undertaken by a person who was very scholarly, intelligent and had an excellent command of five or six languages – all the qualities which were endowed in General Kennedy. As the number of books has increased lately, a thousand rupees have been set aside to prepare a new catalogue but it is not easy to find a capable person in the mould of Kennedy Sahib. It is said that this gentlemen had the names of all the books in this library on the tip of his tongue.

This is a branch of a large library in the city of London called the Royal Asiatic Society. One can imagine the immense size of the London library that is like a tree compared to its branch in Mumbai. Apart from having thousands of books written and published in countless languages, this library houses ancient artefacts from Asia and other continents and the fruits of knowledge of this tree-like library are enjoyed by thousands of people.

The members of the Mumbai branch of this library have to pay an annual subscription fee of one hundred rupees. Members no longer resident in Mumbai have to pay an annual fee of fifteen rupees. The Society holds monthly meetings. Only scholarly and respectable persons who would use the library for purposes of acquiring knowledge are granted membership of this Society. A rich person who is not a scholar is not given membership just to increase numbers. The Governor of the Mumbai Province is typically the patron of this Society and a learned person of the rank of the Chief Justice is the President of the Society. When the Society was first established, Sir James Mackintosh was the President. This illustrious and scholarly gentleman discharged the responsibilities of this position with judgement and discrimination. The philanthropic and scholarly Dr. Wilson was the President of the Society for many years and he is currently the President Emeritus. He has worked very hard for the welfare of this Society and has encouraged the native people to become members and benefit from this Society. When Sir Erskine Perry was the President of the Society, he reduced the fees the native people were charged to fifty rupees to induce them to become members.

It is now imperative for us to know how and when this tree of knowledge came into being and who was responsible for its birth. Everybody should know the name of that wise and thoughtful gentleman who has done us such an enormous favour. A few years back, a very impartial, intelligent and indefatigable judge was appointed to the Supreme Court in Mumbai. He was Sir James Mackintosh.[3] He established this Society in 1804 for the welfare of the people and, as already mentioned, was the first President. Nobody should think that this Society was established only for the English people. There is no doubt whatsoever that it was the intention of this philanthropic gentleman to enable the native people of this country to acquire knowledge through this Society.

In 1861, this Society had sixty-five members resident in Mumbai and forty-five members resident in other places. The number of native people is so few that it is almost shameful to mention it. Most of the native members are Parsis. There are very few Hindus. Isn't this a sad state of affairs? Mumbai is the seat of English knowledge and business and trade. If such an advanced aggregation of people are too lazy to read books in this library or at their residences, what must be the state of people in other areas? Only a city with numerous schools and libraries with innumerable readers will be able to achieve material progress. However many of our rich people believe that there is a natural enmity between Lakshmi and Saraswati. If one of them stays in a particular place, the other prefers not to reside there. This fear makes them abandon the pursuit of knowledge. This is however only an imaginary fear. There is no doubt that knowledge begets happiness. Just observe! The learned Englishmen are more often than not rich, happy and famous.

One is able to judge a man by his actions. When strangers observe our indifference towards education, they will obviously believe we are ignorant. One comes across a story in the books about the Roman Emperor Caesar travelling in state along a road; his eyes alighted on a stranger carrying a puppy and a baby monkey in his arms and fondling them; the following words came out of his mouth, 'Do no women of this people bear children?' In a similar manner, when the English see us relying on our puerile tales, they say, 'How can these Hindus be so ignorant? Is there no scholarly or learned person among them?' A few days back, an Englishman uttered the following words. 'O Hindus! I honour you because of the past scholars of your race, but I pity you for your current indifference towards learning.'

It has been over fifty-six years since this library has been established. Hundreds of Englishmen have been its members in this period. They have done their various researches on Bharat Khand and have published them in mighty tomes under the auspices of this Society, and they continue to do so. How many of our fellow native citizens have used the facilities of this library and published books in their own interest or for public good in this long period? The late Bal Gangadharshastri was a member of this Society.[4] He accumulated as much knowledge as he could in his brief life. One comes across many of his articles written in the English language and published in the annual reviews of this Society and the Geographical Society. One may come across a couple of such scholars on the membership rolls of this Society. This however amounts to nothing when seen against the eight lakh citizens of Mumbai, 'A drop in the ocean.' It would not be wrong to say that these two scholars represent not just the population of Mumbai but also the total population of over two and half crores in the Mumbai Province.

As we did not have the culture of establishing libraries in earlier times, it was very difficult for a person from the ordinary classes to obtain a book for his study. If a book was lent to someone, one was not sure if it would be returned.

One came across the following story in a book; a very aged gentleman in the country of France published a well-written book on agricultural science for the public good in his ninety-fifth year. If one keeps up such excellent practices, one will be able to achieve good results. However our people are under the impression that a deep and vast study of books renders one mad. Many of our people who do not undertake any economic activity in their dotage just while away their time or indulge in useless practices. If these gentlemen spend their time in such libraries, read books and write their opinions, it will greatly benefit them as well as the country. One was taken aback to hear the following question from an English scholar. 'Can man live without reading books?' I would rather not comment on how our people will respond to this question.

Only when our youth and old people behave in a reformed manner will they be able to experience the joys of learning.

General Vans Kennedy, who has been mentioned earlier, used to read Sanskrit books at the age of ninety with the help of pundits. He used to read new books in Marathi, Gujarati, and English in his spare time. Many of the Englishmen use their lives in a similar manner to acquire knowledge.

In 1852, a very important event occurred in this city. The native citizens of all castes including rich businessmen, government servants and other prominent citizens established a society. The objective of this society was to address the problems and difficulties, if any, faced by the *ryot* and present it before the Company Sarkar and try to ensure the happiness of the *ryot*. If required, they could write to the Chief Sarkar with the permission of the Company Sarkar to ensure the peace and happiness of the country. These were the praiseworthy goals of this society. This society was called the 'Bombay Association'. When the first meeting of the organization was held, the grandeur and intelligence of the participants made one feel that they would forthwith expel poverty and unhappiness from this country. Many also felt that this organization had been modelled on the lines of the Parliament of England and represented the interests of the people. However, nothing of note has been achieved by this organization to date. They have not investigated the nature of ills facing the *ryot*, and do not seem to intend to do so in the future. People are not wrong when they say that our folk are not persevering enough to complete tasks undertaken by them. The society was reduced to a state of torpor. While citizens of different castes and races may sit in the same forum, there is no unity of thought in them. They do not behave in a free and frank manner with each other. They do not behave with a spirit of generosity that is imperative in such forums. This has led to the failure of all our ventures that are designed to promote the welfare of our country. While they may have cordial relations with each other, either the basic differences of caste or some other reason creates doubts in their minds. This is our biggest enemy. Only when the native people of Mumbai interact with each other in a frank and generous manner will there be happiness; otherwise, the establishment of even a hundred such organizations and a thousand schools will be futile. Everybody should have the same level of national pride for these things to be successfully concluded. All men should behave equitably with each other without discriminating on the basis of caste. The following article on this subject was published in the *Dnyanodaya*.

A meeting of the native people was held at the *Elphinstone Institution* at four in the evening on the fifth of last month. The objective of this meeting was to establish an organization that would work for the welfare of our people when new laws would be drafted. The Shrimant Rajamanya Rajashree Jagannath Shankarseth was the chief guest and he aptly said that since the English Sarkar was working for the welfare of the *ryot*, it was not their intention to work against the government; rather they would convey to the government, well-considered suggestions for the welfare of the *ryot*. We should be ardent in rendering this assistance to the government. If proper requests are made to the government, it is unlikely that they will be rejected. After many speeches in the same vein, it was decided to establish an organization called the 'Bombay Association' which after consultations with similar organizations in Calcutta and Madras would present the suggestions which were considered as appropriate. Contributions were collected to fund the activities of the organization. The objectives, rules and regulations of the organization were decided and representatives were nominated as follows:

Sir Jamsetjee Jejeebhoy, Knight	Honorary Chief
Shrimant Jagannath Shankarseth	President
Bomanjee Hormuzjee	Vice-President
Cursetjee Jamsetjee	Vice-President
Dr. Bhau Daji and Vinayak Jagannathji	Secretary

Fifteen other prominent gentlemen were nominated to the Committee. The principal contributors to this Society were as follows.

	Rupees
Sir Jamsetjee Jejeebhoy	3,000
Jagannath Shankersethji	1,000
Sakharam Lakshmanji	1,000
Dhunjeebhoy Nusserwanjee Cama	1,000

Contributions were received from other people and a total of twenty thousand rupees were collected by 26 August 1852.

We are grateful that the report of this organization reached us. The report describes the achievements of this organization, but these, which undoubtedly are for the welfare of the people, seem very trivial. It does not seem that these issues will make a fundamental difference to the welfare of the country. It will not improve the state of the country. There are two ways to improve the fortune of a country – firstly through rules and secondly through the efforts of its people. This organization should present the means of improvement through the proper framing of rules to the law-making body and urge them to convert their suggestions into laws. If such an organization makes a request, the law-making body will accept it. They will repeal unnecessary laws and introduce new rules that are currently required. This organization should work in this manner while its members should set an example before the people about how they have reformed themselves, and help their fellow citizens in following their model. It is hoped that the members of the Association will muster enough courage and will reach new heights of success.

Dnyanodaya
4 July 1856

There is a society of learned men known as the Mechanics Institution. Its objectives are the spread of knowledge and happiness through the study of the English sciences of Architecture, Art, Chemistry, and Material Science. Its members include government employees and other gentlemen. They present lectures in turns, about eight to ten times a year for the public good. Everybody is welcome to attend these lectures. They also read essays every week when meetings of the society are held. These meetings can be attended only by invitation. The meetings of the society are held at the Town Hall. Its library has also been set up in the same place. The Chief Engineer of the railway company, Mr. Blackie was the President of this society for many years. Colonel Barr is currently the President. Many native scholars are members of this society. A small subscription has to be paid every month by its members. The best speeches and essays in the English language are awarded prizes worth one or two hundred rupees on each occasion. Gold and silver medals are also awarded to deserving individuals. The goals of this institution are also praiseworthy. If students from our community enrol themselves as members of this society and regularly write essays and deliver speeches, they will be able to completely understand the intricacies of the English language and will have the same command over the language as the English people themselves. The presence of these societies enhances confidence and improves oratory skills. One is confident of one's writing abilities and is able to distinguish between good and bad writing. If one is called upon to speak in front of a strange audience, one normally develops the jitters. These societies are essential to be able to overcome such difficulties.

In 1849, a society engaged in the production of books in the Dakshini languages called the Deccan Vernacular Translation Society was established in this city. The driving force behind this society were Colonel French, who replaced General Outram as Resident in Baroda a few years back, and the late Captain Hart, who managed the Pensions Office. Both these gentlemen had a great deal of affection for the native people and were committed to raise the levels of ability in all areas amongst our people. They were of the opinion that producing numerous entertaining and informative books on various subjects in the native languages could cure the present distaste for books among the native people. This would create an interest for learning in them and they would automatically gravitate towards learning English and the modern sciences. They pursued this idea for the sole purpose of the welfare of the people and wrote letters to prominent citizens and convened a meeting in this regard. The Governor was also a member of this society. Many prominent local citizens including Ram Lal, Jagannath Shankarseth, and Bomanji Hormuzji also became members. Shamsher Bahadur Raja Sahib Ganpatrao Gaikwad had visited this place in 1849. He gave five thousand rupees to this Society. The Honourable Willoughby Sahib, Councillor was the President of this Society. The Society collected twenty-five thousand rupees for this commendable task. This sum was kept as a deposit and the interest was used to employ a couple of people and when the occasion demanded, they would use part of the original sum, with the permission of the members to translate the best English books into Marathi and publish it. The books were sold at a nominal cost. Any surpluses were added to the original sum. This rule of keeping the original sum of money sacrosanct is very good. In this manner, they have published eight to ten books of excellent quality to date. But what do our people think? Their current state of appreciation is similar to 'dancing for the blind and singing for the deaf'. They do not have any desire to improve their lot. This Society prints thousands of books but that does not make any difference to our people. The Society has diverted its funds for this great task but as our people are not willing to spare any money to buy these books, they have run out of money and this has led to a slowdown in their work, though they still continue to publish books. The first Secretary of this Society was Captain Hart who carried out his duties with a great sense of commitment. His desire was that all the Dakshini noblemen and kings in the Bombay Province should patronize this Society. He suggested that entertaining books be sent to them to enable them to develop an interest in reading. He had considered this as the chief objective when he agreed to become the Secretary. He however died about two years before this could be achieved. This was a great loss to our people. This gentleman alone could have worked a lot to spread the love of knowledge among our people. The present Secretary of this Society is the Chief Translator of the Supreme Court, Mr. Flynn and he is assisted by Narayan Dinanathji.

A library called the Native General Library was established in the year
1845. It had many supporters among the natives and the English, but the
prime force behind this organization was Raghoba Janardhan. He is
currently the Deputy Collector and Magistrate at Belgaum. He was earlier
the Chief Clerk in a government office known as the Military Board. He
undertook this effort for the welfare of the people. It is said that the Late Bal
Gangadharshastri also helped to set up this library. The library is currently
situated at Dhobi Talao. It has books on two thousand and thirty-five
subjects in the English, Marathi, and Gujarati languages. The monthly fee
ranges from four *annas* to two rupees. There are three categories of members
who pay rupees two, rupee one or four *annas*. The more you pay, the more
books you can issue and take home. Many educated men visit the library in
the morning and evening to read newspapers and other books. One can
read books in Marathi, English, Gujarati and other languages, and is free to
take any book home. It has to be returned back on the specified day. In
1862, the Secretary of this library was Sir Ardaseer Framjee, who was
committed to the welfare of the native people.[5] When this library was first
established, the Court of Directors granted one thousand rupees for the
purchase of books. Many of our Marathi kings and nobles have also
provided considerable help to this Society. Sir Erskine Perry donated five
hundred rupees on the eve of his departure to England.

People generally stop reading books once they have completed their studies
and start working in offices or businesses. They forget what they have learnt
and in due course lose their belief in learning and spend their lives in idle talk
and lethargy. This library was built with the objective of enabling such people
to devote an hour or two every day to reading and study. The fees were
initially fixed at four *annas* per month, but since the Hindus have hardly any
interest in reading books to acquire knowledge, those whose welfare it was
supposed to serve did not frequent this institution. It had generally languished
but it has recovered since the Parsis, Portuguese and English have become
subscribers. There are but a few who use it for the purposes it was conceived
for. The Hindu community has still not developed a penchant for the
acquisition of knowledge and the reading of books.

There are thirty to forty such libraries in this city. Our people show
enthusiasm only in the early stages and do not have the energy to complete
the tasks they have undertaken. There are about a hundred and fifty shops
which sell books in Marathi, English and other languages.

The Government Depot (which sells text-books and books in numerous
languages published by the government) is presently on the Kalbadevi
Road. It has a stock of two lakh rupees' worth of books on various subjects
and in numerous languages. English books and maps are imported from

England and published here in local languages. They are sent from here to all the villages in the Mumbai Province.

It has been the habit of the English to find new means to acquire knowledge and happiness, and more often than not, they succeed. In the year 1856, the Sarkar collected exquisite and unique objects from various regions and organized a general exhibition in the Town Hall. Thousands of men, women, and children of this city saw it. The various objects were exhibited in a most fetching manner. Grains, clothes, animals and birds from various countries were exhibited. There were huge snakes and pythons on display. Dr. Buist, who has involved himself in activities concerning the welfare of the people, first mooted the idea of this general exhibition. We have been treated to this great marvel at his behest. Many generous native gentlemen eventually supported this idea. There was also some misunderstanding among a few who said, 'What is this? What is to be gained by collecting such objects from various countries and exhibiting them to the people at a cost of hundreds of rupees? We have seen such objects thousands of times and it has made not an iota of difference to our lives. This is just the madness of the English and an utter waste of money'. Our people are capable of a very wild imagination.

A museum is the principal place for education and entertainment. People are motivated to industry and diligence when they see the skilled work of people from various parts of the world and other wonderful objects. A naturally lethargic person may also be motivated to work diligently. One is unable to say how a particular object will affect a particular person, and what heights he may be motivated to reach. The museum is a place of education for the people. There are many such places in Europe. There is a very famous museum in London that is supposed to be the best in the world.[6] The building itself costs 8,500,000 rupees and valuable articles have been collected from all parts of the world. It has a collection of ancient inscriptions, books, coins and seals. The presence of such a place in a city affords a place of relaxation to the industrious and diligent citizens and provides them with the means of acquiring valuable knowledge.

A meeting between the English and the native people was held on 15 December 1858 at the Town Hall. The objective of this meeting was to perpetuate the memory of that important event of 1858 when the Queen took over the reins of the government of Bharat Khand from the Company Sarkar. To demonstrate the loyalty of the population of this country a general museum set amongst picturesque gardens was proposed to be established in this city to create a unique place. It was decided to name it after the reigning sovereign of England and Bharat Khand as the 'Victoria Museum and Gardens'. Many people made excellent speeches about the appropriateness of Mumbai city as a location for such a place. The

Honourable Jagannath Shankarseth was the President of this society and Dr. Birdwood and Dr. Bhau Daji were named as Secretaries. Jagannath Shankarseth gave a donation of five thousand rupees for this venture. Many Parsi, Vani and other gentlemen from different castes contributed according to their capacity and about one lakh of rupees were collected. This was just the contribution of the native people. Besides, the Sarkar has given one lakh of rupees and a large sprawling location at the far end of Byculla near Chinchpokhli has been allocated for the construction of a building. The government garden at Sewri has also been moved here. The construction of this building has started and it should be ready in a couple of years. It is 180 feet long and 80 feet wide. The objects meant for exhibition are currently being gathered in the Town Hall. This museum has also been named after the consort of the Queen, and consequently its name is the 'Victoria and Albert Museum'.[7]

The Governor himself laid the foundation stone for this enormous building on 19 November 1862. The Governor had declared a holiday for half a day in all the government workshops and offices to enable the lower sections of society to witness this function.[8]

A grand victory banner had been erected in front of the building area and a huge and beautiful gateway had been created with green palmyra leaves as a good omen. The people passed through this gateway and entered an open area where over a thousand chairs had been neatly arranged. The Governor and his wife reached the venue at five o'clock. Two special chairs cushioned in velvet had been ordered for them. The President of the society, Namdar Jagannath Shankarseth addressed the gathering. The Governor Sahib replied to this address and heaped praises on the natives for their loyalty and affection. The ceremonial rites were then completed as planned. There was a huge crowd of people on this occasion and the students of the school run by the Students' Literary and Scientific Society were specially dressed for the event. About a thousand of the prominent people of Mumbai had been invited to witness this function. Another couple of thousand uninvited guests had also gathered. There was a mad rush of vehicles and chariots. An English band played during the function to entertain the guests. Lady Frere, the Governor's wife, also inaugurated the Victoria Garden on this occasion. The Government garden at Sewri run by the Agri-Horticultural Society has also been merged with this garden.

Under the stone laid by the Governor at the main portal of the building is a strong copper chest. It contains a copy of all the newspapers published on that day, the coins used then in Mumbai, all the papers relating to the establishment of the museum, and the names of all the individuals who contributed to this cause. The following inscription is etched on the lid of this box.

ON WEDNESDAY, THE 19TH DAY OF NOVEMBER 1862
IN THE TWENTY-FIFTH YEAR OF THE REIGN OF HER MOST
GRACIOUS MAJESTY
QUEEN VICTORIA
HIS EXCELLENCY THE RIGHT HONOURABLE
THE EARL OF ELGIN AND KINCARDINE, K.T.G., G.C.B., K.S.I.,
BEING VICEROY AND GOVERNOR-GENERAL OF INDIA,
HIS EXCELLENCY **SIR HENRY BARTLE EDWARD FRERE, K.C.B.,**
GOVERNOR OF BOMBAY,
LAID THE CHIEF CORNER STONE OF THE
VICTORIA AND ALBERT MUSEUM,
TO BE ERECTED BY THE INHABITANTS OF BOMBAY,
IN TESTIMONY OF THEIR LOYAL AFFECTION, AND IN MEMORY
OF THE ASSUMPTION,
BY HER MAJESTY
OF THE DIRECT SOVEREIGNTY OF INDIA,
PROCLAIMED NOVEMBER 1ST, 1858.

THE HONOURABLE JUGONNATH SUNKERSETT,
President of the Museum and Gardens Committee.

WILLIAM LOUDON, ESQ.
Sheriff of Bombay
WILLIAM TRACEY, ESQ.
Architect

BHAU DAJI, ESQ., G.G.M.C.,
G. C. M. BIRDWOOD, ESQ. M. D.,
Honorary Joint Secretaries.

The following inscription is carved on the stone itself.

THIS,
THE CHIEF CORNER STONE
OF THE
VICTORIA & ALBERT MUSEUM
WAS LAID
ON THE 19TH DAY OF NOVEMBER A.D. 1862
BY HIS EXCELLENCY
SIR H.B.E. FRERE, K.C.B.
GOVERNOR OF BOMBAY

Chapter 12

Drought — Framji Cowasji's Talao — Water channels — Nakhuda Tank — Panjarapole — Remand homes — Industrial Schools — Lunatic asylums — Scheme to unite Mumbai and Thane — Plans for new docks — Notice to demolish the Fort — Eating houses — Inns — Restaurants — The birthday of the King of England — Tennis - Gymnasia — Gymkhana — Talimkhana — Bandstand

Every eight to ten years, a drought occurs in Mumbai. There was a drought in 1822 when the water was hardly a hand or two deep in the wells even in the month of August and by the time it was May, there was an acute shortage of water. Ceremonial rituals were conducted at various places but this did not appease the rain-gods. As the Dhobi Talao had completely dried up, two huge wells were dug in the tank. As the water in them was sweet, the tank was named as the Sakhar Talao or Sugar Tank. Seth Framji Cowasji further strengthened this tank in 1831 at an expense of twenty-five thousand rupees. This Parsi gentleman was a very generous person and a member of the Board of Education. He strove hard to encourage the spread of education among the natives and also spent a lot of money on this account. The Sarkar then announced that the tank had been renamed as the Framji Cowasji Talao. Since the name Dhobi Talao has been in use for many years, both the names, Sakhar Talao and Framji Cowasji Talao have fallen by the wayside and Dhobi Talao is still current.[1]

When this gentleman expired, many Parsi and Hindu students decided to perpetuate his memory by erecting a monument in this city and about forty thousand rupees were collected. It was decided to erect a building known as the Framji Cowasji Institute on the Camp near the aforementioned Talao which will contain a library and a collection of unique and educational objects and provide the Students Literary and Scientific Society with a proper venue for its meetings and public addresses. This building is presently being built adjacent to the tank. Its foundation stone was laid in January 1862 in the presence of prominent English and native gentlemen. Shrimant Ra. Jagannath Shankarseth laid the foundation stone of this building. The guests were welcomed with rose *attar* and garlands. This building should be ready in a short while. While Sir Jamsetjee Jejeebhoy may have moved on to another world, there are many in the Parsi community who can match the generosity of Sir Jamsetjee. One among them was Seth Manikji Nusserwanji Pittie; he died about two years back. He was a very religious, kind and philanthropic person. He did charitable work worth thousands of rupees which benefited hundreds of people. This gentleman set up the spinning mill at Tardeo.

Framji Cowasji was a very generous and industrious person. At a distance of about nine *kos* from here, in a village named Powai in the Sashtee (Salsette) district, this gentleman set up a workshop for the manufacture of sugar, lump-sugar, silk, tea, cotton and other articles which are produced in China. He employed Chinese people and set up a workshop in which various experiments are undertaken. He brought silk worms to establish a silk farm. He planted mulberry trees for their consumption. His efforts in improving the state of land in this village led Sir John Malcolm to felicitate him in 1830. When this workshop was operational, it attracted many visitors. This workshop is not being run properly because of the lack of committed workers, but it still generates an annual revenue of around twenty-five thousand rupees. Though it is practically derelict currently, it is still worth a look. It has got some enormous machines and furnaces. Many varieties of sugar cane and fruits are grown here.

In the year 1838, Framji Cowasji presented Queen Victoria of England and Bharat Khand with mangoes grown in Mumbai and the Queen gratefully and happily received this present. No other mangoes except those grown in Gomantak can match the quality of mangoes grown in Mumbai.

The *ryot* of Mumbai undergo great distress in the years of scanty rainfall. This matter had been raised at the level of the Court of Directors for many years. The Company Sarkar, had over the years, devised many schemes to solve this problem. A permanent solution to this problem was found only in 1845 during the tenure of Sir George Arthur as Governor. He instructed Dr. Leith and Dr. Graham to conduct a survey of all sources of water in Mumbai, and detail their location, quality and quantity. They submitted a report in due course.[2] Further consideration was given to devise plans to address the scarcity of water and places from where the water could be brought. Many English employees and engineers were also appointed for this task. Somebody made a suggestion that a tank be built in Walkeshwar to store rainwater which could then be supplied to Mumbai; somebody suggested the hill at Mazagaon. Many such ideas were mooted. Mr. Henry Conybeare took the lead in this initiative for a while.[3] Finally Major

Crawford put forward a plan for bringing water from the hills of Vihar and everybody accepted this. No praise will be sufficient in this case. A book has been published containing the various papers and letters written by the Government with regard to this project.[4] Nothing can compare to this effort for public welfare undertaken by the English Sarkar.

There was a drought in the year 1856 which brought a lot of suffering among the people. There was absolutely no rain during the monsoon months; all the wells and tanks ran dry; people wondered how they would last out the year. Various rituals were performed – oblations over holy fires were conducted; the Bhuleshwar Temple was worshipped at throughout the day; the Tulsi was venerated; images of Samba were buried – but to no avail. It was then decided to conduct the ultimate rain-making ritual as per the Hindu scriptures. This involved bringing about two to three cartloads of mud for the erection of a life-sized statue of Shringarishi at the edge of the Bhuleshwar Tank. This idol was duly installed and consecrated and Brahmins conducted rituals. This went on for seven to eight days. This Shringarishi was venerated in various ways daily. Thousands of men and women, young and old used to visit this place to pay homage to the idol. The Brahmins got a lot of money for conducting these rituals. All those who visited this place made offerings of money, rice, betel nut, coconuts, bananas and other fruits. They also gave *dakshina* to the Brahmins who were reciting prayers. Flowers worth over ten rupees were showered on the idol every day. However, in spite of all this, the rain fell only when it was destined to, and only in as much quantity as was decreed. Rainfall is only in the hands of the gods themselves.

The legend of Shringarishi is as follows. Many ages ago, there was drought in a kingdom for a period of five to ten years. Narada Muni told the king that there was a holy Brahmin, a blessed sage named Shringarishi in a particular forest whose prayers could induce rainfall. The king invited Shringarishi to his kingdom; he prayed and rain fell in due course.

In a similar manner, the Parsis prayed on the seashore; Christians, Yahudis, Mussalmans and people of other castes also prayed in their respective fashions for the drought to end.

That year, there was an acute water shortage between January and June and the poor were the worst affected. Many people would carry pots and pans over their heads and roam the streets looking for water. The Sarkar ordered that all the cows, buffaloes and other animals in Mumbai be taken to Mahim. Poor women would wait until midnight at the Camp Maidan to fill a pitcher or two of water after a lot of effort. Many would descend into the field-well and fill their pitchers using a small cup. Many Parsis, a couple of Vanis and employees of the Sarkar dug a few wells in the Camp Maidan and other places to try and alleviate the sufferings of the people caused by drought. Crowds of hundreds gathered to collect the dirty water which trickled when these wells were being dug. In addition, the Sarkar made arrangements for the transportation of thousands of barrels of water from other places by the steam-train and poured them into wells at Dongri, Chinch Bunder and Bori Bunder. Many such efforts were made by the English Sarkar to mitigate the suffering of the people.

In the same year, Nakhuda Mohammed Rogay built a large octagonal tank on the Camp Maidan, opposite the Maruti Temple, for the welfare of the public. It is said that over fifty thousand rupees were spent on the construction. The tank has been built from stone; and long benches have been built at each corner for people to rest and enjoy the cool breeze in twilight hours of the morning and evening. Similarly eight other stone benches have been built at various places. Passers-by use them to rest a while during the morning and evening. While there are wells in every house in this city, the water from all of them is not potable. The sweetest water is available only in the Camp Maidan and is used all over the city. Water of good quality is available at Girgaon, Babulnath, Mahalaxmi, and Walkeshwar. As these places are very far, only the rich can use these.

To ensure that similar problems are not faced again by the populace of the city, the Sarkar planned a project to lay pipes in the city and transport water from elsewhere; the work on this project was started shortly thereafter in 1857. The plan involved constructing a beautiful reservoir in the Vihar Hills to store water and building a pipeline to transport the water from this reservoir to supply water to all parts of Mumbai. The pipes for this purpose have been all laid under the streets of Mumbai. In a similar fashion, this water has been taken to all parts of the Fort. Vihar is about seven or eight *kos* away from Mumbai and the Sarkar has given a contract worth fifty-six lakhs of rupees to an Englishman for building the tank and laying the pipelines. The Sarkar at its own expense has imported iron pipes and other machinery from England. The cost per pipe is two hundred rupees. It is said that there are four hundred and fifty such pipes buried under a stretch about half a *kos* long. The design of this reservoir and its construction is wonderful. The Sarkar continues to strive for the welfare of the *ryot* in this manner. As the English Sarkar is constantly spending money for the welfare of its subjects, there is a perpetual flow of wealth into its coffers.

The area of this reservoir is about 1,242 acres or approximately 2,484 *bighas*.

Water from Vihar

The poor in a big and prosperous city like Mumbai used to suffer from a scarcity of water. This led the Sarkar to spend lakhs of rupees to build a tank at a distance of about six *kos* from Mumbai. The villages in that area had to be relocated. The circumference of this tank is currently between ten and twelve *kos*. Anybody who sees it feels that they are standing in front of a sea. The Sarkar has accomplished a great deed because of its compassion for the poor.

Induprakash

The Shravak, Vani, Bhatia and other Gujar people are guided by the following principle – '*Ahimsa* is the highest religion'. They take great pains to protect the lives of animals and birds. They believe that saving the life of any living organism will earn them blessings. Many also believe that saving the life of a dumb animal will lead them to salvation. This leads them to feel more compassion for animals than for people. There are many *yatis* – mendicants of the Shravak sect in this city. They take all efforts to ensure that they do not inadvertently kill even an ant or a germ. They do not wear shoes and walk around with either naked feet or wooden clogs. They tie a small cloth curtain around their mouths to ensure that no organism enters the mouth during the breathing process and gets killed. They filter water through a cloth folded four to five times before using it. If they have to drink water, they get it boiled from somebody else and cool it before consuming it. They take this pot of water with them during their rounds. This is their general practice.

A famous businessman named Motichand Amichand belonged to the Shravak caste. His trade was conducted in many countries and ran into crores of rupees. He built many temples for the men of his own caste in Mumbai. It is reliably reported that he has built similar temples in his native land and also established a free feeding-house. His community members declare that this generous and kind trader spent over a crore of rupees in charity during his lifetime. Whatever may have been the figure, he was certainly a very religious-minded person and very compassionate and generous towards the poor, and if anybody approached him with a plea, he never sent him back disappointed. This is public knowledge.

In 1834, this gentleman felt that, just as there are hospitals and hospices where the ill and the infirm can go to cure their ailments, there should be a place in Mumbai for the care of diseased and dying animals and birds. With this in mind, he bought a large estate near the Cowasji Patel Tank, and built a building and named it 'Panjarapole'. Sick and infirm animals like cows, horses, buffaloes, goats, donkeys, and dogs and birds such as crows, pigeons, hens, and sparrows are brought to this place. There are hundreds of such creatures here. Separate enclosures have been built for different kinds of animals and birds. The sight of these suffering animals is enough to wrench any man's heart – crows with broken wings; hens with swollen legs; ducks with no feathers; blind kites; horses with swollen knees; lame sheep; and similar such cases. There is a separate enclosure for dogs towards one side. When we visited this place, there were over three hundred dogs which kept up an incessant harsh barking and tried to spring on any human within their range. This sight brings back the description of Yamapuri as given in the Garuda *Purana*. About fifty sheep roam around in the courtyard; some rich person who might have purchased them from a butcher must have released them here. The Vanis, on making good profits in their business or on some other happy occasion, buy cows and goats from butchers at twice or thrice the normal price and take care of it in this place. One Vani gentleman carries a cupful of sugar and goes around looking for anthills in the area to feed them with little pinches. The following extract is from the *Vartamandipika* of 8 June 1861.

> A rich Vani gentleman, by name Gangadas, who was the manager of the Panjarapole died last week. He was worth about twelve lakhs of rupees. As a means of preventing his death, his friends bought a hundred bullocks and hundred sheep from butchers and brought them to the Panjarapole. However, he died the following day.

The goddess Mahalaxmi is one of the Shaktis, which are manifestations of power of a deity generally in the form of his consort; cocks and goats have to be sacrificed to propitiate her. Earlier, Koli, Bhandari, Ghanti and other Hindu folk killed goats and hens in front of her to satisfy her. Or they would release them in the temple and the resident Bhopis (the person that officiates in village temples, generally a Shudra) would do the necessary deed. Presently, a watchman of the Panjarapole is posted at the temple, and if any offerings of goats or hens are made to the goddess, he sends them to the Panjarapole. This is his only job. It is however not known whether the goddess agreed to this act of the *mahajan!* Only by sacrificing the lives of these animals can the *Devi* be propitiated. Perhaps in Kalyug, the *Devi* has been tutored by the Shravaks! A sacrifice for the Devi cannot be equated to killing. The scriptures themselves say that the souls of these animals are blessed by the sacrifice.

In September 1862, this city was swamped by caterpillars. They were on the walls, and on the roads and died as people trampled on them. When the rainfall is not adequate, these creatures emerge from all places. They disappear automatically in about fifteen days to a month. The owners of the Panjarapole had devised a strange plan for saving the lives of these caterpillars. They employed a score of people to collect the caterpillars from the streets and bring them to the Panjarapole. These collectors were equipped with a pot, a small bamboo basket and a short stick. They would first put them into the bamboo basket with the help of the stick and then after a few had been collected, they would put them into the pot. Once the pot was full, they went to deposit it in the Panjarapole. They were paid four to six *annas* for their labour. Many weak and lazy labourers were thus able to find some work in those days. This is certainly a strange way of spending money and practising religion! The same people who are so keen on saving the lives of these dumb creatures would not cast a second glance at a man dying of hunger! Such is the nature of their universal benevolence!

The following arrangements have been made to fund the expenses of this organization. A toll known as 'Dharmav' is collected on all goods arriving at the ports, at the rate of one anna per *khandi* and this money is distributed for various charitable purposes. Part of this money is allotted to the Panjarapole and Seth Motichand has also set aside thirty thousand rupees to cover its expenses. Gujar folk also donate money for charitable purposes to the Panjarapole. They take excellent care of the animals that are brought into this asylum. They are regularly supplied with fodder, grass, grains and water, and about twenty-five people are employed to take care of them. They spend hundreds of rupees to take care of those animals that are no longer useful. Just the pigeons are fed with over four *paylee* of grains every day. There is a small bungalow in the middle of the Panjarapole; the upper portion houses the accounts and administrative offices of the Panjarapole. If an honourable gentleman needs a cow or a horse, they get him to sign an undertaking that he will not sell the animal and that he will take good care of it; and then give him the animal for free. There are some good animals here.

The New Panjarapole: this estate had actually been allotted for the grazing of cattle. There are no other animals here but the people refer to it as the New Panjarapole. This place is adjacent to Namdar Jagannath Shankarseth's school at Girgaon and had been purchased by Sir Jamsetjee Jejeebhoy for around twenty thousand rupees and donated for the grazing of cattle. Arrangements for drinking water for cattle have also been made. This charitable deed was done about ten years ago. Until 1838, all the grazing animals of the city including cows, buffaloes, sheep, and goats were taken to the Camp Maidan for grazing. The *dhobis* washed their laundry at various spots in the Maidan. Not only was grass available for grazing, drinking water was also available. A couple of gentlemen had built tanks in the Camp Maidan to provide drinking water for animals. The Sarkar then introduced a grazing fee of three pies per buffalo, two pies per cow, and one pie per goat. This went on for a few years. Finally grazing was completely banned in the Camp Maidan. This caused immense problems for cattle. Their caretakers let them free on the sandy seashore near Sonapur so that the grazing animals could roam about. However, the animals were troubled by the hot sand during the summer, the lack of drinking water and the salty sea breeze. Pained by the condition of these animals, Sir Jamsetjee Jejeebhoy bought this piece of land and donated it for grazing purposes.

Though there are no large grazing grounds in Mumbai, the cattle are well taken care of and the best arrangements have been made for their food and water; the Vani and other religious folk consider it a religious merit to feed cattle with grass and fodder. Cattle are fed on holy days, after the death of a person, or if business prospers. There is a Ghaas Bazar near Byculla where grass and rice straws are sold. Huge bales of grass can be seen piled in front of the Bazaar. Hardly any grass grows in Mumbai but hundreds of cartloads of grass are brought from adjoining areas like Thane, Turbhe, Marol, and Chembur. People can earn thousands of rupees in the grass trade. The price of grass peaked a few years ago and grass available at four rupees per thousand was being sold at sixteen rupees per thousand.

The Gawlis or herdsmen boil millet and add coconut or sesame-seed oilcakes, dried grass, and the husk of various grains like *harbara, moong,* and *urad*; this is then fed to the cattle. Cattle-feed is sold at another place where fodder of different varieties are available. The Jaffarabadi buffaloes, milked in the morning and evening, yield about three-quarters of a *man* of milk in a day while the Surat cows yield about fifteen to twenty *sher* of milk.

There are two jails in this city – one civil and the other criminal. The civil jail is known as the Old Jail while the criminal jail is known as the New Jail. Debtors are jailed in the civil jail for the duration of their sentence. The creditors are supposed to give a food allowance of three *annas* every day to their debtors during their stay in the prison. If this allowance does not arrive on a particular day, the prisoner is immediately released.

The Criminal Jail is used to house criminals like robbers and other malefactors. Many of the prisoners have to perform hard labour. Many instruments have been made available to ensure that they work. One is reminded of the *Yamadanda* when one visits the prisoners in this jail. The Sarkar has to incur the expense of feeding these prisoners. Even though this is a jail, it has been built in an airy place and is kept very clean and neat. When the quarterly Sessions of the Court are held, the representatives of the

Grand Jury who examine the cases visit the jail and superintend its operations. As per the rules, a prisoner who is punished has to be well looked after and his body and health has to be protected. The Magistrates of the Court have directed the jailers and the police inspectors not to beat the criminals and extract confessions from them under torture. How excellent is this rule of theirs!

In 1859, Dr. Ogilvy was named as the Superintendent of all the prisons in the Mumbai Province. He inspected all the jails and submitted a report enumerating the number of prisoners and the state in which they had been jailed, the labour they were engaged in and the output from this labour and made an estimation of the costs incurred by the Sarkar in this regard. From this report, one understands that the Sarkar spends 293,072 rupees annually on all the jails in the Mumbai Province. Based on the number of prisoners in these jails, he estimated that it costs seven rupees to maintain one prisoner. The Sarkar thus has to incur expenditure to punish these vile people. These rogues are a trouble to others wherever they may be.

A different kind of jail was established in 1835 to house underage criminals who are punished according to their ages and then trained to take up a vocation so that they may not lead a life of crime in the future. This has been named as the 'School of Industry'. Underage criminals who may be punished for one to five years depending on the nature of their crimes are taught trades of their liking and are sent home after they have been reformed. Facilities are available to teach the children the 3Rs and to also provide them with food and clothing. The generous David Sassoon has deposited a sum of thirty thousand rupees with the Sarkar to fund this venture. This kind and generous gentleman belongs to the Yahudi caste and is a prominent businessman. He has built an English school for the men of his own caste. He has built a huge synagogue in Byculla and has undertaken many other charitable deeds. Seth Mangaldas Nathubhai has also donated twenty thousand rupees for this venture. The following article about the industrial school was published in a Marathi newspaper known as the *Dhumketu*. This school was earlier located in Sewri, but has now been moved to Grant Road.

Industrial school at Sewri

A meeting was called at this place on the evening of the 26th of the last month. Our Governor Lord Elphinstone was in the chair and there was a huge crowd of native and English gentlemen. When the Governor Sahib's carriage reached this place at five in the evening, the children brought out various kinds of machines and worked on them.

The children exhibited the process of making clay utensils; the European ladies were amazed to see the speed with which they worked. After the exhibition of various trades by the children, Dr. Buist delivered a speech. On hearing the speech, one realized that there were thirty-nine students in this school. Many of them were vagrant children who roamed the streets and indulged in petty theft. This kind of school is certainly necessary for such children. Dr. Buist also mentioned that there is a similar school in Jabalpur which mainly houses dacoits who terrorize the people in various ways. Later our Governor also made a short speech. There is no doubt that such schools will teach a trade or two to our idlers and put an end to their vagrancy and harassment of the people. We believe that it will be for the welfare of this country, if the Sarkar establishes such schools in every district and punishes those who are guilty of petty theft, minor fights and rioting by sending them to such schools. If such schools are established, the Sarkar will not refuse to help them. We have heard of many people who admonish the roving beggars and ask them to take up a trade instead of roaming around like vagrants. On occasion, the beggars retort that if they could teach them a trade, they will gladly do it. These schools can be used to train such beggars.

There is a place in Colaba for consigning people who have become mad. This building has been designed very intelligently. Once a lunatic has been locked in one of these rooms, none of his contrivances to escape will succeed however crazed he may be. All facilities have been made for the care of these lunatics. A permanent English doctor has been appointed to this madhouse. The mad men are taken care of and attended to without being beaten. Quite a few have been cured after spending some time in this hospital.

About a few years back a prince who had just stepped into adolescence was taken to a portrait painter who was requested to draw an exact likeness of the prince to be sent to the Emperor as a present. The painter requested to be excused from this assignment as he could not fulfil the expectation. He reasoned that this royal prince had just entered the years of his youth and was yet to develop into full maturity, so one could not make an estimate of his beauty and visage unless some more years elapsed. If one drew his likeness at the present moment, it would no longer remain a likeness by the time the picture reached the Emperor and the painter would be discredited.

Mumbai is also in a similar situation. It is at the height of its youthful years and there is no telling how it will develop in the years to come. New plans are proposed every day and the design of the city changes accordingly.

In the November 1862 issue of the *Gazette* newspaper, it was written that as there was an extreme shortage of space in the city, and no place is available for rent at even twice or thrice the normal rates, the Sarkar intends to merge that part of the Thane district which is adjacent to Mumbai to form a big city. The government offices could then be established in Thane, Kurla or any other place in Sashtee (Salsette), and this will eliminate the shortage of space in Mumbai by increasing the area which it covers. The government can also save on the expense of appointing a separate Collector, Magistrate and Revenue Officer. One cannot say when this plan will come to fruition. The situation should improve by some degrees with this plan.

The population in Mumbai is increasing rapidly, and the extreme shortage of space is causing a lot of distress to the people; the traders are finding the cost of unloading goods from ships and storing them in warehouses prohibitive and no suitable places are available. Many have suggested that the bay between Colaba and Walkeshwar which is about a *kos* long and a *kos* and a half wide should be filled; a new port be constructed and the space used for erecting houses. This is a very difficult task and the expenditure will be enormous. A monthly newspaper, *Prabhodaya* has written the following on this subject.

> To address the ever-increasing shortage of space in Mumbai, it has been proposed that a sum of two crores of rupees be paid to acquire the sea between Colaba and Walkeshwar to build new settlements. It is hoped that Ratnakar Pant will be agreeable to this amount.' As this creek is very deep at the centre, the plan has been currently suspended. However there are plans to recover the area directly to the East of this creek, that is the area directly adjacent to the Sinal Tekdi[*] behind the Mint, or at least build a bridge and construct a new dock.[5] Some others are of the opinion that the creek from the Mazagaon Dock to the Mandvi at the Fort should be filled up and new settlements be developed there. This project will cost about three to four crores of rupees. If the project is completed, the owners will make a lot of money and it will add to the beauty and strength of the city. Looking at the rate of activities, it is expected that this project will be completed in the

---

[*]   Our people call this place Chinal Tekdi; however the Portuguese had named it the Sinal Tekdi. When they had first come to this island, they had raised their standard on this Tekdi or hillock. In their language, the standard is referred to as Sinal, and hence the name.

near future. Mumbai will then become comparable to Liverpool, a famous trade port in the country of England. Concrete plans have already been made to install iron pillars in the sea from Mazagaon to build docks and godowns and a managing committee has also been appointed. As it has been estimated that this work will take sixty lakhs of rupees, twelve thousand shares have been made and it has been decided to allot them to each shareholder for five hundred rupees.

A majority of the businessmen and government employees of Mumbai requested the Sarkar in August 1861 that, as the increasing shortage of space in the city of Mumbai was causing a lot of distress to the people, the walls of the Fort, excepting those to the East and South be demolished, the moat surrounding the Fort be filled up, and this area be merged with the Camp Maidan, and the whole of it be sold off to the public for building houses, offices, and bungalows. The plan will have two benefits – it will provide an extended space for the citizens, and it will result in a substantial inflow of money for the Sarkar. This request has the signatures of the Magistrate, Councillors and other important English gentlemen.

GOVERNMENT ORDER

Decision of the Government to demolish the walls on the Western side of the Fort was taken on 22 November 1862, under which the Justices of Peace have named a committee consisting of Colonel Barr and Sir Jamsetjee Jejeebhoy, Baronet to grant permission in this regard. Mr. R. Shovell has been named as the Officiating Secretary of the Committtee and Lieutenant Colonel A. D. Lille has been named as the Superintending Engineer.

The above extract is from the Government Gazette dated the 12 December 1862.

There is a constant flow of passengers and a multitude of goods into this city from Europe, America and other countries through the steamships and three-masted schooners. These are manned by the captain, sailors and other mariners who are Englishmen. These sailors are typically unlettered and ill-mannered. When they come ashore, they tend to roam the city causing considerable disruption. They spend as much as fifty or a hundred rupees in a day on occasion. Most of them run after women. Residents are upset when they come into the city. The disturbances are typically concentrated on Sundays. When they are well behaved, they do not bother anybody, but if they are in a mischievous mood, they do not even care about the police. In earlier days, they caused a lot of trouble, but currently they do not venture too much into the streets because steps have been taken to contain their harassment. Their eateries used to be located among residential settlements in the areas of Dhobi Talao, Kalbadevi Road, Kolbhat, Bhendi Bazaar, and Hanuman Sheri; but they have now been moved to a place in Duncan Road. If one visits this road, one can see different flags fluttering in each house, and a board has been affixed indicating the name of the owner of the eatery. This has however not put an end to their gallivanting in the streets. Some of these eateries are in the Hindu colonies. They are served with liquor, meat, bread, *roti*, tea, coffee and anything else they may desire. They have to pay from one to five rupees per day for food. These rates are quite steep. There are around thirty to forty such eateries in Mumbai, run by Parsis, Mussalmans, Christians, and Englishmen. As these sailors wander in the streets, and consume excessive liquor and upset the ordinary folk, some English gentlemen, with the help of the Sarkar, have built a huge building on the Camp Maidan next to the Maruti Temple at an expense of one lakh rupees to house these sailors comfortably. This has been named as the Sailors' Home. Once they come here, steps are taken to ensure that they do not commit any excesses.

This building has been built very adroitly. This building was inaugurated in the English fashion on 29 March 1862. The captains, officers, mariners, and sailors from the ships were invited for dinner on that day. An English band played from five in the evening till nightfall, accompanied by the good-natured shouting and singing of these sailors, which could be heard at a distance of over a quarter of a *kos*. Hundreds had gathered to witness this function; the area was patrolled by foot soldiers and mounted police.

While inaugurating a house, the English do not need to take into consideration any specific day, month, date, phase of the moon or the position of the stars; neither do they have to do any charitable acts or fire-rituals. They enter a new house on any day that takes their fancy. If somebody has built a new house or building, they may invite a few of their friends for lunch, and if they are particularly religious, they may thank the formless god for providing them with a new house and pray for their welfare and the long life and happiness of their children and relatives. If a prominent government building or charitable structure is built, they may invite a few prominent citizens to inaugurate the building. They do not have any practice of distributing coconut and sugar or arranging for a dance performance on such occasions. They do not have any holy or unholy days like *vaidhruti, amavasya, grahan, mrutyuyog, kuyog, suyog, grahbal, chandrabal, amrutsiddhiyog, sankranti, et cetera.* They are of the opinion that God has made all days equally good, and our fate is in his hands.

There are somewhere around twenty eating-houses for the use of respectable English folk located in the Fort, Byculla, Mahalaxmi, Mazagaon, Girgaon and other pleasant locations. the full-board cost can range from five to fifteen rupees per day in these eating-houses. One can obtain all the best facilities at these places – rooms to stay; beds to sleep; chairs to sit; couches to lounge on; tables to write on; and servants to serve you. These eating-houses have been constructed at an expense running into thousands of rupees, and their monthly budget is in the hundreds. The paraphernalia and design of these houses are worth a look. They may be called eating-houses but they are more comparable to palaces of Nawabs.

The inns of the Mussalmans are located in Bhendi Bazaar, Market, Fort, Dongri and at many other places. A variety of victuals are available in these inns. Down-and-out Mussalmans, Fakirs, strangers and travellers subsist on such food for years on end. The Arabs, Moghuls and other travellers do not bother with lodgings; they buy and eat food worth two to four *annas* and sleep in the masjid. They do not have any respectable eating-houses like the English. If a prominent gentleman comes visiting, he has to take separate lodgings.

There are no *annachhatras* or facilities for providing free food for poor Brahmins and *Shudras*. During the reign of the Marathas, it was a common practice to establish *annachhatras* and the poor could go and eat there. As there are no respectable eating-houses like those for the English, respectable visitors have a lot of problems in securing lodgings. Such facilities will be most useful to visitors, but the observance of caste differences amongst our people will render this task most difficult. If a separate eating-house has to be set up for each caste, one or two hundred of them will have to be built.

There are about ten to twenty *savkari annachhatras*, that is, eating houses established by the Brahmins. These are similar to the English eating-houses but they do not have similar facilities. The prices are very low. Each meal costs from one to four *annas*. For an anna, one gets plain rice, buttermilk *kadhi*, a vegetable and just enough ghee to purify the food; one does not get any water for a bath or a place to sleep. Those who pay two *annas* are provided with hot water for their bath, a room to sit and sleep, and a meal consisting of pulses, rice, a couple of vegetables, *saar*, curds, ghee, pickles and *chapatis* made of wheat. For four *annas*, one can get clothes laundered and meals are served with *puris* and a sweet. One is served very liberal portions. Such an establishment is known as *khanaval*. However it is difficult to get food that is exactly to one's liking for any kind of money in most such places or to be served liberally. Our people are not accustomed to giving liberally. Most of the diners in these *khanavals* are travellers, foreigners, and orphan students. The buttermilk served in these places is as dilute as lime water. Our people consider it beneath themselves to eat in an eating-house, but the English do not seem to think so. People of the highest rank like Magistrates gladly spend six months to a year in these eating-houses.

It has become common practice among the Vani, Bhatia, Lavane, and other Gujarati folk to throw a feast during weddings and other festive occasions. A rich man might well spend ten to twenty thousand rupees on these feasts and arrange for fifteen to twenty different caste-meals and meals for Brahmins. They believe that donating food procures them the highest religious merits. They serve eighty-four different castes of Brahmins in a ritual known as the *Chouryashi*. One Brahmin caste is invited for a feast on each day known as the *samaradhana*. If a wealthy Vani businessman prospers in business, or begets a child or commemorates his parents' death anniversary, he feeds the Brahmins and makes presents of various brass and copper utensils like *parati, ghagri, tope, tamba, sandhypatre, et cetera*. The Vanis are very careful about their money and account for every paisa, but when it comes to weddings, birth or death ceremonies, they are very liberal with their wealth.

They do not throw these feasts in their respective houses. Their caste *mahajan* have built extensive buildings for the purpose of these feasts which are built along the lines of a *dharamshala* and *samaradhana* functions are conducted here. Feasts can be comfortably arranged for numbers ranging from a thousand people to over ten thousand. The required paraphernalia like huge cooking vessels and seating boards are provided for by the caste *panchayat*. Unlike the Dakshinis, they are not particularly concerned about ritual purity and do not follow such restrictions. Their feasts are typically held in the evening. About two hours before nightfall, the women and children are served. Once they have eaten, the men are served. A variety of sweetmeats are served in their meals, and even their very food is generally sweet to taste. They also do not have any restrictions on the purity and staleness of food; if somebody does not like what he is eating, he puts it back into the serving vessel.

It has been a practice since early times to observe the birthday of the King of England and celebrate it enthusiastically. On 22 May 1724, the Governor of the day decided, on the occasion of the King's birthday on the following 28th, to make a gift of four decrepit horses from the government stables to fourteen of the prominent businessmen of Mumbai. As they were old, thin and weakly, it was decided to cover them with thick red horse-cloth known as *kharva*. These covered horses were then presented to the businessmen who were mighty pleased that they had received gifts from the Sarkar itself. As the saying goes amongst our people 'Courtly honours should never be spurned'.

In the years gone by, the King's birthday was celebrated at Parel with a decoration of lights and bursting of fireworks. The Sarkar would invite the prominent residents of the town for this occasion. Thousands of other people would also gather to witness this spectacle. Presently, the birthday of the Empress Victoria is celebrated on the 24 of May every year. All employees of the government and trading houses are granted a holiday on this day. An inspection of the white and black troops is conducted at five o'clock in the evening. The nobles, decked in fine attire, ride on horseback. A drill is conducted for a while. The rich people, besides thousands of others come in chariots, horses and palanquins to see this spectacle. After the drill is over, cannons are fired and a gun salute is given. The robes of the nobles, and the glint as the sun reflects off their arms are a sight to behold. An English band plays pleasant tunes. It is a very entertaining function. The Sarkar had to incur an expense of twenty-five thousand rupees in earlier days for the lighting and the fireworks during this function; this has presently been suspended.

An extensive structure has been constructed next to the *Elphinstone Institution*; there is a similar one in the Fort. High-ranking Englishmen and other prominent people play tennis in these grounds. The ball is made of rubber and is as hard and smooth as stone. It is white in colour and imported from England. Our people might consider it strange that prominent Englishmen should play a game of toss and catch with a ball. They might exclaim, 'Why do the English play like small children? They don't seem to be mature at all.' However, this will be a grave mistake. This is a faultless game and is a good way of maintaining one's health. The learned and diligent play this game not just for fun but mainly to exercise their bodies, keep it in shape and remain healthy. They have therefore spent thousands of rupees on these buildings. This is the reason for their healthy and fit bodies. They also have another sport by the name of cricket which they play on the Camp Maidan.[6] Colonels, captains and other army folk play this game to keep their bodies fit and strong. They formulate the rules of the game in specially convened meetings, which are even attended by Councillors. They adopt various means to ensure that their health is maintained. It would certainly be good if our Hindus had some such practices. Our people perpetually complain about the quality of air in Mumbai and the consequent deterioration of their health. Many just slouch in some corner. If these people are provided with the means of maintaining their health, it will be excellent. Most of the Hindus in Mumbai are insipid and weak; the reason being that they are not able to exercise their bodies. Every Englishman has at least a pair of dumb-bells in his house; besides they also play games to ensure that their bodies have enough exercise.

Recently the Parsis have started a school near Dhobi Talao to teach children various forms of exercise. This school has all the equipment present in a gymnasium. Our Hindu folk seem to lag behind in all matters. If our Hindus send their children to this school, they will benefit greatly.

A gymnasium (place for doing exercises) has been built on the Camp Maidan opposite the Elphinstone School. The Sarkar has allocated the land, and it is heard that they may even support it. Children of all castes are free to exercise in this gymnasium. If man maintains his health and increases his strength by means of such exercises, he will not be afraid to undertake any work or travel to any country. A healthy body is a means of acquiring knowledge and wealth. This is the reason why the English folk are particular that their children are strong and healthy. There is an English proverb which goes 'A Healthy body leads to a healthy mind'.

There is a society by the name of Gymkhana which is devoted to keeping the body strong and healthy and developing the muscles. They exhibit various bodily skills like jumping from a horse, running and leaping beyond a certain point, jumping from a height, and crossing obstacles. The persons who are the strongest and most skilful are awarded prizes ranging from fifty to one hundred rupees. They are also presented with silver cups and other utensils. Such facilities are available in this city.

There is an English sport known as the Billiard Table. Even even the most learned scholars and judges play it. The paraphernalia for this game costs between two and three thousand rupees.

The *talimkhanas* or *palaestra* of the Hindu, Mussalman, Beni Israeli, and Parsi people have been around for many years. Respectable people do not frequent them, as these places are filled with headstrong and uncouth people who are always squabbling and fighting. Our people believe that going to a *talimkhana* is equivalent to learning how to pick up fights and quarrels. They therefore forbid their children from exercising. The *talimkhana* of one locality is always at loggerheads with the *talimkhana* of the adjacent locality resulting in frequent fights erupting between them, and they end up destroying themselves. There are many strongmen among the Parsis, Mussalmans, Ghantis, Gawlis and the Israeli folk who come out of these *talimkhanas*. As these people have indulged in frequent rioting, the Sarkar has closed down many of these *talimkhanas*.

Just a little ahead of the Palo Bunder, there is a very entertaining place called the Band Stand on the Camp Maidan. It is open on all sides and is only large enough to accommodate performers. Benches are provided on the lower side for the accompanying orchestra. Benches are also provided all around for spectators. At about five in the evening, the performers gather at this place. As these people are employed by the Governor and play English instruments at his residence, they are known as the Governor's Band. These players are from the white regiment and play beautiful new tunes three times every week for the entertainment of the public. Many people throng the location at this time. It is the favoured location of the English for an evening stroll with their families. Hundreds of their vehicles are parked here at that time. As there is also a pleasant breeze at this time of the day, the whole atmosphere turns magical. The English are equally keen on ensuring the health of their bodies and the peace of their minds.

In the second century of the Christian era, that is seventeen hundred years ago, a Greek geographer named Ptolemy had described all the parts of the earth then known. In his description of Bharat Khand, he has named Mumbai as Heptanesia (place with seven islands). It is clear that in those days Mumbai consisted of seven different islands. Presently seven islands have been united into one, but this may well not be the final shape. When the creeks on all the sides have been reclaimed to increase the land, and when Sashtee (Salsette) and other villages are merged with Mumbai, it will never occur to anybody that Mumbai was an island once.

Chapter 13

Sky-chariot – Tamasha – Animals of various types – Plays – Horse acrobatics –
Dance of the harlots – Bankoti - Teliraja – Gosavi – Tumdi Bawa – Tales of
the Haridas – Bawa – Atmaram Bawa – Paud, Pangul, et cetera – Jogi,
Sanyasi and other beggars – Blind men – Jogini – Joshis who cast horoscopes

Every few months, there is some spectacle or dance or some other wonderful
event that showcases some of the best skills in this world. In 1853, a man
named Kight came to Mumbai from the European continent and he created
a buzz among the people of Mumbai and the surrounding villages. There
were reports that this man could ride a sky-chariot that reached a height of
three *kos* and travelled as far as fifty to sixty *kos* in the air. It was the talk of
the town among all the people in Mumbai some fifteen days prior to when
this event was planned. The newspapers published new rumours daily about
this sky-chariot. This sky-chariot is referred to as a 'balloon' in English. Our
people have given it names like sky-chariot, box, and *vimaan*. Many
newspapers have described this sky-chariot but the following account from
the *Dnyanodaya* describes it perfectly.

A balloon means a flying machine. The people of Mumbai witnessed
the flight of this balloon on the eighteenth of January. The flight of the
balloon was well planned and it was decided that certain people would
ride on the balloon; the flight was well advertised and the Sarkar had
declared a holiday on that day. This function was held at the Byculla
grounds. A *mandap* had been erected for the spectators and seats with
prices ranging from two, three and five rupees were demarcated. As
this spectacle was certainly worth seeing, crowds thronged the site from
eleven in the morning till about four in the evening till it seemed like a
sea of people had come from the Fort. The dense crowds prevented
women from venturing inside and many of them climbed the roofs and
terraces of the buildings nearby. The crowds were unprecedented. They
were amused at the sight of the machine that was bobbing in the air in

spite of being tied down. It was flown at around five in the evening. It rapidly ascended to a height of about half a *kos* and turned towards the South where it seemed as small as a star. It was then swept towards the East where it landed near Panvel.

The only shortcoming was that the man who was supposed to sit in the balloon did not ride in it. Those who had paid money to witness this spectacle fretted because they had paid money to witness a man riding in the balloon. Many reasons are being given for his not riding the balloon. Some say that not enough sand had been filled for a man to ride in the balloon. Some feel that the device that was to carry the man had malfunctioned. Some say that as he was high on alcohol, he was not allowed to ride the balloon. When the practice runs were being held, he had demonstrated where and how he would sit but when it came to the real thing, he cut the rope binding his waist and ran away when the balloon took off. If there was nothing wrong with the machine and if he was drunk, then he has made a big mistake and wasted one whole day of work in the government, and it would not be wrong to call him a criminal and a rogue. He has not been worthy of the respect accorded to him.

Whatever may be the reason for his not riding the balloon, one cannot however conclude that this machine cannot be used to ride in the air. People have travelled hundreds of times in such flying machines. This machine was first invented in 1783, about seventy-nine years ago. Montgolfier was a paper-maker from the French nation. He observed that gases rise in the air and used the same logic to fly a machine in the air. He first made a strong airtight bag of silk and filled it with steam; it went up and quickly came down. He then opened the mouth of the bag and burnt some stuff in a bucket underneath it and flew the whole apparatus. He could not perfect the technique. It then occurred to him to use hydrogen gas which worked perfectly. He then perfected the technique of ascent and descent in this machine and informed the people of Paris. About three lakhs of people had gathered to witness this spectacle. Nobody sat in this machine. It went up very rapidly and after about two hours it burst because of the pressure of the gas. It fell at a spot that was eight *kos* distant from the place where it took off. The unlettered people of that area were shocked and thought that it was a demon or an animal. They first shot it and then they all charged at it and killed it jointly. When the gaseous matter inside started smelling badly they tore it to shreds. They then used their horses to haul it for about a *kos* and decided to completely exterminate the organism. This news finally reached the government and they ordered them to refrain from doing so and bring the remnants back to Paris.

To understand the complexities of landing the balloon, animals were first flown in them. Humans then ventured to sit in these balloons. This has happened many times since and it is no longer a novelty in those places. A man named Green has travelled in these machines over five hundred times. Horses and bullocks have been tied to these balloons and flown in the air to offer a strange spectacle. A madam once sat on a bullock in a balloon. As there are proper facilities for manufacturing hydrogen gas in the cities of London and Paris, these flying machines are flown there frequently.

On Saturday, the 10th, Mr. Kight sat in the balloon at about four in the evening and took off. The air currents propelled him up rapidly and swept him towards the sea and people could see the balloon until it fell into the sea. The chief of the Indian Navy sent a steamboat from Walkeshwar to look for him and other boats were also mobilized. They searched till midnight but could find no trace of him. It was concluded that he fell into the water and drowned.

Late news. On Thursday, the 14th, Mr. Kight arrived in Mumbai from Surat by a steamboat. He says that he landed in the sea at a distance of about five *kos* from Mahalaxmi and was helpless. A steamboat going towards Surat was passing that way and picked him up. Otherwise, he might well have died.

The streets of Mumbai are witness to new kinds of shows and spectacles practically every day. Snake charmers, tumblers and rope-dancers, monkey and bear performers and such other showmen roam the streets with their paraphernalia and will put up a show for four to eight *annas*. But the famous snake charmers and showmen from Europe set up camp for two to four months and their takings range from ten to twenty thousand rupees. They prepare an arena on the Camp Maidan or another central venue and hold their shows there. They perform very difficult shows like dancing on a horse, somersaulting while riding the horse and other gyrations. The other magicians and conjurers put up all kinds of shows. Each person is charged from one to five rupees. Our people are glad to spend their money on such events. A wave of enthusiasm runs through the populace of Mumbai when these showmen land here. The Europeans are very skilled in all things and as they are very shrewd, they can convert any vocation into money. These showmen typically come from France, Italy or England.

As there are no forests in the vicinity of Mumbai, neither does one see beasts roaming about freely nor does one hear the melodious notes of birds. However the English and among the natives, the rich Parsis buy various kinds of exotic birds and keep them as pets. They also bring different kinds of animals from various countries. Numerous types of pigeons are also maintained in gardens and houses. A few years back a pair of lions had been brought here; thousands rushed to see it. They also put huge tigers in vehicles and parade them around the streets. One can see all kinds of forest and village animals like giraffe, zebra, rhinoceros, ostrich, *sambhar,* deer, elephant, camel and bison. A huge dog was brought for sale in the month of November 1862 and one has heard reports that a Bhatia bought it for five hundred rupees. One can see about fifty to a hundred different varieties of dogs. Hunting dogs are bought from Arabia. Each dog is priced between five to six mohurs. Cats from Basra, which are very beautiful, cost over fifty rupees each. In sum, one can see all the animals of this world in this city.

In 1840, the English built a drama-school in a place called Grant Road. This is called the 'theatre'. Initially, only the English staged plays in this theatre. As the craze for plays has spread amongst the citizens of Mumbai, the Hindus and Parsis have also started staging their plays here.[1] Presently, there are four to five drama companies in Mumbai who are always staging new plays. Many seem to have developed an opinion that these plays are agents of reform. This bizarre opinion is backed by idiotic arguments.[2] England produces hundreds of plays and if a scholar like Shakespeare could produce plays, why can't our children do so? However the playwrights of that country are learned and write plays on various topics in pursuit of knowledge. Most of our playwrights are enemies of the lettered word. Most of their plays are just parodies. One never comes across any playwright who has written a few good books. There are many excellent plays in Sanskrit. They were composed by scholarly playwrights; not plain artistes. If a child enters a theatre, one can safely assume that he will come to a bad end. Even in England these are not considered proper plays. A few years back, showmen would come to Mumbai from Karnatak, Sangli, Rajapur, Gomantak, Gujarat, Pune, and other places and perform shows at various houses – hand-puppets, dancing-puppets, the Dashavatars or ten *avatars* of Vishnu, tambourines and drums. The Dashavatars are however made here these days. All the scriptures of the world have condemned the work of a theatre artiste, and the Hindu *shastras* have particularly singled them out. Respectable and learned people spurn them. It is certainly strange that such things have captivated the people of Mumbai. After the arrival of these plays in Mumbai, many children have been spoilt and many have abandoned their ancestral professions. Once a child is hooked on plays, one can safely assume that he is lost to both this world and the next. In Mumbai, parents have to take special care of their children, because if they fall into bad company or into bad practices, it is impossible to restrain them. While there are some facilities for learning in this city, the opportunities for fulfilling one's baser instincts are a thousand-fold. Only the man who can overcome these temptations will be able to succeed and prosper.

Horse racing is just a form of gambling for the rich and the famous. The racing area is on the Mahalaxmi Road in the fields. An area with a circumference of around one and a half *kos* has been set aside for this purpose. A bungalow, named the Sarticha Bungalow has been built at an expense of around twenty five thousand rupees.[3]

Races are held here every year in the month of February. English officials of the highest rank from the civil and military departments, businessmen and many Moghuls subscribe money to run this venture. The racehorses are exercised on these grounds every day. They are trained every day to prepare for these races. They spend hundreds of rupees on each horse. Once they are fully trained, they are entered into the races. Many Englishmen have lost thousands of rupees on these horses and have become paupers. These horses can run the distance of one and a half *kos* in two or three *pal* and reach the finishing line. The owners of these horses bet four to five thousand rupees on these horses. Thousands of people come to see these races and they also bet amongst themselves. On every racing day, about fifty thousand rupees worth of gambling is conducted openly. Crowds of about twenty-five to thirty thousand people gather on each occasion.

A racing horse named *Copenhagen* is praised universally. It is said that this horse has earned its weight in gold for its owners. If this horse ran a race, the owners of the other horses lost hope and would say, how can our horses stand up to this lion among horses? In March 1861, this horse was sent back to England by its owner in its old age to lead a relaxed life. This account was published in the newspaper called the *Gazette*.

Prominent English gentlemen get together to race boats. They have built excellent racing boats and employed the best captains. On an appointed day, four of five of these boats are got ready and the boat which reaches a particular place first is named the winner and is awarded cash prizes. This show is watched by hundreds of people from land and sea.

Dancing girls have cast an eclipse of sorts on Bharat Khand. One cannot estimate the destruction caused by these dances in each city. Women of the loose sort are spread all over Mumbai. Their numbers are increasing daily. If a rich man has to honour his guests, he invites a couple of these dancing girls to grace the occasion, and everybody is happy! Many of the people of Mumbai are of the opinion, that this sort of entertainment is the best available in Bharat Khand. These ladies have become very rich and do not listen to anybody. About eight or ten years back, Danby Seymour, a famous Englishman who was a member of Parliament in the city of London, had come to take a stock of the state of this country. Our people had organized such a dance in his honour. When the Jangbahadur had come from Nepal, Sir Erskine Perry held a dance reception in his honour at the Supreme Court.

Some few days ago, a dancing lady conducted a mock marriage for her daughter. She spent around four thousand rupees on this wedding. The wedding procession consisted of nearly thirty fabulous carriages and two huge chariots drawn by horses, all fully caparisoned. When this regal procession of women slowly strolled down the streets to the accompaniment of instruments like kettledrums, English instruments, and tabors, one was reminded of the stories of the matriarchates mentioned in the *Puranas*. It has been reliably reported that this woman invited all the women belonging to her caste to this function and presented each of them with a cup worth a rupee.

Amongst the Hindus of this city, it is common practice to maintain a couple of servants once they have achieved some minimal prosperity. These servants are *Shudras* from places like Shrivardhan, Harnai, Bankot, Chiplun, Ratnagiri and Rajapur. They do all the domestic work like grinding grains, pounding rice, washing, sweeping, smearing cow dung on the floor, and taking care of the children. Being poor, they are very good at such domestic work. In the houses of the rich, five or six such servants are maintained. They have to be paid between one and three rupees a month besides their board. There must be about three to four thousand such servants in Mumbai. Irrespective of their native villages, they are commonly referred to as Bankotis. They of course have different names, but all Bankotis are named Balu. Those who are paid a monthly salary with board are referred to as being paid wet wages; those paid only a monthly salary are on dry wages – this ranges from five to six rupees a month. However hardly anybody is employed on dry wages for domestic work. *Shudras* and people from other castes come from many other regions but are not much employed in domestic work. They have now begun to be employed in the houses of Vanis and other people. These servants have also started to learn the work of the gardener, watchman, and spice-grinder.

During the month of *Bhadrapad*, on the festival days of Ganpati and Gauri, these people, for a few days, sing a variety of wild songs accompanied by drums and cymbals and contort their face and body in strange manners.

Many of them wear rattles on their feet. Their dances are very uncultured and vulgar. They move about in groups numbering about fifty playfellows. On these days, they dance in the evenings in front of the houses of their employers and other acquaintances. One has to make a present of eight *annas* or a rupee. Their dance movements are however faultless. During the months of *Aashad* and *Shravan*, they take up residence in a house and gather there to practise their dancing. All through the night, they play their drums, and scream and dance.

The following lines of verse have been published in a newspaper called the *Deepdarshak* illustrating the necessity of the Bankotis.

Ovi
Balu works in the police || Many Balus in other offices too||
Not a house without a Balu || Can you see in Mumbai ||
Balu brings the water || Balu shops in the market ||
Balu tends to the old || Balu looks after the kids ||
Balu massages legs || Balu cleans tables ||
Balu drives the *shigram* || Also does the clothes ||

In spite of the numerous arrangements and facilities provided by the Sarkar and the rich, there are hundreds of beggars who roam the streets of Mumbai.[4] They sit on the streets, make plaintive sounds and strike weird poses to beg for money. Some of them may be blind, crippled, lame, old or abandoned; many fraudsters also abound. There are very few beggars among the Parsis and their Panchayat takes care of the beggars. They never beg from other people; neither do the Bohras. They may do some trade for a few *annas* but they would never beg at another's doorstep. This is a very praiseworthy quality of theirs which should be emulated. Among the Christians and English, no able-bodied man will beg from another. Only those who are utterly destitute and orphaned with no support whatsoever may beg on occasion. Even if they are forced into a situation where they have to beg, they are very reluctant to do so.

In 1833, a Bairagi by the name of Tumbdi Bawa had come to Walkeshwar; he had very long matted hair. He wore just a loincloth around his privates and carried a big *tumba*, a vessel made of hollowed gourd, from which his popular name had been derived. He had a group of five to ten disciples. He assumed a very enlightened pose and distributed expensive gifts of cloth − *dhotarjoda, pagoti, shela, lugdi* − to learned men like *shastris, pundits, vaidics* and other Brahmins and their wives, besides presenting them to beggars of various castes. On the first day, he gave away such expensive presents as *pagotis* in the Paithani style and *dhotarjodas* with exquisite serrated edges worth a thousand rupees or two. Brahmins who could not afford to wear a torn *pancha* would go to Walkeshwar and come back decked out like a bridegroom. Many were reminded of the tale of Sudama by his actions. What does one expect next from the people of Mumbai! From the very next day, Walkeshwar became a place of pilgrimage. Practically every Brahmin was on the road to Walkeshwar. The Telegana Brahmins practically took over the place. Somebody would fan the *Bawa*; somebody would wash his loincloth; and a third would clean his matted locks. The Maruti temple, where he had taken up residence, could not be entered. On hearing about this *Bawa*, the cloth bazaar of Mumbai moved to Walkeshwar. Vani, Bhatia, and Shimpi traders came to Walkeshwar with bundles of expensive cloth and urged the disciples of the Tumbdi *Bawa* to buy their goods. Within about five or six days, the *Bawa* managed to run through goods worth ten or fifteen thousand rupees. He paid some money to the traders from whom he had procured these goods. He would bring the money in his *tumba*, and give the impression that he was so powerful that money was being produced in the *tumba* itself. What happened next? All the businessmen and traders went to pay their respects to Tumbdi *Bawa*. Finally, the Bawa could successfully execute his plot. He stayed in Mumbai for some fifteen odd days amid a lot of fanfare and then ran away one night with goods worth over twenty thousand rupees procured from the traders. The traders could not get their hands on even the *tumba*. Fraudsters of this type come to Mumbai frequently and cheat the simple folk, but people never seem to learn. After he disappeared, it was said that this Tumbdi Bawa had cheated people in numerous villages in a similar manner.

Both the Hindus and Mussalmans are much taken up with asking for alms under various pretences. Strong, well built and solid individuals act as if they have renounced the world and beg in various disguises. They assume numerous roles – *Bairagi, Gosavi, Sannyasi, Shivhare, Dhavle Bawa, Kowle Bawa, Brahmachari, Digambar, Paramhansa, Bhajin Bawa* – and move from house to house harassing people. Hindus of all castes can be seen begging for alms. They seem to believe that it is their divine duty to ask for alms. Hundreds of Gujarati and Dakshini Brahmins can be seen knocking on doors asking for uncooked food; even Mahars and Chambhars disguise themselves as holy men and beg for alms. The Mahars beg in the name of Chokamela while the Chambars invoke Rohidas. The Vanis and Shimpis use Namdeo and Tukaram as their standard bearers. They sling a bag under their arms and ask for rice in the morning; come evening and they equip themselves with the *veena* and a lantern, and singing *powadas* and *padas* beg for a few pice. In this manner, from morn till midnight, beggars beset the people of Mumbai.

Some days back, a person called Teli Raja came visiting; his dress and manners were very strange. He was a devotee of Hinglaj Devi and claimed to have come from Hinglajpuri. Two disciples, who took care of his needs, accompanied him. He had tied a kerchief around his head, and wore a vest soaked in oil on his body; oil also dripped from his *dhoti*. He would go and stand on the doorstep of houses and his disciples would ask for oil to be poured on his body or that he be given an oil-bath. Many people would actually venerably do so and ask him for his blessings! They would also give him food and money. He would then forecast their future. His strange appearance would shock the people. If he stood in a place, streams of oil would flow from his body. Such new and novel methods of moneymaking can be seen in Mumbai. Such wiles beguile many of our people.

As the esteem of Pandharpur has increased in the eyes of the people, there has been an increasing trend among the Hindus to assume the habit of a holy man and beg for alms. This has reached its heights in Mumbai. Practically everybody descends on the roads clutching cymbals and sticks. In addition, beggars from other regions congregate in Mumbai. Many women behave like religious devotees, recite stories, sing *bhajans,* beg for alms and move about in a stately manner in the company of their acolytes. One such 'saint' came here in 1838. She recited the *katha* at numerous places. During the nine nights of Rama Navmi, she recited stories at the temple of Atmaram Shimpi. This lady was a child widow. It is the opinion of a learned English economist that as the number of beggars increases in a population, it gets impoverished further. This is certainly true. Just look! Compared to the other people, the state of the Hindus is deteriorating rapidly. This is because of the number of beggars. If somebody sits outside with about a *khandi* of grain on his doorstep and distributes it in handfuls to passing beggars, he will exhaust his stock by the evening, such is the huge number of beggars in Mumbai. Many of them are idlers, frauds, and rogues. One verse composition that is quite long accurately describes the activities, as they are, of *Kowle Bawa, Dhawle Bawa,* and others; it has not been reproduced here because it contains some disgusting words. Mumbai contains numerous such *Bawas*. A Brahmin named Gujaba Nana composed these verses; he has written many such verses.

The resident population of Gosavis and Haridases in Mumbai is quite large, but at the end of the month of Shravan and during the Rama Navami, these people gather in Mumbai from various regions in large numbers. The reason being that the Ganpati festival is celebrated with great ceremonial in the houses of many Hindus. During the festival, they organize *kathas* – one or two according to their capacity. The *katha* reciters are paid quite a lot of money. Many of the Haridases are quite learned and good speakers. They earn from one hundred to a hundred and fifty rupees per night. If he is of the ordinary sort, he may get about twenty odd rupees. When they get the opportunity, they also beg for alms from door to door, a *veena* in their hands, accompanied by a retinue of cymbals and drums and servants carrying their bags tucked under the shoulder. Many take up residence in a temple for a month or two, deliver *kathas* in the night and during the day, making a pretence of having done the ablutions and become pure, they roam the streets accompanied by a *shastri* and the usual instruments asking for alms. When they leave their houses, they arrange a few coins – rupees, *chavli, pawli, adheli* – and some essential oil on a dish, wrap a shawl around themselves and assume a very dignified manner. They then go about collecting money from householders. This kind of alms is known as the *mahabhiksha* or supreme alms and many collect this under the pretext of going for a *mahayatra*, the supreme pilgrimage to Kashi.

A few years back, a holy man named Atmaram Bawa resided in this city. He was a very saintly person and was very compassionate. It is said that he would recite *kathas* that evoked god and were very melodious. He was generosity personified. He spent his life doing good deeds. He has been awarded an *inam*, a village with an annual revenue of five hundred rupees at Baroda, by Sayaji Maharaj. He built a temple to Rama on the Palo Road at an expense of thirty to forty thousand rupees. He was much venerated by the people of Mumbai and other places. His ascetic lifestyle, lack of avarice, and munificence inspired the people to serve him. People would give him thousands of rupees. He would distribute the money to the poor or use it for other charitable purposes. This philanthropic *sadhu* attained *samadhi* around 1836, that is on Shravan Shudh 7 of *Shaké* 1758. It is said that he was around ninety at that time, and had led a very disciplined life. His memorial is in the *mandap* opposite the temple of Rama. This temple is known as Atmaram Bawa's Thakurdwar. The people of Mumbai assisted him with the finance to build this temple.

Hordes of Gosavis, Bairagis, and Sanyasis congregate annually in Mumbai, and many more camp out here through the year smoking their *ganja*. They stay in Mumbadevi, Bhuleshwar, Babulnath, Gaondevi, Bhavani Shankar, Mahalaxmi and Walkeshwar. They come into town only to beg for alms. Some light up their *dhumris* and smoke *ganja* or *bhang* through the day or chew opium. They subsist on whatever they receive from devotees who visit the temple. They also earn their share of alms from their disciples who come to beg in town.

Mumbai abounds in exorcists and dispossesors of all sorts – *panchakshari* who exorcise by chanting the *panchakshari mantra* consisting of five letters; *devrishi* who summon gods and devils; *samudriks* who interpret spots, lines and other marks on the body; *dhutara* who invoke the divinities like Kanoba, Khandoba and others in the body. Most of the Hindus believe in them. They tie threads, rub *vibhuti*, give ashes, ritually invoke gods, give rice to eat, or just plain water after whispering some *mantras;* it is indeed surprising that there are so many who cannot see through their fraud.

The beggars start roaming the streets a few hours before sunrise. Before it is bright enough to discern a man properly, the *paud* makes his presence known. The *paud* wears a *langoti*, and has a small black blanket over his head, a staff in his hand and a bag hanging from his shoulders. He shrieks loudly from the road and announces his arrival about ten to twenty times. On hearing his shouts while sleeping on a mattress, one's chest beats with fear as if hearing an enemy approach. He stands on the doorsteps of houses and babbles ceaselessly. He advises the people thus: 'donate in the name of your ancestors during this holy time of the day; donate a few clothes in the name of your god; donate some money to earn some merit; donate in the name of your parents.' If somebody comes out and gives him a paisa or two or a rag or a torn blouse, he jumps up and down like a madman, and in slightly hushed tones rattles off the name of a few hundred gods as they occur to him. The Kunbi, Ghanti, Maratha and Vani folk hold him in esteem. Many simple folk believe that he is invested with great powers just because he shouts loudly, and offer him rice, money, old blouses, *lugdi, angarkha, bundee,* or rags. Within a couple of hours, he manages to collect about ten or twenty rags, loose change of about four *annas,* and about a *paylee* of rice.

Even as the *paud* continues to scream, the *vasudev* comes along. He wears a crown of peacock flowers on his head, a long tattered gown over his body, and rags wrapped around his hands. He has a bag on his shoulders, cymbals in his right hand and plays the *tipri* with his left hand. He wears tinny bells on his ankles. Decked in this fashion, he comes dancing down the road, shouting out to people and playing his cymbals. He calls out many different words. He babbles just like the *paud.* Some of his sentences are as follows. 'Karna Raja did charity do; Dharma Raja did charity do; Ramachandra did charity do; Ahilyabai did charity do; Gopikabai did charity do; Changdeva did charity do; Damajipant did charity do; Pundalik did charity do; Janabai did charity do; *et cetera.'*

Just as the *paud* and *vasudev* are winding up their prattles, the *pangul* comes along with a *nandi* bull. It is not as if these arrive at the same place at the same time; but the times of their arrival are about the same. Occasionally, the *vasudev* and *pangul* create a racket at the same place, but more often than not, they avoid each other; the obvious reason being that they may not both get the rewards they are after.

A boy beating a *dholka* and a *nandi* bull, also referred to as the *pangul* bull or *ghansa* bull, accompanies the *pangul*. The bull is festooned with chains and bells around its neck and castanets around its legs. Rags of different colours and baubles are tied to its horns. Besides this, rags weighing about a couple of *man* are hung from its back and on its forehead is tied a brass image of either Mahadev or Maruti. It is thus decorated. When the cow is made to dance to the beat of drums and the *pangul* himself sings loudly, the racket is deafening. He lies on the ground on his back and makes the bull stand on his chest on all four legs. He performs many such stunts. Students, the old and infirm and people of the contemplative sort are much affected by the sound of the rasping words of the *pangul*, the jangling of the bells on the bull, and the vulgar beat of the drums in the early hours of the morning.

Some years back, a Thandoji Bawa used to come at dawn and roam the streets singing loudly. He would wear a wet *dhotar* and don a hat made from oleander leaves; he would stand at the doorstep of houses and get his disciples to pour cold water from a pot over him. He would do his rounds mainly during the cold season. On days of extreme cold or rain, he would make it a point to come very early and get lots of water poured over himself. It is not well understood why people honour him. These sort of people are not to be encountered these days.

It is certainly very pleasing that, of late, the number of such people has been decreasing. In the last ten to fifteen years, one has rarely seen the *nandi* bull and the Thandoji Bawa. Perhaps as the people have reformed they have stopped giving money to these people or maybe they themselves have tired of this profession; the reasons are not very clear.

Various sorts of vicious people used to come to Mumbai in earlier days, but they do not come here now. Many beggars known as *Nanakpanthi* used to come here, wielding cudgels made of smooth black wood, their mouths babbling away and forcibly taking money from the shopkeepers. If someone refused to give money, they screamed at him and cursed him loudly in the most vulgar manner. Other even more savage types also used to come here. They would carry a wooden cot with them when they made their rounds, and if somebody refused to give them money, one of the accompanying boys would be made to lie on the cot. He would pierce his chest with knives, or push a nail through his cheeks, and make a hole in his tongue and pass a string through it. Suddenly a gang of twenty or so eunuchs might appear, spouting a variety of profanities and clapping their hands very loudly, and coerce the shopkeepers into giving them a paisa or two. They terrorize the people very greatly and refuse to go away until they are paid.[5] The Gosavis put on various gruesome stunts. Some pull their intestines out through their mouths. They stage such disgusting displays and trick the people into giving them money. The English have very slowly and tactfully eliminated all these monstrosities from the city.

About forty years back a Bairagi came to this place and asked the people to honour him with a purse of five thousand rupees. As he was not given the money, he climbed to the top of the pole installed in the centre of the tank at Mumbadevi, lay prone on his stomach and refused to come down. Some people offered to give him a thousand rupees or two but he refused to listen. He was on the pole for two consecutive days. Finally some simple and godfearing traders convinced him to come down after they gave him the money. Many such stuntmen used to come here. If somebody tried to pull such stunts in the present day, Forjett Sahib would frogmarch him down the road to jail within the hour.

Bairagis and Bairaginis roam the streets singing couplets of various kinds.

In a similar fashion, Mussalman fakirs come from Delhi, Mecca, Sindh, Kabul, Kandahar, Hyderabad, and Punjab in their hundreds. They base themselves in the masjid at Bhendi Bazaar and other masjids. Nakhuda and other rich Mussalmans feed them. They roam the streets of Mumbai singing the couplets of Kabir or other songs and collecting money. Many of them also provide threads, magical water and practise other hocus-pocus. Many Hindus and Parsis gather these fakirs together and distribute money. They are of the opinion that giving charity to the Mussalmans is of special religious merit as compared to giving alms to other beggars. Many fakirs come to the doorsteps of the Hindus to beg by singing couplets of gods like Rama and Krishna. These are just wiles to get money out of the Hindus; in reality they despise the Hindu religion and are very cruel in nature. Many fakirs stay in the masjids and some build huts for themselves. While the Hindus may worship the Mussalman gods, a Mussalman would never pray before a Hindu god even at the cost of his life.

A recent trend among the beggars of Mumbai is the arrival of phoney *vatandars*, hereditary officers from the Dakshini country. They are mostly fraudulent Marathas, Vanis or Brahmins from the Nizam's kingdom or other regions. Somebody masquerades as a *kulkarni* with accounts hanging from his neck; another becomes a *patel* with ledger books tied around his waist; a third poses like a *deshmukh* with chains around his hands; another acts like a *deshpande* and has an iron ring on his feet; and yet another acts like a *zamindar* with a small plough hanging around his neck. They adopt a variety of disguises, forge some papers and come with their wives and children to beg on the streets. They then claim that they have to pay five hundred or a thousand rupees to the Sarkar; hence the chains and rings around their legs and they claim that their kin are in jail. Their women proclaim their sad state of affairs in a loud tone and sing strange songs.

One can see beggars from Telegana on the streets accompanied by their wives – with a tableau hoisted onto their shoulders or with some pictures displayed on a plate. Some bring along some five or ten cows, and ask for money for their care. At every step, one is hassled by such conmen in Mumbai.

Every morning one can see at least a couple of *pingle, medhe joshi, gondhali, vadhye,* and *kaan-fatye* on one's doorstep. Gangs of women posing as Khandoba's *murali* roam the streets; these women unleash a reign of terror in the name of religion. People can only be led to destruction by such fraudsters. There are too many inducements towards bad behaviour in this city. People spend their ill-gotten wealth in acts of charity and feel happy. What does one call this? Most beggars are proud and arrogant in spite of their wretchedness.

In the mornings, there is a rush of the Gondhali people, and their importance increases during the Navaratri. They wear chains made from cowries around their necks and wear an oil-soaked robe on their body. They carry a huge, fiery torch and dance boisterously. They have an oil bottle slung from their shoulders and are accompanied by a boy playing a one-stringed instrument. They sing a variety of songs in praise of Bhavani. Their signature tune is '*Udobhavani, ambabaicha jogwa*'.

Blind men from various regions and provinces come into this city in hundreds; they beg from morning till about ten in the night in a variety of plaintive tones. Some bring a cow or two along with them. They form a chain of eight to ten people by placing their hands on each other's shoulders. Many have two wives. Some time back, there was a beggar who was crippled in both legs; he would walk like an animal on the streets and beg for money. He would earn a rupee or two every day. He had three wives.

In the month of Ashwin, during the nine days of Navaratri, the Vaadval, Gurav and other *Shudra* castes beg for alms in the name of *Jogwa*. These famous beggars move with their entire families and clans and collect a handful of rice from each house. During an eclipse, Mahar, Mang, Dhed and Halalkhors roam the streets shouting out '*De daan sute grahan, de data sute grahan*', that is, 'Give charity and the eclipse will go away' from the commencement of the eclipse until it is over.

The Motyale Brahmins from Gujarat who cast horoscopes, *yaadvan* (the paper on which are recorded the lunar day, natural day, aspect of the planets, and other circumstances of a nativity), *varsh fal* (the events or fortunes of the year as determined astrologically on the first day of it), and *trimasik fal* (fortunes for three months) have been resident in Mumbai for many years. They are mostly settled around the houses of Antoba Gosavi and Anant Rishi. Their numbers are depleting in recent years as their feeble voices are drowned in the loud clamour created by English knowledge.

A few years back, the Hindus, Parsis, and Yahudis put a lot of store in their horoscopes, and their business prospered. Some would spend over a hundred rupees for getting a horoscope done. They believed that these horoscopes were literally written by Lord Brahma himself. If they came up against any trifling loss or some other obstacle, they would take their horoscope bundles to one of these Joshi Bawas. Each horoscope is about two hundred hands long with a drawing of the Tulsi plant or the banyan tree on the top. It contains drawings of various kinds of *rashichakras* (the circle of the signs of the zodiac), positions of the planets, and *kundalikas,* all coloured in a multitude of shades. Many bring freshly prepared horoscopes into their houses with ceremony at the appropriate holy time and invite a Joshi Bawa to read it out and worship it. They then honour the Joshi Bawa with gifts. The main reasons why they have fallen out of favour with the public – English schools and hospitals.

Chapter 14

The Churches of the English – The igrejas and khurus of the Portuguese – The temples of the Hindus – The dere and yati of the Shravaks – The raul of the Kamathis – The masjids and pirs of the Mussalmans – The Synagogue of the Bene Israeli and Yahudi – The agiary of the Parsis – Festivals of different people – Kapilashasti – Songs of the goddess – Kanoba's Math – Ganesh Chaturthi – Deepawali – Moharram – Yatra and Jatra – Urus – Missionary – Company of Paramhans – Vishnu Bawa Brahmachari

For many years, there was no priest or preacher of the English in Mumbai and the English did not have any place of worship either. In 1714, the Court of Directors sent Reverend Richard Cobbe as the head priest. In 1700, the then Governor, Sir Nicholas Waite wrote a letter to the Court of Directors in which he said, 'Please send a Bible (a religious book) and two prayer books to Mumbai'. The building of the big church at the Fort was begun during his tenure but it could only be completed during the tenure of Mr. Charles Boone due to the efforts of Mr. Cobbe. It is known as the Cathedral.[1] To keep this church in good repair, it was decided to endow it with an annual sum by levying an additional customs duty of eight *annas* on every hundred rupees' worth of goods landed in the port of Mumbai. The following note can be encountered in the Government Archives, 'In 1733, a sum of 2,674 rupees and in 1734 a sum of 8,893 rupees collected from customs was handed over to the church officials'.

Of all the English places of worship, the Cathedral is the largest. It took three years to construct and it was completed in 1718.[2] The Governor, Charles Boone gave a lot of money for installing the large bell in the Cathedral. His name and the year are inscribed on it. He also made great efforts to collect money from other Englishmen. The Company Sarkar gave 10,000 rupees for this task. The total expenses of this church amounted to 53,992 rupees. There is a large musical instrument here that is played every Sunday when the meetings are held in the church.

This church was renovated in 1838 and its height was increased. On this occasion, a similar contribution was collected. There are clocks on all four sides. They ring on the hour, half hour and the quarter hour. Prominent Englishmen have been buried in this church. One of the tombs is that of Governor Duncan Sahib. His qualities have been described on it. A picture of a Brahmin and a Lady has been sculpted, with the Lady writing down the description of his kindness while the Brahmin mourns his death with folded hands. This Brahmin was an astrologer in Calcutta. When Duncan Sahib was working as a clerk in Calcutta, the Brahmin had prophesied that he would attain political heights in the future. As this prophecy had come true, it is said that a close relationship developed between the Brahmin and the Sahib. As this kind Sahib had attempted to put an end to the practice of female infanticide among the Rajputs, two children mourning his death are also depicted. A beautiful banyan tree has also been carved. The sculpting work on this tomb is of the highest quality. As this Sahib was very committed to public welfare, the citizens of Mumbai raised a collection to erect this mausoleum, and a marble stone sculpted with pictures was ordered from Vilayat and installed in 1817. There are seven English churches in this city.

There are thirteen igrejas of the Portuguese and Christian people in this city. Three of them are in Mahim. Besides, there are *khurus* or crosses at numerous places. Just as the Hindus venerate the road-side peepul tree, the Portuguese worship the wooden crosses installed at various places. They are about seventy-eighty in number. They must have been installed during the reign of the Portuguese in this city. Many of them have been renovated recently. Just as a Tulsi tree at the doorstep of every Hindu house that is worshipped in the morning and the evening, the *khurus* are treated in a similar fashion. These people kneel in front of the *khurus* three times a day and pray in a very dignified manner.

There are three *khurus* on the Camp Maidan. As they are the gods of the Portuguese people and are monuments of their rule, the English have left them standing. Of these, the large one near the Marine Lines is venerated by many of them in the morning and evening. They kneel in front of it and pray. In the evening one can see about twenty to twenty-five of them praying in unison. An old Christian woman who is a devotee of this *khurus* is always present with a basket containing some earthen lamps, oil, candles and similar items. Many take a vow to light a lamp or a candle in front of this *khurus* and there are around ten or so lamps burning in front of this *khurus* every day. Many throw flowers over it while some offer fruits. Older devotees have many tales regarding the greatness of this *khurus*. Many

Hindus and Parsis also take vows in front of this *khurus*. One lady says that this *khurus* will get you a job; grant you children; cure your diseases and do anything else that you wish for! It is not clear whether the Hindus venerate this *khurus* because they believe that god is ubiquitous or because they feel that this *khurus* is more powerful than the thirty-three crores Hindu gods.

The most important Portuguese temple is the one on the road running behind Bhuleshwar known as the 'Nossa Senhora da Esperança'. It is set in a sprawling compound. The church contains many paraphernalia including statues of saints. They worship these idols just like our people. This church was earlier located at the Camp Maidan quite near to the large *khurus*. It was renovated in 1833. The church at Mazagaon is also very old. It is said that the Koli people built it.

The ancient temples of the Hindus in this city are Mumbadevi, Kalbadevi, Gaondevi, Bhuleshwar, Walkeshwar, Babulnath, Mahalaxmi, Mankeshwar, Prabhadevi, Venkatesh at the Fort and the temple of Rama at Ramwadi.

The Vageshwari is at Sewri. It is not known who installed the idol in this temple. It is currently under the care of Janardhan Balaji. This gentleman is affluent and a member of the Grand Jury. His father, Balaji Shamshet was very famous in Mumbai for many years. There are about seven to eight small temples at Parel, one of them being the Mankeshwar temple built by Vithoba Mankoji. There is a Mankeshwar temple at Mazagaon and it is said, that a Sutar resident of Worli built it about a hundred years ago. It cannot however be determined who first installed the idol in this temple. A gentleman called Purushottam Ramachandraji renovated it. The Shambu Mahadev Temple on the lower side of Worli and the Prabhadevi Temple at Mahim are very ancient. There is a temple in Matunga built by Narayan Seth Shimpi. There are a couple of temples at Sion and about twenty-five temples at Mahim. Most of them are very old.

There is a Ram temple at Ramwadi. It is very ancient. A Prabhu gentleman called Kashinath Sokaji first built it. About sixty or seventy years later, it was renovated by the late Vithoba Kanoji. Since then, his family has been managing the affairs of this temple.

Towards the end of Girgaon, on the road to Mahalaxmi, is the Bhavani Temple built by the famous Shrimant Jagannath Shankarseth. This is a very beautiful place and there is a dharamshala adjacent to it, which has been given out for charity. Guests and strangers stay in the dharamshala. The poor can stay here for free. His residence is next to this temple. It is full of invaluable articles. There are fountains at various places. A pleasant breeze wafts down the garden. This place is worth seeing. Many others have also built their bungalows on this road.

The temple of the Devi of the Kansars is just below the Mumbadevi Temple. These people have settled here since a long time. One of them named Bapushet was very famous and charitable. He would give five rupees for the last rites of the poor irrespective of which caste they belonged to. He was earlier responsible for the minting of coins at the Mint. The Kansars had a lot of prestige at that time; one hardly encounters any illustrious person among them currently. The Kansars claim to be Somavanshi Kshatriyas.

If one compares the inscriptions on the temples done two hundred years ago with those done currently, one can form an idea of the evolution of the language and the diction of the people of this island and can put a date to them. If one reads the inscription in the Sanskrit, Marathi, and English languages at the Dhakjee Dadajee Temple and compares it with that at Prabhavati Temple at Mahim written in the original Marathi of Mumbai, one can understand the vast difference between the Marathi of those days and the current Marathi. Some temple inscriptions have been reproduced below.

A wise old man of the Somavanshi caste wrote the following account of the Gaondevi Temple.

'Shree Gramdevi is very ancient. Her name is Lilavati. About two hundred years back, it was located on the hills at Walkeshwar. She came into the dreams of one Bapaji Mhatre Somavanshi Kshatriya Pathare and asked him to take her into the village; he and the other people of Girgaon collectively brought her to Girgaon and installed her in an open space and planted a banyan tree at that spot. This tree grew to an enormous size but it collapsed in a storm a few years ago; a part of it still remains. Later in the year *Shaké* 1728, Rajashree Balaji Bhikaji Kshatriya Somavanshi Pathare built the temple, which still stands. This Devi is much venerated by the Vaadval, Sutar and Somavanshi Kshatriya Pathare castes. A procession is celebrated in the month of Margashirsh on the Shudh Purnima day. The Rama Navami and Navaratri festivals are also celebrated. These people meet all the expenses.'

A Sutar composed a *shloka* on this *Devi* in earlier days which is as follows.

Mumbadevi Lilavati who sits by a banyan at Girgaon
The old people believe her to be the true goddess
Obstacles are removed even before they are realized
Seeing her devotees in problems, she rushes to their rescue.

The inscription on the temple built by Dhakjee Dadajee is in Sanskrit.

'This temple and the dharamshala adjacent to the temple have been built by Prabhu Dhakjee Dadajee, citizen of Mumbai and consecrated to the five gods Shree Mayureshwar, Shree Rameshwari, Shree Dhakleshwar, Shree Hari Narayan and Shree Vinayakaditya on the 11th day of Vaisakh shudh in the Samvatsara year named Nandan Shaké 1745 as per the religious rites prescribed by the Hindu shastras. May our descendants look after and protect this temple.'

A small temple, about three hands high and two hands broad is located beside the Mankeshwar Temple; the image of a snake has been carved on the stone there. Adjacent to it is a rock about two hands high and a hand broad on which are carved the images of the sun and moon. Below it are images of the lingam of Mahadeva and a Nandi. Further below are inscriptions in the Kannada and Balabodha scripts. The Kannada script reads as follows.

'The writer is from Shrirangapattan in Karnatak. Lingayya, son of Honnarappayya, son of Nyanki Narasappiya. Originally from near Bijapur. May Lakshmi reign. Samvatsara year name Prabhav.'

It is said that a Lingayat, Kannadi Ayya in the service of Badshah Aurangzeb installed this stone. The inscription however does not provide any support for this contention. It is well known that there is a practice among the Kannada people to demarcate the boundaries of their land by installing a stone inscription with images of the snake, sun, moon and Mahadev as witness. This is just the boundary stone of a Lingayat Vani but our people seem to think of it as the image of a god and worship it every day and conduct *poojas* with the help of a Brahmin. This is a very dim thing to do. What can one say about the simple-mindedness of our people?

The farthest part of Mazagaon is known as Upper Mazagaon. The Ghodupdeo is located there. Its actual name is Khadakdeo, the Rock God, as it is a very big rock whose front face has been anointed with vermilion to signify a god. A fraudulent *Shudra* has built this temple. He sticks betel nut on the god and tries to cheat the people of their money. On the roof of this temple, fifty or so small cradles have been hung. Even the gods of Mumbai have very queer names – *Jabreshwar* or the brutal god, *Hatteshwar* or the stubborn god, *Tad Dev*, the god of the palymra tree, *Bab Dev*, the god of the palm tree, *Khokla Devi*, the cough goddess, *et cetera*.

There are about three hundred Hindu temples in Mumbai. Khokladevi, the cough goddess is in Mahim. Her devotees maintain that anybody with a cough will get cured if they pray to her! Of course, every compound has got its own Bab Dev. There are many Maruti Temples in this city and they generate substantial revenue. They are owned by the Bairagis. Many of the female devotees of Maruti are harlots of a depraved nature.

In a few places, the *Puranas* are recited through all the twelve months of the year. The *Puranas* are regularly recited at Bhuleshwar, Kashivishveshwar, Ramachandra (in Ramwadi), Vithoba's temple, Atmaram Bawa's Thakurdwar and other temples. Week-long recitations are held at many places during the months of Shravan and Bhadrapad. In times past, affluent Prabhu, Shenvi, Sonar folk and others used to organize the recitation of various *Puranas* like the *Bhagavad Gita*, the *Mahabharata* and the *Ramayana* at their houses during the monsoon; once the recitation was completed over five or six months, they would present the *puranik* with four or five hundred rupees. Many arrange for the recitation of *Pandavpratap*, *Harivijay*, *Ashwamedh* and other books written in the people's language. As the importance of English education has increased, this practice is on the wane. Only the most religious people now arrange for recitations. The Vanis and Bhatias also do not arrange for the recitation of the *Puranas*. Some five or ten years back, a *puranik* who was blind from birth came here. He had recited the *Bhagavad Gita* in the Vithoba Temple at Vithalwadi. It is said that he could recite the entire *Bhagavad Gita* and the *Ramayana* by heart. Many Gujaratis arrange for week-long recitations the cost of which ranges from five to twenty-five thousand rupees.

Building temples is a meritorious deed as it is the primary duty of man to introduce god to those who are completely unaware and ignorant about the existence of god, inculcate a sense of devotion in them, and motivate their hearts to do good deeds. There is, however, no gain in building small temples that even the priest cannot enter in a place where there are many other temples. Nobody casts a second glance at them. If a temple is not useful for its primary purpose, what is the point of building them? The main objective behind building a temple is nothing but to enable people to reach out to god and inspire them to lead a good life. Such small temples do not help people to know god and they are just a waste of money. There is no religious merit or worldly gain attached to this act; rather it will be much more useful to build temples in places where people do not understand the way of god, and in villages where there are no temples and lead people on the divine path.

Temples have to be very pleasant spots and should allow at least two hundred people to gather easily. People should be inspired to devotion when they see the temple.

There are seven *deras* (temples) of the Shravak folk – five of the Marwadis and two of the Shravak Vanis. These *deras* are built in a very different manner. These temples are very different from ours; mirrors are fixed in apparently random fashion to the ceiling. These people are traders and donate a lot of wealth to god as they are very religious. The Ghorjinath Dera at Bhendi Bazaar is the largest of all the *deras* and it is said that it has a treasury worth fifteen lakh rupees. During the month of Shravan when the Marwadis celebrate their festivals, they decorate the idols with splendid gems and jewellery. These *deras* contain a great many crystal articles. This is typical Marwadi behaviour as they do not have any sense of proportion or delicacy. They embellish the idol with decorations – one day with diamonds, the next with rubies, the third with emeralds, then with pearls and so on. The decoration involves covering the idol from head to toe with stones of the same sort – either by sticking them with gum or in the form of jewels – with the exception of the eyes which are kept open. It is said that the diamond decoration of Ghorjinath is worth a lakh and a quarter of rupees. The nature of their devotion is very strange and quite different from that of the other Hindus. They have devised the following scheme to finance these decorations. A particular Seth will undertake to supply ten *mans* of ghee to fund the decoration. The decoration is undertaken in the name of the person who bids the highest number of *mans* and he has to send money at the rate of twelve rupees per *man* of ghee that he has undertaken to supply. They decide the amount of donation based on the quantity of ghee. People undertake to supply a hundred *mans* or two hundred *mans* of ghee. They then have to pay a corresponding amount of money to the treasury. Just as a particular object is auctioned off, these people auction these festivals. Once all the people are gathered together, the priest of the temple stands up and says, 'Moti Seth undertakes to supply ten *mans* of ghee'. Somebody shouts out, 'Fifteen,' and a third screams, 'I am at thirty'. The name of the person who undertakes to supply the largest quantity of *ghee* is entered in the register. The Shravaks celebrate their festival from the month of Aashad to the Shudh Panchami of Bhadrapad. They fast on these days. Many *yatis*, religious mendicants of this sect, fast for periods ranging from one to three months and do not eat anything at all, so they say. Some rich trader then buys the religious merit derived from these fasts for five or six thousand rupees. Others also contribute money according to their capacity. Ordinary people who fast for fifteen days are invited by the Marwadi people to break their fast at their houses and pay them fifty to a hundred rupees to buy the religious merit due from the fast. In the month of Bhadrapad, a grand procession of the *yatis* who have fasted is led through the streets. Many of these *yatis* are very rich, and they also conduct trade.

During the festival in the month of Shravan, the Marwadis decorate their body with gems and gold and silver jewellery. This festival is known as *Pajusan* and it is celebrated for eight consecutive days.

It is said that in 1862, a *yati* fasted for three consecutive months in the *dera* of Khemchand Motichand. Towards the evening, he would boil about a glass of water, cool it and then drink it, while some say that he drank the water of *Kirayat*. He touched no other food of any kind. One cannot understand how this happens. He looked very thin and emaciated like Jaratkaaru, a holy man who performed severe penances, and hundreds of people used to go to see him. One is very reluctant to believe this story unless one can confirm from contemporary doctors that a man can survive for three months without food.

There are five *rauls* of the Kamathi people in Kamathipura – two of Vithoba and three of Maruti. These people are Hindus and worship the Hindu gods, but their main gods are Jakhai, Jokhaya, Putlai, and Yellamma. These people are from the Madras Province. They have been staying here for over a hundred years. Their population is between five and six thousand people belonging to eight or ten different castes. They mostly work as labourers but some of them are affluent. Their women are diligent and sturdy and quite often earn more money than the men. No labour work or house building or lime pounding is undertaken without them. Both the men and women work very hard to earn money.

The masjids of the Mussalmans, Bohras, Khojas, and Memons number sixty-nine. In addition, there are over a fifty mausoleums of the *pirs* and places where the iron fist or *Panja* is buried.

In 1862, a rich Moghul named Haji Mohammad Hussain built a big mosque near the Babulnath Tank at an expense of one lakh rupees for the use of Moghuls. It is very beautiful. The work on the main door of the mosque is excellent.

The tombs of Magdum Bawa and his mother are located next to each other outside the masjid in Mahim. These tombs are worshipped daily. There are many resident fakirs and this has become a source of perpetual income for them. Many Hindus and Parsis venerate these tombs. They take vows in the name of the Bawa. When his *urus* is held, his tomb is decorated for fifteen consecutive days. The simple folk are very devoted to him.

His account is as follows. The simple folk consider it to be as true as the ancient scriptures. It is up to the scholars of the present day to examine these accounts and determine how much of it is true. Even a ten- or twelve-year-old boy will be able to tell that these traditional accounts are not much to be relied upon. One has to relate these accounts occasionally to illustrate the simple-mindedness of the people in the past. A reader, however, must use some discrimination at the appropriate places while reading them; otherwise, it is a waste of time.

Some years ago, a Mussalman used to stay in Mahim. This Magdum was his son. The father died when he was young. Magdum and his mother struggled to make ends meet. The son loved his mother and was very devoted to her. On one occasion, when they were sleeping next to each other, the mother called out to Magdum at midnight and asked him to get her some water to drink. When he heard it, he immediately got a glass of water and went and stood near his mother. As she had drifted back to sleep, she did not realize that she had called out for water. When she woke up in the morning, she saw Magdum standing next to her with a glass of water in his hand. When she saw this display of maternal devotion, the mother was overcome with emotion. She sang praises of the lord and prayed to him to bless her son. From that time on, the mother and son were very devoted to the worship of god who bestowed his blessings on them. As time went by, the fame of Magdum Bawa spread far and wide. He started performing many miracles! He would bestow children on somebody and cure those lying on their deathbeds! Some also say that he went to Mecca every day! Of the many miracles performed by him, this was related by one of his devotees. One morning, he got up and went towards a pond and started scooping out the water with the hollow of his hands. The people were astonished to see this and asked him why he was doing so. He replied that Mecca was on fire and that he was helping to put out the fire. They did not believe him and felt that he must have been touched by madness. Many businessmen however wrote to Mecca to ascertain the facts and received replies confirming the fact that there was a fire in Mecca on that particular day. He was much venerated since this event. He performed many such miracles! There is however no information on the date of his birth or the period when he performed these miracles.

The Habshee of Habsan has venerated this saint for many years and continues to send money and cloth for the tomb during the days of the *urus*. It is said that, earlier, he used to send to send a swathe of gold brocade to lay on the tomb, and would personally visit the tomb during the *urus* with much fanfare to the accompaniment of music.

The names of Pirs and their locations in and around Mumbai

Sayyad Badruddin Hussaini	Pen
Karamali Shah and Haji Abdul Rahman Sahib	Panvel
Sheikh Ismail Gaza Ali	Upper Colaba
Gaibi Pir	Bazaar

Sheikh Hassan Gaza Ali	Lower Colaba
Gaibi Pir	Camp Maidan
Sayyad Nizamuddin	Near the jail
Sayyad Badruddin Rafai	Bhendibazaar
Madar Chilli	Null Bazaar
Sayyad Jinal Abuddin Rafai	Khara Talao
Mastan Shah and Sayyad Abdullah Sahib	Khara Talao
Bismillah Shah	Camp Maidan
Sayyad Abdullah Sahib	Kitta
Sayyad Ali Mastan	Line
Mulla Fakhruddin	Marine Lines
Sayyad Hussain Andrus	Saat Tad
Gaibi Pir	At the railway station
Sheikh Haji Momen	Near the Jumma Masjid
Vali Yulla	Hanuman Galli
Ashok Shah	Dongri
Sarhang Sayyad Hisamuddin Rafai	Mahalaxmi
Sarhang Madar Chilli	Kitta
Sayyad Moiddin Ghogari	Near the jail
Sayyad Moiddin Basravi	Kitta
Jomay Shah	Duncan Road
Gulab Shah	Rupapad
Sheikh Bari Sahib	Chinchpokhli
Sheikh Talyani Sahib	Kitta
Sheikh Mistri Sahib	Matunga
Pakba Ali Makdoom Sahib	Mahim
Poopleer Sahib	Thane
Gaibi Pir	Thane
Diwan Sahib	Bhiwandi
Haji Ali Sahib	Below Mahalaxmi
Mama Hajani	Besides Worli
Jungli Pir	On the Worli hill

The biggest mosque of the Mussalmans is the Jumma Masjid in the Market. It was earlier in the Camp Maidan; it was demolished and rebuilt here.

The native land of the Bene Israeli people is Arabia. It is estimated that they had to leave this land for Bharat Khand in the sixth century of the Christian era, about twelve hundred years ago, because of the cruelties of the ruler of that area. They came here in two ships – one of these reached Cochin where those people settled down and the other crashed into the rocks at Navgaon near Alibaug. Many people lost their lives and the survivors settled in the surrounding areas. The corpses that were washed ashore were collected and buried in a mass grave. This tomb still exists at Navgaon.

The faces, colour, appearance and costume of the Bene Israeli is very similar to those of the Arabs. As they have settled in this place for many years, their dress is similar to that of the Hindus, and they have also adopted some of their practices. They do not have any castes, but distinguish between those who have had relations with women from other castes, and those who followed a different religion before entering their fold. This extends to not marrying with them and not eating from the same plate with them. They are known as the Black Israelis.

The Yahudis and Bene Israelis are one and the same. Their rituals, prayers, philosophies, codes of conduct and religious tradition are exactly the same. As they have stayed in this country for many years, their colour, language, and dress has changed. The reason for the two different names is as follows. When they had kings among their people, there was an evil king who troubled his subjects; this led them to split into two groups with one calling themselves Israelis and the other Yahudi. They were all known as Israelis earlier.

These people have two masjids,[3] while the Yahudis have one. Their synagogues do not have idols. Idol worship has been condemned very severely in their scriptures. Their boys are circumcised. There is a religious scripture written in the ancient Yahudi language in the masjid, and it is read on Saturdays when they gather together to pray. This community gathers every Saturday. Saturday is a day of rest for them, and their scriptures enjoin them to do nothing else but pray on this day. Their masjids are known as synagogues.

The native places of the Israeli people in Mumbai are Ashtagar, Bhiwandi, Pen, Habsan, Roha Ashtami, Dande Rajapur and Harnai. Some of their people used to hold military offices in the Angre Durbar. They used to trade in oil earlier, and this led our people to call them Shanivar Teli or Saturday Oilers. They also do masonry and carpentry work. In the Konkan, they subsist on farming where they have their lands and estates and are quite prosperous.

Based on certain evidences, one may conclude that this community came to this island around 1750. They came here and entered the military service of the Company Sarkar. In the first instance, a few men came here. They excelled as soldiers and this led to the building of their reputation. In due course of time, others followed them, some with families, and took up various jobs connected with the military. There are many descendants of those who went to fight alongside the English against Tipu. They exhibited courage, intelligence and valour in their soldiery. Many of them attained ranks like Commandant, Major Subhedar, Subhedar, Naik, and Havildar. As they have not revolted or rioted in the army, the English have come to trust them. They have now taken to trade, or learnt English and taken up employment in offices, and some of them are schoolmasters. Education has spread rapidly among these people. Many of them have taken up employment as Draughtsmen (those who sketch maps) and Surveyors. An Israeli by the name of Banaji Bhavji Ghosalkar is the Head Draughtsman in the Chief Engineer's Office and draws a monthly salary of hundred rupees. They are very good at this job and are well-qualified. Abraham Davidji is the Native Commandant of the Police Corps in Ahmednagar.

Since they have come here, they have stayed in the localities of Mandvi, Chinch Bunder and Dongri. The part of Mandvi where they stay is known as the Israeli Mohalla. Many of them have large houses here and are quite affluent.

The original mosque of these people is in Mandvi. The late Azam Samaji Hasaji Divekar built it in the year 1796. It was built for the following reason. When this gentleman fought against Tipu on behalf of the English, the enemy captured him. He prayed to god and vowed to build a masjid if he was able to return safely to Mumbai. He then built this masjid in due course of time. The following inscription can be seen on the masjid.

'This masjid was first built by Azzam Samaji Hasaji Divekar in 1718. As that masjid was small, it was rebuilt with funds generated by the masjid itself and consecrated on Saturday, Chaitra Shudh 2 *Shaké* 1782.'

There are nineteen Parsi agiaries in Mumbai. Their temples are known as agiarys (abode of fire). They are of two types – Aadaryan and Atash Behram. The Aadaryan is an ordinary abode of fire and contains fire lit from fifty or sixty different types of fire. The Atash Behram is lit from one thousand and one different fires. It is brought from various countries. It costs a lot of money. In Mumbai, the Atash Behram was first established by a Parsi gentleman named Dadiseth in Samvat 1838, that is in A.D. 1781. It is near Navewadi and that road is known as Agiary Road. Hormuzji Wadia built the second agiary near Chandanwadi. It is now thirty-two years since it was established. Framji Cowasji has built the third one on the Girgaon Road near the seashore. This sprawling and beautiful place was built seventeen years ago. The Parsis do not allow people of other castes to enter their agiaries.

In this city, some festival or the other is being celebrated every other week. It may be the Dosle of the Parsis; or Papeti; or perhaps Parab; maybe the Gambaar; the Bakr-Id of the Mussalman; or the Moharram of the Moghuls; perhaps the Pureem of the Yahudis; or Valandan; the Gokulashtami of the Hindus; or Pithori; or Muka Padwa; or Aaje Padwa; maybe some Gujarati festival; or the Gowali Agyaras of the Vanis; Randhan Sat; maybe Shili Satam; the Intruj of the Portuguese; Pajusan of the Marwadis; Haritalika of the Bhatias; maybe the Ganpati; Gauri of the Kolis; Shiralshet of the Shimpis; the Deepotsav; the Kojagiri; Bhagat at Vandre; Havan at Mahalaxmi; Rathsaptami; Til Sankrant; or maybe the English celebrating Christmas. In this manner, our people get the opportunity to waste their time and toss their money away under some pretext or the other.

The major festival of Kapilashasti was celebrated in the year 1858, on Bhadrapad Vadhya 6. The enthusiasm with which this festival was celebrated in Mumbai must have been unmatched in the whole of Bharat Khand. The alignment of stars for the Kapilashasti normally occurs only once every sixty years. This time, it however occurred after twenty-eight years. The alignment occurred at about three in the afternoon. Most of the Hindus in Mumbai fasted till the evening. Hindus of all castes celebrated the festival enthusiastically. The Hindu employees of all the government and trade offices had received a holiday. The Vani, Bhatia and other traders and businessmen shut their businesses for the day and kept themselves free for a day devoted to charity, meditation, prayers, and rituals. Hundreds of beggars and Brahmins had camped on the seashore and at Walkeshwar right from the morning. At about three in the afternoon, people proceeded to take a bath. Many people had come from various places to Mumbai to be able to take a dip in the sea. The seashore was densely packed with people right from the Camp Maidan to Chowpatty. An innumerable number of people gathered at Walkeshwar. The crowds were so great that some three or four people were crushed to death on that day. People thronged the roads and were seen walking towards the sea with cows, baskets of fruit, bags of grain, and purses full of coins. After having taken a dip in the sea, they distributed cows, gold, silver, grains, and land to the Brahmins on the seashore and gave alms and returned home. Their charity continued even after they reached home. They donated food, gold, cows or houses. Within a space of two hours, about two lakh rupees' worth of charity must have been done in the island of Mumbai. One Vani donated a three-storeyed house to a Brahmin filled with goods to last a family of ten for a year or two. It had utensils, grains, jars, cots, clothes, a milch cow and other items. This was the manner in which people fulfilled their religious duties. Even poor orphan Brahmins received ten odd rupees while Brahmins under the care of the rich received five hundred thousand rupees.

Once a child is afflicted with smallpox, a huge amount of time and money is wasted; even the native people will have to regretfully agree that it is an extravagance. They may spend two hundred rupees on a vow but a child afflicted with smallpox is put to sleep in a cradle to the accompaniment of songs.

The Hindus have songs on practically every aspect of life and business and on all subjects relating to the city. These songs are composed by girls and women in any manner that takes their fancy and are quite meaningless.

Kanoba's *Muth*. Mumbai is dotted with *muths* or hermitages. In the whole city, there are between fifty and sixty of them. Sonar, Shimpi, Bhandari and, Shudra people own them. One does not come across any *muth* owned by the Brahmins. The managers of these *muths* earn their living like other ordinary people, and also do this job. Kanoba's *muths* are not built like temples; ordinary houses, huts, or even a room in a chawl where a devotee of Kanoba resides can be termed as a *muth*. This devotee is referred to as *bhagat*. These *muths* have a *makhar*, a seat of honour, the size of which depends on the revenue of the *muths*. An idol of Kanoba is placed on the *makhar* along with amulets filled with prayers of a pir obtained from fakirs or the *Panja*. The Hindu idol of Balakrishna and the *Panja* impression of a Mussalman pir combine together to form the Kanoba god. The origin of this cult is in Paithan and its devotees claim that Sayyad Saadat established it. Women particularly venerate Kanoba. The *bhagat* of Kanoba has numerous disciples who are invested with the afflatus, known as Kanoba's wind. One has to struggle a lot to be infused by this wind and open one's purse strings liberally. Unless money is offered, Kanoba does not enter into any body.

It is not possible to properly determine whether Kanoba is Mussalman or Hindu. These people say that both Ram and Rahim are one and the same; the Hindu and Mussalman religions are fraternal, with the Mussalman religion being the senior one and the Hindu religion being the junior one. In this manner, mainly Mussalman rituals are followed in the *muth*. They burn frankincense in front of the god, shower *sabja* seeds over it, throw *abir* all around, speak in the Mussalman language, and recite the *Kalima*. They use phrases like *'Ya allah Bismillah'*. It is sometimes necessary to invite a fakir to conduct the worship of Kanoba. On occasion, they revile the Hindu religion and criticize it. They request the fakirs to officiate in ceremonies.

The Kanoba festival is celebrated in the month of Shravan on the Janmashtami and Gokulashtami days. Its devotees claim that about eleven hundred years back, Sayyad Saadat, a Mussalman pir who was a big devotee of Lord Vishnu in Paithan, intermixed these two religions. The Mussalman religion is predominant. When the Mussalmans were trying to destroy the Hindu religion, the Hindus may, in fear, have invented this combination to protect themselves. There is a huge difference between the Hindu and Mussalman religions, and it is ordained that Hindus should not even enter a Mussalman masjid; in spite of this, these people consider it very holy to fast on the day of Janmashtami and read prayers from the Kuran of the Mussalmans! One is unable to clearly identify the origins of Kanoba. Some say that Kanoba is Lord Krishna himself, while others claim that he was his playmate and a great devotee.

The Ganpati festival is celebrated in great style for ten consecutive days in this city. Many gentlemen spend about six months to prepare the Ganpati idol themselves. It may be made of clay, but it is hard work and they spend over a hundred rupees on it. In some places, beautiful pictures are produced. There are many places that produce hundreds of idols, and some also prepare beautiful *makhars*. The Ganpati festival is only celebrated by the Dakshini Hindus. The Gujaratis and Ghatis do not seem to have even heard the name of Ganpati. In Mumbai, Ganpàti is much venerated by the Prabhu, Sonar, Brahmin, Bhandari, and Shenvi people. A series of functions, recitations, dances, receptions, and meetings are held on these days. The affluent spend around a thousand rupees on this occasion. Some arrange for the *chowgada* to be played outside their houses for all the ten days; they collect urns, chandeliers, lanterns, mirrors and pictures from various sources to decorate their houses, and also apply a coat of whitewash. On the day the Ganpati is immersed, the roads are packed with people, vehicles and palanquins carrying the image of Ganpati. On the Gauri Pooja day, the Bankotis dance on the roads and their fair covers the entire Camp Maidan. They keep up a constant dance of leaps and jumps accompanied by grunts and loud noises.

About twenty years back, people were forbidden to venture out of their houses on the evening of Ganesh Chathurthi. As darkness took over, criminals would hurl stones at houses and passers-by. The Sarkar has put an end to this and the guilty have been punished with prison sentences of five or six years. People used to yearn to see the moon on Chathurthi and these rogues used to harass them by throwing stones at them. The Vani, Parsi, and Gujarati people referred to this day as the *Dhagla Chouth* (stone throwing Chathurthi). People used to lock themselves into their houses by five in the evening on this day.

Deepawali

The pomp and pageantry in Mumbai during this festival must be unmatched anywhere in the world. The revelries continue for five consecutive days, and people come from various countries to see this spectacle. People decorate their workplaces with pictures, mirrors, lanterns, urns and chandeliers in such a grand manner that the glass-houses of the rich pale in comparison. Lanterns and lights are lit in every street and lane in the Fort, Bazaar and all other parts of Mumbai. The decoration in the *pedhi* or counting houses of the *shroffs* defies description. On the day when the new account books are opened and the *Pedhi Pooja* is held, the Fort and Market overflow with people and vehicles.

On this day, the Gujarati stable-hands don uniform costumes, wear trinkets on their legs, and skirts around their waists, and gather in front of houses and sing and dance with two short sticks in their hands. They have to be given a reward of a rupee or eight *annas*. During major festivals, the servant folk have to be given a present of four to eight *annas* – this is known as *post*. The Gawlis celebrate Bali Pratipada in a big way. On this day, they decorate their buffaloes and cows and take them out in a procession accompanied by a music band. The evil eye is then warded off by ceremonially waving the *Pancharati*, a platter of five lights. Some also arrange for an English band to be played on this occasion.

Moharram

This may be a Mussalman festival but it is observed by about a third of the Hindus in this city. This festival is known as *tabut*. Moharram is the name of this month as in the Muslim calendar. In this month, the Mussalmans prepare a *tabut* or bier in which the Panja is installed and decorated with flowers, *sabja* and *abir,* and worshipped with frankincense. This is known as the *tabut* or *dola*. They spend hundreds of rupees on this *dola*. It is decorated by a variety of papers and gold and silver foil. There are about hundred odd *tabuts* in Mumbai, both large and small. The Kamathis and in some places, even the Hindus prepare *tabuts*. This festival goes on for seven to eight days. Our people have named this festival *Imam Jayanti*. As the people of Mumbai are constantly flush with cash, they are able to celebrate these festivals in style.

In these ten days, many Mussalmans and other mischievous folk disguise themselves in various ways and celebrate noisily in the streets of Mumbai. Many become tigers, while others don the robes of a Sannyasi or Bairagi, and quite a few disguise themselves as bears by donning a bearskin. Five or six people get together and form a cloth elephant and roam the streets. On these days, the *tabut* devotees tie green, red and yellow strings around their wrists and their necks. Many Hindus dress their children up as fakirs, drape a cloth bag around their shoulders and send them from door to door shouting 'Imam Hussain' to collect the *fakiri and chirakhi* due to them. Such alms are then surrendered to the *tabut* in the evening. As *kichidi* has to be ceremonially offered to the *tabut*, people donate a mixture of *tur dal* and rice, and if they are acquainted with the boy, they give a paisa or two as *chirakhi*. If they are closely related to the boy, they may give two to four rupees and about a *sher* or two of *kichidi*. As the *tabut* likes the fragrance of *abir* and frankincense, and prefers the green colour, the Hindu and Mussalman devotees wear green-coloured clothes and apply *abir* to their body. On the day of immersion of the *tabuts*, they are ceremonially taken to the seashore in a procession and dipped in sea-water. The urn is then broken and the *tabut* brought back. Some few years ago, soldiers from the army and English employees accompanied the tabuts.

On the previous night, the *tabuts* are ceremonially taken around the streets. This night is known as the 'Night of Assassination'. About twenty years back, the horses of the Moghuls were paraded on this night; it was an amazing spectacle and people used to fall over each other to catch a glimpse of this awesome display. However skirmishes used to break out amongst the Moghuls and Mussalmans resulting in a few deaths; the Sarkar has now banned the parading of horses. Thousands of people gather on the day of the immersion of the *tabuts*, and the Camp Maidan assumes the appearance of a fair and is thronged by thousands.

Every other year, people gather here to embark on pilgrimages, the *mahayatras* to the holy places of Kashi, Rameshwar and Dwarka. Many affluent men undertake these *mahayatras* and they are accompanied by scores of poor devotees. Hundreds of *warkaris*, men who perform periodical pilgrimages to a sacred place gather here in the months of Aashad and Karthik to undertake the *yatra* to Pandharpur. When they embark on their journey, the roads echo with the sounds of their *bhajans* and music, and all of them, young or old, are bedecked with chains around their neck. In addition, there are pilgrimages undertaken to places in the neighbourhood. Thousands of people go to Wai, Nasik, Gokarn Mahabaleshwar, Alandi and Nirmal every year, and with the coming of the railroad, people have begun to undertake *yatras* more frequently. The Mussalmans go to Mecca for their *yatra;* it is called the 'Haj'.

Every year, many temples in Mumbai hold *jatras*, fairs where toys, sweets and other trinkets are sold. The temple and its surroundings are elaborately decorated. Firework displays also take place at appropriate times. The Mussalmans also have their *jatras*, which are known as *urus*.

Two *jatras* are held at Walkeshwar every year – one on the Shravan Amavasya and the second on Karthik Poornima. The *jatras* last for a couple of days at present. In earlier times, bets worth two or three lakhs of rupees used to be wagered every day. The gambling attracted desperadoes from Thane, Vasai, Panvel, Alibaug and other places and the *jatra* used to go on for five or six days. The Sarkar banned the gambling some eight or ten ago; and as the outsiders stopped coming here, the *jatras* are just a shadow of their earlier splendour. It winds up in a day or two. About twenty-five years ago, many Parsis used to come to this fair; they would pitch their tents at various places on the hill. These Parsi gentlemen were accompanied by mimics, pranksters, frauds and gamblers who indulged in boisterous fun and teased the women who came to the fair. The *mahajan* then complained to the Sarkar about this problem and built a wall around the Walkeshwar establishment and got the Sarkar to ban the entry of Parsis into this area. The *jatra* has lost its prestige since then. There are two *jatras* at Mahalaxmi – the one at Mahalaxmi on the Chaitra Poornima and the other at Dhakjee Dadajee's temple on the Vaishakh Poornima. The Navewadi *jatra* is held on Karthik Amavasya while the Kalikadevi *jatra* is on Margashirsh Amavasya. In addition, *jatras* are held at Prabhadevi, Gaondevi, Shimpi Oli, Jagannath Shankarseth's temple, Mankeshwar, and Bhuleshwar temples. The Mumbadevi *jatra* is held on Dusserah. About a thousand rupees' worth of *apta* leaves (standing in for gold) is sold on this day. People buy these leaves, and present two or three of them to their friends as representative of gold praying for their prosperity and their enemies' defeat. A big fair is held at the seashore near the Camp Maidan on the Narali Poornima. People worship the sea and throw coconuts into it so as to calm its fury. A *jatra* is held on Shivratri at Gharapuri and it attracts quite a crowd. In a year, thirty or forty such *jatras* are held in Mumbai.

People from the Gujarat Province have a widespread practice of dancing the Garba during Navaratri. The women of the Kharvi, Koli, Ghodewale and other communities of the lower classes place a clay pot in a basket with a coconut on top. About twenty of them gather and visit the houses of the Vani and Parsi folk and dance the Garba in the following manner. They place the basket on the floor and light a few lamps. They then dance around these baskets for an hour or so singing songs in the Gujarati language and clapping their hands. This festival continues for ten or even fifteen days.

Even women from affluent Vani homes dance the Garba at various houses in the month of Ashwin for around fifteen days. This is done as follows. A rich Vani gentleman arranges for a Garba programme in his residence and sends invitations to his friends. The ladies gather around eight or nine at night at the appointed house and dance the Garba till eleven at night. They then distribute cups, glasses, plates or pans to the guests, each according to their capacity.

The *urus* of Gaza Ali Sahib at Colaba is held in the month of Bhadrapad. The tomb of Bismillah Sahib is along the edge of the Fort at the end of Bori Bunder; his *urus* is held in the month of Margashirsh. In addition, ten to fifteen other *urus* are held at Matunga and other places. The most prominent *urus* is the one at Mahim. About two hundred large shops are set up and the *urus* goes on for seven or eight days. Earlier, trade worth thousands of rupees used to be conducted here for fifteen to twenty days and it attracted people from distant places. While gambling can be conducted openly, it leads to some real trouble in Mumbai. Many gamblers go totally bankrupt and lose all their belongings and property during the Walkeshwar *jatra* and Mahim *urus*. The Parsis used to participate in this *urus* in a big way and used to camp here for four or five days. However after riots broke out between the Parsis and Mussalmans, the Parsis have stopped going to the *urus*.

A chariot is taken out in procession in the Fort on Kartik Vadhya 5. This establishment is maintained by the Shenvis. Many affluent Shenvis used earlier to stay in the Fort. A *jatra* was held, followed by a *brahmanbhojan*. The Gujaratis celebrate a festival known as the Gowali Agyaraas on the Shravan Vadhya 11. On this day, boys aged five or thereabouts are made up as Gopal and their bodies decorated with gold and gems. About a hundred such boy Gopals gather at the Thakurdwar at the Fort. Their heads are decorated with flowers like women. If a rich man sends his boy to this function, he may be bedecked with ten to fifteen thousand rupees' worth of jewellery. Once these five-year-old boys and girls have paid their respects to the Lord, they are then taken around to the houses of friends to be exhibited. Many Dakshinis also decorate their children in a similar manner on this day. They send them around to the houses of their acquaintances, who have to give them a rupee or two; they are also given something to eat.

When the English first established a factory in Surat to conduct their trade, most of the men who had come from that country were hardly religious and had very little faith in the Christian religion; this did not however prevent them from wishing to spread their religion in this country. In 1616, Mr. Joseph Salbank wrote a letter to the Court of Directors in which he fervently and earnestly requested them to send a few Christian preachers to this country to work for the welfare of the people. He also said that, they should be so saintly in their behaviour that the people amongst whom they reside should be impressed by their behaviour. It is also written that a Moghul servant in the Factory at Surat was admitted to Christianity.

Missionary

Their main aim is to preach the Christian religion among the native people and convert them to Christianity. In 1807, a missionary named Dr.

Taylor decided to come to Mumbai and preach the Christian religion among its people, but he was not given leave to stay in this city by the Sarkar and had to proceed to Surat and accept some employment with the government. In 1811, three missionaries came to Bharat Khand from America. When they first came here, their situation could well be described as dire. They first went to Calcutta, where the Sarkar expelled them. They then proceeded to Kochi, where their situation was no better. When they came to Mumbai, what do you think was their fate? They were not even allowed to enter the harbour. After a lot of trouble, they somehow managed to get on to boats and land on the wharf; they were served with the Governor Evan Napean's orders to leave the island of Mumbai in two days. They were not allowed to stay here because they might speak against the religions of the natives, and besides, the Court of Directors had ordered that no missionaries should be allowed to stay here. Even though they were hard-pressed by many difficulties, the missionaries did not yield in any manner. They put their trust in god and behaved in a very courageous manner. They pleaded with the Sarkar and also wrote to England for permission to conduct their business. They received orders from them not to stay in the territory of the Company Sarkar and that they should proceed for home immediately. This put paid to their hopes but they still did not give up their mission. In the end, they somehow managed to achieve the objective for which they had set out from their native country and obtained permission to stay here. In 1814, they gradually commenced their activities in Mumbai. They first learnt the local language. They published translations of various books in English and started preaching to the people. They then set up a school for young boys and girls and conducted their activities with great fortitude.

If any of our local self-righteous religious men had had to face even a fraction of the obstacles which these missionaries had to face in Bharat Khand, they would have thrown in the towel and retired to Kashi a long time ago. The obstacles which they overcame proved their mettle and made them strong. Since these unique religious men committed themselves fully to all their activities, they were able to achieve their objectives. They have recently spent lakhs of rupees to build schools and their education department compares favourably with that of the Sarkar. The three schools of the missionaries are The Free Church School, The General Assembly School and The Money School. Thousands of children are learning the Marathi, Gujarati, and English languages through these schools and these missionaries themselves teach in the schools in addition to spending thousands of rupees on their upkeep. They also establish schools in various other places to teach boys and girls. The missionaries from America were the first to come here and establish schools. They had also started an English school but now all their schools teach in the Marathi language. There are only four prominent missions and they have established schools in Pune, Surat, Nasik, Baroda, Kolhapur, Satara and other places in the Mumbai Province.

Report on the government and mission schools

One can get an idea of the number of students in the government and mission schools from the following report. The Sarkar spends 2,500,000 rupees on the government schools while it spends only 165,000 rupees on the mission schools. There must be about 30,000,000 children of school-going age in the whole of Hindustan. Of these 100,000 children study in mission schools while 127,513 students study in government schools. The details of the mission schools are as follows: – The Church Missionary Society runs 781 schools with the help of twelve European and 846 native teachers and has an enrolment of 27,000 students. The London Missionary Society has 319 schools, 589 native teachers and about 15,000 students. The Wesleyan Mission has 53 schools, 100 teachers and approximately 3,000 students. The Free Church Mission School has 9,132 students while 2,500 students study in the Baptist Mission schools. If one includes the students who study in other mission schools, the total number of students studying in mission schools will be 100,000. The details of the government schools are as follows: - The Bengal Province has a total of 281 government schools and 14,498 students attend these schools every day. There are 142 schools in the Madras Province and 8,593 students attend them everyday. The Mumbai Province inclusive of Sind has 610 schools, and the number of students who attend these schools daily is around 25,187. There are 156 schools in the Punjab Province including Delhi with about 8,301 students. The Northwest Provinces have 2,944 schools and 68,689 students. The total number of schools is 4,131 and the total number of students comes to 125,268. If one includes the schools at Agra and other places, the total increases to 4,158 schools and 127,513 students.[4]

When the missionaries first started distributing books related to the Christian religion in the Marathi language for free, they used to urge our people to accept them, but many of our people refused to even touch them. If somebody accepted it, they would tear it up in the presence of the missionaries. Children were not allowed to join their schools. Our people are now eagerly purchasing books that were earlier delivered free to their houses at full price from the Tract Society. Parents were urged to send their children to these schools and the children themselves were given gifts, but they were not sent regularly; now the same parents are quite willing to pay the monthly fees and request the missionaries to enrol their children. This is the outcome of their commitment. Now neither do the preachers distribute books for free any more nor do they teach children at no cost. The Tract Society sells books worth hundreds of rupees.[5]

There are two organizations which prepare books for the missions – Tract and Book Society and the Bible Society. The Tract Society sells small books explaining the Christian religion at a very low price while the Bible Society publishes the Christian scriptures in many native languages. In addition, such is their industry that they have translated these books into 200 languages in other continents. Two hundred languages might seem like an exaggeration but the English have determined that there are 3,054 distinct languages in the world and over a 1,000 different religions. Subscriptions worth thousands of rupees are collected to undertake missionary work. After the arrival of these people, the poor and depressed people of Mumbai, indeed, the whole of Bharat Khand, have been exposed to education, and many have been motivated to think about and understand their religions. They have translated their religious books into sixteen native languages and sell them at cheap rates. They have prepared a Bible in Sanskrit. This can be truly regarded as diligence and commitment; what is the point in aimlessly chattering about religion squatting beside the cooking stove?

When the Firangis ruled this place, they forcibly converted thousands of people to their religion and made them Portuguese. Such Hindus who are now known as Christians are scattered all over Mumbai and even all of Hindustan. In a similar manner, when the Mussalmans were in power, they converted thousands of Hindus into Mussalmans. There are many Konkani Mussalmans in Mumbai. They work as sailors and in other jobs. These conversions cause real problems for the people.

While the main objective of the missionaries is to teach the people about their religion and get them into their fold, they do not restrict the religious teaching in their schools only to Christianity. They also teach them other philosophies and scriptures. The positive aspect of their behaviour is that they do not forcibly convert anybody to their religion. They teach them and try to interest them in their religion and if they so desire, convert them to Christianity. In spite of all this, they have managed to convert 112,425 natives into Christians. This was the number in 1852 and must have increased considerably by now.

By 1863, about three hundred people from various castes had been converted into Christianity by the missionaries who are based in the city of Mumbai. In 1839, the famous Rev Dr. Wilson accepted two Parsi students of the Free Church School into the fold of Christianity. They were the first Parsis to accept the Christian religion. This caused a lot of uproar on the day of their conversion, and efforts were made by the Parsis to get them back into their fold for a month or two. The *panchayat* dragged the case all the way to the Supreme Court but could do nothing. Dr. Wilson is a great scholar and conversant in many local languages. He has a lot of influence in government circles and is renowned amongst the natives.

Around 1852, many youths educated in English and others felt that the presence of the caste system was a disservice to the Hindu people and that it should be destroyed and all Hindus should belong to only one caste. They established a secret society by the name of Paramahansa Sabha and many youths were amongst its members. One of their rules was that when members from different castes met in a private place, they were to dine without following any caste restrictions. The society had between fifty and seventy-five members from different castes, and they had established branches of their society in other places by sending letters secretly. It is said that they had branches in Calcutta, Madras, and Kashi. Their efforts were mainly directed towards eliminating the strict restrictions on inter-dining placed on the various Hindu castes. This was their secret goal but they would not divulge their opinions openly. Their strategy was to enrol sufficient numbers and subsequently emerge in the open to achieve their goals. Their meetings were held on specific days, and they had a long list of rules and regulations. However, when the parents of some members came to know of the society, they forbade them from participating in its activities. This caused considerable disruption in many houses, and people kept a close watch on their children. There was a lot of idle talk in the newspapers. Even though they did not know who the members of the society were, and who its leaders were, they began to criticize anyone associated with the society. The society was then dissolved and all its efforts came to nought. However it was not completely exterminated and there are members who still continue their activities.[6]

Many self-righteous Christians were happy to hear about the objectives of this society, and felt that once the caste restrictions of the Hindus were broken down, they would be able to freely dine with the English, which would accelerate the spread of Christianity. However, other events overtook them and the members of the society reverted back to observing the caste restrictions. Many strictly enforced the inter-dining rules and returned to their religion with greater vengeance and took to meditating with their hands in the *gaumukh*. This has been the outcome of all the reform efforts undertaken by our people. It can only be said that our people are eager to jump into a new venture without carrying it through.

In 1856, a Konkani Brahmin named Vishnu Bhikaji Gokhale came to this city. He wore saffron robes and sported a loincloth around his privates; he carried a *tumba* in his hands and wore sabots. He used to call himself a Brahmachari but did not actually follow the rules and restrictions of Brahmacharya. He did not believe in any inter-dining restrictions. He always chewed *paan-supari*, and whenever he felt like it, he would wear white clothes and shoes on his feet. He was quick-witted, a good orator and could debate very well in the Marathi language. If he could not find a proper reply to a question, he would parry it successfully without digging his heels in. He was well versed in Vedanta and other subjects but was not comfortable in Sanskrit. People were attracted by his felicity of speech. Though he was a Vedanta scholar, he kept changing his opinions depending on the situation. On occasion he would criticize idol worship, while on other occasions, he would advocate its necessity. His primary objective was to revile the Christian religion. This led to a debate in the papers for over a year. Once there was a debate between him and some *shastris* of Mumbai in a meeting held at the Thakurdwar on the subject of remarriage; this led to some differences between them. His opinion was that widows from the Brahmin and other castes should be able to remarry, while the *shastris* were opposed to it. He was not a scholar, but he was intelligent and not afraid to speak his mind. He would say that a kind goddess had laid her beneficent hand on him and instructed him in the various fields of knowledge!

When he first came here, a few meetings were held at the residence of the late Dhakjee Dadajee. He would speak in support of the Hindu religion in those meetings. People from all castes were free to attend these meetings. Missionaries, Christians and people from all castes would question him in those meetings and he would respond to them all in some manner or the other. After a while, these meetings were held at any of five or six different venues and attracted around five hundred people. On particular occasions, over a thousand people attended these meetings. These meeting would go on till eleven at night. They were then held for a season opposite the Thakurdwar on the seashore when crowds of over two thousand people attended the meetings. These meetings mainly featured debates between him and the preachers. In every meeting, there were a couple of preachers and four or five native Christians. These meetings were popular for between eight and ten months.

He had written a small book called *Bhavarthasindhu* in the *ovi* metre. Towards the end of 1858, he wrote and published a book titled *Vedoktadharmaprakash*. It had 790 pages in octavo and was priced at two rupees. When people realized that there was nothing great about this book, they lost interest in him. He then went to Calcutta, Kashi, and Madras. His debates with the preachers on the seashore have been collected and published in English by the Rev. George Bowen. It contains the questions and answers of both the parties. People supporting the preachers published another small book in Marathi. It was entitled '*Bawacha Kawa*' or the 'Wiles of the Bawa'.

Chapter 15

General topics – Inconsiderate views about the English people –
The misrule of our Kings, their prodigality and cowardice – Doll weddings –
Tendency to marry small children – Monkey weddings – Watchfulness of the
English Sarkar – Drawbacks of the caste system – Unhappiness –
True compassion

Many inconsiderate people are of the opinion that the English obtained their territories in Hindustan through unfair means. These thoughts are however quite meaningless when examined in the light of logic. In 1530, the Portuguese obtained the island of Mumbai from the Moghul Badshah.[*][1]

The immense wealth earned by the Portuguese, French and the Dutch through their trade with Hindustan induced the English to come here. In 1599, many affluent and rich traders in the city of London formed a company to conduct trade with Hindustan. After they came here, they took every opportunity they got to amass wealth and expand their trade. They then obtained Mumbai serendipitously and they also bought some territory from our Sheikh Chilli kings, who were stupid enough to cut the very branch of the tree on which they were seated.

The haphazard governance of our kings, the malicious interactions between the king, his ministers and practically every other official, and the endless internecine rivalry and fighting between them led the English to further their interests in this manner. Our durbars may seem united on the surface, but they all behave in a very selfish manner, and if the opportunity presents itself, the prime minister himself plots the downfall of the king. Amid such confusion in the kingdoms, the English seized every opportunity to further their interests and increase their influence, and in due course,

---

[*] Many authors have written that the Moghul Badshah presented the island to the Portuguese on account of their having undertaken some delicate task for him.

obtained political power. When the English first came here from their country, their only objective was to make profits from trading, and they could have hardly imagined that they would be able to obtain a kingdom. However, the stupidity and mutual distrust of our people led to the destruction of these kingdoms, and they found themselves in a situation where they could profit from this anarchy.

'Man is the servant of wealth'

All of us very well know that the English did not come to India to assume *Brahmacharya,* or to be ordained as *Sanyasis;* or to perform austere devotions in front of the *Panchagni*; or perform *Gayavarjan* at Kashi for the souls of their ancestors; or in search of divine bliss. They believe that their religion, their teachings, their principles and their means of attaining divine bliss are a thousand times superior to ours. They undertook every task with commitment and saw it through with their strength and intelligence. Their main objective of coming to this country was to amass wealth and attain fame. They did this by mediating in the ceaseless strife carried on by our ignorant people. If one reads the history of Hindustan, one realizes how meekly and humbly they behaved in front of our kings in the early days. As the days went by, they profited from their shrewdness, and there is no point in blaming them at this point. If our people had been alert and careful, they would never have applied to strangers to mediate in their internal quarrels, and would not have sold parts of their territory to foreigners to finance battles with their fellow-countrymen. Where a nail would have sufficed, an axe was wielded; what is the point in talking about its effects thereafter? The English were clever and capable, and have therefore obtained political power in a foreign country and continue to prosper. This is an example of 'The fool grinds while the smart one eats', and 'Two fight while a third benefits'. There is no point in blaming somebody else for our problems. We are reaping the fruits of our own actions.

The rule of our Marathi kings was anarchical, and this led to their destruction. When the Peshwas were on the ascendancy, there were extravagances everywhere! A tremendous waste of time and money! It is said that the Peshwa built seven government residences in seven different boroughs of Pune, and every day similar arrangements for dining were made in each of these houses. A grand dinner with many exquisite dishes was prepared every evening in these houses. The Peshwa would then proceed to the house that took his fancy and have his dinner there, while the servants and officials consumed the food in the other houses.

An old gentleman recalls the following incident that occurred in Gomantak that illustrates the cowardice of the Hindu people. When the

Firangis first came from Portugal in their battleships (this may have been in 1510 when Albuquerque conquered Goa), they dropped anchor outside the harbour and reviewed the state of affairs in Gomantak. Their troops were on their ships and were clearly visible to all the people from the fort at Goa. They would eat biscuits and drink liquor. The biscuits were hard and white in colour, while their alcohol was reddish in colour. Their diet led the simple folk to spread the story that these people, in strange ships and in outlandish costumes, ate bones and drank blood. They could well be demons from another world. This totally terrified them and led them to believe that they would not be able to stand up to them, and they ran away into the woods and wilds. What do you think happened next? When the king heard this story, he also abandoned the city with his army! On the following day, when the Portuguese observed the desolation in the city, they landed ashore and captured the fort. They also assumed control of the royal palace and other military apparatus, and started ruling the country. Our people were real cowards.

On the Karthik Shudh Dwadashi of 1861, a Palshe Joshi gentleman conducted a Tulsi wedding with superb ceremony. He had no children but he was much interested in conducting a wedding, with all the attendant activities, to gain the merit of *kanyadaan*, and entertain a lot of guests. He conducted this ceremony to satisfy his desire. In this grand wedding, the priest acted as the father of the groom, that is, an idol of Balakrishna while the gentleman imagined himself as the father of the bride (the Tulsi shrub). Just like in an actual wedding, invitations were sent out, the bridegroom's party was assembled and the bridegroom was brought in a ceremonial procession to the accompaniment of musical instruments. The wedding was conducted as per tradition, dakshina given to the Brahmins, and guests were presented with coconuts, *paan-supari*, and flowers. Married women were treated with the usual honours. The bride was also brought in according to the *shastriya* traditions.

Some years back, a gentleman held a ceremony to commemorate the Satti or the sixth day of the wedding of his cats. He invited Brahmins to conduct a Shasti *pooja* and gave them *dakshina*, and invited many people for a dinner of sweet viands. A Shenvi gentleman conducted a *munj* for a peepul tree. Our people spend their lives and their wealth on such activities instead of devoting themselves to the welfare of their children, friends and relations, and ultimately they amount to nothing.

There is a village called Nadia near Calcutta which had many pundits. In 1790, about seventy-three years back, a Raja named Ishwarchandra conducted a grand wedding between two monkeys according to the Hindu tradition by spending over a lakh of rupees. The wedding procession consisted of elephants, horses, palanquins, camels, a train of decorated horses, a thousand torches, and the groom (the monkey) was seated on a gem studded palanquin. A scholarly Brahmin also conducted the wedding. How stupid can it get! How surprising is this story!

Some years back, Ganpatrao Gaikwad Maharaj conducted a wedding of dolls at an expense of twenty-five thousand rupees. The ceremony was conducted in the traditional manner and lasted for fifteen days.

In 1860, a son was born to the Maharaja of Indore and one heard reports of the celebrations held at his Durbar. Soon after, one read in the *Vartamandeepika* that about five lakhs of rupees were spent in the Durbar on the occasion of the *Balantvida* of the royal prince's mother. In the same year, the Maharaja of Baroda spent some ten lakhs of rupees on two diamond bracelets to wear on the occasion of the Dasara celebrations, in addition spending thousands of rupees on the festival. When the Mussalmans kept their *roza,* the Maharaja distributed over sixty *khandies* of sugar to fakirs!

One comes across many people who will spend lots of money to display their high status. There are many who will wear bracelets weighing two to four *shers* and their wives will have a nose-ring worth a thousand rupees while they pay a monthly interest of twenty-five rupees to the Marwadi. Some years back, the daughter of an affluent Prabhu gentleman conducted a wedding of dolls and spent some five hundred odd rupees. Many people were invited and a procession with horses was led around the streets. Our people spend wealth in such a thoughtless manner. Hardly anybody is willing to spend their money for a good cause or for the welfare of the country. Everybody is in the race for money – from clerks earning a salary of ten rupees a month to businessmen earning two thousand rupees a month. Hardly anybody is willing to recognize their true station in life.

Our people strongly believe that unless they conduct the marriages of their children, they continue to remain in debt. This has led the Hindus to be in the same position as a man who steps on a rope in the darkness, and believing it to be a snake shivers with fright. Once a boy or a girl is born, the parents start worrying about the child's marriage; even if the boy lounges around in a *chandolkhana,* or mopes around in a betting room, or assumes the role of Veerbhadra on the stage, or just hangs around chatting at Dhobi Talao, they would be happy as long as they arrange to get him married. Most of the marriages conducted among our people are similar to just chanting the mantra – 'Eat grass, drink water, and be happy'. Many people conduct marriages of poor people as acts of charity and also believe that they will gain religious merit by conducting weddings between trees and animals.

Some get married at such a young age, that the parents have to perform the rituals which are supposed to be done by the married couple.

It seems to be the family tradition of the citizens of Mumbai to conduct the marriages of their young children and spend money without limit on this occasion. Even if the Mehta or accountant of a Parsi conducts his son's wedding, he spends between ten and twenty thousand rupees on just the nuptials. A few years back, an affluent Vani gentleman named Murlidhar Shambhu erected a grand marquee on the occasion of his son's wedding; it is said that the marquee itself cost forty thousand rupees. He bought a large three-storey *haveli*, demolished it, and built this marquee on that plot. At least a couple of marquees are constructed on this scale every year.

In 1861, a Memon's son got married; the wedding procession was praised to the skies. It consisted of five hundred large vehicles and a couple of hundred grandly decorated horses; about seven to eight *khandies* of coconut oil were consumed just to light the *hilals*. About five hundred rupees' worth of candles were lit on this occasion. These candles were placed in lanterns to provide light for the affluent men who were part of this procession. The procession consisted between two and four thousand people. This was just the cost of the marriage procession for one night; just imagine the money spent on the entire wedding!

Not only do the people of Mumbai not value money, they sometimes throw it away on unreasonable expenses. If somebody spends two thousand rupees on a wedding procession, someone else would spend three thousand rupees. A third would spend four thousand rupees on a *kelvan* ceremony while a fourth would spend five thousand rupees on a procession for the *seemanth pooja*. There are very few in this city who actually spare a thought on how, when, where and why to spend money and who should spend it. They seem to believe that spending money would make them rich. How hollow their beliefs are!

They may well spend thousands of rupees on a shraddha or a couple of lakhs on a wedding ceremony, but they cannot be bothered to pay any attention to the fact that the nation is getting impoverished and is sinking deeper into the depths of ignorance, or take any steps to improve the lot of the people. Even if they have the money, many are not willing to spend it on the education of their own children. They are however willing to display their boundless generosity on such occasions.

Just observe the skill of the English in business! If a place of worship, or road, or a structure to enhance the beauty of the city or for public welfare has to be built, they collect a contribution from everybody, so that it can be completed without being burdensome either to themselves or to others.

They have used this method from the very beginning to increase the grandeur of Mumbai. If our kings undertake any such venture, they will spend two lakhs where one lakh would have sufficed, or exact a heavy toll from a businessman and make him bankrupt in the process. Contrast this with the shrewdness of the English on such occasions! They do not think it below their dignity to receive contributions ranging from half an anna to fifty thousand rupees. They respectfully accept whatever has been contributed voluntarily without taking on unnecessary burdens, and both the giver and taker hold each other in esteem. This has enabled them to fulfil all their plans.

The Fort in Mumbai, its moat, the docks, bridges, tanks, wells, schools and roads have mostly been built through contributions.

The English Sarkar carefully considers the amount of money that needs to be spent on a particular venture. On the occasion of the wedding of the daughter of the Empress who reigns over us, all the innumerable expenses to be incurred were approved by Parliament about a year in advance; and all expenses were incurred as per this plan. Just look! The Queen has many children, but has one ever heard of even one incident where wasteful expenditure was undertaken? The Governor of Mumbai occasionally invites the members of the Durbar for a dinner reception, but there has never been any wastage of food or any excessive expenditure.

Most of the Hindus in this city seem to be under the sway of their caste, and believe it to be supreme over all other castes. The Hindu patriarch imagines himself from a high-born family with illustrious ancestors, and feels it beneath his dignity to associate with others. This idiocy infects everyone from the Brahmins to the Shudras, but the factual situation is obviously very different. No single caste is dominant in Mumbai and all this puffing up is just vain pride. It just generates hatred, jealousy, ill-will and a perpetual state of strife, and people are circling each other snarling like fighting tigers. There is nothing to be gained from this.

This caste system has prevented the Hindus from bonding together. Not a single day passes by without some quarrels on account of caste. Somebody might accuse his fellow-caste member of having eaten some trifle in a house owned by a person of a different caste and demand that he be ejected from the caste; another might say that he drank some milk at somebody's house and should therefore be ostracized. A third might say that he wears his *pagota* in the Shindeshahi style and should be ostracized. These puerile matters raise a huge storm. Many consider it prestigious to identify such faults and cause disruption by highlighting domestic foibles. A united front gets divided in three and this has led to the formation of so many castes. It is crazy to fight over the supposed high status of one's caste and the impugned low status of others. Once we are born, it is not possible to change one's parents or abandon one's caste; it is therefore futile to fight over such matters. In 1861, an inquiring gentleman prepared and published a book called the *Jatibhed Viveksaar* for the welfare of the public. With the help of many examples, he has clearly shown that it is utterly stupid to fight on the basis of the false pride of one's caste. The only thing that needs to be said here is that man should prove his mettle by his actions. The family that stresses positive qualities devotes itself to god, and has many philanthropic members who will be able to ascend to the heights of greatness. It is useless and vain to believe in the prestige of caste. Men should behave in a manner that is thought prestigious by other people.

The book *Jatibhed Viveksaar* contains numerous evidences from the *Vedanta* and other books regarding the futility of caste. People should certainly read this book.[2]

Our people moan that it is not possible to earn money under the rule of the English, and whatever little is earned gets spent very easily. It is not possible to accumulate any wealth or leave money for the next two or three generations because the English money is not lucky. They dream up such idiotic notions. Some people place a *mohur* or paisa from the time of Akbar Badshah in their small shrines and worship it every day in the hope of prosperity. Yet they do not take the trouble to realize that they are spending much more than they earn; if they waste their precious time which is the key to wealth and happiness, how are they going to be prosperous? 'If your expenses are more than your income, you will always be at a loss', so goes a local saying. How can money then be saved? This is not the fault of English rule but the fruits of our own behaviour. If we examine the facts carefully, we will realize that if we proceed shrewdly and carefully, the income under the English is more than that under the previous kings; it is the greatness of Kaliyug that those who are willing to work hard and spend money carefully will ultimately become prosperous. Those citizens of Mumbai who are watchful in their actions and astute in their trade become affluent and happy.

A lot of charitable work is done in Mumbai and the poor and the orphaned do get food and clothing, but there is a lack of true compassion. One may come across people who altruistically work for the welfare of others in a loving and generous manner amongst other communities, but hardly ever, if at all, among the Hindus. It is not as if this is limited to Mumbai, but seems to be the case with our people everywhere. Shrimant Jagannath Shankarseth has established an English school for the Hindus while Seth Goculdas Tejpal has established English and Gujarati schools for the Gujaratis. Sir Jamsetjee Jejeebhoy has started English and Gujarati schools for the Parsi community. Nakhuda has established an English school for the Mussalmans. In a similar manner, Kasim Natha has started a school for the Khoja children while the Portuguese have established a school for their children. The Prabhu community has started a school for themselves. These are certainly generous deeds, but one has never come across a single school that has been started by all the communities of this city together for the welfare of mankind and to inculcate positive qualities in children. All that has been achieved by our people has been done under the auspices of the English Sarkar and other English folk, and with the intention of winning laurels from them. What this boils down to is that there are very few who do charitable work because they have been moved by the condition of the poor.

In 1863, a prosperous Parsi gentleman set aside three lakh rupees for the purpose of building a home for the sick, where the poor people of his community can stay until they recover from their illness. He has bought a plot of land near Colaba for this purpose and proposes to build a large structure with every facility for recuperation.

Similarly, another Parsi gentleman has set aside four or five lakhs of rupees for charitable purposes within his community. The money is to be used in the following manner. If any Parsi falls into bad times and becomes impoverished, he is given a certain sum of money from the interest earned from this sum to help him overcome his poverty and begin a new life.

In Karthik 1862, the Shinde Maharaj served *bhojan* to one lakh Southern Brahmins on a single day and gave a *dakshina* of one rupee to each Brahmin. To make up this number, it was proposed to serve a similar meal at places where these Brahmins resided. Of these, ten thousand Brahmins at Pune were served a meal with *boondi laddoos*. On this occasion, many Brahmins from Mumbai had gone to Pune. Arrangements were made to convey the information regarding the number of people who dined at each place through the telegraph machine. It is said that this function cost three lakhs of rupees.

It is certainly praiseworthy to spend money on philanthropic activities. However the above instance is an example of single-focused charity, and very different from anything done with true compassion and patriotism. Charitable work must be done with the welfare of mankind as its objective. Its recipient may well be a *dashgranthi* Brahmin or the stupidest of stupid untouchables. The act should benefit everybody equally.

Sir Jamsetjee Jejeebhoy has built a hospital and Seth Cowasji Jehangirji Readymoney has given one lakh rupees for building the Elphinstone

College. These are examples of true compassion and patriotism. Only when our people are similarly motivated in all their actions will there be unity amongst them and will they be happy and regain power.

In an English paper published in England, one came across the following account regarding education in that country. In 1861, the patriotic people of England donated ninety lakh rupees to various educational institutions in that country. In addition, money was collected through annual subscriptions. There are such generous people in that country. When they donate this money, they intend it to benefit not only a certain class of people but humanity in general.

Notes to the Text

Preface

1. J. T. Molesworth, who had prepared a Marathi-English dictionary which was first published in 1831, was again invited to India by the Bombay Government in 1851 to prepare an updated version of his dictionary. This classic Marathi-English dictionary, which is still in print, came out in 1857. The situation regarding other Indian languages was not very different. See Molesworth, *A Dictionary, Marathi and English.*

2. Martin Haug (1827–76) came to India in 1859 and was made the Superintendent of Sanskrit Studies at Deccan College in Pune. Apart from his Sanskrit studies, he also made pioneering contributions to the study of Parsi culture. He resigned from his post in 1868 to take up the Sanskrit Chair at the University of Munich. He was replaced by another German, Dr. J. G. Buhler (1837–98) who had arrived in Mumbai in 1863 for a job in the Education Department of the Presidency with a recommendation from Professor Max Mueller. As there was no suitable vacancy, the Elphinstone College created a Professorship in Oriental Languages and named him to that post. Leifer, *Bombay and the Germans*, p.204.

3. For most of the nineteenth century, there was raging debate about the suitability of Marathi as a language of higher learning. Both Indians and Europeans expressed opposing views and the issue was never completely settled though Marathi generally came to be used as the language of school education with English being the exclusive language for higher instruction.

4. The glossary mainly consisted of English and Sanskrit words used in the Marathi text and has not been appended to this English work. It also included a few words from other European languages – mainly Portuguese, and a few French and Greek words. Persian and Arabic words are also listed. Words from Indian languages like Gujarati,

Hindi/Urdu (which is referred to as Hindustani) and even Marathi are also explained. Interestingly there is a category which is styled as Mumbai slang but it contains only one word. A glossary of non-English words retained in the text has been provided.

Chapter 1

1. The Europeans were generally referred to as *topiwalas* or 'hat-wearers' as most of them sported hats in contrast to the Indians who wore turbans or *pagdis*.
2. Oliver Cromwell (1599–1658), in fact, was the Lord Protector of England, Scotland and Ireland from December 1653. The Court itself had been abolished after the execution of King Charles I in 1649 and a republic declared.
3. '... in 1653, the President and Council of Surat again brought the subject under the consideration of the Directors, pointing out how convenient it would be to have some insular and fortified station, which might be defended in times of lawless violence, and giving it as their opinion that for a consideration the Portuguese would allow them to take possession of Bombay and Bassein. The following year the Directors drew the attention of Cromwell, the Protector, to this suggestion.' Anderson, *The English in Western India*, p. 110. Anderson himself refers to Bruce, *Annals of the Honorable East-India Company*.
4. This actually happened in the year 1668 when, by the Royal Charter of 27 March 1668 the port and island of Bombay were transferred to the East India Company. Malabari, *Bombay in the Making*, p. 106.
5. The government of the East India Company was commonly referred to as the Company Sarkar by the Indians and this terminology has been retained throughout the book.
6. 'The whole area of the island is about sixteen square miles. Its shape approaches a trapezoid, with its shorter side, six miles in length, towards the sea, and its longer side extending eleven miles parallel to the main-land. Between the two hilly ridges, which form these sides, there is a level plain, about two miles in width, now called the Flats. The greatest breadth of the island is little more than three miles.' Anderson, *The English in Western India*, p. 109.

Chapter 2

1. Sashtee, or Salsette as it was spelled by the Portuguese and then the English, was the large island directly north of Mumbai with Thane as its capital. It was the major bone of contention between the Portuguese and the English when Mumbai was handed over by the former and remained so until the Portuguese lost it to the Marathas in 1739. The English conquered it from the Marathas in 1774 and it became the first major territory to be acquired by military means by the English in Western India. It was always treated as an appendage of Mumbai by the English and continues to be so. The island, whose name has been obliterated from public memory is now split between suburban Mumbai and the neighbouring city of Thane.

2. This *bakhar*, or Marathi chronicle, which Govind Narayan refers to seems to be a manuscript containing both the *Mahikavatichi Bakhar* and the *Sashteechi Bakhar*. The former was published by the eminent Marathi historian, V.K. Rajwade in 1924 (Reprinted. Pune: Varda Books, 1991). The latter was first serially published in the Marathi magazine *Kavya-itihas-sangrah* in 1882 and later published in book form by G. G. Naik (ed), *Sashteechi Bakhar*. Mumbai: Worli Gopchar va Bhoye Sansthan, 1935.

3. This narrative was published by R. X. Murphy in the first volume (1836–38) of the *Transactions of the Bombay Geographical Society* and titled 'Remarks on the History of Some of the Oldest Races now Settled in Bombay; with Reasons for Supposing that the Present Island of Bombay Consisted, in the fourteenth century, of Two or more Distinct Islands'. It was reprinted again in 1844 when it was accompanied by a map showing Mumbai as consisting of seven distinct islands; this map was the prototype for many subsequent reproductions to support the Heptanesia theory for Mumbai. Also see biographical note on Murphy.

4. Govind Narayan is referring to the article which George Buist wrote on the geology of Mumbai. George Buist, 'Geology of Bombay', *Transactions of the Bombay Geographical Society*, Vol. 10 (1850–52), pp. 167–238. Also see biographical note on Buist.

5. John Fryer, a medical doctor in the employ of the East India Company wrote a famous account of his stay in Mumbai and Surat during the 1670s; it was first published it in 1698. As it was not published again till 1909, it is unlikely that Govind Narayan would have had access to this book; he may have seen its reference in Anderson, *The English in Western India*. He quotes Fryer again in later chapters. The second edition is

John Fryer, *A New Account of East India and Persia*, William Crooke (ed), 3 vols. London: Hakluyt Society, 1909–1915.

6. In fact, as Govind Narayan himself narrates later in Chapter 5, the Siddis, who were based in the nearby island of Janjira and were in the service of the Mughal emperor, Aurangzeb, attacked the island of Mumbai in February 1689. They occupied a greater part of the island for over 16 months, and finally withdrew in June 1690, after the English signed a humiliating treaty with the Mughals. Only after the Siddis withdrew, did an epidemic of plague strike Mumbai which decimated what was left of the English garrison.

7. Rustom Dorab (1667–1763) actively helped the English defend the island of Mumbai during the invasion of the Siddis in the 1690s. He was appointed the Patel of Mumbai and the title was granted to his family in perpetuity. By all accounts, a vigorous and virile man, he is credited with two sons, Cowasjee and Dorabjee, born in 1744 and 1754 respectively.

8. Cowasjee Rustomjee Patel (1744–99), became the Patel of Bombay in 1763 on the death of his father, Rustom Dorab. When the English conquered the neighbouring island of Sashtee (and its captial Thane) in 1774, he was appointed the Patel of many villages in that island. He was actually presented a Dress of Honour in 1775 by the Governor, William Hornby for his services. He held the lucrative contract for supplying shipping vessels to the East India Company. He encouraged the Parsis to migrate to Thane where in 1780, he built for them a Tower of Silence and an Agiary, both of which are still in existence. In 1776, he constructed a tank at Khetwadi, the area still popularly known as C. P. Tank. A road in the Fort area is named after him as Cowasjee Patel Street, the name still officially in use. He was also an early member of the Parsi Panchayat.

Chapter 3

1. The transfer of power from Surat to Mumbai actually happened only in May 1687. Later that year, Mumbai was elevated to the dignity of a Regency in order to enable the government of the East India Company to assume the rank of an Indian power. Malabari, *Bombay in the Making*, p. 205.

2. 'Indeed the Factors at Bengal seemed to doubt whether he *could* die. On the 13th of December, 1680, having heard of his death from the Governor and Council of Bombay, they wrote thus: "Sevagee has died so often, that some begin to think him immortal. T'is certain little belief

can be given to any report of his death, until experience tell the waining of his hitherto prosperous affairs, since when he dies indeed, it is thought he has none to leave behind him that is capacitated to carry on things at the rate and fortune he has all along done."' Anderson, *The English in Western India*, p. 372n.

3. Mrs. Rose Nesbit, was the widow of Commodore Nesbit, Harbour Master of Bombay, under the East India Company. She owned property in Mazagaon and built a private chapel there in 1787. On her death in 1819, the chapel and her property were transferred to the Roman Catholic church. The St. Mary's Institute currently functions from these premises.

4. 'For many years it [Colaba] was only used "to keep the Company's antelopes, and other beasts of delight."' Anderson, *The English in Western India*. p. 144.

5. The Governor's residence, now called the Raj Bhavan, became the official residence of the Governor of Bombay only in 1883 when Sir James Fergusson's wife died of cholera in the Government House at Parel. Set in 50 acres of lush forest land, it is now the official residence of the Governor of the state of Maharashtra.

6. Rev. Richard Cobbe, Chaplain of Bombay from 1715–20 published an account of the building of the church (now the Cathedral) at Bombay in 1766; most probably, this book was not available to Govind Narayan and he relied on Anderson for the reference. Richard Cobbe. *Bombay Church: or, a True account of the building and finishing the English Church at Bombay.* London: John Rivington, 1766.

7. Mahabaleshwar, at an altitude of 4,500 feet above sea level in the Sahyadri ranges was acquired by the Governor of Bombay, Sir John Malcolm in 1829 from the Raja of Satara to be developed as a sanatorium for the English. The new town was originally named Malcolmpet but has now reverted back to its old name. Its invigorating climate and spectacular views made it one of the favoured hill-stations of the English.

Chapter 4

1. The Ghodapdeo Hill was demolished by the Bombay Port Trust in stages during a fifteen year period from 1893–1908. As was usually the case with the small hills which earlier stood on the island of Mumbai, the adjacent low-lying areas, in this case, Mazagaon, were filled up with the rubble. S. T. Sheppard. *Bombay*, p. 57n.

2. The Sewri Fort is still standing, though it is in a completely ruined and unkempt state, and constantly threatened by encroachment from the surrounding slums. The salt pans themselves have moved northwards gradually, first to Sion and Matunga on the island of Mumbai, and then, early in the twentieth century, further north to the island of Sashtee, in places like Mulund and Bhandup, where they are still worked.

3. The government gardens at Sewri were under the management of the Agri-Horticultural Society of Western India. When this land was required for a newly planned European cemetery, the gardens were shifted to their present site in Byculla in the 1860s. Earlier known as the Victoria Gardens, it is now the Jijamata Bhosale Udyan. The cemetery still occupies the site at Sewri.

4. The Government House at Parel was earlier a Jesuit monastery which the English confiscated late in the seventeenth century on account of the Jesuits' allegedly treasonous behaviour. The first Governor to use it as an official residence was William Hornby (1771–84). It remained so for over a century when it was given up in favour of the Raj Bhavan by Sir James Fergusson. It was used as a plague hospital during the great epidemic of 1897–98. Vaccines for plague and cholera were developed here by Dr. Waldemar Haffkine and since 1925, it has been known as the Haffkine Institute.

5. The Kabul Church is the Church of St. John the Evangelist which, though commenced in 1847 with designs by Henry Conybeare of the Bombay Engineers, was finally consecrated only in 1858. It is now commonly known as the Afghan Church.

6. Bori Bunder is the site of the present Chhatrapati Shivaji Terminus (earlier the Victoria Terminus) which was built in the 1870s. The monumental edifice of the terminus of the Great Indian Peninsular Railway (now the Central Railway) is now some distance away from the coastline because of series of reclamations over the years.

7. The hill was named after Naoroji Rustom Manek Seth (1663–1732), son of Rustom Manek, the famous Surat broker to the East India Company. He was the first Parsi to visit England in 1723 to fight a dispute with the Court of Directors of the East India Company. He was also a member of the first Parsi Panchayat in Bombay. The Naoroji Hill no longer exists, because the Bombay Improvement Trust commenced demolishing it in 1910 to provide plots for houses and provide access to the docks from the railways. The only traces of the hill are cross-roads which bear the name of Naoroji Hill Road, just outside the Sandhurst Road railway station.

8. The *bombil* or Bombay Duck (*Harpadon nehereus*) is a lizard fish which is native to the waters of the northern part of the Arabian Sea around Mumbai. It is consumed either fresh or dried, when it gives off a rather powerful smell. The fish is also common in the South China sea.

9. The road at Mahim is still named Lady Jamsetjee Road in honour of Lady Avabai Jamsetjee Jejeebhoy (1792–1870). She was the first Indian woman to bear the title of Lady. Darukhanawala, *Parsi Lustre on Indian Soil*, p. 82.

10. The Sion fort is still standing, albeit in an extremely dilapidated condition, on a small hillock adjoining the Sion railway station.

11. The Rewa fort, also known as the Kala Killa (or the 'Black Fort') is now overrun on all sides by the slum settlement of Dharavi and much encroached upon.

12. The construction of the bridge commenced in 1797 but it was only completed in 1805. It was constructed in stone and had a drawbridge in the centre. It was popularly known as the Duncan Causeway.

13. See James Hervey. *Meditations among the Tombs. In A letter to A Lady*. London: 1746.

Chapter 5

1. The Angrias, based in Vijaydurg, were associated with the Maratha kingdom and in 1698, Kanhoji Angria was designated the Admiral of the Maratha Navy. Their fast-sailing boats and large fleet could not be contained by the English, who conveniently branded them pirates. Until they were finally overwhelmed in 1756, they were a constant threat to Mumbai. The Habshees were the Siddis of Janjira, originally immigrants from Africa. When the Mughal power started waning in India, the Siddis made peace with the English and continued as a subsidiary state until they were absorbed by the Republic of India in 1947.

2. Dr. John St. John was appointed as the Judge-Advocate of Mumbai under Royal Charter. In fact, he did not arrive in Mumbai on 9 August 1683, as can be inferred from the despatch which the Court of Directors of the East India Company sent to their President at Surat on 7 April 1684. 'We have chosen', they wrote, 'Dr. St. John, Doctor of the Civil Law, to be Judge of the Admiralty Court in the East Indies and of all our maritime affairs there, to be erected in pursuance of His Majesty's additional charter of the 9th August last (1683) at the salary of £200 a year, and to have the accommodation of his own diet at the Governor's table at Bombay, but all other accommodations for himself

and his two servants are to be at his own charge, and to take place at the Governor's table as second.' He could not land in Mumbai when he first came as it was in the grip of Keigwin and his company of mutineers. He played a major role in negotiating with the rebels and obtaining their surrender on 19 November 1684. The formal opening of the Admiralty Court in Mumbai took place shortly thereafter. He was soon in conflict with the Company's employees about the extent of his jurisdiction, and by all accounts, left Mumbai with an unblemished record around 1690. For more details see Malabari, *Bombay in the Making*, pp. 158–69.

3. For a detailed description and analysis of these interesting cases from the early eighteenth century, see Malabari, *Bombay in the Making*, pp. 289–363.

4. This case became famous as the 'Dirzie Case' and was discussed excitedly in the Mumbai newspapers, especially since Meason, who resigned from the Bombay Army, was the editor of *The Bombay Telegraph and Courier*. For a detailed account of this case, see A. K. Priolkar, *Dr. Bhau Daji*, pp. 149–59.

5. 'According to Fryer, the fort was guarded by three hundred English troops, "four hundred topazes or Portugal firemen," "a militia out of Portugal, comprising five hundred men with English leaders, and three hundred Bhundaries armed with clubs." There were also in the harbour three men-of-war, the largest carrying thirty guns, and five French ships which were ready to assist the English.' Anderson, *The English in Western India*, pp. 125–26.

6. For a detailed narrative of this episode in the history of Mumbai, see Ray and Oliver Strachey, *Keigwin's Rebellion (1683–4): An Episode in the History of Bombay*.

7. 'By way of increasing their military strength, the Court applied to the King for a Company of regular infantry, and one of the Marquis of Worcester's companies was ordered to be sent out under the command of Captain Clifton, the Adjutant, who was to have a salary of thirty pounds in addition to Captain's pay, and was to be junior member of Council.' Anderson, *The English in Western India*, pp. 237–38.

8. The volunteer corps was formed in 1798 in response to perceived threats from the French. Known as the Bombay Fencible Regiment, it was a predecessor of the Bombay Volunteer Rifles. For an account of its formation and activities, see S. T. Sheppard, *Bombay Volunteer Rifles*, pp. 1–18

9. 'The Mogul troops left behind them a pestilence, which in four months destroyed more than had perished in the war, so that only thirty-five

English soldiers were left on the island.' Anderson, *The English in Western India*, p. 249.

10. Extracted from Bruce's Annals by Anderson, *The English in Western India*, p. 248n.

11. These drawings of Captain Pyke were, in 1785, published by Alexander Dalrymple as an 'Account of a curious pagoda near Bombay, drawn up by Captain Pyke, ...' in *Archaeologia, or, Miscellaneous tracts relating to antiquity.* Vol. 7 of 1785.

12. This is not true as there are accounts of the Elephanta island by both Fryer and Ovington. There are also a few Portuguese accounts, the earliest being the one by Garcia da Orta, the famous physician, who visited the island in 1534. See *Colloquies on the simples & drugs of India*. Conde de Ficalho (ed), Sir Clements Markham (tr) London: H. Sotheran and Co., 1913.

13. Govind Narayan is completely mistaken about the great age of Vans Kennedy and the date of his death. For more details see biographical note on Kennedy. For his Marathi dictionary see Vans Kennedy. *A Dictionary of the Marat,ha Language, in two Parts: ... Marat,ha and English; ... English and Marat,ha.*

14. The area adjoining the Dockyard Road railway station is still known as 'Darukhana' or Gunpowder Factory, though the factory has long since been dismantled. There is also a Gunpowder Lane in the same locality. It is now the centre of the wholesale timber market in Mumbai.

Chapter 6

1. Though Govind Narayan comments that Palogate is a corruption of Apollo Gate, most authorities believe that the name has nothing to do with the Greek god. 'The origin of Apollo (Bandar) is still undetermined. In Aungier's agreement (1672–74), it appears as Polo, while in 1743 it is written Pallo; and the original form of these words is variously stated to have been Palva (a large war-vessel) and Pallave (a cluster of sprouts or shoots). A fourth derivation is from Padao (small trading vessel) known to Bombay residents of the seventeenth and eighteenth centuries as the class of vessels chiefly used by the Malabar Pirates. Of the four derivations that from Pallav is perhaps the most plausible.' *Gazetteer of Bombay City and Island*, Part I, p. 25.

2. When Bombay Green was remodelled to form the Elphinstone Circle in 1869–72, the Cornwallis statue was moved into a location in the newly

laid gardens. In 1965, it was removed to the backyard of the Bhau Daji Lad Museum near Byculla where it has now rotted beyond recognition.

3. The 'new and brilliant layout' for the Bombay Green was the Elphinstone Circle which retained only the original Town Hall building towards the East; all the other buildings were acquired and demolished. The redevelopment of the Green in the late 1860s was superintended by Charles Forjett, then the Municipal Commissioner of Mumbai. With its classical-Italianate structures, it provided a welcome relief from the Gothic revival Mumbai was experiencing during the same period.

4. Queen Victoria's statue arrived in Mumbai only in 1872. Though it was to be placed in the Victoria and Albert Museum (now the Bhau Daji Lad Museum), it was considered too exquisite to be placed in a closed structure. It was consequently placed on the Esplanade Road (now the Mahatma Gandhi Road). Vandalised in 1965, it finally reached its originally intended location, albeit in the backyard where ravages of time and apathy have taken their toll on the statue.

5. The statue of Marquis of Wellesley was erected in the year 1814 by the merchants of Mumbai, on a site close to the present Flora Fountain. This statue is also presently in the backyard of the Bhau Daji Lad Museum. Only the main body of Wellesley's statue survives and the rest of the grand paraphernalia have long since disappeared.

6. The same listing of census details for Mumbai also appears in the 'Guide to Bombay' printed in the *Bombay Calendar and Almanac of 1855*, p. 250.

7. The fire actually happened in 1803.

8. 'On the 17th February [1803] a most alarming fire broke out in the very extensive and populous Bazar situated within this garrison. It is not exactly known whence the fire originated. Notwithstanding surmises and suggestions to the contrary, in our opinion there is no sufficient reason to consider it arose from any other cause than accident. The fire broke out early in the day and the wind continuing unusually high the flame increased with astonishing rapidity. So great and violent was the conflagration, that at sunset the destruction of every house in the Fort was apprehended. The flames directed their course in a south-easterly direction form that part of the Bazar opposite to the Cumberland Ravelin quite down to the King's barracks. During the whole of the day every effort was used to oppose its progress, but the fierceness of the fir driven rapidly on by the wind baffled all attempts; nor did it visibly abate till nearly a third part of the town within the walls had been consumed.' *Bombay Government to the Court of Directors*, 22

February 1803, reproduced in the *Gazetteer of the Bombay Presidency, Vol XXVI: Materials towards a Statistical Account of the Town and Island of Bombay*, Part I, pp. 431–35.

9. Ardeshir Dadyseth (1756–1810) was a leading cotton merchant of Mumbai, and one of the pioneers of the cotton trade. He was also a banker, and apparently, much respected in his own as well as other communities.

Chapter 7

1. Govind Narayan is referring to the Crimean War (1854–56) which England, allied with France and the Ottoman empire, fought with Russia. The main cause of the war could be traced to the fight over the overlordships of the Christian population in the Ottoman empire between France and Russia.
2. This victory is perhaps the one at the Siege of Sevastopol which commenced early in 1854. The city was taken finally in September 1855.
3. 'The Kabul War' referred to is the First Anglo-Afghan War (1839–42). It marked the direct involvement of the British in Afghan affairs after they tried to instal a king of their choice in Kabul. They initially tried to win over the support of the Afghan tribal chieftains with money, but when this dried up, both the British agents were murdered and a retreating army was massacred. The British retaliated by sending an army which ransacked Kabul and killed over 20,000 citizens.

Chapter 8

1. In fact, the Earl of Marlborough left only in March 1662 and arrived in Mumbai in September of that year. Malabari, *Bombay in the Making*, p. 93.
2. Sir Abraham Shipman appointed Humphrey Cooke, his Secretary as Vice-Governor on 5 April 1664, and on the former's death, he succeeded to the Governorship. Malabari, *Bombay in the Making*, p. 97.
3. After the representatives of the East India Company at Surat took charge of the affairs of Mumbai, it was administered by a Deputy Governor who reported to the President of the Council at Surat. Captain Young was nominated the first Deputy Governor but was soon dismissed for gross misconduct. For a brief while during George Oxenden's tenure, a commission was appointed to administer the affairs of Mumbai. Aungier, who frequently visited Mumbai, successively appointed Matthew Gary, Philip Gyfford, Henry Oxenden

and Ward. During the tenure of Sir John Child, in 1687, Mumbai became the main base of the English in Western India and Surat was gradually reduced to the status of a minor out-post.

4. This list of the Governors of Bombay is not very accurate; it contains some glaring errors of the dates of appointment, especially relating to those of William Hornby and Mountstuart Elphinstone. Some names, like W. H. Macnaghten, who was only nominated but never actually the Governor, are included and acting Governors are occasionally mentioned. No changes have however been made.

5. This building was earlier known as the Admiralty House as the Admiral of the Marines stayed there. It is unlikely that William Hornby built this structure but he must have acquired it during his long tenure as Governor. On his departure from Mumbai in 1784, he rented it to the Bombay Government. In 1800, the Recorder's Court moved to this building, and subsequently, the Supreme Court also functioned from this building. When the High Court buildings were ready in 1878, Hornby House was converted into a hotel – The Great Western. The building is still standing, opposite the Lion Gate of the Bombay Docks – a warren of tenanted offices – with just a decayed plaque to commemorate its 250-year history.

6. This material is based on a letter from the President, Gerald Aungier and Council of Surat to Bombay, dated 22 March 1677. For more details see, *Gazetteer of the Bombay Presidency, Vol XXVI: Materials towards a Statistical Account of the Town and Island of Bombay, Part I*, pp.74–6. In fact, Nima Parakh was not the only one to have received the so-called privileges; the Bombay council had already granted similar rights to '... Girdhar, the Moody and some others ...'. Anderson, *The English in Western India*, p. 127.

7. Charles Boone was the Governor from 1715–22. However, responding to a petition from the inhabitants of Mumbai, he did try and secure Mumbai from attack by completing the town walls and strengthening the gates of the Fort. S. T. Sheppard. *Bombay*, p. 38.

8. This impressive statue of Jamsetjee Jejeebhoy is still in the Town Hall, in a niche above the northern stairwell, in premises occupied by the Asiatic Society of Mumbai.

9. 'In 1678, the Court were informed by Henry Oxenden that the Customs had risen to thirty thousand, and the duty on Tobacco to twenty thousand Xeraphins. (Letter from the Deputy Governor, dated 24th January, 1676–7).' Anderson, *The English in Western India*, pp. 141–42 n.

Chapter 9

1. All the years mentioned are inaccurate; the Recorder's Court actually functioned from 1798 to 1825 (see Descriptive Index for more information) while the Mayor's Court existed from 1726 to 1798.

2. Manekjee Cursetjee was actually the first Indian to be appointed Sheriff of Bombay in 1856; Bomanjee Hormuzjee Wadia was the second Indian named to this office in 1859. See biographical notes on both for more details.

3. This refers to the famous Maharaja Libel Case which took Mumbai by storm in 1862. All the papers relating to this case were published in the *Oriental Christian Spectator* 3 (4th series). pp. 288–451. Also see biographical note on Karsandas Mulji.

4. Panvel, Alibaug and Uran are places in the mainland which are about an hour or two from Mumbai by sea. As the English consolidated their rule in India, the exiled prisoners were sent to more distant places like Singapore. After the Sepoy Mutiny of 1857, the Andaman islands in the Bay of Bengal was the preferred destination for *Kala Pani* and much dreaded.

5. The Parsis formed a Parsi Law Association to draft a set of laws specially designed to 'enforce the observance of time-honoured customs, ancient laws, and immemorial usages of their community'. For a detailed analysis of the context and the laws, see Dobbin. *Urban Leadership in Western India*, pp. 99–110.

6. Black leprosy, a particularly dreaded form of elephantiasis, was characterised by burning ulcers diffused all over the body.

7. This impressive statue of Sir Jamsetjee Jejeebhoy is now in the main foyer of the Sir J. J. Hospital.

8. The University of Bombay (now the University of Mumbai) was started in 1857. It was one of three universities started in each of the Presidencies of Bombay, Calcutta, and Madras. The first colleges to be affiliated with the University in 1860 were the Elphinstone College, the Poona College, the *Grant Medical College* and the Government Law School. In the next year, the Free *General Assembly's Institution* (now the Wilson College) was the first private college to be affiliated to the University. Govind Narayan was closely associated with the Free *General Assembly's Institution* for nearly three decades.

9. Perhaps, Govind Narayan is referring to Sir William Hamilton's *Lectures on Logic and Metaphysics.*

10. Dr. Harkness' statue is still in the Framji Cowasji Institute at Dhobi Talao. Also see biographical note on Harkness.

Chapter 10

1. The fighting referred to here is the American Civil War (1861–65). The export of cotton, grown mainly in the Southern states, was prevented by the blockade of the southern ports by the superior navy of the northern states. Govind Narayan recounts the cotton boom in Mumbai only for the first two years of 1861–62; the following two years were more spectacular and fuelled the 'Share Mania' which ultimately led to the doom of many a Mumbaikar.

2. This is perhaps based on George Buist, who writing as the editor of the *Bombay Times* on 4 December 1855 comments that 'We have met with no information as to the original establishment of a Printing Press in Bombay, but the production before us (Bombay Calendar) shows that we in this matter anticipated Calcutta, which first boasted of a Printing Press in 1780. The Calendar of course must have been set up in 1779 and it seems reasonable to be presumed that an enterprising Parsee must have opened his establishment not later than the end of 1778 ... and it is particularly creditable, under these circumstances to the Parsees, who have always shown themselves the most enterprising of our natives, that one of their number should have provided us with the first Printing Press established in India.' Priolkar. *The Printing Press in India*, pp. 71–2. In fact, both Buist and Priolkar seem to be mistaken as the first Calendar printed in Calcutta was for the year 1778. See Graham Shaw. *Printing in Calcutta to 1800*. London: The Bibliographical Society, 1981.

3. The Governor, Lord Falkland did not participate in the opening run of the railways as he had already left Mumbai on the end of his tenure. The new Governor, Lord Elphinstone, had perhaps not yet arrived in Mumbai. The train left Mumbai at twenty-five minutes to four in the afternoon on 16 April 1853.

4. This is a description of the Bombay Spinning and Weaving Company founded by Cowasji Nanabhoy Davar in 1854 with machinery supplied by Ms. Platt Brothers of Oldham. Davar followed this up with the Bombay Thorstle Mill soon after, both of which were great commercial successes. This inspired numerous other entrepreneurs to enter the textile industry in Mumbai. For more details see S. M. Rutnagur. *Bombay Industries: The Cotton Mills*. Bombay: The Indian Textile Journal Limited, 1923.

5. The Mughal Emperor Akbar (1549–1605) had died long before the English established a factory in Surat in 1613. This decree may have

permitted the sale of intoxicating spirits to Europeans in general in his empire. Anderson, *The English in Western India*, p. 63.

6. In fact, gas lights had been introduced in Mumbai as far back as 1834. Ardeshir Cursetjee Wadia (1808–77) was the first to introduce gas lights to Mumbai when he lit up his own house on 20 February 1834. The Governor, Earl of Clare, inspected the installation and presented him with a Dress of Honour. He was a member of the famous shipbuilding family of Wadias. An enterprising engineer, he went to London in the 1840s to train in marine engineering, and published an English account of his European experiences. He was the first Indian to be elected Fellow of the Royal Society. He is reputed to be the first to introduce the sewing machine and among the pioneers of photography and electroplating in Mumbai. He retired as the Chief Engineer of the Bombay Dockyard in 1857. Darukhanawala. *Parsi Lustre on Indian Soil*, Vol. I, p. 353.

Chapter 11

1. The reference is to the Literary Society of Bombay. See Descriptive Index for more information.

2. The two famous organizations were the Agri-Horticultural Society of Western India and the Bombay Geographical Society. See Descriptive Index for more information.

3. Sir James Mackintosh was actually associated with the Recorder's Court, a predecessor of the Supreme Court at Mumbai. He was the second Recorder and lived in Mumbai during 1804–11. For more details, see biographical note on Mackintosh and Descriptive Index for the Recorder's Court.

4. Though widely regarded as the leading scholar amongst the Indians of his time, Balgangadhar Shastri was never a member of the Bombay Branch of the Royal Asiatic Society. He may well have conducted research under the aegis of the Society and helped its members in translating ancient inscriptions and tablets.

5. Ardaseer Framjee (Moos) was never knighted. As Secretary of the Native General Library for over two decades from 1860, he revitalised the organization. See biographical note on Moos.

6. Govind Narayan is referring to the British Museum in London.

7. This was renamed the Bhau Daji Lad Museum in recognition of Dr. Bhau Daji's contribution to its establishment. It is now the City Museum of Mumbai.

8. A similar account of this function is available in the fifth volume of the *Bombay Miscellany*, a short-lived magazine published from Mumbai between 1860–63, pp. 252–54

Chapter 12

1. Dhobi Talao was located at the Northern end of the Esplanade Road (now the Mahatma Gandhi Road). Fed by freshwater springs, it was the site where washermen or *dhobis* washed clothes from as early as the seventeenth century. It was partly filled up in the 1860s to construct the Framji Cowasji Institute. The rest of the lake was gradually filled in as pressure for land mounted in Mumbai and it vanished completely before the end of the nineteenth century. The area is, however, still popularly known as Dhobi Talao.

2. This report was later printed as No. 80 of the New Series of 'Selections from the records of the Bombay Government'. A.H. Leith, *Report on the sanitary state of the Island of Bombay*. Bombay: Printed for Government at the Education Society's Press, Byculla, 1864.

3. Conybeare's first report was printed as No. 11 of the New Series of 'Selections from the records of the Bombay Government'. Henry Conybeare. *Report on the sanitary state and sanitary requirements of Bombay*. Bombay: printed for Government at the Bombay Education Society's Press, 1855. Also see biographical note on Conybeare.

4. This book was No. 22 of the New Series of 'Selections from the records of the Bombay Government'. It contained Conybeare's second report and Major Crawford's suggestions. Henry Conybeare, *Second report, with appendices, on the supply of water to Bombay; also, Observations on Mr. Conybeare's second water report by Maj. J. H. G. Crawford*. Bombay: Printed for Government at the Bombay Education Society's Press, 1855.

5. This was the Mody Bay Reclamation Scheme. Initially launched by the Bombay Government, but completed by a private enterprise, it reclaimed eighty-four acres of land from the Mint northwards and provided a site for the building of a terminal station for the Great Indian Peninsular Railway. Albuquerque. *Urbs Prima in Indis*, p. 178.

6. The Parsis took to playing cricket in the 1830s and in 1848 had formed their first club, the Oriental Cricket Club. The first Hindu club, the Bombay Union Club was formed in 1866 by youth from the Prabhu caste, to which Govind Narayan belonged. As cricket became more popular among the Indians, a multitude of clubs were formed, and matches arranged. For a review of the early history of cricket in

Mumbai, see Ramachandra Guha. 'Cricket And Politics In Colonial India'. *Past and Present.* November 1998.

Chapter 13

1. The first Hindu theatre company was the Hindu Dramatic Corps, which first staged a play at the Grant Road Theatre on 8 March 1858 under the leadership of Vishnudas Bhave, now considered the 'Father of Marathi Theatre'. The success of his play inspired many others like the Chawoolwady Hindu Dramatic Corps, Sangleekur Hindu Corps, Poona Hindu Dramatic Corps, and the Subodh Bodhuk Hindu Dramatic Corps to produce plays in Marathi and Hindi, mainly based on mythological themes. Albuquerque. *Urbs Prima in Indis*, pp. 93–4.

2. Govind Narayan was not alone in voicing his disgust at the popularity of plays. His opinion was shared by such worthies as the Bishop of Bombay who delivered a sermon against the 'abomination of a theatre and the great dangers which such a building would create if erected, in any central part of Bombay'. Notwithstanding such opposition, theatre flourished in Mumbai because of support from the Bombay Government and Indian notables like Jagannath Shankarseth who donated a piece of land in Grant Road for the construction of the theatre and Dr. Bhau Daji Lad who patronized several playwrights. Albuquerque. *Urbs Prima in Indis*, pp. 92 and A. K. Priolkar, *Dr. Bhau Daji*, pp. 160–71.

3. Racing began in Mumbai in the late eighteenth century and by 1800, the Bombay Turf Club was formed. It held races on a course in Byculla which was gradually abandoned because of its dusty nature in preference to a course in Mahalaxmi, though the present site of the Mahalaxmi Race Course was only laid out in 1882. By 1864, a West of India Turf Club was proposed, which is now the Royal Western India Turf Club. S. T. Sheppard, *Bombay*, p. 145.

4. For a detailed description of the beggars of Mumbai, see a late nineteenth century text by K. Raghunathji, *Bombay Beggars and Criers*.

5. Many of these beggars and extortionists may have vanished from the Mumbai scene but the eunuchs, who continue to be marginalized and discriminated against, have come to dominate it. They still operate in groups, clap their hands loudly and coerce shopkeepers into giving them a rupee or two.

Chapter 14

1. This church is the Church of St. Thomas, built just off the Bombay Green, which was designated the Cathedral Church in 1835 when the first Bishop was appointed. It was renovated again in 1864 and this structure, recently refurbished, still exists in the Fort area.
2. A first-hand account of the building of the church at Mumbai was published in 1766 by Richard Cobbe, *Bombay Church*. A copy is available in the library of the Cathedral at Mumbai.
3. Govind Narayan refers to the synagogues of the Jews as 'masjids', perhaps because they, like the masjids of the Muslims did not have any idols.
4. The data on schools for India is from a snippet titled 'Details of school children in India' which appeared in 1862 in the Oriental *Christian Spectator* 3 (4th series), p. 516.
5. This is the Bombay Tract and Book Society; see Descriptive Index for more information.
6. Many of Govind Narayan's associates were linked with the Paramahansa Sabha, chief among them being Dadoba Pandurang Tarkhadkar; see Descriptive Index for more information. Also see Priolkar. *Paramhansa sabha va tiche adhyaksh Ramachandra Balkrishna*.

Chapter 15

1. Before the advent of the Portuguese, the island of Mumbai (then just an adjunct of the mainland with Vasai as the chief town) was under the rule of the Gujarat Sultans. The Portuguese demanded the island of Diu in the Gulf of Cambay which was not acceded by the Sultan Bahadur Shah. In 1531, the Portuguese captured Diu and Daman and in 1533, also overran Vasai (and the neighbouring islands of Mumbai and Mahim). In 1534, a formal treaty was executed between the Portuguese and Sultan Bahadur Shah by which Vasai and all its dependencies (including Mumbai) were handed over to the Portuguese. This eventually became the famous 'Province of the North' which was finally conquered in 1739 by the *Marathas*. *Maharashtra State Gazetteers. Greater Bombay District*. Vol. 1, pp. 163–37.
2. The book was published under the name of 'A Hindu', a pseudonym used by Tukaram Tatya Padwal. *Jatibhed Viveksaar*. Mumbai: Vasudeo Babaji Navrange from the Ganpat Krishnaji Press, 1861. A second edition, completely revised by the renowned social reformer, Mahatma Jyotirao Phule was published soon after in 1865.

3. Cowasji Jehangirji Readymoney, in fact, donated rupees 200,000 towards the Cowasji Jehangir Building of the Elphinstone College. His bust is mounted on the frontal wall of the building. He further contributed Rs 100,000 towards the building of the Cowasji Jehangir Convocation Hall of the University of Bombay (now the University of Mumbai). See biographical note for more details.

Biographical Index of Mumbai Men
of the Nineteenth Century

Any biography of Mumbai would not be complete without a mention of its prominent citizens and the people who helped to shape its course and Govind Narayan's is no exception as well. The narrative includes short biographies of the more eminent inhabitants of the city, accounts of the activities of its more famed English governors, references to authorities on various subjects and many others who are mentioned in passing, assuming that the Mumbai reader of the 1860s is familiar with them. Most of these men, both British and Indian, have passed into obscurity and it is difficult to readily obtain any information about them. These biographical notes provide introductory information about the Mumbai men of the nineteenth century who have been mentioned in the book; further sources of information are included where available. The biography of Govind Naryan also refers to a few more Mumbai men with whom he was associated; they have also been included in this index. This index is far from being a representative list of all the Mumbai men of the nineteenth century as it excludes those who were active only in the last third of the century.

Note on spelling of Indian names

Through most of the nineteenth century, the orthography of Indian names in English was in a constant state of evolution. This was further complicated by the fact that most Indians did not sport a family name in everyday life but merely used a patronymic. Only after the establishment of schools in the Western mould, when surnames were demanded of enrolling students, did surnames come into vogue. For example, the famous physician of Mumbai, Dr. Bhau Daji never used the surname Lad himself. Only after his descendants started using the surname in the later part of the nineteenth century did his early biographers append it to his name.

There has been no attempt to standardize the spelling of Indian names to make them conform to twenty-first century orthography; as far as possible, nineteenth century spellings as spelt by the individuals themselves during their lifetimes have been used. Unfortunately, there were significant variations in the spelling of the same name; for instance, Bhau Daji is written in over six different combinations in a single annual volume of the *Journal of the Bombay Branch of the Royal Asiatic Society*. In such instances, the most commonly used spelling has been preferred.

The Biographical Index lists individuals alphabetically according to their surname (where known, else by their first name) and cross references have been provided for names as they appear in the text.

Names in parentheses refer to surnames which have been added retrospectively, though the individuals themselves never used them in their everyday life. While the main entry is entered against the surname, the individuals are cross-referenced through their first names. Names in square brackets refer to alternate spellings which were in common use.

ANANT CHANDROBA, see (DUKLE), ANANT CHANDROBA

ANDERSON, REVEREND PHILIP (1816–57), of the Bombay Ecclesiastical Establishment, was appointed a chaplain in the East India Company's service in 1842. He was initially based in Malegaon and was designated Pastor of Colaba in about 1850. He officiated in a temporary church built at Colaba Point near the entrance to Bombay Harbour and devoted much of his energies into the building of the Church of St. John the Evangelist in Colaba (now popularly known as the Afghan Memorial Church). He however died just before the church was completed in 1858 and his name is commemorated at the base of the Anderson Memorial Window. He is deservedly famous for his book, *The English in Western India* (London: Smith, Elder & Co., 1856), in which he provides an independent and critical view of English activities on the Western coast of India in the seventeenth century. He was also the editor of the *Bombay Quarterly Review*, a popular periodical published in Mumbai from 1855 to 1858, which did not survive long after his death.

ARTHUR, LIEUTENANT GENERAL SIR GEORGE, 1ST BARONET, (1784–1854), was the Governor of the Bombay Presidency from 1842 and 1846. A colonial administrator, he served in the West Indies (where he quelled a slave rebellion), Australia (setting up a penal colony in Tasmania and carried on a policy of oppression against the Aborigines) and Canada (where he helped entrench British control), and was honoured for his illustrious services by being appointed the Governor of Bombay. His reign was not particularly notable except that it further strengthened the British rule in Western India. Many of the developments which overtook Mumbai in the 1850s and 1860s were intially explored during his tenure, especially the railways, the water supply and sanitation system, and various schemes for land reclamation. He was provisionally appointed the Governor General of India in 1846 but did not take up the position due to ill-health.

BAL GANGADHARSHASTRI, see (JAMBHEKAR), BAL GANGADHARSHASTRI

BALA MANGESH, see WAGLE, BALA MANGESH

BANAJI, FRAMJI COWASJI, (1767–1851), a Parsi businessman who straddled both the eighteenth and nineteenth centuries was witness to many of the monumental changes which Mumbai underwent during that period. He was among the foremost businessmen in Mumbai and in the vanguard of the China trade from Western India. He was one of the first Indians to be appointed a Justice of the Peace. He took a leading role in the activities of the Agri-Horticultural Society of Western India and conducted many agricultural experiments successfully in his Powai estate on the adjoining island of Salsette (now included in Greater Mumbai). He was one of the founders of the *Bombay Times,* a promoter of the Bombay Bank in 1840 and in 1844, a Director of the Great Indian Peninsular Railway (now the Central Railways). The Framji Cowasji Institute at Dhobi Talao was built in his honour and his major biography in English is by his grandson, K.N. Banaji, *Memoirs of the Late Framji Cowasji Banaji,* (Bombay: 1892).

BELL, JOHN, (fl. 1830s–40s), was one of two teachers to arrive from England in 1834 to teach in the Bombay Native Education Society's English School. He was responsible for teaching the subjects of Mathematics, Natural Philosophy and Chemistry. He is credited with initiating the spread of European science in Mumbai by holding extra-curricular lectures and demonstrations of chemical processes. He was extremely popular with his students. In 1845, he resigned his position and returned to England. The Professor John Bell Prize was instituted at the Elphinstone College in 1848 to be awarded to any student who produces the best essay on any subject connected with Chemistry and Natural Philosophy.

BHANDARKAR, RAMAKRISHNA GOPAL, (1837–1925), M.A., in the first batch of graduates of the University of Bombay in 1862, is now recognized as a pioneer Indological researcher and Sanskritist. He was born in Ratnagiri and moved to Mumbai in 1853 to study at the *Elphinstone Institution.* He joined Educational Department and was a teacher for over 30 years, including a stint as Professor of Oriental Languages at Elphinstone College and Professor of Sanskrit at Deccan College, Pune, from which position he retired in 1893. He published numerous landmark works on religion and literature including *A Peep into the Early History of India* and

Vaishnavism, Saivism and Minor Religious Systems. On his eightieth birthday, the Bhandarkar Oriental Research Institute was founded in Pune. His Sanskrtit primers (first published from 1864) are still in print and used for learning Sanskrit. His writings can be accessed at N.B. Utgikar and V.G. Paranjpe (eds), *Collected Works of R.G. Bhandarkar*, 4 Vols., Poona: Bhandarkar Oriental Research Institute, 1927–33. The standard Marathi biography is by S.N. Karnataki (Pune, 1927) while the only available English biography is H.A. Phadke, *R.G. Bhandarkar.*New Delhi: National Book Trust, 1968.

BHAU DAJI, see (LAD), DR. BHAU DAJI [BHOW DAJEE]

BIRDWOOD, SIR GEORGE, (1832–1917), M.D., born at Belgaum in India, graduated from the Edinburgh University and entered the Bombay Medical Service in 1854. He was prominent in all aspects of Bombay society from the foundation of the University of Bombay to the creation of the Victoria and Albert Museum and Victoria Gardens. He was at various times Professor of Grant Medical College, Curator of the Government Central Museum, Secretary of the Bombay Branch of the Royal Asiatic Society and the Agri-Horticultural Society of Western India and Sheriff of Mumbai. He returned to England in 1868 due to ill-health and joined the India Office where he published an *Report on the old records of the India Office* (London: 1891). He was the author of many books on Indian art and religion, chiefly the *The Industrial Arts of India.* London: Chapman and Hall, 1880 in two volumes.

BOWEN, REVEREND GEORGE, (1816–88), educated at the Union Theological Seminary at Richmond, Virginia was sent to Mumbai in 1847 by American Board of Commissioners for Foreign Missions. He was initially associated with the Presbyterian Board and then the Methodist Church. Seeing the abject poverty around him, he refused his salary and supported himself by leading a very spartan life. He became Secretary of the Bombay Tract and Book Society, and was also the editor of the *Bombay Guardian.* He produced numerous tracts in local languages during his stay of three decades and his editorials were also collected into three volumes.

BUIST, GEORGE, (1805–60), LL.D., F.R.S.E., F.S.A. Scot., arrived in Mumbai in 1840 to take charge of the *Bombay Times*, a paper promoted by a group of leading Indian and European traders. He was already an experienced editor, having successively edited the *Dundee Courier*, the *Dundee Guardian*, and the *Fifeshire Journal.* He was very active in the Bombay social scene and enthusiastically involved in almost all the organizations of his time. He was the prime mover and Secretary of the Bombay

Geographical Society for many years; his articles on geology and meteorology dominate the Society's *Transactions* during the 1850s. He was appointed the superintendent of the Bombay Observatory in 1842 and helped in the establishment of observatories in other parts of Western India. He was also a founder of the Bombay Reformatory School of Industry and its Superintendent for a few years; likewise, he was founder of the Royal Bombay Golf Club and its Secretary. He actively participated in the activities of the Agri-Horticultural Society of Western India, oversaw the Government Gardens at Sewri, and was at the forefront in founding the Victoria Museum and Gardens. He was the Sheriff of Mumbai in 1846 and was also briefly appointed its Municipal Commissioner in 1859. He was a prolific writer, and besides his role as journalist, published over thirteen independent works and numerous articles in learned journals of organizations like the Society of Antiquaries of Scotland, the Royal Geographical Society, and the Highland and Agricultural Society. However, his career in Mumbai ended in ignominy, as he was dismissed by the Indian proprietors of the *Bombay Times* for adopting an irrational and intemperate attitude in his reportage in the wake of the military uprising of 1857, now famous as the First War of Indian Independence. After an abortive attempt at setting up a rival newspaper in Mumbai, he moved to Allahabad in 1859 as the Superintendent of the Government Press, but died shortly afterwards on a visit to Calcutta. For a modern assessment of his Mumbai career, see Aroon Tikekar, 'Dr. George Buist of the Bombay Times: *A Study of the Self-Proclaimed Messianism of an Anglo-Indian editor, 1840–57*', in N. K. Wagle (ed), *Writers, Editors and Reformers: Social and Political Transformations of Maharashtra, 1830–1930*, (South Asian Studies No. XXXIV, South Asia Institute, Heidelberg University), New Delhi: Manohar Publishers & Distributors, 1999, pp. 98–113.

CAMA, CURSETJEE NUSSERWANJEE, (1815–85), rose from humble beginnings to become one of the leading Parsi merchants conducting trade between India and China. He established the first Parsi trading firm in London. He actively supported various initiatives for reform within the Parsi community and took a lead in furthering female education. He helped establish a Gujarati newspaper, *Rast Goftar*, in 1851. He mobilised support among the Parsis for the Bombay Association and was later a Vice-President of the Bombay Branch of the East India Association. Though he suffered financial setbacks in the Share Mania of 1865, he recovered to become a prominent player in Mumbai's growing textile industry.

CANDY, MAJOR THOMAS, (1804–77), born in East Knoyle, Wiltshire, arrived in India in 1822 with his twin brother, George Candy to take up military service. They both showed a remarkable facility for Indian languages and were drafted to assist Molesworth in the compilation of his monumental bi-lingual Marathi-English dictionary. While George left the army to become a missionary, Thomas became Superintendent of Native Schools in the Deccan and also of the Poona Sanskrit College; in 1847, the Board of Education entrusted him with the responsibility for preparing text-books for use in Marathi schools. He was eventually designated the chief Marathi Translator to Government, in which role he wielded great influence, to much resentment by many Marathi scholars, on practically all Marathi publications in Western India for over three decades until his retirement in 1876. While he initially published a few tracts on the Christian religion, his later work mainly involved the translation, edition and production of books and graded text-books for use in Marathi schools. His other important works include the English-Marathi dictionary completed in 1847 and the translation of the Civil Procedure Code and Criminal Procedure Code, two landmark British legislations of the 1860s, into Marathi. His all-pervasive role in the development of the Marathi language in the mid-nineteenth century is exhaustively analysed by K.B. Kulkarni, *Adhunik Marathi Gadyachi Utkranti* [Development of Modern Marathi Literature], Mumbai: Mumbai Marathi Granth Sangrahalya, 1956 and A.K. Priolkar, '*Thomas Candychi Marathi Vangmayachi Seva*' ['Thomas Candy's services to Marathi literature'], *Marathi Samshodhan Patrika* 4 (1956–57), pp. 181–230.

CHHATRE, SADASHIV KASHINATH, (1788–1830), respectfully known as Bapusaheb Chhatre, is considered to be the foremost amongst the makers of modern Marathi literature. A native of Mumbai, he was one of the first Maharashtrians to learn English, and worked for a few years as a 'Writer' in the Engineer's Department. He was appointed as the Native Secretary to the Bombay Native School-book and School Society in 1823; in this position, he translated a number of books from English and Sanskrit into Marathi. His *Vetalpanchvishi, Balmitra, Esapnitikatha,* and other books proved very popular and were written in a modern Marathi prose style. He resigned his position in about 1830 intending to establish a press to publish Marathi books but unfortunately died soon after. A brief biography of Chhatre is available in C.G. Karve, *Marathi Sahityatil Upekshit Mankari* [Forgotten Notables of Marathi Literature], Pune: Venus Prakashan, 1957, pp. 1–6, while a contemporary estimate is provided in A.K. Priolkar, *Ra. Ba. Dadoba Pandurang: Atmacharitra va charitra* [R.B. Dadoba Pandurang: Autobiography and Biography], Mumbai: Keshave Bhikaji Dhavale,1947, pp. 60–2.

CLARE, SECOND EARL OF, JOHN FITZGIBBON, (1792–1851), educated in Harrow and Oxford, succeeded to the earldom in 1802 and entered the House of Lords in 1820. He was appointed a Privy Councillor in 1830, and later in the same year he was appointed Governor of Bombay, a post he held till 1835. He later became the Lord Lieutenant of Limerick city in Ireland.

CONYBEARE, HENRY, (1823–84), arrived in India in the mid-1840s as a qualified engineer to assist in the Bombay Great Eastern Railway, an early railway project which did not fructify. He then became Superintendent of Repairs to the Board of Conservancy and produced two reports on the sanitary situation in Mumbai which proved influential in designing a modern water supply system for Mumbai which is still extant. He designed and supervised the construction of the Vihar and Tulsi waterworks. However, his passion was for Gothic churches and he provided the designs for the Church of St. John the Evangelist in Colaba (now popularly known as the Afghan Memorial Church). On his return to England in 1858, he established a civil engineering practice in London which ran until 1870; he also indulged in his passion by contributing to the design of various churches in England and published a scholarly book, *The Ten Canons of Proportion and Composition in Gothic Architecture ... Practically Applied to the Design of Modern Churches* in 1868. However, only the first volume was published as it was not well received. He migrated to Venezuela in 1878, and died in Caracas in 1884.

COWASJI NANABHOY, see (DAVAR), COWASJI NANABHOY

DADOBA PANDURANG, see (TARKHADKAR), DADOBA PANDURANG

(DAVAR), COWASJI NANABHOY, (1814–73), the founder of the cotton mill industry, joined his father's broking business at the age of sixteen. After his father's death, he started a firm called Nanabhoy Framji & Co. in partnership with his brother. He recognized the potential of establishing a cotton spinning and weaving mill in India, and in 1854 started the Bombay Spinning and Weaving Company, whose financial performance defied all expectations. In 1857, he opened another mill, the Bombay Throstle Mill, which was sold soon after. He was also active in the banking sector and helped found the Commercial Bank in 1853 and the Orient Bank.

DHAKJEE DADAJEE (1760–1846), was born in a family settled in Mumbai for the previous two generations. After acquiring some basic education, Dhakjee initially worked in the Police Department and then in an English trading firm. He then became ship broker to Rivett-Wilkinson and finance broker to Forbes & Co. and Leckie & Co., and also obtained numerous supply contracts from the East India Company, thus amassing a huge fortune. He acquired numerous properties in Mumbai, his native Thane and in Baroda where he was also appointed as Diwan. His later life was dogged by many scandals and personal tragedies.

(DUKLE), ANANT CHANDROBA, (1829–84), came to Mumbai from Calangute in Goa with his family as a young boy. After the death of his father, he and his brother had to discontinue their studies and accept menial jobs in the Mint. His brother then started a pharmaceutical agency for importing European medicine which enabled Anant to pursue his studies, first in the Elphinstone Institution and then in the Grant Medical College, when it started in 1845. He was among the first graduates in 1851 and joined government service, first in Central India and from 1854, in Karachi. In 1859, He was promoted and transferred to Mumbai as the Vaccination Superintendent, a post he held for twenty-five years. His efforts led to the acceptance of the small-pox vaccine by the general populace of Mumbai. He also assisted his brother, Madhav Chandroba in the publication of a series of books of classical Marathi poetry titled *Sarva Sangraha* which helped in their revival.

DUNCAN, JONATHAN, (1756–1811), joined the East India Company's service in Calcutta in 1772 and held various positions of responsibility, including a prominent role in the takeover of Avadh, when he was British Resident at Benares (Varanasi); he also instituted the Benares Sanskrit College in 1791 which is now the Sampurnanand Sanskrit University. After a brief stint in the Southern province of Malabar, he was appointed Governor of Bombay in 1795 and continued for an unprecedented sixteen years before he died in 1811 in the Old Secretariat building. He is buried in the St. Thomas' Cathedral, where a grand memorial was erected in his honour. The Duncan Docks which were erected during his tenure are still in operation today under the Indian Navy. The Duncan Road (now Maulana Abul Kalam Road) opened up for settlement many new parts of what is now Central Mumbai. During his tenure, many large public building were built and Mumbai began to view itself as a city. He had a very good command over many Indian languages and was considered by many to be completely Indianized. His early Indian career is examined by V. A. Narain, *Jonathan Duncan and Varanasi* Calcutta: Firma K. L. Mukhopadhyay, 1959.

ELPHINSTONE, LORD JOHN, (1807–60), a nephew of Mountstuart Elphinstone, was the Governor of Bombay in 1853–60, and dealt quickly to prevent the spread of the Sepoy Mutiny into the city. He was Governor of the Presidency of Madras in 1837–42. He again returned to India in 1853 to become Governor of Bombay. The infrastructural changes which happened in the 1860s in Mumbai were begun during his tenure. The old Bombay Green in front of the Asiatic Society was elegantly redesigned and named Elphinstone Circle (now Horniman Circle) in his honour. The Elphinstone Road local railway station is named after him.

ELPHINSTONE, MOUNTSTUART, (1779–1859), considered to be one of the most illustrious of the Governors of Bombay, arrived in India in 1796 to join the civil service of the East India Company. He was appointed to the post of Resident in the Court of the Peshwas in Pune, and oversaw the demise of that regime and on the annexation of the Peshwa's territories in 1818, he was appointed as the Commissioner of the Deccan. The following year he became Governor of Bombay, and very deftly handled the tricky process of establishing a Western order of things while endearing himself to the locals. One of his major contributions was the introduction of a Western education in Mumbai, though he foresaw that it would eventually lead to the end of British rule in India. His name is perpetuated in Mumbai by the Elphinstone College. He twice refused the post of Governor General of India to complete his monumental *History of India*, published in 1841, just one of many scholarly tomes he produced. His biography is by T.E. Colebrooke, *Life of Mountstuart Elphinstone*, (London: 1884) while his miscellaneous works have been collected in G.W. Forrest (ed), *Selections from the Minutes and Other Official Writings of the Honourable Mountstuart Elphinstone*. London: Richard Bentley and Son, 1884.

FORBES, SIR CHARLES, (1773–1849), after a brief spell of education at Aberdeen University, came to Mumbai in 1789 and joined his uncle's trading firm of Forbes & Co., the first one to be established in India after the Charter of 1793, which partial threw upon the India trade, earlier the preserve of the East India Company. He came to the aid of the Company, financially and otherwise, during the many wars it fought in the early nineteenth century in India and thus made his name. He was the first Treasurer of the Literary Society of Bombay, a predecessor of the present Asiatic Society of Mumbai; his statue can still be seen in its premises. He left Mumbai in 1811 after a long stay of twenty-two years, still a young man. He spent much of his time in England, both in Parliament and outside in championing the cause of India and strongly condemned its impoverishment by the English. He strongly opposed the sending of missionaries to India and was against the trade in slaves and opium, common-place in those days. He was knighted in 1823. Well-known for his generosity to all, he was particular liberal with his own employees, distributing gratuities at frequent intervals. A brief account of his life is by R.A. Wadia, *A Forgotten Friend of India: Sir Charles Forbes 1st Bart.*, Baroda: Padmaja Publications, 1946.

FORJETT, CHARLES, (1810–90), of Anglo-Indian parentage was the son of an officer in the Madras Fort Artillery. He joined the police in the Bombay Presidency and achieved fame for his police reforms in the Belgaum Division of the Southern Maratha country. In 1855, when he was Superintendent of Police in the Mofussil, he was part of a Committee which investigated corruption in the police at Mumbai, leading to the dismissal of European policemen. He was then made the Chief of Police of Mumbai (1855–64) where he introduced major reforms. His dark skin and linguistic skills enabled him to pass off as an Indian and conduct investigations in *mufti*. He is credited with preventing any incidents occurring in Mumbai during the First War of Indian Independence in 1857 after he discovered a plot among Indian soldiers to mutiny in Mumbai. He narrates his Indian experiences in *Our Real Danger in India*. Bombay: Cassell, 1878. He was also briefly the Chief Municipal Commissioner of Mumbai.

FRAMJI COWASJI see BANAJI, FRAMJI COWASJI

FRERE, SIR HENRY EDWARD BARTLE, G.C.B.,G.C.S.I, (1815–84), a product of the Haileybury College, arrived in Mumbai in 1834 and joined the India Civil Service in the Presidency of Bombay. He worked his way up the hierarchy through many assignments, including Political Agent to Satara in 1846, and Chief Commissioner in Sind (1850–59), and a member of the Supreme Council of the Governor General (1859–62). He was appointed Governor of Bombay in 1862 and is credited with the redesign of the city from an old fort town to a modern metropolis. His order to demolish the walls of the Fort led, among other reasons, to a building spree which produced many of Mumbai's current landmark buildings. He was back in England as member of the Council of India (1867–77) and then Governor of the Cape and first High Commissioner of South Africa (1877–80). However, his administrative career ended in ignominy as his stance precipitated the Zulu War and he was recalled. As early as 1870, his Mumbai utterances were compiled by B.N. Pitale (ed), *The Speeches and Addresses of Sir H.B.E. Frere*. Bombay: 1870. His Indian career was reviewed in Richard Temple, *India in 1880*, while his biography is by John Martineau, *The life and correspondence of Sir Bartle Frere*. London: John Murray, 1895. A more recent work examines his African career:

Damian P. O'Connor, *The Zulu and the Raj: The life of Sir Bartle Frere.* Knebworth: Able Publishing, 2002.

GANPAT KRISHNAJI, (1800–60), the leading printer in Indian languages in Mumbai, established a lithographic press in 1831. The machine was of his own design and he also made his own inks. His first production was a *Panchanga* or Hindu almanac, which eventually proved very popular. He designed his own typefaces in 1840 and the elegance of their design was considered to be unmatched. Though he had initially worked at the American Mission Press, he was largely self-taught and introduced many innovations in Devanagari typography. He printed numerous books in Marathi and English, and his Press survived into the twentieth century when its assets were auctioned off.

GOKHALE, VISHNU BHIKAJI, (1825–71), popularly known as Vishnubawa Brahmachari, and a proponent of the superiority of Vedic religion, wrote the book *Vedokta Dharmaprakash* to promote his reforms. It generated a fair amount of controversy and he was also opposed by many progressive Hindus, who accused him of being obfuscatory. His disciples established the Marathi newspaper, *Vartaman Deepika*, to propound his views. Though cast in the traditional mould, he also propogated progrssive views in relation to caste and female emanicipation. His seaside debates on religion with Christian missionaries were famous and collected together in *Samudrakinari Vadvivaad* [Seaside Debates] in 1862, albeit from the Christian perspective. His work is briefly reviewed in S.V. Puntambekar, 'Vishnu Bawa Brahmachari (1825–71) – An Utopian Socialist', *Indian Journal of Political Science* 6 (1945): pp. 154–66.

GRANT, SIR ROBERT, (1779–1838), was born in India and was the son of Charles Grant, Chairman of the East India Company. After a brilliant academic career at Cambridge, he was called to the bar in 1807. He was elected to Parliament many times and knighted in 1834. He became Governor of Bombay in 1835 and died of illness in Dapoli in 1838. He was a strong advocate of the value of Western education among Indians and carried out useful public works during his short reign. His name is commemorated in the Grant Medical College and the Grant Road (now Maulana Shaukat Ali Road) and the synonymous railway station were named after him. He published *A Sketch of the History of the East-India Company* in 1813.

GRANT, SIR ALEXANDER, (1826–84), arrived in Mumbai, *via* Chennai, in 1860 to become Professor of History and Political Economy in the

Elphinstone College, and soon after, its Principal in 1861. Born in New York, he had been educated at Harrow and Oxford and was a specialist in Greek philosophy. He became the Vice-Chancellor of the Bombay University in 1863, a post he held till 1868, when he returned to become the Principal of Edinburgh University, where also he had a successful career. In Mumbai, as the Director of Public Instruction since 1865, he also oversaw all the educational activities in the Bombay Presidency. Under his direction, the first *Catalogue of Native Publications in the Bombay Presidency upto 31st December 1864* was published, and further updated in 1867, providing a valuable primary source for research in Marathi incunabula.

HARI KESHAVJI, see (PATHARE), HARI KESHAVJI

HARISHCHANDRA CHINTAMAN [HURRICHUND CHINTAMON], was one of the early practitioners of photography in Mumbai; in 1860, he published a book on photography in Marathi. By the late 1860s, his was the oldest photographic firm in Mumbai; he made significant photographic contributions to the book, *The People of India.* London: Indian Museum, 1868–75. By 1873, he had already travelled to England and on his return, had escaped excommunication from his caste. Involved in various reform initiatives, he was President of the Arya Samaj in Mumbai by 1876 and the main architect of its brief union with the Theosophical Society; however he embezzled funds sent by the Society for the use of the Samaj and was expelled in 1879 once the charges were proven. He then permanently settled in England. His commentary on the *Bhagvad-Gita* was published in 1874 from London.

HARKNESS, JOHN, (1807?–83), M.A., LL.D, arrived in India in 1835 as Professor of General Literature in the Elphinstone Institution. He was one of two professors who were personally selected by Mountstuart Elphinstone. He became the first Principal of the Elphinstone College in 1845, a position he held until his retirement and return to England in 1862. He was a member of the Dakshina Prize Committee which awarded prizes to new Marathi books and was also the Inspector of Schools. He is credited with making improvements to the orthography of the Gujarati script. He acted as a benefactor to a whole generation of students of Mumbai and was given a fond farewell on his departure. From the funds collected to commemorate his memory, a bust was installed in the Framji Cowasji Institute at Dhobi Talao to perpetuate his memory in the city; it still exists there. The Harkness Road (now the Jamnadas Mehta Road) at Walkeshwar was named after him because he had a bungalow there.

HENDERSON, WILLIAM (–1850) one of two teachers to arrive from Scotland in 1834 to teach in the Bombay Native Education Society's English school, was responsible for teaching English literature. He obtained an M.A. from Aberdeen College and completed his education at the University of Edinburgh. He achieved early success as a teacher of youth and was the classical master of Heriot's Hospital at Edinburgh before coming to Mumbai. He was briefly entrusted with the editorship of the *Bombay Times* in 1839. He resigned his position in 1846 to join the Free Church of Scotland as a missionary. He left Mumbai in 1849 due to his poor health and died soon after he reached home. A long obituary notice appeared in the *Oriental Christian Spectator* 2 (3rd Series): pp. 268–76.

HORNBY, WILLIAM (–1803), Governor of Bombay from 1771 to 1784, who had one of the longest tenures in this position, was an old India hand. Going against instructions received from the Directors of the East India Company in London, in 1774, he invaded Salsette, the island adjoining Mumbai, and conquered it from the Marathas, thus heralding the start of the territorial acquisition by the English in Western India. He is also credited, though undeservedly, of first damming the breach between Worli and Mahalaxmi, reclaiming thousands of acres of land for Mumbai; the road was known as Hornby Vellard . For his many transgressions, he was dismissed by the Court of Directors in London, but since he first opened the letter of dismissal in Mumbai, he took the opportunity to resign. Hornby House, owned by him, is one of the oldest standing structures in Mumbai (now known as the Great Western Building); it was called the Admiralty House as it was the residence of the Admiral from 1764 to 1792; from 1800, it was the seat of successive judicial courts till the present High Court building was built. On conclusion of his India career, Hornby was granted land in the village of Hook in Hampshire, where he built a mansion modelled on the Government House at Mumbai. He also speculated in land in the United States of America through the Pulteney Associates. One of the main throughfares of Mumbai (now the Dadabhai Naoroji Road) was named after him as Hornby Road. His career in Mumbai has been studied by Eugene D'Souza, *William Hornby: The Governor of Bombay (1771–1784)*, Ph.D. Dissertation (unpublished), Bombay University, 1986.

HOWARD, E.I., the Director of Public Instruction for the Bombay Presidency from the mid-1850s to 1865, introduced many innovations in education in Mumbai. He was the first to introduce the concept of graded text-books in Mumbai and established a Class-book Committee. He also supported Indian students of law in their request to start practicing in the Small Causes Court, which earned him the ire of European lawyers. He also donated his personal collection of over a 1,000 law books to form the core of the Law Students' Library.

JAGANNATH SHANKARSETH, (1803–65), leader of the Hindu community in Mumbai for over four decades, belonged to a rich family of traders which had settled in Mumbai for over three generations. His sagacity, honesty and forthrightness impressed a succession of English governors who consulted him on many delicate issues relating to governance. Popularly known as Nana, he patronized almost all Mumbai institutions of his time, was the first President of the Bombay Association from 1852 to 1857, when he briefly came under suspicision for possible involvement in the uprising. He was a member of the Bombay Legislative Council during 1862–65. Though not very rich, his charities were legendary, especially in the field of education. His impressive statue is located in the stairwell of the Asiatic Society at Mumbai, while the arterial Girgaon Road now bears his name. The subject of numerous biographies in Marathi, his English biography is G.S. Vedak, *A Life Sketch of the Hon. Mr. Jagannath Shankerseth.* Bombay: 1937. In oblivion for over a century after his death, he is enjoying a revival of sorts in Mumbai public memory – a postage stamp was issued by India Post in 1991 to commemorate his involvement with the inception of railways in India.

(JAMBHEKAR), BAL GANGADHARSHASTRI, (1812?–46), from the Ratnagiri district of Konkan, was a precocious child with a great memory who completed his initial education in Sanskrit in his native village. He came to Mumbai in about 1824 and studied at the Elphinstone Institution. He joined as a teacher in government schools after he finished his education in 1828 and succeeded Chhatre as the Native Secretary of the Bombay Native Education Society (initially as the Deputy Secretary because of his youth) in 1830. He eventually became a professor of Mathematics and Astronomy at the Elphinstone Institution, and was well-versed in both traditional Indian knowledge and modern Western sciences. His numerous literary works include an adaptation of Montstuart Elphinstone's *History of India* in Marathi and other works on Geography and Grammar. He is popularly credited with being the founder of the Marathi press - in 1832, he founded and edited the Marathi newspaper, *Bombay Durpun* which was published simultaneously in English and Marathi. When it folded up in 1840, perhaps due to a libel case, he associated himself with the first Marathi monthly magazine, *Digdurshan* founded in 1840 with a view to spreading knowledge on various scientific subjects in the Marathi language. He was rightly considered the leading light amongst the 'natives' and his untimely death was much mourned by his fellow-citizens. For more details on Jambhekar and his pioneering work, see G.G. Jambhekar (ed), *Memoirs and Writings of Acharya Bal Gangadhar Shastri Jambhekar (1812–1846)*, 3 Vols., Poona: 1950.

JAMSETJEE JEJEEBHOY, SIR, 1ST BARONET, (1783–1859), was undisputedly the leader of the Indian community in Western India for many decades and the foremost businessman of his day. He made his fortune as an early participant in the opium trade with China and by exporting cotton to Europe during the Napoleonic wars. His initial business was in partnership with his uncle who was also his father-in-law; later his firm had Motichand Amichand and Mohamedali Rogay as partners. His charities were legendary and of an enduring nature; many of the institutions which he funded continue to thrive to this day, chiefly the J.J. Hospital and the J.J. School of Arts and Architecture. The first Indian to be knighted in 1842, he was elevated to a baronetcy in 1857. He is the subject of numerous biographies in Gujarati and English – a full-scale English biography is by J.R.P. Mody, *Jamsetjee Jejeebhoy, the first Indian knight and baronet (1783–1859)*, (Bombay: R.M.D.C. Press, 1959) – and numerous articles in scholarly journals.

JERVIS, COLONEL GEORGE RITSO, (1794–1851), educated at the Royal Military Academy, arrived in India in 1811 and joined the Bombay Engineers, eventually becoming the Chief Engineer at Mumbai. He made pioneering contributions in the establishment of educational facilities for Indians at Mumbai as the first European Secretary of the Bombay Native School-book and School Society (1823–30), Superintendent of the Engineer Institution (1823–32), and member of the Board of Education (1843–49). In the raging debate about the medium of instruction, he strongly advocated the use of local languages. As Secretary of the Printing and Publishing Branch of the Educational Department, he himself translated about ten books on Mathematics and Science into Marathi and Gujarati. The first book was published in 1826 and many of them were still used in schools in the 1860s. He was also the first editor of the *Bombay Government Gazette* which commenced publication in 1831.

JOHNSON, WILLIAM, (1820?–8?), arrived in Mumbai in the 1840s and was a Clerk in the Bombay Civil Service during 1848–61. He was one of the earliest commercial photographers in Mumbai and ran a daguerreotype studio in Grant Road between 1852–54. He was also a founder member and secretary of the Bombay Photographic Society (founded in 1854) and edited its journal. He started a photographic studio in 1855 which he ran well into the 1860s. In collaboration with another photographer, William Henderson, he produced *The Indian amateurs photographic album,*which ran for 36 issues between 1856–58, each number containing three original prints. His three volume collection, *Photographs of Western India,* one on *'Costumes and Characters',* and two of *'Scenery, Public Buildings'* is now considered a pioneering effort. He also published *'The oriental races and tribes, residents and visitors of Bombay'* in two volumes, in 1863 and 1866.

KARSANDAS MULJI, (1832–71), was educated at the Elphinstone Institution and one of the leading social reformers of the Kapol Bania caste. He actively participated in the activities of the Buddhivardhak Hindu Sabha and managed its schools for girls. He wrote many articles for the Gujarati newspaper, *Rast Goftar* and in 1855, started another Gujarati newspaper targeted at the orthodox Hindus, *Satyaprakash* of which he was also the editor. He is famous for exposing the Vallabhacharya scandal, which led to a libel case against him. After returning from England, where he had gone as an employee of a trading firm, he incurred the wrath of his caste but defied them. In 1867, he was appointed by the Bombay Government as Special Assistant to the Political Agent in Kathiawar, Gujarat. He became a Fellow of the University of Bombay in 1868. His earliest biography in Gujarati with an introductory English sketch is by Mahipatram Roopram, *Uttam Kapol Karsondas Mulji Charitra* [A Memoir of the Reformer Karsandas Mulji], Ahmedabad, 1877 while a critical biography was published on his centenary by B.N. Motiwala, *Karsondas Mulji: A Biographical Study.*Bombay, 1935.

KENNEDY, MAJOR-GENERAL VANS, (1784–1846), a leading linguist and scholar of his day, was one of the first Oriental scholars. A member of the Literary Society of Bombay since 1817, he advocated its affiliation with the Royal Asiatic Society at London, and eventually became President of the Bombay Branch of the Royal Asiatic Society in 1831. He was the driving force behind its activities for many years, and contributed many articles on Indological subjects to its journal, besides publishing many major independent works, including *A Dictionary of the Marat'ha Language* in 1824, and *Researches into the Origin and Affinity of the Principal Languages of Asia and Europe* in 1828. After he resigned as President because he was transferred out of Mumbai, he became the Honorary President of the Society in 1835. He and his works have largely become obscure, partly because his theories did not find enough adherents and partly because of his belligerent attitude. He was court-martialled in 1836 but was soon reinstated. He offered to prepare a new catalogue of the library of the Society which was completed in 1845; however like the earlier catalogue of 1834, it is anonymous. His work has been briefly noticed by Ludo Rocher, 'Vans Kennedy (1784–1846) a Preliminary Bio-Bibliography', Journal of the American Oriental Society 109, No. 4 (October – Decmber 1989), pp. 621–25 and a small biographical note is available at A.K. Priolkar, *'Gayatri Mantra japnara Hindudharmapremi Kennedy'* [The Gayatri Mantra chanting Kennedy: A lover of Hindu religion], *Loksatta*, 31 December 1967.

KOLHATKAR, MAHADEV GOVINDSHASHTRI, (1818–62?), a career government servant, was a famous orator of his time, and proficient in both the English and Marathi languages. He authored five books, translations and adaptations from English into Marathi – one of them being Shakespeare's Othello – which were considered to be very felicitous. He enthusiastically participated in the activities of the Students' Literary and Scientific Society from its inception and was a teacher in one of its Marathi schools. He was the progenitor of the famous Kolhatkar family which produced a series of social reformers and writers, including his son who was one of the first Brahmins to marry a widow, and his grandson who conducted a Marathi newspaper, *Sandesh* – the most influential one in the early twentieth century.

KUNTE, GOVIND VITHAL, (1815–90), popularly known as Bhau Mahajan, and originally from the Konkan, was another brilliant product of the Elphinstone Institution. He worked at the *Bombay Durpun* for Jambhekar before starting his own weekly newspaper, *Prabhakar* in 1841. Over the next twenty years, it grew to be the most influential of all vernacular newspapers in Mumbai and covered a variety of contemporary issues relating to politics, economics and social reform. He was a radical critic of the English policy of expansionism and used his newspapers to vituperate against their policies. He was also highly critical of the autocratic role assumed by a few Englishmen in the development of the Marathi language, and was in frequent conflict with them. He also acquired control of the first Marathi monthly magazine, *Dig-durshan* in 1843. In 1853, he started a low-priced weekly called the *Dhumketu* to counter the views of ultra-orthodox Hindus. He also managed a printing press, the *Prabhakar Chhapkhana* until he retired to Nagpur in 1862 where he seems to have lived in uncharacteristic retirement until his death in 1890. A recent assessment of his contribution to the intellectual climate of Mumbai can be accessed at J.V. Naik, 'Bhau Mahajan and his *Prabhakar, Dhumketu* and *Dnyan Darshan*: A Study in Maharashtrian Response to British Rule', in N.K. Wagle (ed), *Writers, Editors and Reformers: Social and Political Transformations of Maharashtra, 1830–1930*, (South Asian Studies No. XXXIV, South Asia Institute, Heidelberg University), New Delhi: Manohar Publishers & Distributors, 1999, pp. 64–81.

(LAD), DOCTOR BHAU DAJI [BHOW DAJEE], (1824?–74), a man of many parts, left his impress on almost all organizations extant in Mumbai in the second half of the nineteenth century. He announced his arrival on the Bombay scene with his prize essay on female infanticide in 1844 when he was an Assistant Teacher in the Elphinstone Institution. He joined the Grant Medical College and was amongst the first batch of graduating doctors in 1851. He established his own private practice and quickly made both his reputation and fortune. He played a leading role in the formation of the Bombay Association, the first Indian political organization, in 1852 and was its Secretary. He was also a member of the Board of Education and the Bombay Temperance Union, a patron of Marathi theatre in Mumbai, besides playing a leading role in the establishment of many libraries in Mumbai – the Native General Library, the Mechanics' Institution, and the Juvenile Improvement Library. He was the first Indian member of the Bombay Branch of the Royal Asiatic Society to be elected to the Managing Committee and became a Vice-President of the Society in 1864. Most of his Indological researches have been published in this Society's journals. As joint-secretary of the Victoria Museum and Gardens Committee, he worked hard for their establishment; the museum is now known as the Dr. Bhau Daji Lad Sangrahalaya. He was also the first Indian president of the Students' Literary and Scientific Society. He attempted a synthesis of the Indian and European forms of medicine and was famed to have identified a cure for leprosy. He was twice appointed the sheriff of Mumbai, in 1869 and 1871. A road in Matunga is named after him. He has been the subject of many biographies, the most comprehensive being A.K. Priolkar, *Doctor Bhau Daji: Vyakti Kal va Kartrutva* [Doctor Bhau Daji: The Man, His Times and Work], Mumbai Marathi Sahitya Sangh, Mumbai, 1971. His writings have been gathered in T.G. Mainkar (ed.), *Writings and Speeches of Dr. Bhau Daji*, UNIVERSITY OF Bombay, Bombay 1974.

(LAD), DOCTOR NARAYAN DAJI [NARAIN DAJEE], (1830?–75), one of the early graduates of the Grant Medical College in Bombay, had a brilliant academic career like his elder brother, Bhau. Unlike his fellow-graduates, he went into private practice. He conducted scientific investigations into the medicinal properties of Indian plants and published a number of learned papers on that subject. He was also the first Indian professor to be appointed to the Grant Medical College, when in 1861, he was named Professor of Chemistry and *Materia Medica*. He published two books in Marathi and one in English on these subjects for use of students of the college. He was named Professor of Botany in 1874. One of the first Indians to master the art of photography, he helped his brother in the study of Indian antiquities by photographing ancient monuments. He was a council member of the Bombay Photographic Society and 30 of his photographs were displayed at the 1857 exhibition of the Photographic Society of Bengal. He was also a member of the Managing Committee of the Fort Improvement Library (now the J.N. Petit Reading Room and Library). He served as the sheriff of Mumbai in 1875, just before his demise.

MACKINTOSH, SIR JAMES, (1765–1832), reputedly one of the most cultured and distinguished men of his times, trained as a doctor in Edinburgh University before he joined the legal profession and was called to the bar in 1795. His well-deserved legal reputation led to his posting in 1804 as the Recorder of Bombay, the chief judicial official. He discharged his duties in the most impartial and exemplary manner. On his arrival, he established the Literary Society of Bombay, the precursor to the many scholarly societies which were afterwards established in this city. He was not particularly taken up with the atmosphere in the city and when he fell ill, was glad to return home in 1811. He became a Member of Parliament in 1813, a Privy Councillor in 1828 and the Commissioner for the affairs of India in 1830. He published numerous scholarly books on various historical and legal subjects including a *History of England.* The *Memoirs of the Life of Sir James Mackintosh,* in two volumes edited by his son, R.J. Mackintosh in 1835 provide details about his stay in Mumbai and the founding of the Literary Society. His *Miscellaneous Works* were published in 1846 in three volumes.

MAHADEO GOVIND, see RANADE, MAHADEO GOVIND

MAINWARING, W.B., (1801–?), born in Brecknock, South Wales, and initially with the artillery in the Bombay Presidency was appointed as a teacher in the Bombay Native Education Society's school in 1827. He was not a scholar, but he was considered a good teacher. He however left this school before 1833 and started a private school, which flourished till the 1840s. He is listed in the 1851 census of European residents in the

Presidency of Bombay as residing in Thana (in the adjoining island of Salsette) as a land proprietor, where he perhaps also ran a school.

MALCOLM, MAJOR-GENERAL SIR JOHN, (1769–1833), joined the East India Company in 1782; his early career was characterised by a marked facility for learning Indian languages and customs. He distinguished himself in many military expeditions, and also led many important negotiations with Indian kings. He held many important positions before he became Governor of Bombay in 1827–30. He was also a scholar and the author of many important works including *A History of Persia*, *Memoir of Central India*, *Political History of India from 1784 to 1823*, and *Life of Lord Clive*. The famous hill station of Mahabaleshwar was named Malcolmpet because of the important role he played in its acquisition and establishment. An active benefactor of the Bombay Branch of the Royal Asiatic Society, his impressive life-size statue stands in the premises of the Society. J.W. Kaye published his biography, *The Life And Correspondence Of Major-General Sir John Malcolm* (London: Smith, Elder, and Co., 1856).

MALHARI, RAMRO CHITNIS, (–1823), a high-ranking court official in the service of the Maratha kingdom at Satara was also a poet. He composed *bakhars* on six kings of the Bhosale dynasty, starting from Chhatrapati Shivaji. They are composed in a simple style in Marathi with a few Sanskrit and Persian words thrown in. His poem on Mumbai (of which only the first sections have survived) is in Hindustani.

MANGALDAS NATHUBAI, (1832–90), a wealthy Bania merchant was born into a family that had a long-standing presence in Mumbai. He became one of the largest land-owners in Mumbai and completely abstained from speculating in cotton and shares during the Share Mania of 1865, which led to the downfall of many a Mumbai citizen. A leading social reformer, he helped establish a school for girls under the auspices of the Students' Literary and Scientific Society. He was a member of both the Bombay Branch of the Royal Asiatic Society and the Bombay Geographical Society. In 1866, he was appointed a member of the Legislative Council of Bombay. He attempted a revival of the Bombay Association in 1867 and was its President from 1867–71. He was knighted in 1872.

MANEKJEE CURSETJEE, (1807–87), scion of a wealthy merchant family, had to accept government service in 1835 owing to a reversal of his family fortunes. In the 1830s, he was a proprietor of the *Bombay Gazette*. He was an Assistant Collector in the Customs House in 1840 but resigned this position to practice as a lawyer; he had progressed to become a Magistrate in the Small Causes Court by the 1860s. He retired in 1873 after over thirty-five years of government service. A committed Anglophile, he visited England and Europe in 1841–42, where his command over the English language was greatly admired. His English poetry earned him the mock-epithet – 'Byron of the East'. The acerbity of his articles written under the pen-name 'Q in the Corner' stirred a hornet's nest in the Parsi community. He adopted an adversarial attitude against almost all Indians and courted a series of controversies and the odd libel charge. In his long life, he published numerous books touching upon various aspects of social reform including *A Few Passing Ideas for the Benefit of India and Indians*. Having first applied in 1833, he became the first Indian member of the Bombay Branch of the Royal Asiatic Society in 1840. One of the first Indians to send his daughters to the United Kingdom to complete their education, he helped establish the Alexandra Native Girls' English Institution in 1863. He was nominated the Sheriff of Mumbai twice – in 1856 and 1863.

MANOHARDAS ROOPJI, (1727–92) was one of the three sons of Shah Roopji Dhanji, considered to be the first Gujarati trader to have come to settle in Mumbai. Roopji is recorded as having came to Mumbai in 1692 from Ghogla, a small village in the Portuguese dominion of Diu, and became a contractor to the East India Company supplying miscellaneous articles. Manohardas continued in this line of business after his father's death, and also opened a banking business. He was soon considered a 'Nagarseth' of Mumbai.

MANSFIELD, SIR WILLIAM, (1819–76), was educated at the Royal Military College, Sandhurst. He first saw action in India, chiefly in the North-West from 1844. He took part in the Crimean War of 1885 before returning to India as Chief-of-Staff during the Mutiny from 1857 to 1859. He was then Chief of the Army at Mumbai before becoming Commander-in-Chief in India from 1865 to 1870. He then became Commander of the Forces in Ireland from 1870 to 1875. He was made a member of the Irish Privy Council in 1871 and raised to the peerage as Baron Sandhurst. His son, William Mansfield, 1st Viscount of Sandhurst was Governor of Bombay from 1895 to 1900.

MITCHELL, J. MURRAY, M.A., LL.D., (1815–1904), graduated from Marischal College, Aberdeen in 1833 and ordained in 1838. He arrived in Mumbai to teach in Free General Assembly Institution. His book, *In Western India*, recalls his early missionary life in the region. Though he retired from India in 1863 on account of his wife's ill-health and returned to Scotland, he came back to work in India twice. He was reputed to be a master of fifteen languages and was particularly interested in the Marathi language. He wrote many books on Indological subjects and was Vice-President of the Bombay Branch of the Royal Asiatic Society.

MODAK, WAMAN ABAJI, (1837–97), was born near Dapoli in the Ratnagiri District. After his initial schooling, he came to Mumbai and joined the Elphinstone College. One of the first four graduates of the University of Mumbai in 1862, he was also a Dakshina Fellow. He then became a headmaster in high schools at Ratnagiri, Pune and Surat, one of the few with modern education to continue teaching in schools. He was the first Indian to be headmaster of the Elphinstone School, a controversial decision when it was made. He was a prominent member of the Prarthana Samaj. He published essays on various social and philosophical questions, both in English and Marathi.

MOLESWORTH, JAMES THOMAS, (1795–1872), after completing his preliminary education in Exeter, came to India at the young age of sixteen and enlisted as an ensign in 1812. His extra-ordinary linguistic skills – a command over the Western classical languages, proficiency in Sanskrit and Persian and a quick grasp of Marathi and Hindustani – were immediately evident and his proposal for a Marathi dictionary was accepted by the Bombay Government. Working in close concert with a group of Sanskrit pundits, he first oversaw the completion of a Marathi-Marathi Dictionary (published in 1829) and then published the seminal Marathi-English dictionary in 1831. His work on the English-Marathi dictionary was interrupted by ill-health and he had to return to England. He resigned his military commission in 1837 and dropped the military rank from his name. He was invited back to India to work on the second edition of the Marathi-English dictionary which was completed in 1857; this work is still considered by Marathi scholars to be the best dictionary of its kind and is available in numerous editions. He also published a few Christian religious tracts. A brief study of Molesworth's contribution to Marathi literature has done by A.K. Priolkar, *'Major Molesworth va tyacha Marathi-Engrezi Kosh'* [Major Molesworth and his Marathi-English Dictionary], *Maharashtra Sahitya Patrika,* October–December 1965, pp. 30–45.

MOOS, ARDASEER FRAMJEE, (fl. 1850s–80s), educated at the Elphinstone Institution was the Secretary of the Bombay Native General Library for over two decades from 1860 and is credited with its revival and growth. Active in both Parsi reform movements and the Mumbai political scene, he became Treasurer of the Bombay Association in 1876. Moos was one of the first Indians to write an account of his travels across India with Dr. Bhau Daji and Cursetjee Nusserwanjee Cama – *Journal of Travels in India* (Bombay: Education Society's Press, 1871).

MOREHEAD, DOCTOR CHARLES, M.D.(Edinburgh), F.R.C.S., (1807–82), joined the Bombay Medical Service in 1829 and played an important role in the acceptance of the European system of medicine in Western India. He took the lead in the establishment of the Grant Medical College and was its first Principal. He was also the Chief Surgeon of the J.J. Hospital until 1859. He was the Secretary of the Medical and Physical Society of Bombay from 1835 to 1859 which published all the latest developments in medical science through its journals. Among his various public appointments, he was the Secretary of the Board of Education from 1840–45. He retired in 1862 and returned to England to marry late in life. He later became the first Professor of Military Medicine at the Army Medical School in Chatham. His pioneering work on clinical research still deserves mention; he also published a book titled *Clinical Researches on Diseases in India* in two volumes in 1856.

MOTICHAND AMICHAND [MOTISHA] (1782–1836), was the son of Sha Amichand Sakarchand, whose family was long established in trade in Mumbai. He had extensive shipping interests and was dominant in the trade with China, in partnership with Jamsetjee Jeejebhoy. He was an extremely religious person and famed for his charities both in Mumbai and in Gujarat. There is a Motisha Lane in Girgaon and a Motisha Road in Mazagaon where he built a grand Jain temple which is still in use. His life has been documented in detail by M. G. Kapadia, *Mumbaino Namankit Nagrik Seth Motisha* (Mumbai: Shree Godiji Jain Derasar ane Dharmada Khateyono Trusteeyo, 1991).

MURPHY, ROBERT XAVIER (1803–57), an Irishman, came to Mumbai as the first English teacher in the Bombay Native Education Society's school and continued in this position until 1826. He was also a private English tutor to rich Mumbai families. He subsequently became the editor of the *Bombay Gazette* and for a brief while edited the *Bombay Times*. He was well-versed in various Indian languages and was appointed as Oriental Translator to Government. He wrote well-researched articles on the early history of Mumbai, published in the *Transactions of the Bombay Geographical Society*. His depiction of early Mumbai with its seven constituent islands is very famous and the basis of all subsequent map reproductions. His deep interest in nature led to his involvement in the development of gardens in

Mumbai. He left Mumbai in 1855 because of his poor health and died in Dublin in 1857.

NARAYAN DAJI, see (LAD), DOCTOR NARAYAN DAJI [NARAIN DAJEE]

NARAYAN DINANATHJI, see (VELKAR), NARAYAN DINANATHJI

NEPEAN, SIR EVAN, (1751?–1822), after a three-decade long career as a British politician during which he held many administrative posts including a stint at the Commissioner of the Admiralty, became the Governor of Bombay in 1812. His seven-year tenure witnessed a great consolidation of English power in Western India, and the acquisition of the Peshwa's territories in 1818, marking a turning point in the history of the region. The Nepean Sea Road (now the Lady Laxmibai Jagmohandas Road) in Walkeshwar was named after him.

ORLEBAR, PROFESSOR ARTHUR BEDFORD, M.A., came to Mumbai in 1835 as Professor of Mathematics and Natural Philosophy in the Elphinstone Institution. He was one of two professors who were personally selected by Mountstuart Elphinstone. He was an active member of the Bombay Branch of the Royal Asiatic Society and contributed articles on subjects as varied as geology, hygrometry, and architecture to its journal in the 1840s. He commenced geomagnetic and meteorological measurements in Mumbai in 1841. He later migrated to Australia and settled in the town of Malvern, now a suburb of Melbourne. In 1857, he became an ordinary member of the Philosophical Institute of Victoria (renamed the Royal Society of Victoria in 1859). His work on tidal phenomena is still considered important.

(PATHARE), HARI KESHAVJI, (1804–58), a native of Mumbai, was one of the earliest Indians in Mumbai to learn English to an advanced level. He had a successful government career and retired as the Chief Translator to the Sudder Adawlat at Bombay. He became a member of the Bombay Native Education Society in 1831 and retained this position till 1851. In this position, he translated numerous books from English into Marathi for use in schools which proved to be very popular. The subjects included Chemistry, Economics, and Natural Sciences and a History of England. He was also a member of the Students' Literary and Scientific Society. Dadoba Pandurang devotes one chapter to him in his autobiography: A.K. Priolkar, *Raobahadur Dadoba Pandurang: Atmacharitra va charitra* [R.B. Dadoba Pandurang: Autobiography and Biography], Mumbai: Keshave Bhikaji Dhavale, 1947, pp. 55–9. His son Ramachandra Hari also published a small Marathi biography in 1911.

PERRY, SIR THOMAS ERSKINE, B.A., (1806–82), educated at Trinity College, Cambridge and Munich became a member of Lincoln's Inn in 1827. He became Honorary Secretary of the National Political Union of London and founded the Parliamentary Candidate Society. He left Lincoln's Inn in 1832 and was admitted to the Inner Temple. In the same year he was called to the Bar. He was knighted in 1841. He came to Mumbai in 1842 as a judge in the Supreme Court and acted as the Chief Justice from 1847 to 1852. He lectured on law after court hours and in his honour, the Perry Professorship of Jurisprudence was instituted in 1855 in the Elphinstone Institution; this formed the core of the present Government Law College at Mumbai. On his return to England, he became Member of Parliament from the constituency of Devonport. He sought the abolition of the East India Company and the constitution of an independent council under the executive government and as Member of the Council of India, strenuously advocated the employment of Indian nationals to official posts in India. He wrote numerous books of a legal nature.

RAMAKRISHNA GOPAL, see BHANDARKAR, RAMAKRISHNA GOPAL

RANADE, MAHADEO GOVIND, (1842–1901), M.A., LL.B., a student of the Elphinstone College was among the first batch of graduates of the University of Bombay in 1862. He also acquired the M.A. And LL.B. Degrees in 1864 and 1865 respectively. He joined the Educational Department in 1866 and was for a few years Acting Professor of English Literature in the Elphinstone College. He then joined the judicial cadre and was appointed Judge of the Bombay High Court in 1893 and occupied this post till his death in 1901. He was elected a member of the Bombay Legislative Council several times and occupies the first position amongst Marathi men of the nineteenth century for his sagacity and virtue. He was also a man of letters and many volumes of his works have been published. His statue stands near the Churchgate station. His excellent biograhy is by J. Kellock, *Mahadev Govind Ranade: Patriot and Social Servant,* Calcutta: Association Press, 1926.

READYMONEY, SIR COWASJI JEHANGIRJI, (1812–78), was born in Mumbai into a prosperous business family. After a brief schooling and the acquistion of the rudiments of English, he worked in a series of English trading firms for ten years, before he was appointed guarantee broker to two European firms. He made his huge fortune in the China trade. He was first appointed a Justice of the Peace in Mumbai, became a member of the Board of Conservancy, and in 1860 was named as the Commissioner of Income Tax. He was knighted in 1872. His charities were legendary leading to the acquistion of his family name, and he endowed numerous public institutions including the Convocation Hall of the University of Bombay and the building of the Elphinstone College.

RIVETT-CARNAC, SIR JAMES, (1785–1846), was born into a family with established connections with India. He was the British Resident at the princely state of Baroda from 1808–19, turbulent times when the Maratha power was finally quelled, not without help from the Gaikwad of Baroda. He was Governor of Bombay from 1838–41, before he returned to England to be come Chairman of the East India Company for two years in succession. He was eleveated to the baronetcy in 1836 and was also an MP representing the constituency of Sandwich.

ROGHAY, MUHAMMAD ALI, (fl. 1800–40), from a Konkani Muslim family with a long tradition of shipbuiliding owned a large number of ships. He traded with China in partnerships with the Readymoneys in the early part of the nineteenth century before partnering with Jamsetjee Jejeebhoy. He was among the first group of Indians to be appointed Justices of the Peace in 1834. He also served on the managing committee of the Elphinstone Institution. The Roghay family continued to play a prominent role in Mumbai through the nineteenth century, especially exercising their influence on the Muslim community.

SASSOON, DAVID, (1792–1864), was the most prominent of the Baghdadi Jew community which settled in Mumbai after being persecuted by the Muslim rulers of Baghdad. He arrived in Mumbai in 1833, made his fortune in the trade with China, particularly opium. The seizure of his opium chests provoked the First Opium War, which ended with the Treaty of Nanking, and practically guaranteed Sassoon's opium fortunes. He was a major philanthropist and his fortune benefitted educational institutions, libraries and hospitals. His name is associated with the Mechanics' Institution after he donated funds for a construction of a building in 1863. He built two synagogues in Mumbai – one in the Fort area and the other in Byculla. Mumbai's first wet dock, the Sassoon Docks built in 1875 in Colaba is named after him.

(TARKHADKAR), DADOBA PANDURANG, (1814–1882), an early product of the Elphinstone Institution, is justly famous for his books on Marathi grammar and his autobiography which vividly depicts the genesis of a class of Indian intelligensia in Western India in the mid-nineteenth century. He joined the Educational Department and established his reputation as head-master of the Surat High School (1841–46). He returned to Mumbai to lecture at the Elphinstone College and was also the Inspector of Schools of the Northern Division of the Bombay Presidency. In 1852, he was appointed Deputy Magistrate and Collector at Ahmednagar; in 1861, he resigned from government service. He was the inspiration behind the Hindu reform movement in Western India, founding the Manavdharama Sabha in 1844 in Surat, and later inspiring the Paramahansa Sabha in 1852 in Mumbai. He became the first President of the Marathi Dnyanaprasarak Sabha in 1848. His autobiography has been edited and augmented by A.K. Priolkar, *Raobahadur Dadoba Pandurang: Atmacharitra va charitra* [Raobahadur Dadoba Pandurang: Autobiography and Biography], Mumbai: Keshave Bhikaji Dhavale, 1947.

TEJPAL, GOCULDAS, (1822–67), was the son of a hawker who migrated from Kutch and became a rich merchant in Mumbai. Goculdas invested his fortune in the cotton trade and rose to be the leading Bhatia merchant of his day, making extremely large profits during the American Civil War, but was also ruined in the bust that followed. He was also a patron of education and religious organizations. He was made a fellow of the Bombay University when it was established in 1857.

(VELKAR), NARAYAN DINANATHJI (1818?–70), one of the early students of the Elphinstone Institution, joined the Supreme Court in 1840 as a Translator. He was the second President of the Marathi Dnyanaprasarak Sabha and a Vice-President of the Students' Literary and Scientific Society; he was active in both these organizations until his death and took the lead in the education of women. He was one of the founders and also the Secretary of the Framji Cowasji Institute. Besides these, he was involved with the drafting of petitions for the Bombay Association. He was a member of the Board of Conservancy, a predecessor of the Bombay Municipal Corporation. He published numerous articles in English magazines like *The Students' Miscellany* and *Dublin University Magazine.*

VINAYAKRAO VASUDEOJEE is (fl.1840–80) Oriental Translator to the Bombay Government, after completing his education at the Elphinstone Institution, continued as a teacher in the same oraganization. In 1840, he joined the Persian Department as a translator and in due course became the Head Translator. He was appointed a Deputy Collector and Magistrate in 1852 in recognition of his good service. He was the Oriental Translator to the Bombay Government from 1854–79, the first Indian to hold the post for such a long period. He was a member of the the Class-book Committee for the preparation of graded text-books. His brief biography appears in Z.A. Barni, *Romance of the Oriental Translator's Office*, (Karachi: Ta'alimi Markaz, 1950).

VISHNUBAWA BRAHMACHARI see GOKHALE, VISHNU BHIKAJI

WADIA, BOMANJEE HORMUZJEE, (1808–62), was born into the Wadia shipbuilding family but was apprenticed at the age of sixteen to Forbes & Co. He then traded in partnership with his brother and acquired a few ships. In 1830, he built a huge agiary in Dhobi Talao in honour of his father's memory which is still in use. He was among the first Indians to be appointed Justices of the Peace in 1834. He became the first Indian Commissioner of the Court of Requests. He was also a Vice-President of the Bombay Association and in 1859 was appointed Sheriff of Mumbai. A memorial fountain (still standing) was erected in the Bazar Gate Street in the Fort area after his death to perpetuate his memory. A brief biography is available in *The Death of Bomanjee Hormarjee Wadia, Esq.*, Printed at the Imperial Press, Kalbadevi Road, Bombay, 1871.

WAGLE, BALA MANGESH, (fl.1850–80), M.A., LL.B., a product of the Elphinstone College (where he was awarded the prestigious West scholarship), was amongst the first four students to graduate from the University of Mumbai in 1862 and followed it up with the M.A. Degree the next year. He then taught at the Poona College for a brief while before graduating in law and practised in the High Court at Mumbai. He actively participated in the management of the Bombay Native General Library and was member of the Prarthana Samaj. Through the Bombay Association and as Secretary of the Bombay Branch of the East India Association, he was involved in the political movements in Mumbai from the mid-1860s. He was ostracized by his caste for a minor trangression but refused to buckle under the pressure to perform rites of expiation.

WAMAN ABAJI, see MODAK, WAMAN ABAJI

WESTROPP, SIR MICHAEL, (1817–1890), was called to the Bar in 1840 and came to Mumbai in 1845. He was a practising counsel in the Supreme Court and its successor, the High Court before he was raised to the Bench in 1863. He was named the Chief Justice in 1870, a post he held till 1882. He is famous for his extremely lengthy and learned, but highly dilatory judgements. He was also a Vice-President of the Bombay Branch of the Royal Asiatic Society.

WILSON, JOHN, D.D., F.R.S., (1804–75), came to Mumbai in 1829 as a representative of the Scottish Missionary Society. He was the most active among all the Christian missionaries and his spirit of enquiry led to significant reseacrhes in Indological subjects. He was the President of the Bombay Branch of the Royal Asiatic Society from 1835–42 and its President Emeritus thereafter. The General Assembly's Institution, a school founded by Wilson in 1832, soon gained a reputation and following in Mumbai, and continues to function as the Wilson School and College. He started the *Oriental Christain Spectator* in 1830 which had an uninterrupted run of nearly 40 years, a rarity among periodicals of that era. Besides numerous articles, he published many books including textbooks for use in his school. He actively engaged in debate with Hindu, Muslim and Parsi religious officers to prove the superiority of Christianity over other religions and his conversions created a lot of controversy. In 1868, he was the Vice-Chancellor of the University of Bombay, which purchased his extensive collection of books from his heirs. His first full-fledged biography, written shortly after his death is by George Smith, *The Life of John Wilson, F.R.S.* London: John Murray, 1878 while a recent one is by M. D. David, *John Wilson and his institution*,Bombay: John Wilson Education Society, Wilson College, 1975.

Descriptive Index of Mumbai Institutions of the Nineteenth Century

The text mentions or describes a bewildering number of institutions which flourished in Mumbai during the nineteenth century. Some of them have been described in vivid detail while some are just mentioned in passing. This index provides a brief description of the activities of some of the major institutions of Mumbai which have been mentioned in the text. An additional few which have been referred to in the Biographical Index and Govind Narayan's biography have also been included.
Names of individuals profiled in the Biographical Index are capitalized.

AGRI-HORTICULTURAL SOCIETY OF WESTERN INDIA. The Society was formed in 1830 in imitation of similar societies in the Presidencies of Calcutta and Madras; they were mainly formed with the objective of disseminating modern practices in agriculture to the Indian colonies and introducing plantation crops like coffee and tea into India. Even though it was a private society, it had close links with the Bombay Government with the Governor as its patron. In 1835, the Bombay Government allotted a large piece of land in Sewri to the Society to develop a botanical garden. During this period, FRAMJI COWASJI was involved in the activities of the Society and conducted various agricultural experiments in his estate in Salsette (now in Greater Mumbai). DR. GEORGE BIRDWOOD was the Secretary of the Society for many years from the mid-1850s. In 1855, as the Sewri land was required for an European cemetery, the Victoria Gardens (now called the Jijamata Bhosale Udyan) were moved to their present position in Byculla; its management was transferred to the Municipal Corporation in 1873. The Society published two parts (1843) and then a volume (1852) of its *Transactions*. Its sphere of influence has waned over the years, but it still functions out of Pune where it manages the Empress Gardens.

BOARD OF CONSERVANCY. Until 1846, the management of the civic functions of the city of Mumbai were vested in the Bench of Justices of the

Peace, but that arrangement was found to be extremely unsatisfactory. In 1846, an executive body of seven members consisting of three European Justices and three Indian Justices with the Senior Magistrate of Police as the Chairman was constituted. They managed all the municipal funds collected from the taxes on property, fines, and penalties and on the issue of licenses. As this Board was subject to the control of the Bench of Justices, and continued to conflict with the Bombay Government, it was replaced by a triumvarate of three Municipal Commissioners in 1858.

BOARD OF EDUCATION. The Board was the successor to the BOMBAY NATIVE EDUCATION SOCIETY. It had six members, including three members of Indian origin, besides the President, always an European. The first members included W.C. Bruce as President, DR. CHARLES MOREHEAD as Secretary and JAGANNATH SHANKARSETH, JAMSETJEE JEJEEBHOY AND MAHOMED IBRAHIM MAKBA as its Indian members. When SIR T. ERSKINE PERRY was the President of the Board (1843–52), he strongly advocated the use of English as medium of instruction in the Board's schools, which was strongly opposed by the Indian members. As a compromise, English was chosen as the medium for higher education while. the regional languages were used as the medium of instruction in primary schools; however, as knowledge of English became mandatory for employment in government and other jobs, it was the privileged mode of instruction. The Board opened primary schools in villages with a population of two thousand or more, and managed over two hundred schools. With the formation of the Department of Education in the Bombay Government in 1855, the Board of Education was wound up. It published the *Report of the Board of Education* annually.

BOMBAY ASSOCIATION. After many years of debate in local newspapers regarding the benefits of British rule to India, the Bombay Association was formed in 1852, on the eve of the renewal of the Charter of the East India Company, to communicate the views of Indians directly to the British Parliament. It was an exclusively Indian organization with leading citizens – including traditional businessmen and the newly educated – from all communities becoming members. While SIR JAMSETJEE JEJEEBHOY was the President Emeritus, JAGANNATH SHANKARSETH was the President; BHAU DAJI and Vinayakrao Jagannath were the joint secretaries. Its first petition (chiefly drafted by Nowrozjee Furdoonjee) to the British Parliament was despatched in 1853 sought significantly higher levels of involvement for Indians at the highest levels of government; however, differences of opinion between the members led to many of them including Sir Jamsetjee to resign and the organization soon languished. It was sought to be revived in 1867 by its then President, MANGALDAS NATHUBAI, and submitted another petition in 1871 in which it condemned the entire financial administration of the British Empire in India and sought significant involvement for Indians in the decision-making process. It however became moribund by the mid-1870s. While its achievements may have been meagre, the Bombay Association can claim to be the first indigenous political organization in Western India, and predecessor to the more illustrious Indian National Congress which was first convened in Mumbai in 1885.

BOMBAY BRANCH OF THE EAST INDIA ASSOCIATION. The East India Association was started in London by Dadabhai Naoroji in 1867 to present Indian problems in the British Parliament. The Bombay Branch was established in 1867 to provide information about the India situation and funds to its London parent. It was conceived as an organization which would provide a platform to the newly educated elite without depending on the money-power of the traditional businessmen. Its chairman was BHAU DAJI, while BALA MANGESH WAGLE and Pherozeshah Mehta were the secretaries of the Managing Committee. It attained a certain level of prominence by having over seven hundred members on its rolls by 1871, but did not achieve anything of practical significance. MANGALDAS NATHUBAI became its President in 1877. However, with the control of its parent organization having passed on to its European members, the Bombay Branch became practically defunct by the mid 1880s.

BOMBAY BRANCH OF THE ROYAL ASIATIC SOCIETY. The new name of the LITERARY SOCIETY OF BOMBAY after its affiliation to the Royal Asiatic Society at London. It moved into the Town Hall after its construction in 1830 and continues to occupy the same premises. It has one of the largest collection of books in India and is the premier centre for Indological research in Western India. The *Journal of the Bombay Branch of the Royal Asiatic Society* (1841–1954) ran into two series (with 26 and 29 volumes respectively). The Society was renamed the Asiatic Society of Bombay in 1955 and further renamed Asiatic Society of Mumbai in 1999.

BOMBAY GEOGRAPHICAL SOCIETY. The Bombay Geographical Society was formed in 1832 to investigate and report on questions relating to the geography of India, and further afield in West Asia and Africa. It sought to affiliate itself with the Royal Geographical Society, formed just two years earlier at London. Soon after his arrival in Mumbai in 1840, GEORGE BUIST became the Secretary of the Society, a post he held for nearly two decades. The *Transactions of the Bombay Geographical Society* (1836–73) run into 19 volumes and constitute a rare record of exploratory geographical research undertaken during the mid-1800s. It shared premises with the BOMBAY BRANCH OF THE ROYAL ASIATIC SOCIETY at the Town Hall, and merged with it in 1873.

BOMBAY NATIVE EDUCATION SOCIETY. The new name of the BOMBAY NATIVE SCHOOL-BOOK AND SCHOOL SOCIETY, it functioned from 1827 to 1840 as the primary agency through which all efforts of the Bombay Government in the arena of education for Indians was channelized. By 1840, it ran as many as 115 schools in the Bombay Presidency and had published numerous books for use in schools. Around this time, the debate over the medium of instruction in Indian schools raged both in the United Kingdom and India with English finally being chosen as the language of instruction, especially for higher education. This led to a restructuring in 1840, with the Society's school being amalgamated with the Elphinstone School to form the ELPHINSTONE INSITUTION, while a BOARD OF EDUCATION was constituted to oversee the education in the entire Bombay Presidency. The *Report of the Bombay Native Education Society* was published at irregular intervals, numbering about seven during its thirteen years of existence.

BOMBAY NATIVE SCHOOL-BOOK AND SCHOOL SOCIETY. In 1820, the Native School and School-Book Committe was formed at the initiative of MOUNTSTUART ELPHINSTONE, as a branch of the Bombay Education Society. Its role was to publish text-books in English, Marathi, and Gujarati, give grants to the traditional schools working at that time, and establish new schools. It was felt that the medium of instruction in these schools should be the regional languages of India. The native members of the Committee included Raghunath Krishna Joshi and SADASHIV KASHINATH CHHATRE, with Venkoba Sadashiv Naik as the first Native Secretary, while Dr. Taylor was the European Secretary. In 1822, this Committee was designated as the Bombay Native School and School-Book Society, by which time the Native Secretary was Chhatre with GEORGE JERVIS as the energetic European Secretary. In 1824, a school building was constructed on the Esplanade and the Society's school (sometimes called the Central English School) started functioning, the first attempt to use English as a medium of instruction in Mumbai. The production of books, though initially sluggish (only two in the first four years), gathered momentum with both Jervis and Chhatre translating many books themselves. It was renamed the BOMBAY NATIVE

EDUCATION SOCIETY in 1827. Three volumes of the *Report of the Bombay Native School-Book and School Society* published in 1824, 1825, and 1827 document the activities of the organization.

BOMBAY PHOTOGRAPHIC SOCIETY. The Society was formed in 1854 to provide a forum to its members to exchange notes and technical information on the new art of photography which was becoming popular in Mumbai. The joint secretaries of the Society were WILLIAM JOHNSON, a civil servant and William Crawford, a businessman. They also edited the *Journal of the Photographic Society of Bombay* which commenced publication in January 1855. The Society was patronized by LORD ELPHINSTONE, Governor of Bombay and had as its members many prominent citizens of Mumbai including BHAU DAJI, NARAYAN DAJI, GEORGE BUIST and HARISHCHANDRA CHINTAMAN. As the Bombay Government was very keen on promoting photography, classes were commenced at the ELPHINSTONE INSTITUTION by William Crawford which did much to further the spread of photography in Mumbai. The Society seems not to have survived into the 1860s though many of its members flourished as photographers in Mumbai during this period.

BOMBAY TRACT AND BOOK SOCIETY. The Bombay Auxilliary Religious Tract Society was established in 1827 (renamed the Bombay Tract and Book Society in 1832) with the avowed objective of presenting 'to the Natives of [India], in languages they understand, the truth of god's word in forms adapted to arrest their attention, enlighten their understandings, and affect their hearts'. To this end, it published innumerable tracts in all the local languages of Western India, chiefly Marathi and Gujarati. It also published a series of text-books for use in schools conducted by Christian missionaries. GEORGE BOWEN was its Secretary for a long period in the mid-1800s. It continues to function from an old church near the Azad Maidan in Mumbai, albeit in a more circumscribed manner.

DECCAN VERNACULAR TRANSLATION SOCIETY. The Society was established in 1849 at the initiative of Colonel T. French, then English Resident at Baroda and Captain Hart, Chief of the Pensions Department at Mumbai, who was also the Secretary. The first President of the Society was J. P. Willoughby, Secretary of the Bombay Government. As the Society mainly consisted of European members, it could collect a large corpus of funds which enabled it to fund the translation and publication of a number of books in Marathi. As Secretary from 1850, THOMAS CANDY wielded great influence on the quality of translations published by this Society. However the books published by it did not have a popular appeal and the Society languished for a while until 1860 when about 10 to 12 books were published in a few years. It again lapsed into inactivity before it was resurrected in 1884 by M. G. RANADE.

ELPHINSTONE INSTITUTION. The BOMBAY NATIVE EDUCATION SOCIETY established a school with English as a medium of instruction in about 1824 (sometimes referred to as the Central English School). After acquiring a good knowledge of their native tongues, a student could gain admission to the English School. R. X. MURPHY, one of the first teachers in this English school, taught till 1826. He was succeeded by W. B. Mainwaring who left in 1833 to start a private school in Mumbai. The first teachers to specifically arrive in Mumbai to work in this school were JOHN BELL and WILLIAM HENDERSON in 1834. The Elphinstone College Class was started on the arrival of Professors JOHN HARKNESS and A. B. ORLEBAR in 1835, while the lower classes were referred to as the Native Education Society School. In 1840, after the BOARD OF EDUCATION was constituted, the two were united to form the Elphinstone Native Education Institution. In 1856, the Elphinstone Institution was bifurcated into the Elphinstone High School and the Elphinstone College, both of which continue to function under the same name today. The Elphinstone College is housed in neo-Gothic edifice, completed in 1866 with donations from SIR COWASJEE JEHANGEER READYMONEY and has been recently renovated.

FORT IMPROVEMENT LIBRARY. The Library was established in 1856 under the aegis of the Philosophic Institute. Its reading rooms were to be supplied with such books and newspapers which would result in 'the increased intelligence of the community'. Its management and membership were overwhelmingly from the Parsi community. In 1891, on the receipt of a generous grant from the Petit family, it was renamed the J.N. Petit Reading Room and Library. It occupies a venerable building on Dadabhai Naoroji Road in the Fort area and maintains a respectable collection of books.

GRANT MEDICAL COLLEGE. A predecessor 'Medical School for the Instruction of Native Practitioners' was started in 1826 by Dr. John McLennan at Mumbai, but it did not flourish. However the need for well-trained Indian medical practitioners was strongly felt and in 1838, SIR ROBERT GRANT, then Governor of Bombay recommended the establishment of a medical school at Mumbai. JAMSETJEE JEEJEBHOY provided the funds for the construction of the medical school and an associated general hospital which are now known as the Grant Medical College and Sir J.J. Hospital respectively. The College opened in 1845 with DR. CHARLES MOREHEAD as Professor and the first batch of eight doctors – including BHAU DAJI and ANANT CHANDROBA - graduated in 1851 with the degree of G.G.M.C. (Graduate of the Grant Medical College). In 1860, the College was affiliated to the Bombay University and in due course, started awarding M.B.B.S. degrees. It is still one of the premier centres of medical education in the city of Mumbai.

HIGH COURT. The Bombay High Court was established on 25 August 1862 on the re-organization of the entire judicial system of India and replaced the SUPREME COURT. The first Chief Justice of the High Court was Sir Mathew Sause. The High Court initially functioned from the Hornby House before moving to its own premises in a custom-built neo-Gothic structure in 1878 from which it still functions. The initial sanctioned strength of the Bench was 15 justices while the current strength is 60.

JUVENILE IMPROVEMENT LIBRARY. In the initial spurt of the library movement in Mumbai, this library was founded in 1852 with an exclusively Indian management and audience. It was perhaps modelled as a circulating library for young men. Its patrons were BHAU DAJI and Vinayak Jagannath. In 1888, this library and three others merged to form the Bombay Benevolent Library.

LITERARY SOCIETY OF BOMBAY. Formed in 1804, with SIR JAMES MACKINTOSH as its President and William Erskine as Secretary, the Literary Society of Bombay was modelled on the Asiatic Society founded in Calcutta about a decade earlier. A detailed account of its establishment is available in the memoirs of Sir James Mackintosh. It acquired the library of the Medical and Literary Society of Bombay and quickly grew it to over 10,000 books. The *Transactions of the Literary Society of Bombay* (1819–23) ran into three volumes. It affiliated itself with the Royal Asiatic Society (formed in 1823 at London) and was called the BOMBAY BRANCH OF THE ROYAL ASIATIC SOCIETY from 1829.

MARATHI DNYANAPRASARAK SABHA. In September 1848, under the auspices of the STUDENTS' LITERARY AND SCIENTIFIC SOCIETY, was formed the Upayukt Dnyanaprasarak Sabha, working towards the diffusion of useful knowledge as its name denoted and perhaps modeled on the Society for Diffusion of Universal Knowledge, founded in 1828 in London. DADOBA PANDURANG TARKHADKAR, the eminent Marathi grammarian was its first President while its first Secretary was MAHADEO GOVINDSHASTRI KOLHATKAR. This society, soon after renamed the Marathi Dnyanaprasarak Sabha met twice a month in the premises of

ELPHINSTONE INSTITUTION where members delivered lectures in Marathi. These were subsequently published in the Marathi Dnyanaprasarak, a monthly magazine which the Sabha started publishing in April 1850. A range of subjects – scientific, historical, geographical, social – were covered in the magazine and occasionally stories and plays would be serialised. Overtly political subjects and religious themes were prohibited. The magazine ran uninterruptedly for seventeen years, a major achievement in those years when most publications were short-lived. This publication has been extensively discussed by V. L. Kulkarni in *Marathi Dnyanaprasarak: itihas va vangmayavichar*, (Mumbai: Popular Prakashan, 1965).

MECHANICS' INSTITUTION. In lines with similarly named institutions being established in the United Kingdom after the 1820s, a Mechanics' Institution was started in Mumbai by the European employees of the Government Mint and the Dockyard in 1847. Its objectives were to provide adult education, particularly in technical subjects as well as host lectures on a variety of topics. While it functioned in rented premises in the Fort for many years, its own building was constructed in 1870 through the generosity of SIR DAVID SASSOON. The building was named the David Sassoon Library and Reading Room and the original name died out. The building, still standing on the Mahatma Gandhi Road continues to fulfil its original objectives.

MEDICAL AND PHYSICAL SOCIETY OF BOMBAY. Founded in 1835, its objective was to provide a forum to disseminate modern medical knowledge to Indian traditional doctors. The Society had DR. CHARLES MOREHEAD as Secretary, who was at the forefront of initiatives to establish a medical college for Indian students at Mumbai. This finally led to the establishment of the GRANT MEDICAL COLLEGE. The Society eventually became a platform to discuss new advances in medical science and published 34 volumes of *Transactions of the Medical and Physical Society of Bombay* (1838–89) in three series. It was perhaps merged with the BOMBAY BRANCH OF THE ROYAL ASIATIC SOCIETY in 1890s.

NATIVE GENERAL LIBRARY. The pioneer in the library movement of Mumbai in the mid-1800s, this library was formed initially to cater to the needs of the Indian clerks in the employment of the Military Board at Mumbai on the initiative of Raghoba Janardhan, Head Native Clerk to the Military Board. However, the popular response from the general public and donations from leading citizens converted it into a general library. The first President was J. Mullaly of the Military Board; BHAU

DAJI was the Chairman of the Managing Committee for many years. After the initial enthusiasm, there were hardly any readers and the library languished for a few years before being revived by ARDASEER FRAMJEE MOOS, who was its Secretary for over two decades from 1860. It moved to new premises in the Framji Cowasji Institute in 1863 and continues to operate from there in a desultory fashion. Its dark reading room contains many busts of Mumbai men of the nineteenth century. Further information on its early history can be obtained in A.F. Moos (ed.), *Annual Reports of the Bombay Native General Library ... from its commencement to the year 1879,* (Bombay: Union Press, 1880).

PARAMAHANSA SABHA. The reform movement among the Hindus found various manifestations – one of them being the Paramahansa Sabha, which sought to break taboos and other caste restrictions. It operated in a fairly secretive manner though many of its members aired their views in other fora. It was inspired by DADOBA PANDURANG, who wrote its manifesto when he started the Manavdharma Sabha at Surat in 1844. The Paramahansa Sabha was founded around 1850 with Ramachandra Balakrishna as its President and its members were mainly young men who had been recently educated in the Western fashion. Though it was a secret organization, it was discussed frequently in the contemporary press and the threat of unmasking finally led to its dissolution. Its members then formed the Prarthana Samaj which was less radical in its approach but espoused social reform in a formal manner. Dr. Atmaram Pandurang and R.G. BHANDARKAR, prominent members of the Sabha, were respectively the first President and Secretary of the Prarthana Samaj. It continues to function in Western India, with its headquarters in Mumbai but plays only a marginal role in contemporary religious life and thought.

RECORDER'S COURT. The Recorder's Court was established in 1798 by the British Crown in Mumbai with a view to control the unbridled activities of the employees of the East India Company. It replaced the Mayor's Court which had been in existence from 1726. The Recorder, appointed by the Crown, had to be a barrister of not less than five years standing. The first Recorder was Sir William Syer; he was succeeded by the more eminent SIR JAMES MACKINTOSH. Both of them periodically came into conflict with the Bombay Government. The Court functioned from the Hornby House or Admiralty House. It was the first time in Mumbai that Indians were involved in the administration of law under British rule, with a Hindu pundit and a Muslim *moulavi* advising the Recorder on the applicable Indian laws under which locals were judged. When the Court was replaced by the Supreme Court in 1825, the Recorder was Sir Edward West.

STUDENTS' LITERARY AND SCIENTIFIC SOCIETY. The Society was formed on 13 June 1848 by a group of ex-students of the ELPHINSTONE INSTITUTION under the guidance of their professors. The prime movers included BHAU DAJI and Dadabhai Naoroji, who later emerged as a major leader of India's freedom movement. Its main activities included lectures on various topics – literary and scientific – and provided a platform for continuous learning for its members. Soon after, the organization established two linguistically distinct branches – the MARATHI DNYANAPRASARAK SABHA and the Gujarati Dnyanaprasarak Sabha – so that members could easily understand the lectures. In April 1851, a new branch, the Hindu Buddhivardhak Sabha was constituted with Gujarati as its medium, since the Gujarati Dnyanaprasarak Sabha had evolved into a Parsi bastion. The *Students' Miscellany* published the lectures delivered at the Society and each of the branches also published their own journals. The Society took upon itself the cause of female education and established a few schools in Mumbai for girls, providing education in the Gujarati and Marathi mediums. The teachers also compiled school-books for use in these schools. The Society however soon languished, perhaps due to lack of funds; it was briefly revived by Bhau Daji in the late sixties. The schools however continued to function for well over a century.

SUPREME COURT. The Supreme Court was established in Mumbai in 1825 and succeeded the RECORDER'S COURT. While it had more powers than its predecessor over European subjects, it was not permitted to interefer with any matters relating to revenue. The Supreme Court functioned from the Hornby House just as the Recorder's Court. The last Recorder, Sir Edward West, became the first Chief Justice of the Supreme Court – he was severly censorious of the activities of the Bombay Government and fought hard to maintain the dignity of the Court. His death under mysterious circumstances in 1828 only served to deepen the schism. The Chief Justice was assisted by a Puisne Judge. SIR T. ERSKINE PERRY was appointed Puisne Judge in 1842 and retired as the Chief Justice in 1852, and played an important role in involving Indians in the administration of law. After the British Crown took over the reins of Indian administration from the East India Company in 1858, the legal system in India was completely reorganized to provide a uniform system of justice and the Supreme Court was replaced by the HIGH COURT in 1862.

BIBLIOGRAPHY

The first section list books and periodicals published prior to 1863 which could have been used by Govind Narayan while writing Mumbaiche Varnan. *They have also been used to clarify various aspects of the text as have the books listed in the subsequent sections of the bibliography.*

Works published before 1863 in English

A Brief Account of St. Thomas' Cathedral, Bombay from the year 1715 to the present period with Notices of the Building and of individuals and events connected herewith. Bombay: The Telegraph and Courier Press, 1851.

ANDERSON, Philip. *The English in Western India.* 2nd ed. London: Smith, Elder & Co., 1856.

Bombay Calendar and Almanac for ... Published annually. Bombay: Times Press, 1853–1861.

Bombay Civil List ... showing the names of the Civil, Military and Uncovenanted Servants of Government, etc. Published half-yearly. Bombay: Bombay Education Society's Press. 1850–82.

Bombay Miscellany. Also titled *Chesson & Woodhall's Miscellany. A Monthly Magazine.* 7 vol. (semi-annual). Bombay: Alliance Press, 1860–64.

Bombay Quarterly Magazine and Review. 3 vol. Bombay: Bombay Education Society's Press, 1850–53.

Bombay Quarterly Review. 7 vol. (semi-annual). Bombay: Smith, Taylor and Co., 1855–58.

BRUCE, John. *Annals of the Honourable East-India Company, from their establishment by the charter of Queen Elizabeth, 1600, to the union of the London and English East-India Companies, 1707–8.* 3 vol. London: 1810.

[BUIST, George]. *'Guide to Bombay' printed in the Bombay Calendar and Almanac of 1855.* Bombay: The Times Press, 1855.

CAPPER, John. *The three presidencies of India: a history of the rise and progress of the British Indian posessions, from the earliest records to the present time.* London: Ingram, Cooke & Co., 1853.

COBBE, Richard. *Bombay Church: or, a True account of the building and finishing the English Church at Bombay.* London: John Rivington, 1766.

[EASTWICK, Edward]. *A Handbook for India; being an account of the three presidencies. Part I- Madras, Part II-Bombay.* London: John Murray, 1859.

ELWOOD, Anne Katharine. *Narrative of a journey overland from England, by the Continent of Europe, Egypt, and the Red Sea, to India; including a residence there, and voyage home, in the years 1825, 26, 27, and 28.* 2 vol. London: 1830.

FALKLAND, Viscountess. *Chow-Chow: being selections from a journal kept in India, Egypt, and Syria.* 2nd ed. 2 vol. London: Hurst and Blackett, 1857.

FORBES, James. *Oriental Memoirs.* 2 vol. 2nd ed. London: Richard Bentley, 1834.

FRYER, John. *A new account of East-India and Persia, in eight letters: being nine years travels begun 1672, and finished 1681*. London: R. R. for R. Chiswell, 1698.

GRAHAM, Maria. *Journal of a residence in India, etc*. Edinburgh: A. Constable, 1812.

GRANT, Robert. *A sketch of the history of the East-India Company*. London: Black, Parry & Co., 1813.

GRAY, James. *Life in Bombay, and the neighbouring out-stations, etc*. London: Richard Bentley, 1852.

GROSE, John Henry. *A voyage to the East-Indies, with observations, etc*. London: S. Hooper and A. Morley, 1757.

HALL, Basil. *Fragments of voyages and travels*. London: Edward Moxon and Co., 1860.

HAMILTON, Alexander. *A new account of the East Indies ... 1688 to 1723*. 2 vol. Edinburgh: J. Mosman, 1727.

HAMILTON, Walter. *The East India Gazetteer; containing particular descriptions of ... Hindostan, and the adjacent countries, India beyond the Ganges, aud the Eastern Archipelago*. 2 vol. 2nd ed. London: 1828.

HEBER, Reginald. *Narrative of a Journey through the Upper Provinces of India ...* 4th ed. 2vol. London: 1844.

HERVEY, James. *Meditations among the Tombs. In a letter to a lady*. London: 1746.

KAYE, John William. *The administration of the East India Company ...* 2nd ed. London: Richard Bentley, 1853.

—, *The Life and correspondence of Major-General Sir John Malcolm*. 2 vol. London: Smith, Elder, and Co., 1856.

MACKINTOSH, J. *Memoirs of The Life of The Right Honourable Sir James Mackintosh*. London: Edward Moxon, 1835.

MANEKJEE Cursetjee. *A few passing ideas for the benefit of India and Indians*. Bombay: 1853.

Memorandum of the life and public charities of Sir Jamsetjee Jejeebhoy. Printed for private circulation. Bombay(?): 1854.

MILBURN, William. *Oriental commerce; containing a geographical description of the principal places in the East Indies, China and Japan, with their produce, manufactures and trade ... also the ... progress of the trade of the ... European Nations with the Eastern World, particularly that of the English East India Company, etc*. 2 vol. London: 1813.

MILL, James. *The history of British India*. 5th ed. London: James Madden, 1858.

MOLESWORTH, J. T. *A dictionary, Marathi and English*. 2nd ed., rev. and enl. Bombay: Printed for government at the Bombay Education Society's Press, 1857.

NOWROZJEE Furdoonjee. *On the civil administration of the Bombay Presidency*. Bombay: Education Society's Press, 1853.

Oriental Christian Spectator. 38 volumes in 4 series. Bombay: 1830–67.

OVINGTON, John. *A voyage to Suratt, in the year 1689*. London: J. Tonson, 1696.

PECHEL, Samuel. *A historical account of the settlement and possession of Bombay by the English East India Company, and the rise and progress of the war with the Mahratta nation*. London: Robson, 1781.

PERRY, Thomas Erskine, *A bird's-eye view of India, with extracts from a journal kept in the provinces, Nepal, etc*. London: 1855.

—, *Cases illustrative of oriental life, and the application of English law to India, decided in H.M. Supreme Court of Bombay*. London: 1853.

POSTANS, Marianne. *Western India in 1838*. 2 vol. London: Saunders & Otley, 1839.

ROBERTS, Emma. *Overland journey to Bombay*. London: 1845.

—, *Scenes and characteristics of Hindostan with sketches of Anglo-Indian society*, 3 vols. London, 1835.

STOCQUELER, J. H. *Memoirs of a journalist*. Bombay: Times of India, 1873.

—, *The hand-book of British India*. 3rd ed. London: 1854.

Transactions of the Bombay Geographical Society. 19 vol. Bombay: 1836–1873. Index for volumes 1–17 (1836–64) in separate volume.

Transactions of the Literary Society of Bombay. 3 vol. Bombay: 1819–23.

Transactions of the Medical and Physical Society of Bombay. Bombay, 1838–89. First series: 1–10 (1838–49/50); New Series, 1–12 (1851/52–76); New Series, 1–12 (1882–89); Index 1–10 (1838–49/50) in separate volume.

The Mahomedan riots of Bombay in the year 1851. Compiled by a Parsee. Bombay: Bombay Summachar Press, 1856.

*The 'Times of India' Calendar and Directory for the year ... *. Published annually. Bombay: Times of India Press, 1862–70.

Works published after 1863 in English

ALBUQUERQUE, Teresa. *Urbs Primus in Indis. An Epoch in the History of Bombay. 1840–1865*. New Delhi: Promilla, 1985.

APTE, B. K. *A history of the Maratha navy and merchantships*. Bombay: Maharashtra State Board for Literature and Culture, 1972.

ASHLEY-BROWN, William. *On the Bombay coast and Deccan: the origin and history of the Bombay diocese: a record of 300 years work for Christ in Western India*. London: Society for Promoting Christian Knowledge, 1937.

BANAJI, K. N. *Memoirs of the late Framji Cowasji Banaji*. Bombay: 1892

BANGA, Indu (ed.) *The city in Indian history: urban demography, society, and politics*. New Delhi: Manohar Publications and Urban History Association of India, 1991.

—, *Ports and their hinterlands in India, 1700–1950*. New Delhi: Manohar, 1992.

BARNI, Z.A. *Romance of the oriental translator's office*. Karachi: Ta'alimi Markaz, 1950.

BHANDARKAR, R. G., *Collected works of Sir R. G. Bhandarkar*. 4 vol. Pune: Bhandarkar Oriental Research Institute, 1927–33.

BHATE, Govind Chimnaji, *History of modern Marathi literature, 1800–1938*. Mahad, District Kolaba: 1939.

BUCKLAND, C. E. *Dictionary of Indian biography*. London: Swan Sonnenschein, 1906.

BURNELL, John. *Bombay in the days of Queen Anne*. S. T. Sheppard (ed.) London: Hakluyt Society, 1933.

DA CUNHA, Joseph Gerson. '*The Origin of Bombay*'. Bombay: 1900; *Journal of the Bombay Branch of the Royal Asiatic Society*. Extra number.

DARUKHANAWALA, H. D. *Parsi lustre on Indian soil*. Vol. I. Bombay: G. Claridge & Co. Ltd., 1939; Vol. II. Bombay: 1963.

—, *Parsis and sports and kindred subjects*, Bombay: 1935.

DAVID, M. D. *History of Bombay, 1661–1708*. Bombay: University of Bombay, 1973.

—, *John Wilson and his institution*. Bombay: John Wilson Education Society, Wilson College, 1975.

DESHPANDE, Kusumawati and M. V. Rajadhyaksha, *A history of Marathi literature*. New Delhi: Sahitya Akademi, 1988.

DOBBIN, Christine. *Urban leadership in western India: politics and communities in Bombay city, 1840–1885*. London: Oxford University Press, 1972.

DOSSAL, Mariam. *Imperial designs and Indian realities. The planning of Bombay city. 1845–1875*. Bombay: Oxford University Press. 1991.

DOUGLAS, James. *A book of Bombay*. Bombay: 1883.

—, *Bombay and western India. A series of stray papers*. 2 vol. London: Sampson Low, Marston & Co., 1893.

FALCONER, John. *India: pioneering photographers. 1850–1900*. London: The British Library, 2001.

FAWCETT, Charles. *The English factories in India ... new series ... 1670–1677 (1678–1684)*. 4 vol. Oxford: Clarendon Press, 1936–55.

FORJETT, Charles. *Our real danger in India*. Bombay: Cassell, 1878.

Gazetteer of the Bombay Presidency, Vol XXVI: materials towards a statistical account of the town and island of Bombay. 3 parts. Bombay: 1893–4.

Gazetteer of Bombay city and island. 3 vol. Bombay: The Times Press, 1909–10.

HEWAT, E. G. K. *Christ and Western India. A study of the growth of the Indian church in Bombay city from 1813*. 2nd ed. Bombay: J. Kellock, 1953.

HOUSTON, John (ed.) *Representative men of the Bombay Presidency*. Bombay: C.B. Burrows, Care William Watson & Co., 1897.

HULL, E.R. *Bombay mission history*, 2 vol. Bombay: 1930.

JALBHOY, R. H. *The portrait gallery of western India*. Bombay: Education Society's Press, 1886.

JAMBHEKAR, G. G. (ed.) *Memoirs and writings of Acharya Bal Gangadhar Shastri Jambhekar (1812–1846)*. 3 vol. Pune: 1950.

JOHNSON, William. *The Oriental races and tribes, residents and visitors of Bombay. A series of photographs, with letter-press descriptions*. 2 vol. London, 1863–66.

KARKARIA, R. P. (ed.) *The charm of Bombay: an anthology of writings in praise of the first city of India*. Bombay: D. B. Taraporevala, Sons & Co., 1915.

KELLOCK, James. *Mahadev Govind Ranade: patriot and social servant*. Calcutta: Association Press, 1926.

LEIFER, Walter (ed.) *Bombay and the Germans*. Bombay: Shakuntala Publishing House, 1975.

LONDON, C. W. *Bombay Gothic*. Mumbai: India Book House, 2002.

MACLEAN, J. M. *A guide to Bombay: historical, statistical and descriptive ...* Bombay: Bombay Gazette Steam Press, 1875. Published annually until 1902.

Maharashtra State Gazetteers. Greater Bombay District. 3 vol. Bombay: Gazetteers Department, Government of Maharashtra, 1986.

MALABARI, P. B. M. *Bombay in the making. Being mainly a history of the origin and growth of judicial institutions in the Western Presidency, 1661–1726*. London: T. Fisher Unwin, 1910.

MODY, J. R. P. *Jamsetjee Jejeebhoy, the first Indian knight and baronet (1783–1859)*. Bombay: R.M.D.C. Press, 1959.

MOOS, Ardaseer Framjee. *Journal of Travels in India*. Bombay: Education Society's Press, 1871.

MOTIWALA, B. N. *Karsondas Mulji: a biographical study*. Bombay: 1935.

NARAIN, V. A. *Jonathan Duncan and Varanasi*. Calcutta: Firma K. L. Mukhopadhyay, 1959.

NATESAN, G. A. (ed.) *Famous Parsis: biographical and critical sketches*. Madras: 1930.

Old and new Bombay: a historical and descriptive account of Bombay and its environs. Bombay: G. Claridge, 1911.

NOLTIE, H. J. *The Dapuri Drawings. Alexander Gibson and the Bombay Botanic Gardens*. Ahmedabad: Mapin Publishing, 2002.

PARULEKAR, R V. (ed.) *Selections from educational records (Bombay) Part II. 1815–1840*. Bombay: Asia Publishing House, 1955.

PATEL, Sujata and Alice Thorner (eds.) *Bombay: mosaic of modern culture*. Bombay: Oxford University Press, 1995.

PINTO, D. A. *The Mayor, the Commissioner and the metropolitan administration (Bombay)*. New Delhi: Vikas Publishing House, 1984.

PHADKE, H. A. *R.G. Bhandarkar*. New Delhi: National Book Trust, 1968.

PRIOLKAR, A.K. *The printing press in India: its beginnings and early development*. Mumbai: Marathi Samshodhana Mandala, 1958.

Raghunathji, K. *Bombay beggars and criers*. Bombay: Education Society's Press, (n.d).

—, *Hindu Temples of Bombay*. Bombay: Fort Printing Press, 1896–1900.

ROHATGI, Pauline, P. Godrej and R. Mehrotra. *Bombay to Mumbai: changing perspectives*. Mumbai: Marg Publications, 1997.

RUTNAGUR, S. M. *Bombay industries: the cotton mills*. Bombay: The Indian Textile Journal Limited, 1923.

SHEPPARD, Samuel T. *Bombay*. Bombay: The Times of India Press, 1932.

—, *Bombay place-names and street-names. An excursion into the by-ways of the history of Bombay city*. Bombay: The Times Press, 1917.

—, *The Bombay volunteer rifles. A history*. Bombay: The Times Press, 1919.

SMITH, George. *The life of John Wilson, D.D., F.R.S.* London: John Murray, 1878.

STRACHEY, Ray and Oliver Strachey. *Keigwin's rebellion (1683–4): an episode in the history of Bombay*. Oxford: Clarendon Press, 1916.

TIKEKAR, Aroon. 'Dr. George Buist of the Bombay Times: *a study of the self-proclaimed messianism of an Anglo-Indian editor, 1840–57*', in Wagle, *Writers, Editors and Reformers*, 98–113.

TINDALL, Gillian. *City of gold: the biography of Bombay*. London: Temple Smith, 1982.

VEDAK, G. S. *A life sketch of the Hon. Mr. Jagannath Shankerseth*. Bombay: 1937.

WADIA, Ruttonjee Ardeshir. *A forgotten friend of India: Sir Charles Forbes 1st Bart*. Baroda: Padmaja Publications, 1946.

—, *Scions of Lowjee Wadia*. Bombay: 1964.

—, *The Bombay dockyard and the Wadia master builders*. Bombay: 1955.

WAGLE, N.K. (ed.) '*Writers, editors and reformers: social and political transformations of Maharashtra, 1830–1930*'. South Asian Studies No. *XXXIV*, South Asia Institute, Heidelberg University. New Delhi: Manohar Publishers & Distributors, 1999.

YULE, Henry, Sir. *Hobson-Jobson: a glossary of colloquial Anglo-Indian words and phrases, and of kindred terms, etymological, historical, geographical and discursive*. New ed. edited by William Crooke. London: J. Murray, 1903. Internet edition: http://dsal.uchicago.edu/dictionaries/hobsonjobson/.

Works published in Marathi

ACHARYA, Balkrishna Bapu and Moro Vinayak Shingne. *Mumbaicha vrittant*. Bombay: Nirnayasagar Press, 1889.

DADKAR, Jaya *et. al.* (eds.) *Sankshipt marathi vangmayakosh*. 2 vol. Mumbai: G. R. Bhatkal Foundation, 1998.

DATE, S. G. *et. al.* (eds.) *Marathi niyatkalikanchi suchi (1800–1950)*. 3 vol in 7 parts. Mumbai: Mumbai Marathi Granth Sangrahalya, 1969–81.

JOG, R. S. (ed.) *Marathi vangmayacha itihas. Khand chautha*. 2nd ed. Pune: Maharashtra Sahitya Parishad Prakashan, 1973.

KARVE, G. G. *Marathi sahityatil upekshit manakari*. Pune: Venus Prakashan, 1957.

KHANOLKAR, G. D. *Arvachin marathi vangmayasevak. Pancham khand*. Pune: Venus Prakashan, 1962.

KULKARNI, K. B. *Adhunik marathi gadyachi utkranti*. Mumbai: Mumbai Marathi Granth Sangrahalya, 1956.

KULKARNI, V. D. (ed.) *Marathi niyatkalikancha vangmayin abhyas. Khand ek: 1832–1882*. Pune: Mumbai Vidyapeeth Marathi Vibhag and Shrividya Prakashan, 1987.

KULKARNI, V. L. *Marathi Dnyanaprasarak: itihas va vangmayavichar*. Mumbai: Popular Prakashan, 1965.

LELE, R. K. *Marathi vrittapatrancha itihas*. Pune: Continental Prakashan, 1984.

MONDHE, M. K. (ed.) *Anant Fandi yanchya kavita va lavanya*. Pune: Padmagandha Prakashan, 2004.

Padmanji, Baba. *Arunodaya*. 3rd ed. Mumbai: Bombay Book Tract and Book Society, 1968.

PRIOLKAR, A. K. *Dr. Bhau Daji – vyakti, kaal va kartutva*. Mumbai: Mumbai Marathi Sahitya Sangh, 1971.

—, *Paramhansa sabha va tiche adhyaksh Ramachandra Balkrishna*. Mumbai: 1966.

—, *Raobahadur Dadoba Pandurang: atmacharitra va charitra*. Mumbai: Keshav Bhikaji Dhavle, 1947.

—, 'Thomas Candychi marathi vangmayachi seva' *Marathi Samshodhan Patrika* 4, nos. 1 and 2 (1956–57): 181–230.

SAMANT, Bal (ed.) *Brihanmumbai mahanagarpalika mukhyalaya shatabdi granth. 1893–1993*. Mumbai: Mumbai Mahanagarpalika, [1993].

VARDE, S. M. *Marathi kavitecha ushakal kinva marathi shahir*. Edited by S. G. Malshe. 2nd ed. Mumbai: Mumbai Marathi Sahitya Sangh, 1985.

Works published in Gujarati

DIWANJI, Shakarram Dalpatram. *Mumbaino Bhomiyo*. Mumbai: 1867.

KAPADIA, M. G. *Mumbaino Namankit Nagrik Seth Motisha*. Mumbai: Shree Godiji Jain Derasar ane Dharmada Khateyono Trusteeyo, 1991

Mahipatram Roopram. *Uttam Kapol Karsondas Mulji Charitra*. Ahmedabad: 1877.

SAMPAT, Dungarsi Dharamsi. *'Mumbai ane tena juna mahajano.'* *Shree Forbes Gujarati Sabha Traimasik* 3 (1938–39): 81–90, 183–92, 381–93 and 500–12 and continued as *'Mumbai na mahajano.'* in *Shree Forbes Gujarati Sabha Traimasik* 4 (1939–40): 91–98, 183–81, 283–98 and 460–63. Further instalments appeared in Volume 5 (1940–41): 40–49 and 450–7; Volume 6 (1941–42): 37–47, 205–11, 362–9 and 541–50; and Volume 7 (1942–43): 57–66.

VACHHA, Ratanji Framjee. *Mumbaino Bahar*. Mumbai: Union Press, 1874.

ZABWALA, S. H. *Pahela Sir Cowasjee Jehangir Readymoney*, Mumbai: Jame Jamshed Printing Works, (n.d.).

Glossary

Abhang	Marathi prosody; a form of poetry usually used for religious compositions and hymns, those composed by Sant. Tukaram being the most famous.
Abir	A fragrant powder comprised of sandal and other ingredients.
Apta	Tree with beautiful double-lobed leaves in the shape of a heart; *Bauhinia recemosa*.
Arya	Marathi prosody; a metre with each foot equal to four short syllables or to two long and two short. The *arya* of the poet Moropant are very popular.
Ashrafi	A coin popular in the Portuguese-ruled territories, generally considered to be worth half a rupee. Also known as *Xerafine*.
Attar	A perfume or essential oil obtained from flowers, from mainly, the petals.
Bakhar	A genre of prose narrative in Marathi, usually a history or a memoir; many have now been printed in critical editions. For more information, see Sumit Guha, 'Speaking Historically: The Changing Voices of Historical Narration in Western India, 1400–1900'. The American Historical Review 109, No. 4.
Balantwida	The roll of betel nut, leaf *et cetera*, together with various articles of baby-clothing, presented by her relations to a woman on the twelfth or other day after her delivery.
Bhajan	Religious devotional songs; repetition of the name of a god.
Bhakri	Bread, made from the unleavened flour of a variety of grains, chiefly millet.
Bharat Khand	The Indian land-mass.
Bigha	Measure for land-area; varies widely but generally about half an acre.
Botello	A shipping vessel of 50 to 500 khandies used mainly off the Gujarat coast.

Brahmanbhojan	Ritual feeding of Brahmins.
Bunder	A landing place or harbour.
Chawl	Literally, a line of houses, now used for buildings with one-room tenements.
Chirakhi	Religious offering done in a Muslim shrine.
Chowgada	An assemblage of four kettledrums beaten by two men, two by each man; the two large drums are called nagara and the two small ones *timkya*.
Chowki	Police-station.
Churan	Literally, a coarse powder, used generally to designate digestives.
Dakshina	Presents given to Brahmins on certain occasions, generally to obtain religious merit.
Dashgranthi	Brahmin who has read the *dashgrantha* consisting of the ten books of the *Rigveda*.
Dastur	Parsi high priest
Dharamshala	A building erected for the accommodation of travellers, generally to obtain religious merit.
Dhobi	Washerman.
Dhoti	A garment worn by males around the waist, usually about six feet long; could be made from either cotton or silk.
Dindi	Marathi prosody; a form of musical composition normally sung in religious performances.
Diwan	A prime minister of a kingdom or the chief revenue official in a district.
Fattemar	A fast sailing vessel with masts used south of Mumbai for coastal movement and delivering messages; also spelt *pattymar* in many English works.
Firangis	Generally used to signify an European, with mild disparagement. Derived from 'Frank' or the Franciscan monks who were among the first Europeans to travel in India.
Firman	An order or edict used by a sovereign.
Gandhi	A druggist.
Gaumukh	A glove shaped like a cow's mouth, used to cover the hand while telling the beads of a rosary.
Gayavarjan	Religious ceremonies performed after the death of one's close relatives.
Ghee	Clarified butter, used for cooking and ritual purification.
Gondhali	A caste of musicians and singers who perform in a boisterous style.

Gulal	A red powder, earlier obtained by dying grain flour with red sandalwood.
Handi	Measure of volume; generally signifies a vessel.
Hilal	A light consisting of an iron bowl grate or open-mouthed, containing oil and rolls of cloth and attached to the end of a stick.
Hing	Asafoetida, a resinous gum with an acrid taste and a strong odour, used to season various dishes; obtained from the roots of a plant of the parsley family very common in Afghanistan.
Homa	Ritual fire offering.
Inam	Grant, generally of land in perpetuity on a rent-free basis.
Jatra	Fair, typically held during a festival.
Kaan-fatye	A class of mendicants who wear heavy ear-rings.
Kanyadaan	Giving away of the daughter in marriage.
Katha	Narration of mythological stories, generally from the *Ramayana* or *Mahabharata*.
Kelvan	Ceremony during marriage where the bride or bridegroom is provided careful treatment.
Khalasi	A seaman; a general handyman.
Khandi	Measure of weight; generally equivalent to 20 *maunds*. Also spelt *candy* in many English works.
Kichidi	A cooked dish of rice and pulses.
Kirtan	Religious devotional songs.
Kos	Measure of distance, used most commonly in India; varies hugely according to region but generally considered to reckon about 2 miles. Also spelt *coss* in many English works.
Kotwal	A police-officer, generally the chief of police of a town.
Kulkarni	Village accountant
Lota	A small container for water, usually of brass or bronze.
Mahaal	The sub-division of a *taluka*, itself a sub-division of a *zillah* or district.
Mahajan	A merchant or trader; also an illustrious person, a leader of the community.
Man	Measure of weight; varies widely with region and product, generally equivalent to 40 *shers*. Also spelt *maund* in many English works.
Mandap	A marquee, open on all sides.
Medhe joshi	A fortune-teller and reckoner of dates and seasons.

Mleccha	Generally used to designate non-Indians of all races; also used to describe a class of untouchables in the caste system.
Moholla	Ward, locality or city district.
Mukadam	The head-man, generally of a gang of labourers.
Munj	Ceremony for investiture of the sacred thread for Hindu boys.
Ovi	Marathi prosody; a popular metre used in many important Marathi compositions, particularly those by Sant Dnyaneshwar.
Pada	Marathi prosody; a metre generally used in hymns.
Pagdi	A turban; especially one which has been shaped and sewn into place and generally worn by children.
Pagota	Head-dress.
Pahelwan	A strongman, generally a wrestler.
Pal	A unit of time, sixtieth part of a *ghatika*; a minute equals two and a half *pal*.
Palkhi	Palanquin.
Panchagni	Ritual performed sitting in the midst of four fires kindled in the four directions and under the sun through its daily course.
Paylee	Measure of weight; equivalent to four *sher*.
Pimp	Measure of weight.
Pingle	A fortune-teller who always predicts a good future.
Pooja	Hindu oblation rites.
Powada	Marathi prosody; a ballad which narrates the achievements of a king or recounts a valorous battle; normally sung to the accompaniment of music.
Prasad	Food and other offerings generally presented to an idol or holy person and then distributed to worshippers.
Purana	A sacred poetical work, usually considered to be eighteen in number which comprise the whole body of Hindu theology.
Puranik	A person well-versed in the *Puranas*.
Rattal	Measure of weight, about fifteen ounces.
Roti	Unleavened bread, made of wheat flour.
Ryot	Peasants; tillers of the land; also applied in general to the subjects of a king.
Saar	Vegetable stew.
Sadra	Parsi initiation rite for boys known as *Navjot* when he is given the *sadra* or vest which he must always wear for protection from evil.
Samadhi	Highest stage of meditation.

Samvat	An Indian era, established by King Vikramaditya, reckoned as 56 years ahead of the Christian era.
Saptaah	Religious rituals lasting a week.
Savvakar	A merchant or banker.
Shaké	An Indian era, also known as the Saka era, reckoned as 79 years behind the Christian era.
Shastra	Scripture; of divine origin; also used for treatises on religion, literature or the sciences.
Shastri	A person well-versed with the *shastras*.
Sher	Measure of weight; also sometimes used for volume; generally equivalent to eighty *tolas*. Also spelt *seer* in many English works.
Shigram	A kind of horse-carriage.
Shloka	Marathi prosody; a verse or stanza with two lines.
Shraddha	a funeral ceremony observed at various fixed periods, consisting of offerings with water and fire to the gods and manes, and of gifts and food to relations present and Brahmins.
Shroff	A traditional banker or money-changer.
Shudra	A Hindu of the lowest caste.
Sunnud	A deed of grant by the government conferring a title or a right.
Tola	Measure of weight, chiefly of gold and silver.
Udkadi	A stick smeared with frankincense, burned for its pleasant fragrance.
Vaar	Measure of distance, about an yard; also used to signify square yards.
Vaidic	A person well-versed with the *Vedas*.
Vaidya	A physician, well-versed in the knowledge of medicine as described in the *shastra*.
Veena	A stringed musical instrument.
Vibhuti	Ashes of wood or dung invested with religious significance.
Vilayat	Chiefly employed to designate Europe, and particularly England; derived from the Arabic word for a kingdom or province and used especially in the Transoxanian countries to describe their native lands.
Yamadanda	The punishment inflicted upon sinners by Yama, Lord of Death.
Yatra	Pilgrimage.

INDEX